The Complete Book of North American
Railroading

Kevin EuDaly, Mike Schafer, Jim Boyd,

Steve Jessup, Andrew McBride, and Steve Glischinski

CRESTLINE

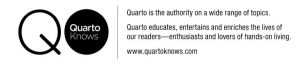

Quarto is the authority on a wide range of topics.

Quarto educates, entertains and enriches the lives of our readers—enthusiasts and lovers of hands-on living.

www.quartoknows.com

This edition published in 2016 by
CRESTLINE
an imprint of Book Sales
a division of Quarto Publishing Group USA Inc.
142 West 36th Street 4th Floor
New York, New York 10018
USA

First published in 2009 by Voyageur Press, an imprint of MBI Publishing Company, 400 First Avenue North, Suite 400, Minneapolis, MN 55401 USA

ISBN: 978-0-7858-3389-5

Acquisitions Editor: Dennis Pernu
Designer: Val Escher

Printed in China

10 9 8 7 6 5 4 3 2 1

Frontispiece: Chris Lambert is busy keeping Western Maryland Shay 6 hot on June 26, 2008, as the three-truck, 162-ton monster climbs the rugged trackage between Cass and Bald Knob, West Virginia. Few things in railroading can compare to hand-firing a steam locomotive, and few operations in North America can compare to Cass for old-time appeal. *Kevin EuDaly photo*

Title pages: On the former Norfolk & Western Pocahontas Division coal is king. This eastbound train of coal loads is making about 15 miles per hour grinding up the grade at Powhatan, West Virginia, on February 28, 2008, during early-morning winds that have the overnight snowfall showering down out of the trees along the right-of-way. This train is destined for Bluefield and eventually Norfolk, Virginia, where this export coal will be loaded into transatlantic ships. *Kevin EuDaly photo*

CONTENTS

Acknowledgments

What started out to be an effort solely by Mike Schafer and me metamorphosed into an effort where many hands were set upon the throttle.

A very special and hearty thanks to Jim Boyd, editor emeritus of *Railfan & Railroad* magazine, who lived in the White River Productions' Kansas City office for over three weeks while writing captions, editing text, and helping with photos. This book would not be as it is without Jim's help, and we're sincerely grateful for the many hours he put in. The fact that he wrote the three locomotive chapters almost pales compared to his contribution to the overall finished product.

Several chapters were written by others, who were called upon to help as deadlines took their toll. White River Productions' Steve Jessup wrote the "Golden Age" and "Freight" chapters, and WRP's Andy McBride contributed significantly to the "Infrastructure" chapter. Longtime friend and colleague Steve Glischinski handled the "Railroading Comes of Age" chapter. To all three, sincere thanks are in order. Thanks also to Ron and Deb Goldfeder, who helped at several stages.

An effort as all-encompassing as this one includes photographic resources from many locations, and our friends in various railroad historical societies with their associated archives helped fill in numerous illustrations. Specifically, we'd like to thank the following archives folks in organizations that made images available:

Joe Oates and Larry Goolsby–Atlantic Coast Line & Seaboard Air Line Historical Society
Joe Piersen–Chicago & North Western Historical Society
Larry DeYoung–Erie Lackawanna Historical Society
Dave Oroszi and Ron Flanary–Louisville & Nashville Historical Society
The Milwaukee Road Historical Association
Dave Schauer–Missabe Railroad Historical Society
Jim Gillum and Harold Davenport–Norfolk & Western Historical Society
Paul Schuch and Dick Hutchins–Rock Island Technical Society

The credit lines beneath each photo recognize the individual photographers and collections that contributed. Our thanks to each and every person who took the time to document the history of railroading in North America, and especially those who have sent material in for use in projects like this one. In this modern digital age, a scan of a photo is as valuable as the original for publishing purposes, and our scanned archive was one of the primary resources for this book.

Kevin EuDaly

One of the biggest diesel locomotives to ever ply North American rails was EMD's DDA40X, built exclusively for the Union Pacific. The twin-engine monsters were nicknamed the "Centennial" because delivery began in 1969, the one-hundredth anniversary of the golden spike ceremony at Promontory, Utah. They delivered 6,600 horsepower in two 16-cylinder engines and rode on rigid four-motor FlexiCoil trucks, the largest truck built for railroad service. Here, the sole operable survivor swings through Lee's Summit, Missouri, with an engineering passenger special on April 15, 2008. *Kevin EuDaly photo*

Using link-and-pin couplers, this tiny train and equally tiny locomotive spent decades running back and forth from quarry to plant on Arkansas Lime's 3-foot gauge railroad in Limedale, Arkansas. The railroad hauled agricultural lime in much the same way as some of the earliest mining railroads until just after the turn of the twenty-first century. This westbound has empties for the quarry on August 29, 1992. Today, the locomotive survives in tourist train service in Hawaii. *Kevin EuDaly photo*

Introduction

By Kevin EuDaly

North American railroading is *big*. Tremendously big. That, in part, is simply because North America is a vast continent, second only to Asia in land mass, and has many population centers with voluminous transportation needs. It is impossible to separate the stunning growth of the United States and Canada from the industrialization that sped that growth forward at an unprecedented rate in the nineteenth and twentieth centuries; it is even a further impossibility to envision such growth without the railroads. If one finds a need to categorize the building of industrial North America and relate that to any single thing, the railroad industry is that thing.

From tiny wooden tracks in the dirt to wooden rails with flat pieces of iron on top on wood cross ties, to the

The rise of coal mining in the Powder River Basin in Wyoming has resulted in unprecedented volumes of coal tonnage on U.S. rails. This heavy coal train has five units on the front—four Santa Fe and one Burlington Northern—and two BN pushers, an SD45 and an SDP45 (bottom photo). They're lifting the train through Wyodak, Wyoming, just east of Gillette, on August 6, 1983, shortly before the C&NW gained access to the basin with partner UP. *Both photos Kevin EuDaly*

Like the Chicago & North Western in the mid-1980s, the Dakota, Minnesota & Eastern is vying for position in the Powder River Basin coal fields. Also like the C&NW, the DM&E needed a larger partner and found that in the Canadian Pacific. Though not yet officially building toward the mines, the DM&E is on the brink of doing so. This eastbound DM&E train slashes across the South Dakota landscape east of Arlington on May 17, 2007. *Kevin EuDaly photo*

tempered and specialized steel rails of today on concrete ties, railroads have grown up with industrial North America, and conversely, much industry has been fueled by the railroads. In the eighteenth and nineteenth centuries, perhaps only coal had more impact than railroads on industry, but the ability to get coal to its endpoints is in part what built the railroads. In that respect, little has changed in the relationship of large industry and transportation with railroads as movers of goods—in bulk. The diminutive cars and locomotives at the birth of railroading in North America have given way to tremendously powerful locomotives and freight cars that now carry what would be to the nineteenth-century railroader inconceivable tonnages. A train consisting of tiny cars carrying a few tons of quarried stone has given way to an endless string of coal trains carrying 15,000 tons of coal from Wyoming's Powder River Coal Basin. Indeed, coal is still the single product hauled in the highest tonnage by North American railroads.

Railroading in North America has for its entire history been fraught with exceptions to the rules, behind-the-scenes negotiation, and all manner of oddities. For a relatively recent example, one only has to look back to the 1970s and witness the Chicago & North Western's expansion into the Wyoming coal fields to see a North American railroad adapting and changing to fulfill a dream. Unable to finance its entrance into the Powder River Basin, the C&NW linked up with longtime partner Union Pacific to help finance building over 100 miles of brand-new railroad. Burlington Northern was already entrenched in the northern part of the coal-mining area that was being developed in the Gillette area, and the Interstate Commerce Commission, the entity that regulated railroads at the time, had made it clear they wouldn't approve two parallel lines—the two roads had to work out a joint operations agreement. That's akin to putting two proverbial 500-pound gorillas in the same cage. After 15 years of legal and financial wrangling, property acquisition, constant negotiations with twists and turns all along the way, and then actually building the railroad, the first trainload of Powder River coal for the C&NW broke through a banner near Alsop at the Wyoming-Nebraska state line on August 16, 1984, doing what many speculated could never be done. That entire scenario is repeating itself today, as the Dakota, Minnesota & Eastern is attempting to access the Powder River Basin.

North of the U.S. border in far western Canada, British Columbia Railway was at the same time expanding into coal territory near Tumbler Ridge, aimed at providing coal for export to the Orient. While the 1980s are not generally thought of as a boom time for railroads, these two expansions resulted in significant new trackage. The Tumbler Ridge line had one aspect that made it entirely unique—it was built to operate with electric locomotives using a 50,000-volt overhead wire system, making it the last new freight railroad built in North America to operate electric locomotives under wire. It was opened in 1982. Two decades later, the bottom dropped out of the export coal business, the wire came down, the line was relegated to diesel locomotives, and it continues in an on-again off-again cycle of operation dependent on the demand for coal overseas. If nothing else, these two expansions illustrate the point that railroading in North America is not done. Indeed, it's as alive as ever, with more tonnage being hauled than ever in history.

In 1983, British Columbia's provincial-owned railroad, BC Rail, opened up the brand-new Tumbler Ridge Division to move coal from new mines to the port at Prince Rupert for export. The new line was built using 50,000-volt electric overhead transmission wires, and seven new General Motors GF6C locomotives were purchased for power. On September 3, 1985, two of the 6,000-horsepower GF6Cs bring empty coal gondolas through remote British Columbia north of Wolverine. When the export coal market dropped, BC Rail pulled down the catenary and mothballed the GF6Cs. In 1985, this operation still included cabooses, and a sharp Canadian National cupola caboose brings up the rear. *Both photos Kevin EuDaly*

By the time this photograph was taken at Harrodsburg, Indiana, on April 20, 1960, passenger operations were already in steep decline. Sitting in the siding are two Alco RS-2s on train 40, the local freight. Swinging into the curve on the main line is F3A 84A on train 5, the *Thoroughbred*, which was discontinued on September 30, 1967. *James F. EuDaly photo*

On the passenger front, the railroads did more than anything else to open up the rush westward as North America was settled. Every town wanted a railroad, and political positioning and sometimes even violence accompanied the tracklayers as they extended rails into every little burgh on the plotted course. As the nineteenth century gave way to the

twentieth, the railroads were tremendously efficient people movers, and as such they were the epicenter of commerce as they moved businesspeople and other travelers about the country. Passenger travel peaked in the early decades of the twentieth century—the railroads simply couldn't compete with the family car for convenience, and today, the automobile completely dominates all forms of travel in North America.

Man has long had a fascination with machines. Essentially every machine invented has devotees, but perhaps none as all-encompassing as railroads. The existence of well over 100 historical societies in the United States alone, each devoted to a specific railroad or region, attests to North America's fascination with railroading—and other countries have their devoted fans, as well. Photographer and author Joe Collias, in his epic attempt at capturing only one element of North American railroading—the steam locomotive in its final years—penned the following in his 1960 book, *The Last of Steam*:

"In his continual search for something better, man has devised and created goods and machines that have left more than a passing impression on his generations. It is a credit to our way of life that though these creations are taken for granted by most people, there

DIESEL DIVISION
GENERAL MOTORS OF CANADA LIMITED
LONDON   CANADA
DATE 12-83   CLASS GF6D
TONS   SERIAL A4343
GM

This builder's plate identifies the December 1983 build date on a GF6C, of which only seven were ever built—all for BC Rail's Tumbler Ridge operation. They served their entire existence on BC Rail's isolated coal line. All were scrapped but one, which resides today in the Prince George Railway Museum. *Kevin EuDaly photo*

On April 1, 1978, VIA took possession of Canadian National's passenger fleet and on October 29 that same year took over Canadian Pacific operations, completing the transfer of passenger operations of those two roads to VIA, a federal Crown Corporation. On August 9, 1983, four F-units with FP7A 6566 in the lead, whisk train 1, *The Canadian*, through Stephen, British Columbia. *Kevin EuDaly photo*

are always those who possess an undying interest in a creation with which they may never have direct contact. Thus it is that while some gaze rapturously at an aged Mississippi stern wheeler and collect souvenirs of its kind, others spend their lives searching for and collecting postage stamps, coins, and the like from the distant corners of the globe. Antique automobiles, modern airplanes, and rockets all come in for their share of attention; in fact, very little that man has created does not gather a following, sometimes momentarily interested spectators or again avid followers whose quest for information and experiences knows no bounds. No other devising of man created such an enthusiastic following as that of the most nearly human of his creations, the American steam locomotive. Since its inception it has been an object of attention and fascination on the part of the American public. Though its construction and operation are really quite simple, its outside motion and near human laborings have never ceased to arouse amazement and fascination on the faces of onlookers. No other machine has so universally captured the public's imagination and affection."

Amtrak had more than a decade under its belt when this photograph of the *Empire Builder* was taken at Summit, Montana, on Marias Pass, with F40PHs 373 and 360 in charge. The National Railroad Passenger Corporation (Amtrak) was formed on May 1, 1971, out of the remaining shreds of U.S. intercity passenger operations. Several roads opted out and retained their own passenger trains, including the Denver & Rio Grande Western, the Rock Island, and the Southern. *Kevin EuDaly photo*

What Joe penned captures how enthusiasts across the world feel about railroads. Although there are many fascinating aspects to railroading, each aspect has its followers: steam, diesel, and electric locomotives each has droves of followers; every major railroad of the past seven decades has a historical society devoted to it; there are those who are experts in signal systems, each nonstandard track gauge has its followers, and people of all ages build models of railroading in North America—from the single loop of track around the Christmas tree to vast detailed empires in basements and outbuildings across the continent. Something as big as North American railroading only has the surface scratched in a single book, but *The Complete Book of North American Railroading* will introduce the appeal of the railroads of this great continent over the two centuries they've been in existence. Climb aboard for a journey through time—by rail.

Just as steam has its followers, diesels, electrics, narrow gauge, and a host of other subsets have enthusiasts following every move. In the 1990s, to the delight of Santa Fe fans, the railroad's president, Mike Haverty, resurrected the classic red and silver warbonnet paint scheme. Two Dash 9-44CWs on their first run west from Chicago were captured just south of Bucklin, Missouri, on October 29, 1997. *Kevin EuDaly photo*

In the 1950s, color film finally came of age, and yet when B&O USRA Pacific 5206 rolled across U.S. Highway 50 at North Vernon, Indiana, on April 8, 1955, with train 51 bound for Louisville, color film speeds were painfully slow. This three-car southbound local connected with the *National Limited* at North Vernon. As the decade of the 1950s closed, so did the widespread use of main-line steam. *James F. EuDaly photo*

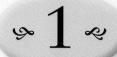

In the Beginning, 1828–1900

by Mike Schafer with Kevin J. Holland

Had North America been settled and developed in the nineteenth and twentieth centuries using only roads and waterways, we'd probably be about a century behind where we are now. As it was, after Jamestown—the first permanent English settlement in what became the United States—was established in 1607, the next 200-plus years were indeed spent settling and developing the continent using only crude roadways and natural waterways. In the early 1800s, North Americans still moved about by horse or horse-drawn wagons, boats, or on foot; the limitations on just how much development could be accomplished remained relatively unchanged.

However, in 1807, the world was in the throes of an industrial revolution, and the 200 years between 1807 and 2007—the year this book went into preparation—would usher in an astonishing transformation. Though the dominance of roadways and air transport today might prompt younger-generation North Americans to assume that the automobile, truck, and airliner were largely responsible for the awesome growth and development of the continent, railroads played a pivotal role.

North American railroading in its infancy looked like this, as a cut of five cars ascends plane 23 at Olyphant, Pennsylvania, from Valley Junction in the 1800s. Railway companies, such as the depicted Delaware & Hudson Canal Company, emerged hauling coal and later passengers on these inclined-plane railroads. The "engineer" and "conductor" have no cabs to ride in here, yet the duty of safely moving the train is their livelihood. *D&H, Jim Shaughnessy collection*

If the railroads were going to make a true dent in the transportation industry, serious motive power would be required to haul passengers and tons of important goods fast and efficiently across the nation. Dressed in their Sunday best, local workers pose alongside five impressive Delaware & Hudson Canal Company 4-4-0 steam engines at the Delanson, New York, roundhouse in 1889. *G. M. Best photo, Jim Shaughnessy collection*

In England around the start of the nineteenth century, and shortly thereafter in America, a small group of people began to experiment with ways to improve and combine two technologies pertinent to the main subject of this book: (1) harnessed energy in the form of steam, and (2) an invention that allowed for a smoother, more effortless manner of moving weighty things: a fixed guideway system or track. Teamed together, these two technologies would revolutionize most of the populated world, with the European and North American continents taking the reins—and the lead.

Track predated steam locomotives by some 300 years at least. The earliest references to trackbound vehicles date from the early 1500s, and these were usually small wagons that rode on wheels bearing flanges on both the inside and outside edge of the wheel—a spool-shaped wheel, if you will. The wheels rode over simple wood beams, and the flanges did the guiding. These wagons were used largely around coal mines; when loaded, the wagons were small enough to be easily moved about by one or two people. The cars were often

moved from mine areas to nearby waterways or points of sale, and invariably the trip for loads was downhill to a waterway, assisted by gravity, with speed kept in check by crude brakes operated by a person riding with the wagon. Once the material was unloaded into boats, the now-empty cars could easily be hauled back upgrade by horses or cables. This whole format, which became known as a tram (a word related to "beam"), also worked well with quarries, particularly slate, which was a prime building material.

One of the better-known examples of an early rail operation involving a coal mine was the Swansea & Mumbles tramway. Built on the south coast of Wales about 1804, it moved coal from the mine downhill to the seaport, and it also laid claim to being the first passenger-carrying railway. One of the earliest recorded instances in North America of a rudimentary track system being used to move freight was near Quincy, Massachusetts, about 1824 at a quarry operation. The stone blocks being quarried for the Bunker Hill monument had to be moved to a waterway; the quarry operator had laid a track consisting of lengths of cut stone between the quarry and the waterway so that horses could move loads of stone to waiting boats. The Granite Rail Road is considered to be America's first official rail operation although it is unlikely that its creation was mandated by a governing body, which would become the norm for nearly all future North American railroads.

Small railways like this boomed in settled areas of England, Europe, and eventually North America wherever there was a need to move commodities of great weight or bulk, notably stone, coal, and lumber.

Of course, for all its virtues, wood rail set on stone slabs or wooden ties was only a step in the evolution to what we have today: high-tensile, continuous-welded steel rail on concrete ties. A great leap forward came with the development of iron rail. Far more durable than wood-railed track, iron rail provided unparalleled strength and longevity. Early iron rails were also mounted on stone slabs, but once the era of "real" horsepower came to an end and the steam locomotive emerged the victor, cross ties quickly became the accepted means of rail support. (For more details about track evolution, see Chapter 9.)

Railway Companies Emerge

At least a few visionaries who witnessed early tram or similar fixed-guideway operations probably saw the vast potential of this new form of transportation. However, canals and similar

The gravity tracks and canal basin at Honesdale, Pennsylvania, are seen in 1898. The inclined plane had been in place some 70 years here before this photo was taken. At left, a heavily laden passenger train starts up plane 13 for Honesdale, while boats are being loaded from coal cars at various points in the basin to the right. The big white horse in front of the coach in the foreground would pull the cars to the front of the plane. Inbound trains moved down the sloping track to the left in the background. *D&H, Jim Shaughnessy collection*

The *Stourbridge Lion* steam locomotive, brought over from England in May 1829, was the first of its kind to operate on American rails. It was too heavy for the Delaware & Hudson Canal Company rails but was used as a stationary steam engine to drive the railway's cabling system. This replica was built for the 1933–1934 Century of Progress Exposition in Chicago. *D&H, Jim Shaughnessy collection*

waterways had already proven themselves a cheap and easy option for moving bulk materials (and people), and early in the 1800s there was a frenzy to build them wherever feasible. In 1817, construction began on the king of them all in North America: the 364-mile Erie Canal system linking the Hudson River at Albany, New York, with Lake Erie at Buffalo, New York; it was completed in 1825. It was a boon to transportation between America's Eastern shores to the interior we now know as the Midwest.

During this period, improved roads and turnpikes were experiencing a boom of their own, with some 5,000 miles in operation in New York and Pennsylvania alone. In 1806, construction of the most famous turnpike of them all, the National Road, was authorized by Congress, but it would take until 1833 for the road to reach Columbus, Ohio. Although these improved roads made travel a bit more comfortable,

travelers were still faced with the limitations of how far a horse or horse-drawn wagon could travel in a given amount of time and how much could be carried.

Canals initially were thought to be the new future of American transportation—and for a time, they were. By 1830, some 1,200 miles of canals would be in operation, mostly in New York, Pennsylvania, and Ohio. But their shortcomings quickly provided sobering realities of this mode's limitations. Canals were easily stymied by rugged terrain and winter weather, the latter freezing the waterway—at least those in northern climes—and shutting down its commerce for the duration. Mountain ranges were a particular problem that not even the most sophisticated lock-and-dam system of the period could overcome. Tramways and their direct descendants, railways, were far less affected by terrain and could be built just about anywhere that a canal could not—as well as where a canal could.

Early visionaries saw the virtues and limitations of all modes then coming into play and, for a short period in American history, utilized combinations of canals, tramways (known as inclined planes in North America), and railways to move freight—and eventually passengers—along a designated route. One of the earliest of these intermodal operations was the Delaware & Hudson Canal & Gravity Railroad.

Use your imagination to transport yourself back in time to January 5, 1825, to fledgling New York City. You're at the Tontine Coffee House on Wall Street enjoying the meeting place's fireplace, but it has a curious, blue-flamed fire that elicits little of the usual oily smoke wrought by burning coal. Merchant brothers William and Maurice Wurtz from Philadelphia are responsible for this unusual warming, having introduced locals—which included several bankers—to a hard, clean-burning form of coal known as anthracite. The Wurtz brothers own an anthracite coal mine at Carbondale,

Pennsylvania, and are seeking financial backing for a scheme to bring this new wonder coal into a whole new, untapped market: New York City.

The scheme was bold for its day, for the transport could not be done via an all-water route. Mined in the vicinity of Carbondale, the coal would have to be hauled up and over Moosic Mountain (950 feet above sea level at its summit) before it even got to Honesdale, Pennsylvania, the head of an intricate, 108-mile system of waterways that would take the coal to Kingston, New York, where it would enter the Hudson River for the final float downstream to New York City.

William and Maurice Wurtz had already received charters in 1823 from New York and Pennsylvania to build their Delaware & Hudson Canal, but they still needed backing to complete that tricky cross-mountain section between Olyphant (near Carbondale) and Honesdale. The plan to accomplish this feat had already been devised by D&H

The community of Honesdale, Pennsylvania, gathers for the arrival of the first Erie Railroad train with its passenger coaches being pulled by classic 4-4-0 American steam engine 310. Honesdale was the end of the branch that extended westward from Lackawaxen, New York. The line reached Honesdale in 1867. Rail transportation was extremely important to such small communities, yet the race was already on to reach larger cities in the nation's interior regions. *Pete Hasler collection*

The Baltimore & Ohio Railroad is considered by many historians to be the first true common-carrier railway company. Initially, B&O trains were horse-powered. In 1829, the railroad experimented with the *Tom Thumb* steam engine. A replica of the *Tom Thumb* is seen here at Halethorpe, Maryland, in August 1980. Even though the *Tom Thumb* once lost a race with a horse, steam engines would prevail, driving the B&O as far west as St. Louis. *Dale Jacobson photo*

Chief Engineer John B. Jervis. He designed a 17-mile railway comprising inclined sections interspersed with landings (relatively level sections); the coal cars were hauled up the mountain with a steam-powered winch-and-cable system. Cars moving downhill would do so by gravity, but were kept in check by cables.

The sell was a success, and the Delaware & Hudson Canal Company opened in 1828, although the railway portion would not move its first load of coal over the mountain until October 1829. On August 8, 1829, however, the D&HCC experimented by operating the *Stourbridge Lion* steam locomotive, brought over from England in May 1829, along a short portion of the railway at the Honesdale end. This was the first time ever that a steam locomotive had operated on American rails, although it turned out to be too heavy for D&HCC rails and subsequently was used as a stationary steam engine to drive the railway's cabling system.

Once in operation, the D&HCC flourished, enjoying long-term success as a common-carrier operation—that is, a company that provided equal-access transportation to the public and to private companies alike, as mandated by its charter. The D&HCC was not alone in its employment of both canals and incline-plane railways; canals were still regarded as the way of the future while railways were still relatively unproven, save for the task of hauling goods over mountain ridges thanks to a century-plus-old (about 1712) mode of stationary power—steam—and a system of cabling.

But even as the D&HCC commenced in 1828, the future of canals was already being threatened by upstart railways that were companies unto their own and not just a small aspect of a transportation entity. In 1826, the Mohawk & Hudson Railroad became the first chartered railroad to actually be completed. (Charters issued by the government did not necessarily result in railroad construction; numerous well-intended charters fell by the wayside without a single foot of rail ever being laid.) The 17-mile railway linked Albany with Schenectady, New York, and served as a high-speed shortcut between the two cities that bypassed the slow, circuitous Erie Canal between those two points. The M&H opened all the way through in 1831.

The success of the M&H inspired a proposal to extend it all the way across the state to Buffalo—a proposal that miffed the State, which had invested heavily in the

Covering 90 miles in about seven hours, the *John Bull* steam locomotive was used on the Camden & Amboy Railroad with scheduled service between New York and Philadelphia. That was half the time it took to travel by horse-drawn wagons. In September 1981, a Pennsylvania Railroad–built *John Bull* replica is captured around the Bordentown, New Jersey, area. *Jim Boyd photo*

Erie Canal. As it turned out, the M&H would never extend west of Schenectady—but other railroads would. In what some historians view as a surreptitious end run around railway foes, eleven locally grown, small railroads sprouted up along New York's Northern Tier (and Erie Canal), serving the likes of Utica, Syracuse, Auburn, Rochester, and other communities, and began linking up end to end. Their names spoke of their original destination intentions: the Auburn & Rochester, the Syracuse & Utica, the Buffalo & Rochester, and so on. But by 1841 these railroads, along with the M&H, had formed an all-rail route between Albany and Buffalo. And then they had the audacity to provide coordinated through freight and passenger service all the way from Albany to Buffalo! In 1853, these railroads merged to form the New York Central Railroad. The Erie Canal was more or less rendered secondary.

Concurrent with the M&H's construction, work had also begun on what many historians consider to be the first true common-carrier railway company in North America, the Baltimore & Ohio Railroad, chartered in 1827. Its name foretold its destiny: to link the port of Baltimore, Maryland, with the then-western frontier at the Ohio River. The heady project was born of rivalry more than a general need to actually get to the interior, as that had already been successfully accomplished by the landmark Erie Canal. Baltimore feared the loss of its status as a great port for traffic destined to and from the interior if the Erie Canal became the preferred route.

Because of the approximately 300 miles of rugged geography separating Baltimore and the Ohio River, backers of the B&O were pretty much forced to use the infant technology of railway construction rather than canals, with basically no prototype to work from except for railroads already under construction in the British Isles—weeks away in terms of travel and communication time.

Construction forged ahead anyway, beginning on July 4, 1828, as Charles Carroll, the last surviving signer of the Declaration of Independence, dedicated the first stone to be placed for track support. The line first opened for public service in 1830, reaching Ellicott's Mills, Maryland, 13 miles out of Baltimore. Initially, trains were horse-powered, but as the steam locomotive evolved in America, the B&O switched to steam early in the 1830s. Reach the Ohio it would, but the B&O did

In 1847, the Pennsylvania Railroad embarked on the daunting project of building an all-rail route from Philadelphia to Pittsburgh through the Alleghenies. The last piece of the puzzle was the construction around the landmark location of Horseshoe Curve west of Altoona, which was completed in 1854. Pennsy successor Conrail is pictured at the curve in October 1987 carrying a westbound freight uphill. *Jim Boyd photo*

not have an easy time of it. Builders had to cut a treacherous path through Virginia (the portion of which would later become West Virginia), Maryland, and Pennsylvania, surmounting the spine of the Allegheny Mountains west of Cumberland, Maryland. The route required steep grades, fills, bridges, and several tunnels. The B&O reached Wheeling, (West) Virginia, on the Ohio River in 1853, 25 years after the construction began in Baltimore. Not all efforts had been concentrated on this main line to the west, however; in 1835 the B&O completed a branch into Washington, D.C., that came off the original main line at Relay, Maryland. As the importance of Washington grew, this branch grew into an instrumental main line for the B&O both in terms of passenger and freight traffic; it served as a gateway to the Southeast by connecting with railroads reaching south from Washington to the Carolinas, Georgia, and Florida. It was also critical to Washington itself during the Civil War, as this was the city's only railroad at the time.

At its apex, the venerable B&O would reach as far west as St. Louis, the future gateway between the East and the American West, as well as to Pittsburgh (originally spelled Pittsburg), Chicago (destined to be the nation's railroad hub), Indianapolis, Detroit, Toledo, and Cleveland. The B&O would

survive as an entity for 160 years before merging into CSX Transportation in 1987, and it illustrates both the manner in which early railroading evolved in North America and how all interstate railroads were formed around charters provided by the federal government for interstate commerce and the well-being of the country.

If the B&O demonstrates how a typical early railroad got under way, the Main Line of Public Works—as well as the Delaware & Hudson Canal Company and others of its ilk—illustrates how railroads overwhelmingly triumphed over canals. What became the MLofPW originally was intended to be an all-canal route across Pennsylvania between Harrisburg and Pittsburgh, one that included a 4-mile tunnel under the spine of the Alleghenies. (Lack of a good water source between Philadelphia and Columbia, near Harrisburg, prevented the canal from reaching all the way east to Philadelphia.) By the time construction of the Pennsylvania Canal began, about 1829, railway technology was just beginning to be accepted in some circles, although it had yet to prove itself as a superior form of transport. Thus, the MLofPW incorporated only short segments of railway to link its canal segments, which opened first between Columbia and Hollidaysburg and between

Johnstown and Pittsburgh in 1832. In 1834, the gaps in the canal system were filled with two railroads, the Columbia Railroad between Philadelphia and Columbia and the Allegheny Portage Railroad between Hollidaysburg and Johnstown. The latter was a fascinating incline-plane railway in which portions of the canal boats were loaded onto railcars and hoisted up, over, and down the summit of the Alleghenies, initially using horse power and, beginning in 1835, a complicated array of cabling and stationary steam power. Today, a visit to the Allegheny Portage Railroad Historic Site near Gallitzin, Pennsylvania, provides an unsurpassed look at this segment of one of America's most historic transportation corridors.

Once the entire route opened, travel across Pennsylvania went from weeks to days. It was a travel sensation!

Of course, a transportation link between the East and the frontier was not the only manner in which the new railways served the colonies. In 1833, the first through railroad, the Camden & Amboy, opened between the metropolitan New York area and Philadelphia, a distance of about 90 miles. This was particularly significant in that its trains were powered by the *John Bull* and its sister locomotives (see Chapter 4). Together, they powered a system of scheduled trains between the outskirts of the growing cities of Philadelphia and New York, with a scheduled running time of about seven hours, perhaps less than half of what horse-drawn wagons might take.

By the 1840s, the tremendous potential of railways had become increasingly clear. Of the nation's 26 states, 22 of them had track—some 3,000 miles total, which at the time equaled that of canals. Prompted by a request from the B&O to build a line into Pittsburgh, the Commonwealth of Pennsylvania on April 13, 1846, issued a charter that sanctioned the creation of the Pennsylvania Railroad (PRR). Its purpose was to build an all-rail route between Philadelphia and Pittsburgh, and if it failed to do so, the B&O could do so instead. The PRR wasted little time, launching this daunting project in 1847. By this time, talented civil engineers for railway construction were beginning to surface, and the PRR hired a brilliant man by the name of Edgar Thompson to survey the new PRR route. He scouted out a nearly level, river-hugging route between Harrisburg and Altoona, at the base of the main ridge of the Alleghenies. Due west from there he envisioned a direct assault on the mountains, with the railroad climbing steadily out of Altoona and gaining much-needed elevation through one particularly large hairpin turn—the future Horseshoe Curve—that hugged parallel mountainsides. Near the top of the climb, Thompson avoided what would have been a particularly nasty, long, winding grade by proposing that a tunnel be bored right under the summit of the Alleghenies and into future Gallitzin,

Pennsylvania. From there, the railroad would have a relatively gentle grade all the way down to Johnstown and then over to Pittsburgh.

Construction commenced in 1847, and various segments were opened as they were completed. In some cases, the new PRR acquired small railroads that had already been started under a separate charter: for example, the Philadelphia & Columbia, which had already been built as part of the Main Line of Public Works system. The last piece of the puzzle— the engineering marvel known as Horseshoe Curve—in PRR's quest to surmount the spine of the Alleghenies in a direct manner was completed on February 15, 1854. That changed everything. The boom that almost instantly followed PRR's emergence as a through rail line between Philadelphia and Pittsburgh would help propel the "Pennsy" to become one of the most powerful railroads in U.S. history, a status it would maintain until the mid-twentieth century.

The impact of the opening of the PRR across the state could be felt on many levels. In 1857, the State of Pennsylvania put its Main Line of Public Works up for sale. Further, the State's own project of building an all-rail route over the mountains west of Altoona—the New Portage Railroad—was nearly rendered moot. (The PRR eventually bought it for use as a lower-grade, though longer, route for heavy freight trains to use in tackling the climb to Gallitzin.) As for the B&O, it was forever relegated to being the "other" carrier between the Atlantic seaboard and Pittsburgh.

Early Canadian Railway Development

In Canada in the first half of the 1800s, a similar unfolding of the new railroad technology was taking place. With commercial interests and population concentrated in today's Nova Scotia, New Brunswick, Quebec, and Ontario, newspapers and business leaders began suggesting railroad construction around 1820. The first short stretch of track was laid in 1829 at Albion Mines, Nova Scotia, to serve a coal mine. The title of Canada's first railroad, however, went to the 14 1/2-mile Champlain & St. Lawrence, chartered in 1832 and opened in July 1836 between Laprairie and St. Jean (St. John), Quebec, using the locomotive *Dorchester*. The line was extended to reach Montreal and the American border at Rouses Point, New York, by 1851. Soon after, in 1853, a new pair of affiliated railroads—the St. Lawrence & Atlantic and the Atlantic & St. Lawrence— connected at Island Pond, Vermont, and linked Montreal with the ice-free harbor at Portland, Maine, to provide Montreal grain merchants with a year-round transatlantic outlet for their cargo.

As in the United States, railroad construction in Canada boomed during the second half of the nineteenth century,

The Canadian Pacific is credited with creating Canada as it exists today. The CPR was North America's first true single-carrier transcontinental railroad. The main line was completed November 7, 1885, as CPR Director Donald Smith drove the last spike at Craigellachie, British Columbia. The stone cairn, built during the 100th anniversary of the last spike ceremony in 1985, is pictured June 3, 1990. *Steve Jessup photo*

and larger lines grew as they absorbed smaller companies. A major force in Canadian railroading during the second half of the nineteenth century was the Grand Trunk Railway, formed by British interests in 1852 and by the end of that decade stretching from Portland through Montreal and Toronto to Chicago. The GTR grew from an amalgamation of existing companies, including the aforementioned StL&A/ A&StL and C&StL in Quebec, and the Ontario, Simcoe & Huron and the Great Western in Ontario. As the head of practical navigation of the St. Lawrence River from both east and west, Montreal was a commercial crossroads long before the arrival of the railroads. The seaport of Halifax, Nova Scotia, was linked with Montreal by the Intercolonial Railway, and the city was also the eastern terminus of the Canadian Pacific Railway's transcontinental main line. Completed in November 1885, when the celebrated last spike was driven at remote Craigellachie, British Columbia, the CPR was North America's first true single-carrier transcontinental railroad, linking Atlantic and Pacific tidewater under one company's management. The CPR is also justly credited with creating the Canadian nation as it exists today; British Columbia agreed to join the confederation in 1871 on the promise of Prime Minister John A. MacDonald that such a railroad would be built.

Chicago and St. Louis Become New Goals

Back in the United States, the heat was on as the 1800s crested at midcentury. The race to link Atlantic seaboard ports with the Ohio River, Great Lakes, and the westward-marching frontier was akin to a frenzy. Joining the New York Central, Pennsylvania, and Baltimore & Ohio was the New York & Erie Railroad, which had been chartered in 1832 to link the Hudson River with Lake Erie. The charter required it to do so entirely within the State of New York, a mission that was accomplished when the railroad opened all the way through between Piermont (on the Hudson River above New York City) and Dunkirk, New York (on Lake Erie).

Although the B&O, NYC, PRR, and Erie attained their initial "frontier" goals—either the Ohio River or Lake Erie— there was a newly targeted destination a little farther west: a trading-post-turning-city known as Chicago. A diamond in the rough, Chicago eventually became the goal for nearly every major railroad built in North America. Our pioneer carriers from the East reached Chicago in 1869 (PRR), 1873 (NYC System), 1874 (B&O), and 1880 (Erie).

A late bloomer rising from the swampy southwestern shore of Lake Michigan, Chicago was incorporated in 1837 and by the end of the nineteenth century would establish itself as *the* transportation hub for the new America—a title held to this day. Chicago was established on the site of Fort Dearborn on a portage between Lake Michigan and the Mississippi watershed, specifically, the future Des Plaines/ Illinois River system. (Today's Chicago has spread entirely over this portage and then some.) Chicago's location at the western end of the Great Lakes system essentially made it an ersatz ocean port, and southwest from Chicago the Illinois and Mississippi rivers linked it to the Gulf of Mexico via St. Louis. Established in 1764, St. Louis was a rival to Chicago due to its ideal location at the confluence of the Missouri and Mississippi rivers as well as its location in an area surrounded by choice farmlands. Railroads that had reached Chicago now added lines to St. Louis, among them the NYC, PRR, and B&O.

Because of the sheer commerce generated by Chicago and St. Louis' advantageous locations, the most intense and dense railroad construction during the last half of the 1800s fell within the 1,200-or-so-mile-long Middle Atlantic Coast– Middle America region, which for our purposes we have dubbed the Trailblazer Belt. And a broad belt it was—300 miles at its widest point—with the New York Central System across its top and the B&O across its bottom. The Trailblazer Belt's east end was anchored in the great port cities of Boston, New York, Philadelphia, and Baltimore, while its west end was marked by Chicago and St. Louis.

The railroad's arrival in the Midwest changed the overall orientation of transportation from north-south along the Mississippi to east-west. And even though the Ohio, Mississippi, and Missouri rivers remain important shipping lanes to this day, the new railroads often provided bypasses. The route between Cincinnati and St. Louis by way of the river system was 702 miles; by the new Ohio & Mississippi Railroad it was only 339 miles—and an all-weather route to boot.

This new orientation became all the clearer when the first railroad bridge opened over the Mississippi in 1856. The span was built to link Rock Island, Illinois, with Davenport, Iowa, by a predecessor of the Chicago, Rock Island & Pacific Railroad building between Chicago and Iowa. Soon, the Rock Island was directing traffic to move between the East and the West via Rock Island rather than along a circuitous river route down through St. Louis to Cairo, Illinois, and then up to Pittsburgh.

The fertile lands of the territories that grew into the states of Ohio, Indiana, Illinois, Iowa, Minnesota, and Missouri drove the development of railroads in the interior while East Coast railroads were still building west. Clearly, this region was destined to become America's breadbasket. Although railroads in the region were quick to build links between Chicago and Milwaukee and the Mississippi River for access to steamboat lines, a multitude of other lines were built as town-to-town and city-to-city links to move agricultural products, grain, and livestock into populated areas for processing and consumption. For this reason, the density of rail lines would be highest in Middle America.

Giant Oaks from Acorns

During the middle 1800s, the process of railroad building took on a new, decidedly aggressive style. By this time, the resounding success and astonishing potential of this newfangled transportation method had become clear to business leaders and politicians alike. Railways were no longer a curiosity: they were the future of a new North America.

Naturally, some railroads were more successful than others. Some never got beyond their charter, while others began construction, only to meet with financial failure. But as the second half of the 1800s began to unfurl, the strongest railroads—like those mentioned earlier—began buying up unfulfilled charters, partially completed railroads, and wholly built railroads as a means of expansion. Similarly, some larger companies acquired control of lesser companies, built them up, and then merged them into the parent company (or sometimes into a totally new railroad). The result was a frenzied growth race among emerging railroad giants. Together, these processes allowed for faster expansion while also wiping out potential competition.

We'll return once more to the New York Central System for an example of how some of these growth methods played out. We've seen how a dozen small carriers strung out between Albany and Buffalo became a single railroad, the New York Central, in 1853. This didn't happen by chance, but at the behest of a budding rail baron known as Cornelius Vanderbilt. Also in 1853, Vanderbilt merged the new NYC with his own company, the Hudson River Railroad, to form the New York Central & Hudson River Railroad; later, Vanderbilt's New York & Harlem was added to the mix. To reach Chicago, Vanderbilt's NYC&HR in 1873 acquired control of the Lake Shore & Michigan Southern, a successful maverick of a line running between Buffalo and Chicago via Cleveland and Toledo, Ohio. To gain a foothold in Michigan as well as an alternate route between Buffalo and Chicago, the NYC&HR exerted its now-considerable influence over the Michigan Central—a Detroit–Chicago carrier—and its Canada Southern subsidiary through southern Ontario between Detroit and Buffalo, making the MC in essence an extension of the NYC&HR in 1900. Interestingly enough, Vanderbilt had owned stock in the MC since 1869, and he owned the CS outright! At about the same time, NYC&HR leased the Boston & Albany, giving the Central an anchor in New England, which was rapidly becoming a manufacturing region. Vanderbilt's firm control of the *Cleveland, Cincinnati, Chicago & St. Louis*—the "Big Four"—also played into the hands of the NYC&HR, allowing it to spread its influence farther into Ohio as well as across south-central Illinois to St. Louis, a new gateway to the American West. Acquisition of the Pittsburgh & Lake Erie brought the NYC&HR right into Pittsburgh, a stronghold of Central's most bitter rival, the monolithic Pennsylvania Railroad. Formal merger of the NYC&HR and LS&MS in 1914 resulted in a new railroad named . . . New York Central. The 1853 name had resurfaced once more, but now it was applied to a sprawling giant whose width (some 700 miles) and breadth (nearly 1,200 miles) and route-mileage (nearly 12,000) made it one of the largest companies in North America. The NYC chose to keep some of its components semi-independent as subsidiaries, hence the Central's adoption of the New York Central System name early in the twentieth century.

For purposes of this book, we've simplified the description of the rather convoluted growth pattern of the NYC, but it serves as an example of how many of the principal railroads of the late nineteenth century grew from almost nothing to the kingpin transportation players they became in the twentieth century. The NYC and its peers—the PRR, B&O, and Erie Railroad—would survive into the 1960s (1980s for the B&O) before they were likewise swallowed up in a whole new round of mergers . . . fodder for a later chapter.

Consolidation took place in Canada, too, culminating in the early 1920s creation of Canadian National Railways. Zealous overbuilding of rail lines and ill-conceived duplication of transcontinental routes in the late nineteenth century combined with a relatively sparse population and traffic base to create financial weakness among most of Canada's railroads by World War I. The federal government stepped in to order—and subsidize—the progressive amalgamation of the weakest companies into one massive, nationalized railroad, the CNR. The Canadian Pacific Railway was not involved, remaining privately owned as the cornerstone of a globe-spanning enterprise that included cargo vessels and ocean liners on both the Atlantic and Pacific. By the mid-1920s, Canada was a country of two major transcontinental railroads, the CPR and CNR, augmented by a handful of regional companies including the Temiskaming & Northern Ontario (known as Ontario Northland after 1947), the Algoma Central, and the Pacific Great Eastern (after 1972, the British Columbia Railway).

Beyond the Trailblazer Belt

The swath of railways—B&O, PRR, NYC, and Erie—that came to define the Trailblazer Corridor as the second half of the 1800s began would serve as a broad anchor for nearly all major railway construction after 1850. New railroads, and those expanding from other areas of the country, tended to anchor themselves to a city or cities within this corridor, especially Chicago, St. Louis, and New York.

In the mid-1800s, the industrial boom had spread to New England. With Boston, Massachusetts, as its epicenter, the region came to specialize in textiles and lumber—goods and materials in great demand throughout the Northeast and the Midwest—as well as dairy products. With this rising crescendo of manufacturing activity in Massachusetts, Connecticut, Rhode Island, New Hampshire, Vermont, and Maine, much of it built around mills reliant on water power (fast-moving waterways being abundant in New England), a web of railroads spread throughout the region. Most principal rail arteries in New England eventually led to Boston, though in a few

Railroad maps from 1830 (left), 1840 (center), and 1850 (right) are shown here. By the 1840s, rails were being laid in the South, and by the 1850s, tremendous growth had taken place in New England. The region specialized in textiles, lumber, and dairy products. With manufacturing on the rise, goods were in great demand throughout the Northeast and Midwest, providing the railroads with much business. *Association of American Railroads*

instances lines went northward to Montreal, Quebec. With roots dating from the 1830s, the Boston & Maine rose to become upper New England's prominent carrier, feeding into Boston from the north, northwest, and west. New England's early link to the Trailblazer Belt was near Albany, New York, where the Fitchburg Railway—a B&M predecessor linking Boston and Albany—connected to the New York Central & Hudson River. The New York, New Haven & Hartford Railroad, the earliest origins of which dated from 1833, would later provide the principal, through, all-rail link between Boston and New York City, the primary east-end anchor for the Trailblazer Belt.

Meanwhile, in the Southeast, agriculture dominated, with cotton being a major commodity that fed textile mills in the Northeast. Naturally, then, the Southeast's earliest railways were aimed at connecting Southeastern commercial centers—notably Atlanta, Georgia; Richmond, Virginia; and the important ocean port cities of Charleston, South Carolina, and Norfolk, Virginia—and the Trailblazer Belt, principally at Washington, D.C. The railroad destined to become the powerhouse railroad of the Southeast, the Southern Railway (SR), was the result of combining myriad small companies in Virginia, Tennessee, the Carolinas, Georgia, Alabama, and Florida in 1894. (Eventually, as traffic to and from the West developed, the SR would also reach into Kentucky, Ohio, Illinois, Missouri, and Louisiana.) One of these predecessor companies was the South Carolina Canal & Railroad Company, which in 1830 hosted America's first scheduled steam-powered passenger train, pulled by one of the most famous locomotives in U.S. history, the *Best Friend of Charleston*. The SR became a crescent-shaped, iron-bound artery linking the upper Atlantic seaboard with the gulf ports of Mobile, Alabama, and New Orleans, Louisiana, by way of Atlanta—the Southeast's most important transportation hub—and the industrial center of Birmingham, Alabama.

Twin principal rivals to the SR were the Atlantic Coast Line and the Seaboard Air Line railroads, with ACL antecedents—the Petersburg Railroad between Petersburg, Virginia, and Weldon, North Carolina—dating from 1830, and SAL predecessors—the Portsmouth & Roanoke, linking Portsmouth and Weldon—being chartered in 1832. Richmond wound up being a key anchor city for both the ACL and SAL once they had grown through the acquisition of several smaller companies. At Richmond, connection was made with the Richmond, Fredericksburg & Potomac, already a critical artery for north-south traffic between Richmond and the Trailblazer Belt at Washington, D.C.

With the emergence of Florida in the very late 1800s as both a destination for travelers and a newer source of agricultural and mineral products, the ACL and SAL's role in Southeastern transportation networks shifted. Formerly rivals of the SR, the ACL and SAL began to compete with each other for the lucrative Florida–Northeast traffic.

At the western frontier of the Southeast, specifically the Ohio River port city of Louisville, another future legend of Southeastern railroading, the storied Louisville & Nashville, was chartered in 1850 to connect its namesakes. Though late in its development compared to the SR, ACL, and SAL, the L&N nonetheless carved out its niche in Southeastern transportation by providing the Trailblazer Belt with another link to the Gulf of Mississippi, and to the Southeast, that

From the mid-1800s to today, Chicago has established itself as North America's railroad capital. Rising from a population of 4,000 in 1840 to more than 2.8 million, the Windy City owes its growth to the railroads. It caters to six of today's seven major railroads and served as the major interchange point for hundreds of railroads between East and West prior to the megamergers. Chicago is pictured with the Sears Tower in the background on March 11, 1998. *Howard Ande photo*

bypassed having to funnel traffic from Middle America over to and through Washington. Further, the L&N played a critical role in the transportation of coal to population centers at a time when coal was becoming America's principal fuel. Coal drove trains and boats; it heated buildings and was critical to the emerging iron and steel industry.

Chicago's Rise to North America's Railroad Capital

Towns and cities in the interior of the continent did not wait for the arrival of railroads from the East Coast before building their own railways. As was the case throughout much of young America, European settlements had been established along rivers—especially the Mississippi and Missouri—and on the Great Lakes as early as the 1700s, though most places above St. Louis were established early in the 1800s. As cited earlier, Chicago, at the far northeast corner of Illinois (which gained statehood in 1818), holds a special place in the story of North American railroading, for early on it became (and remains) the most important railroad center of the continent. Chicago achieved this formidable status through both its geographical location and the fact that, early on, it had established itself as the chief supply center for railroad equipment and construction needs.

One of the fastest-growing cities in American history, Chicago owes its growth to the railroads. Chicago was established by some 350 people in 1833 on the site of Fort Dearborn, itself built in 1803 as a protected trading post for fur traders and ships sailing the Great Lakes. Chicago was incorporated as a city in 1837, and by 1840 it had a population of over 4,000. By 1850, it was close to 30,000; by 1860, it had exploded to 112,000 to become the ninth-largest city in the United States. In 1870, it was close to 300,000, and by 1890 Chicago had become the second-largest city in North America with over 1 million people. The growth was largely driven by the city's place in the country's transportation network, principally its railroads.

Chicago's first railroad, the Galena & Chicago Union, came from within (versus a railroad that built in from somewhere else) and was chartered a year before the city's incorporation in 1837. Construction did not begin until 1847, and in 1848 the first train ran from Chicago to what is today the suburb of Oak Park. The G&CU was headed for the lead mines of northwestern Illinois at Galena, but the Illinois Central, building up from the Ohio River, got there first. The G&CU refocused its efforts and built a new line due west from today's West Chicago to the Mississippi River at Fulton, Illinois, which it reached in 1864. The G&CU was the genesis of the Chicago & North Western Railway, a reigning Midwestern carrier based in Chicago.

The IC was another Chicago-based powerhouse, chartered in 1851 to build a line up from the Ohio River at Cairo, Illinois, to the lead mines of northwestern Illinois as well as a line to Chicago off this "charter line." The IC pulled into Chicago in 1856 and quickly became one of the city's key railroads—and remained so until nearly the end of the twentieth century, when Canadian railroads began to take over U.S. carriers.

Several other Chicago-based railroads were born before any of the westward-building East Coast railroads reached town first in 1869. The Chicago, Burlington & Quincy, destined to become one of the finest American railroads, began in 1849 as the Aurora Branch Railroad, built to connect Aurora, Illinois (now a Chicago satellite city), with the G&CU. The ABRR became the CB&Q in 1864, the same year it built its own line into downtown Chicago. By the end of the nineteenth century, the CB&Q blanketed Midwestern farm country with branches built to serve grain elevators and had main lines to Denver, Colorado; Billings, Montana; the Twin Cities of Minneapolis/St. Paul, Minnesota; and St. Louis and Kansas City, Missouri.

In 1864, the Chicago & Alton opened a through route between Chicago and St. Louis, thereby shortening transit times for freight moving on a rail-water route between Chicago and New Orleans. In the 1870s, the C&A created a through route between Chicago and Kansas City.

The Chicago, Rock Island & Pacific—the fabled Rock Island Lines—had its genesis in an 1845 railroad proposition envisioned to link the Illinois & Michigan Canal, which ran between Chicago and La Salle, Illinois, with the Mississippi River, thereby providing a new transportation route between Chicago and the Mississippi. But in the end, the Chicago & Rock Island Railroad—the foundation of the future CRI&P— was chartered in 1850 to replace the I&M Canal, which is indeed what happened when the railroad opened and the locomotive *Rocket* left Chicago with the C&RI's first train to Joliet, Illinois. This was yet another instance of the railroad triumphing over canals, as was being played out in the East.

Some 90 miles north of Chicago lay its rival city, Milwaukee, Wisconsin, hard against the western shore of Lake Michigan. Though younger than Chicago by nine years, Milwaukee was very much its own commercial center and was seeking its own means of developing railroads to serve its needs. Its earliest efforts in rail transportation were providing impetus for a railway to be built west to link the city with the Mississippi River. This took place in 1857, when the Milwaukee & Mississippi reached Prairie du Chien, Wisconsin, on the east bank of the river. The M&M was one of the earliest predecessor lines of yet another powerhouse Midwestern railroad, the Milwaukee & St. Paul, which soon had lines

This map shows the extent of railway development just prior to the Civil War. The decade 1850–1860 was a period of rapid railway expansion, characterized by the extension of many short, disjointed lines into important rail routes. This decade marked the beginning of railway development in the region west of the Mississippi River. By 1860, the "Iron Horse" had penetrated westward to the Missouri River and was beginning to make itself felt in Iowa, Arkansas, Texas, and California. *Association of American Railroads*

fanning out in all directions from Milwaukee. However, as much as the city tried, the tremendous influence of Chicago could not be ignored, and in 1873 the M&StP opened a through line between Milwaukee and Chicago. This prompted a name change to Chicago, Milwaukee & St. Paul, and eventually The Milwaukee Road, despite the nickname that would last until 1985, would be headquartered in Chicago, with lines radiating in four directions from Chicago.

Westward Ho!

Throughout the turmoil of the Civil War period, the Wild West beckoned. It had been prompted by California's admission to the union in 1850 (not to mention the discovery of gold there in 1849) and the ongoing quest of the federal government to stake out as much territory as it could to accommodate the country's influx of immigrants. But separating California and the Oregon Territory to the north from the westernmost reaches of the fledgling railway network, now approaching the Missouri River, were vast plains and the formidable Rocky Mountain and Cascade ranges. The Missouri was the only navigable waterway that reached from Middle America into the West, though it ended in present-day Montana, well short of the Pacific Coast; further, its shallowness limited its use by shallow-draft steamboats. Other transportation routes penetrating the West were the pathways established by pioneer migration in wagon trains, notably the Santa Fe, Mormon, California, and Oregon trails, all of which had their starting points on the Missouri River.

The railroad was the only means of transportation that could eclipse these barriers, cutting travel time from months

Railroads and the Civil War

The Civil War was the first major conflict in the world wherein railroads were key weapons—for both sides. Railroads played a large part in deploying both materials and troops, which was especially important to the South, which had fewer troops. Trains allowed soldiers to be quickly shifted between fronts, even if broadly separated. Thanks to the railroads, Confederate General Braxton Bragg was able to move his 30,000 troops to Tennessee from Mississippi in less than a week, while General Robert E. Lee was able to quickly reinforce General "Stonewall" Jackson's army in Virginia through use of troop trains.

The critical role of railroads in aiding the Confederacy did not go unnoticed by the Union Army. When General William Sherman made his landmark "March to the Sea" in 1864, creating an arc of devastation to Southern forces, he did so by moving along rail lines down from the north, using them as his supply line—and then destroying the lines behind him so they became useless to the Confederacy.

In fact, the Civil War wound up destroying more than half of the South's railroad infrastructure. The fact that the less-industrialized and undercapitalized South had fielded a substandard railroad network to begin with didn't help matters. The opposite happened above the Mason-Dixon Line, with Northern railroads strengthened by the tragic conflict.

If there was any good to come of it for the South, it was that Southern railroads had to in essence be completely rebuilt, and they would do so without overbuilding as would be the case in the North and Midwest. Further, the South was able to rebuild its rail network using up-to-date technologies. In the long run—particularly in the second half of the twentieth century—and because of this, the South's railroad system would remain robust even as Northeastern roads began to crumble.

The railroad bridge at Harpers Ferry, West Virginia, is a scene of absolute destruction in this photo taken during the Civil War. The war took a much greater toll in the South—half of the entire railroad infrastructure built in this region was obliterated. The South would rebuild using updated technology, and as the Northeastern roads began to wobble, the South's railroads system would remain strong. *C. O. Bostwick photo, U.S. Library of Congress*

to days. Well aware of this, Congress appropriated funding to study potential rail routes to the West Coast. Talk of a true, Atlantic-to-Pacific transcontinental railroad dated from the early 1830s but did not get beyond the talking (and arguing) stage until 1853, when U.S. Secretary of War Jefferson Davis pushed the Pacific Railway Survey into action. Survey parties scouted out four principal routes west of the Mississippi: three in the southern half of the U.S. states and territories and one

across the northern tier. In the end, however, none of these were adopted for what became the first rail line to link the frontier with the Pacific Coast.

Though distracted by the depression of 1857 and impending civil war between the North and South, the Republican Party adopted a platform that envisioned a railroad to the Pacific Ocean. That vision became considerably clearer when President Abraham Lincoln signed the Pacific Railway

In a Civil War–era scene of utter destruction at Richmond, Virginia, a steam locomotive has bitten the dust at the Richmond & Petersburg Railroad Depot. A translation for the five men posing with the steamer might be, "Well, boys, onward we go!" During this time, railroads were looking to expand westward to the Pacific Ocean, and four years after the war, the vision of a transcontinental railroad was realized. *U.S. Library of Congress*

Probably the most famous and significant photograph in the history of American railroading is this image of the joining of the Union Pacific and Central Pacific at Promontory, Utah, May 10, 1869, completing the first transcontinental railroad. On the left is the Central Pacific *Jupiter* facing Union Pacific No. 119, both 4-4-0 American-type steam engines. One could ride from the Atlantic to the Pacific mostly by train using four railroads. *Union Pacific photo*, Railfan & Railroad Magazine *collection*

Bill on July 1, 1862, authorizing the Union Pacific Railroad to build west from Omaha, Nebraska Territory, on the Missouri River, while the new Central Pacific Railroad was to build east from Sacramento, California. The bill also forced the issue of a standardized track gauge, calling for the new line to be built in standard gauge: 4 feet, 8 1/2 inches—the majority gauge outside of the rebellious South, which had a variety of gauges that were all wider than standard.

The two new lines would meet at a location to be determined by the progress of each—with both railroads being paid by the mile. To a degree, this enticement backfired, with track crudely and hastily built so as to lay down as many miles as possible in the space of a day. With Grenville Dodge leading a crew of

10,000 men, the UP began the monumental task on December 2, 1863; the Central Pacific commenced on January 8, 1864, with Chinese laborers. The CP faced a particularly daunting challenge, the Sierra Range, which it negotiated by way of Donner Pass, the current route of Amtrak's *California Zephyr*.

It took more than five years, but on May 10, 1869, at 12:47 p.m., the UP and the CP met at Promontory, Utah, thus completing the nation's first transcontinental rail route. Photos and other illustrations of this driving of the final, golden spike[*] and locomotives *Jupiter* and UP No. 119 meeting pilot

[*] Because the 17.6-carat gold spike would have been too soft to actually drive into the wooden tie, the hole for it was pre-driven and the spike gently tapped into it.

to pilot have been the staple of history books for decades, but the importance of this event could hardly be understated. CP president Leland Stanford drove a regular iron spike with an iron mallet, both of which were wired such that when the two came in contact, a signal was sent out along the telegraph lines all the way to Chicago and Washington, D.C., where fire bells were activated and, in Washington, a ball was lowered over the U.S. Capitol building's dome.

The reference to May 10, 1869, as the completion of the first transcontinental railroad is a bit of a misnomer, the implication being that a single railroad had been responsible for this feat. True, as of May 10, 1869, one could ride from the Atlantic to the Pacific mostly by train, but it involved the use of several railroads: the Pennsylvania Railroad from Philadelphia to Chicago; the Chicago & North Western from Chicago to Council Bluffs, Iowa; the UP from Omaha to Promontory; and the CP to Sacramento—where you were still 90 miles from the Pacific. A steamboat completed that gap until the Central Pacific (later, Southern Pacific) could lay rails to today's Oakland.

And, technically, this wasn't even an all-rail route, since freight and passenger traffic still had to be ferried across the Missouri River between Council Bluffs and Omaha until the first bridge opened between the two cities in 1872.

That said, the floodgates now had been opened for the push to settle the West, and the fledgling railroad industry was poised for the challenge. New railroads marched west from the Missouri River as well as from endpoints of the various granger railroads well under construction by this time. The westward-building lines followed several alternative routes to the West Coast, and in their wake, brand-new towns and cities grew—often at the expense of Native Americans and

Although the Civil War temporarily halted railway development, many projects were resumed or initiated soon after the conflict. The nation's network increased from 30,626 miles in 1860 to 52,922 miles in 1870. An outstanding development of the decade was the construction of the first railroad to the Pacific Ocean, making it possible to travel all the way across the country by rail. Railway development in the Mississippi and Missouri valleys was especially notable during this period. *Association of American Railroads*

In the 10-year period prior to 1880, some 40,000 miles of railroad were built, bringing the total network up to 93,267 miles. In 1880, every state and territory was provided with railway transportation. A second line of railroads to the Pacific was nearing completion, and other transcontinental railroads were under construction. Railway development was exerting a powerful influence upon immigration and agricultural and industrial growth throughout the country. *Association of American Railroads*

vast, roaming herds of buffalo. For the new farmers, ranchers, and commercial wholesalers, the railroad became their lifeline to the East—and West.

This new railway expansion into the Western prairies was greatly aided by a concept that became federal policy about 1850: land grants. To promote expansion and commerce, the federal government provided some 170 million acres of land to about 80 different railroads (Illinois Central being the first to benefit from this practice) in the space of about 20 years—land that is today worth billions of dollars. Not only was the land used for railroad rights-of-way, but the railroad companies themselves sold the land at bargain prices (but 100 percent profit) to immigrants, farmers, and merchants. Towns sprang up all along the new railroads that then brought in merchandise and building materials and shipped out the harvests of agriculture and cattle ranching. Contrary to popular belief, land grants were not a true giveaway, but a form

of credit. In return for the land, the federal government was entitled to use land-grant-driven railroads for transportation at greatly reduced rates. Not until the late 1940s was the balance due paid off.

By the end of the nineteenth century, the single, fragile route between Omaha and Sacramento via North Platte, Nebraska, and Ogden, Utah, which had opened in 1869, had given way to five major transcontinental routes, including that of a carrier destined to become one of the foremost railroads in American history: the Atchison, Topeka & Santa Fe. Like so many other railroads of the era, the Santa Fe was created from a consolidation of several smaller railroads. Upon its completion in 1888, the Santa Fe's transcontinental main line stretched over 2,200 miles from Chicago to Los Angeles (on two different routes, actually) through Illinois, Iowa, Missouri, Kansas, Colorado (Texas on the alternate route), New Mexico, Arizona, and California.

Two other southerly transcontinental routes involved the Southern Pacific. Its route from Los Angeles to Tucumcari, New Mexico, was coordinated with the Chicago, Rock Island & Pacific (Rock Island Lines) at Tucumcari to form the Golden State Route all the way to Chicago via Kansas City. SP's Sunset Route (shared with the Golden State Route between Los Angeles and El Paso, Texas) reached all the way to New Orleans.

Across the northern tier of the United States, both the Great Northern and rival Northern Pacific linked the Twin Cities of Minneapolis/St. Paul, Minnesota, with Seattle and

Tacoma, Washington. Both roads used affiliate Chicago, Burlington & Quincy to close the gap between the Twin Cities and Chicago, along with the Chicago & North Western, the Chicago, Milwaukee & St. Paul, the Wisconsin Central, and the Rock Island. The Spokane, Portland & Seattle Railway allowed NP and GN to reach down into the important inland port and gateway city of Portland, Oregon.

Other late-bloomer transcontinental routes in the United States would open late in the 1800s and early 1900s, some of them as consortiums of cooperating railroads and

The result of a consolidation of several smaller railroads, the Atchison, Topeka & Santa Fe was destined to be one of the foremost carriers in the United States. Linking Chicago with Los Angeles and the Bay Area, as well as reaching into the Gulf Coast, the Santa Fe developed a reputation for excellent service and expedience on both freight and passenger runs. Here, a westbound passenger train arrives at the depot at Burlingame, Kansas, in the late 1800s. *Kevin EuDaly collection*

The period from 1880 to 1890 was one of rapid expansion. More than 70,300 miles of new lines were opened in that decade, bringing the total network up to 163,597 miles. By 1890, several trunk-line railroads extended to the Pacific. In 30 years, from 1860 to 1890, the total mileage of the region west of the Mississippi River increased from 2,175 to 72,389, and the population of that area increased fourfold. *Association of American Railroads*

one other as a single-railroad Chicago–West Coast carrier (The Milwaukee Road). Interestingly, a true Atlantic-to-the-Pacific single-carrier transcontinental U.S. railroad would not appear until the National Railroad Passenger Corporation (Amtrak) began operations in 1971, although at the time, none of its trains actually ran from coast to coast. In 1980, the St. Louis-San Francisco (Frisco) Railroad was merged into Burlington Northern (itself the product of the 1970 merger of Great Northern, Northern Pacific, Burlington Route, and Spokane, Portland & Seattle). This merger provided single-carrier freight service between the Gulf of Mexico and the West Coast, but that was as close to a truetranscontinental freight carrier within the contiguous

United States as there would be as of the writing of this book, although both Canadian National and Canadian Pacific opened newer Atlantic–Pacific transcontinental routes by way of Chicago through the acquisition and/or control of certain U.S. carriers.

In Canada, truly transcontinental railroads were a way of transportation life as early as November 7, 1885. On that day, the Canadian Pacific was completed, making it possible to ship by rail from Montreal to Pacific tidewater at Vancouver, British Columbia. Although Montreal is nowhere near the Atlantic Ocean, its position on the St. Lawrence River/Seaway gave it a direct water link to the Atlantic.

The CPR was envisioned as the land portion of an All Red Route linking Great Britain with its Asian colonies. (On maps of that period, Britain and its possessions were colored red.) CPR ships crossed the Pacific from Vancouver to China and Japan (a significant source of silk traffic until the 1920s), and by about 1910 CPR had its own fleets of passenger and cargo liners between Montreal and the United Kingdom, too.

Standardization Begets Interchange and Efficiency

The Civil War (1861–1865, see sidebar) was a turning point for the United States in several ways, not just cultural. On the railroad side, it prompted the integration and standardization of the wild array of railroads that had mushroomed throughout the East, Southeast, and Midwest. In the North alone, these railroads were using nearly a dozen different track gauges, ranging from the Erie Railroad's

Three track gauges are shown in this photo near Carbondale, Pennsylvania. The D&H gravity lines measure 4 feet 3 inches, the D&H standard line is 4 feet 8 1/2 inches, and the Erie broad gauge line is 6 feet. The majority of railroads used the standard gauge. Standardization would be the critical component for the future interchange of traffic between the railroads, and such a cooperative effort would be the better way to do business with passengers and shippers. *Jim Shaughnessy collection*

Where Standard Gauge Didn't Apply

In the 1870s, when most American railroads were climbing onto the standard gauge bandwagon, several new rail lines went in the opposite direction—to narrow gauge. The best-known example of this fascinating genre of railroading still exists and today is one of the most popular rail-oriented tourist attractions in the United States: the Colorado narrow gauge.

Most narrow gauge lines in Colorado and adjacent New Mexico were built by the Denver & Rio Grande Railway beginning in the 1870s. Why narrow gauge? Because it was more economical to construct and was a better fit in some of the tight confines of the Colorado Rockies. But the D&RG, which became the Denver & Rio Grande Western in 1921, wasn't entirely narrow gauge. In the late 1880s, the railroad assembled a standard gauge route between Pueblo, Colorado, and Ogden, Utah. In addition, it added a third rail along its route between Denver and Pueblo so that it could be used by either standard gauge or narrow gauge equipment.

Eventually, a considerable amount of the railroad was standard gauged, but the Rio Grande continued some of its 3-foot-gauge operations until—amazingly—1979, when it sold off its now-famous Durango–Silverton line to a private operator. It had already sold off another one of its narrow gauge lines to the states of Colorado and New Mexico in 1970 for tourist operations. Both of these lines can still be experienced today as successful tourist railroads.

In the Eastern United States, Maine was a hotbed of 2-foot-gauge railroading, which was well suited for lumber-hauling as well as economical to build, frugality being a hallmark of New England. The famous Sandy River & Rangeley Lakes survived until 1935 but still has a devoted following of historians. Others included the Bridgeton & Saco River, which lasted until World War II, and the Monson Railroad, which went out in 1943 as the last Maine "two-footer."

In Pennsylvania, the East Broad Top Railroad is a well-remembered coal-hauling institution that now, in private hands and supported by a legion of EBT aficionados, serves as a tourist-hauler though with a considerable dose of authenticity. Dating from 1856 but not in operation until the 1870s, the 3-foot-gauge EBT was built to haul coal from Broad Top Mountain mines to the Pennsylvania Railroad at Mount Union; later, it would carry other bulk commodities as well. The EBT holds the distinction of being the last common-carrier narrow gauge line east of the Mississippi River.

Other late-surviving narrow gauge operations largely involved various logging railroads scattered about North America, but particularly in California, Kentucky, Louisiana, Oregon, West Virginia, Mississippi, South Carolina, Tennessee, and other regions where forestry is essential to area commerce. Aside from being economical to build, the tracks of narrow gauge logging railroads could be easily shifted, moved around, or relaid to follow the ever-changing paths of tree cutting. When trucking came of age, it doomed most logging railroads. A few have been revived as tourist attractions.

The Durango & Silverton Narrow Gauge Railroad wanders through the mountains of southwest Colorado as passengers enjoy this spectacular scene in June of 1987. This narrow gauge line was built by the Denver & Rio Grande in 1881–1882 primarily to haul gold and silver ore mined in the San Juan Mountains. Narrow gauge railroads were more economical to construct and were better suited to the tight confines of the Colorado Rockies. *Jim Boyd photo*

6-foot broad gauge to the South's 5-foot "Carolina gauge" and Ohio's 4-foot 10-inch gauge down to 3-foot narrow gauge and even 2-foot gauge in Maine. A majority of railroads, of course, were using the standard gauge of 4 feet 8 1/2 inches set forth by England (specifically George Stephenson) years earlier.

Regardless, the differences wrought transportation havoc, with freight having to be reloaded into different cars at every interchange point and passengers having to change trains, sometimes waiting hours for the next railroad's train to run. Prior to the war, for example, there was even a local statute that no freight car could pass from one railroad to another in Pittsburgh without being reloaded—because until the loads were transferred from one car to another, the crooks and politicians could not get their share of the goods. It was President Lincoln and the threat of Robert E. Lee that cleaned up that corruption.

In fact, the concept of interchanging one railroad's freight (or passenger) car to another to eliminate cartage between carriers at transfer points—which was often in larger cities where railroads still lacked direct connections to each other, anyway—was a foreign concept to most carriers of the era that smacked of giving in to the competition. Not until commercial pressures forced the issue did some railroad companies begin offering faster freight service through joint agreements with participating carriers—agreements that allowed a railroad's cars to operate over a participant's lines. Once this concept caught on as being a better way to do business, standardization became even more important.

The Master Car Builder's Association was organized in 1867 to establish industry standards to enhance the railroad-to-railroad interchange of equipment. Formally adopting the standard gauge mandated by the Pacific Railway Act, the MCBA set standards for external dimensions of the cars, axle loadings, wheel contours, couplers, brake equipment, and other pertinent equipment.

During the remainder of the century, a vast majority of North American railroads standardized their track gauges to 4 feet 8 1/2 inches and, as much as feasible, modified their existing locomotives and rolling stock to MCBA specifications. New locomotives and cars were designed and built to MCBA standards. As a result, by the end of the century, railroad cars were being freely interchanged from carrier to carrier, eliminating the need to transload freight. And passenger trains could operate through from point A to point B over more than one carrier, sparing passengers the discomfort of having to change trains several times throughout a journey between, say, New York and Chicago.

Closing out the Century

With the Civil War out of the way, a transcontinental route now in place, and standardization under way, the North American railroad industry entered another period of phenomenal growth. During the last three decades of the nineteenth century, many railroad companies grew to be large, powerful entities that virtually controlled the country through political and financial clout—and spurious activities. Welcome to the era of rail barons.

Cornelius Vanderbilt, of New York Central fame, is sometimes cited as the father of rail barons, figuratively speaking. He was already worth $11 million when he acquired the New York & Hudson and New York & Harlem railroads in 1862. Vanderbilt's principal foes were Daniel Drew, Jim Fisk, and Jay Gould, all of the up-and-coming New York & Erie. The latter three swindled Vanderbilt out of an enormous sum of money through a surreptitious stock exchange, after which Vanderbilt (who had been trying to gain control of the rival Erie) had a warrant issued for their arrest. The three fugitives, who had escaped to New Jersey, wound up buying off the New York State legislature with a half million in cash to get out of trouble.

These four and their ilk from other railroads watered stock, fueled rate wars, and bought off judges and politicians to secure their own interests. Railroads became bullies as much as transportation companies, often steamrolling their own customers to line the pockets of stockholders. The byproduct of their financial battles was a railroad infrastructure that was redefining how America would live and grow.

In the end, shippers, farmers, and the railroad labor force prevailed, their outrage fueling the Grange, a powerful political entity in the granger (rural agricultural) states, to enact Granger laws in the 1870s that would fix rates. The feds likewise reacted, creating the Interstate Commerce Commission in 1887 to regulate railroad activities—and none too soon. By the turn of the twentieth century, two-thirds of the nation's rail mileage was controlled by only seven railroad entities, despite the hundreds of railroad companies from coast to coast. That's how powerful (and destructive) the big guys had become.

When Theodore Roosevelt became the twenty-sixth president of the United States in 1901, one of his priorities was to curb the reckless endeavors of American railroads by further strengthening the ICC and implementing a system of checks and balances. This suppression initially was a success, fostering rational growth and boosting business with fair rates. But many of these controls would have a long-lasting effect that would haunt the railroads for most of the century that followed.

The Rail Barons

by Steve Jessup

What is the definition of a "rail baron," and who were they? The origin of the term dates back to the Gilded Age (1865–1895), as journalists described greed-driven individuals whose sole ambitions in life were to amass personal fortunes off the nation's largest business—railroading—by means of the carriers' stocks and bonds. These barons were manipulators of finance rather than builders of track, and their fortunes came by acquiring ownership of a profitable industry, then capitalizing on those profits by selling securities to the public. Additionally, shifts in investors' perception of future profits allowed financial gain. The term "rail baron" is linked to those who utilized unethical practices, and since the railroad industry was plagued by corruption with security scandals and rate manipulation, it's sometimes difficult to separate the true pioneers of the industry from the money thugs who had no true interest in railroading and only went through the motions. In pursuing such fortunes, it's safe to say that there was dirt in everyone's closet, including the government. However, the history books give us some information on a few individuals who resorted to questionable tactics to feed their monetary lust.

Daniel Drew (1797–1879): Drew began his career as a cattle drover and floated into stock speculation. He established a brokerage house and invested in the steamboat industry. Drew took interest in the stock of the troubled Chicago & Erie Railroad and eventually became its director in 1857 and elected treasurer. In the 1860s, he brought Jay Gould and James Fisk on to the board of directors, forming an alliance with them. When New York Central's Cornelius Vanderbilt tried to gain control of the Erie, Drew, Gould, and Fisk used their own printing presses to issue millions of dollars' worth of "watered stock" and tried to lure Vanderbilt into buying as many shares as he wanted. The three absconded to New Jersey—thereby avoiding arrest—where New York's laws weren't applicable. Through bribery, the three legalized the stock, but the sham essentially killed the railroad. Pointing the finger at Drew for ruining the Erie, Gould and Fisk turned on him. Drew lost his fortune in the panic of 1873 and died in 1879 with only $500 to his name.

James Fisk (1834–1872): Fisk opened a brokerage house in New York in 1865 and was discovered by Daniel Drew, eventually becoming an agent in Drew's steamboat dealings. Forming a partnership with Drew and Jay Gould, Fisk would move on to become the comptroller of the Erie Railroad in 1868. He had no knowledge or skills in railroading and was primarily "along for the ride" with Gould and Drew. Beyond that, he was known as a New York–area playboy and died in that limelight.

Jay Gould (1836–1892): Gould was regarded by the popular press as the ultimate robber baron. Before forming a tight relationship with Daniel Drew and James Fisk, Gould had a brokerage house in New York speculating in stocks and gold. He was among the richest Americans of his time, and because of that wealth, he was tagged as the ringleader of the trio. Gould was president of the Erie, and beyond the unscrupulous acts of issuing "watered stock," he tried to mend a wrecked and worthless railroad to no avail as stockholders expelled him. In 1874, Gould took control of the Union Pacific, only to give it up in 1878. He continued to buy railroad properties until his death, at which point he had control of more trackage than anyone, at 8,160 miles.

Collis P. Huntington (1821–1900): After opening a general store in New York, Huntington moved to Sacramento, California, at the start of the gold rush. He formed a hardware store with partner Mark Hopkins. In 1860, Huntington took interest in a presentation from Theodore Judah on a proposed railroad over the Sierra Mountains. Along with Hopkins, Charles Crocker, and Leland Stanford, the "Big Four," as they were known (no relation to the railroad of the same name), pledged their support to help finance Judah's attempts to secure government loans. Congress chartered the Central Pacific in 1862, and a year later, Judah died. Huntington took control, and he and his buddies pocketed enormous profits by controlling the construction company that turned in inflated bills for its work. When the acts were uncovered in 1872, a congressional committee sought "the books" only to find them burned in a "mysterious" fire. Huntington, who was the financial agent for the railroad, was also a lobbyist in Washington, D.C., where he fended off the efforts of competitors to secure government loans. Huntington discouraged other railroads from entering Southwestern areas by building the Southern Pacific to El Paso and New Orleans.

Mark Hopkins (1813–1878): Along with Collis Huntington, Hopkins ran a hardware store in Sacramento and later became Huntington's financial assistant for the Central Pacific. He wasn't exactly "into" physical labor, thus he was never out and about on the railroad, preferring to keep a low profile behind company curtains. Hopkins was well aware of the financial deceit and took the blame from Huntington in burning the books, although it was played up as an unfortunate incident. The fire remains a mystery, by their accounts.

Leland Stanford (1824–1893): Stanford practiced law in New York before becoming a merchant in the Sacramento area, where he also toyed with politics. He became the governor of California from January 1862 to December 1863. Stanford was the president of the Central Pacific, though his duties were hardly in the trenches, but rather more ceremonious. Along with the Union Pacific's Thomas Durant, Stanford drove the last spike at Promontory, Utah, where the transcontinental main would meet. Eventually, he fell out of favor with Collis Huntington when Stanford took a Senate seat occupied by one of Huntington's friends. Stanford also founded and endowed Stanford University in Palo Alto, California, in honor of his son, Leland Stanford Jr., who died at age 15.

Charles Crocker (1822–1888): Of the Big Four linked with the Central Pacific, Crocker may be the least known and the one who had the "cleaner" hands among them. Crocker opened up a dry goods store in Sacramento, and in 1854, he was elected to the state legislature. Crocker became associated with Theodore Judah, Collis Huntington, Mark Hopkins, and Charles Stanford in the Central Pacific project. His role was taking charge of building the railroads while leaving the finances up to the others.

Thomas Durant (1820–1885): Before jumping into the railroad world to fill his pockets, Durant practiced medicine for a short time then moved on to the flour and grain business as well as stock speculation. He was associated with the Lake Shore & Michigan Southern, the Chicago & Rock Island, and the Mississippi & Missouri. Next, Durant had his own ideas about extending the Union Pacific westward, organizing the board of directors for his own benefit. He served as vice president and general manager and sat on the executive and finance committees. Two workers, including the first chief engineer, exited under Durant, who then often interfered with engineer Mellen Dodge by increasing route mileage in order to gain financially. Already known for unethical financial practices, Durant's next cure for his railroad's pending economic doom was to produce a charter (with the aid of Congressman Oakes Aimes, Massachusetts) for the Credit Mobilier to build the UP. The bogus Credit Mobilier company piled up generous sums of money that were far more than the actual costs of the line, and profits were nicely shared with stockholders—among them not only the leaders of the road, but also members of Congress and the vice president. The Credit Mobilier scandal, coupled with the financial deceit of the Central Pacific and overcapitalization in the industry, would harm the railroads for more than half a century. As for Durant, he would continue in his schemes all the way to the last spike ceremony in Promontory. Within two weeks, he was dropped from the board and never realized any business success thereafter.

Cornelius Vanderbilt (1794–1877): A financier and railroad promoter, he just might be the most well-known rail baron, but at least he spawned a wealthy, healthy railroad—the grand New York Central System—to show for it.

One of the rail barons was Cornelius "Commodore" Vanderbilt (1794–1877), an American entrepreneur who began in the steamship business. In the early 1860s, he started withdrawing capital from his steamships and began investing heavily in railroads. One of his main rivals, Jay Gould, always seemed to get the better of him. Vanderbilt is associated with the standardization of gauges and the use of steel in rails. *Mike Schafer collection*

Vanderbilt started on the road to wealth in the maritime business, then shifted to investing in the rail industry. He got control of three railroads, including the New York Central in 1867, and eventually built his system to Chicago upon acquiring the Michigan Central and Lake Shore & Michigan Southern railroads. Later, Vanderbilt wrestled with the Gould Ring (Jay Gould, Daniel Drew, and James Fisk) for control of the Erie Railroad but lost due to the Gould Ring's innovative debauchery. The Commodore, as he was known, called for their arrest, but the trio escaped to New Jersey and bribed the New York legislature, which legalized the watered stock. Unfortunately for Vanderbilt, he lost both money and his attempt to control the Erie. But Vanderbilt knew the game, as he had bribed his way into acquiring and merging the Harlem River Railroad with the Hudson River Railroad. Had he not lived a philosophy that law could be overcome by craft and ingenuity (not to mention a ruthless demeanor, by historical accounts), he may have been remembered for more than just being the richest man in America in 1877.

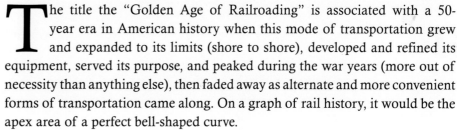

The Golden Age, 1900–1950

by Steve Jessup

The title the "Golden Age of Railroading" is associated with a 50-year era in American history when this mode of transportation grew and expanded to its limits (shore to shore), developed and refined its equipment, served its purpose, and peaked during the war years (more out of necessity than anything else), then faded away as alternate and more convenient forms of transportation came along. On a graph of rail history, it would be the apex area of a perfect bell-shaped curve.

In a way, it seems to convey the idea that the railroads never enjoyed better times. Stand on a street corner and ask the average U.S. citizen to determine America's finest hour in railroad history, and the answer will likely hinge on the latter side of this time frame. We all know the story. Sometime in the classroom, we learned about the railroad boom and how it dominated the transportation industry back in the late 1800s and early 1900s. Then we heard the stories from our grandparents or aunts and uncles about rail travel back in their day, tied that to photographic images we've seen in

No better image represents the "Golden Age of Railroading" than this scene at the Rockwell City, Iowa, depot in the first decade of the twentieth century. Two Chicago, Milwaukee & St. Paul Railroad trains heading in opposite directions are stopped at the station. Three modes of on-land transportation are seen: train, horse-drawn carriage, and walking. Note the classic 4-4-0 American steam engine and the short wooden railcars. *Milwaukee Road photo, Milwaukee Road Historical Association archives*

Transferring from the steamboat *Sagamore* to the afternoon local train to Albany, New York, passengers step aboard at Lake George station in 1906. Leading the train is a Delaware & Hudson Camelback or "Mother Hubbard" steam engine 536 with its cab toward the center. The station was built in 1882 and replaced in 1912. Riders taking the boat and train into town likely resided up the lake at Pilot Knob or Silver Bay. *J. S. Wolley photo, Jim Shaughnessy collection*

family albums, books, museums, and so on (not to mention rail advertisements, which hardly exist today), and we concluded that the railroads really had something going in mid-twentieth-century America.

Even though the railroad industry today is about as healthy as it's ever been, railroading isn't on the general public's radar because the general public doesn't interact with or experience the railroad like they did in the past. Further, many of today's railroads, with the exception of Amtrak, prefer to be isolated from the public, which railroads perceive as being hostile and a nuisance. It's often been said that Americans love railroading but have no love for the railroads themselves. Part of this is because railroads today have become megacorporations, far removed from the era when they were integral to all on-line towns and cities, nearly all of which enjoyed direct freight and passenger service. Most of these towns have since been bypassed by the railroads, with goods being delivered to larger station points and then redistributed to the smaller towns and cities by truck.

Today, railroading has little perceived impact on the lives of people (or perhaps a negative impact when they grumble

about being delayed at a road crossing when they were in a hurry to get somewhere). Yet they forget that the automobile they're driving was shipped by rail in a protected autorack railcar before landing on the dealership lot, the wine they tasted at their friend's house the previous night was shipped by rail in a boxcar before being stocked on the market shelf, and that new high-definition TV they bought to watch games and movies night after night came overseas in a container and was loaded onto a flatcar to be shipped by rail before hitting the electronics shop.

Consider this: If you told a student to go outside and measure the snowfall at school, the answer could be 3 inches or about 7 1/2 centimeters, depending on which side of the ruler was read. So, depending on the measuring stick, today's railroading might be the Golden Age or even better. For example, as of the year 2005, railroads held a staggering 41 percent of the freight market in terms of ton-miles. In other words, trains are hauling more tons of freight and at greater distances than ever before. Most people believe that trucks—second to railroading at 30 percent—haul the majority of freight tonnage because they're so often seen tearing down the nation's highways.

It's easy to see why there are misconceptions about railroading's most prosperous times. Statistics tell us the railroads flourished and peaked in many areas in the early 1900s, they had good equipment and offered unrivaled travel experiences in the mid-1900s, and today, modern design and technology are allowing the railroads to move millions of tons over many miles quickly and efficiently.

For the sake of history, what we *can* say about the Golden Age of Railroading is that the first 50 years of the twentieth century laid a solid foundation for the future success of the industry. And those who are monitoring the railroad scene into the twenty-first century are beginning to catch a glimpse of a railway age that may redefine the success of transportation on the high iron.

Overview

At the turn of the century, the vast majority of America's railways were firmly established across the nation. Not only was railroading the dominant transportation source of people and goods, it was the nation's largest business. Competition was stiff as the railroads battled for superiority, and what they couldn't gain financially in the states, they sought overseas in capital.

Needless to say, hostilities developed between the railroads themselves as well as between the railroads and the shippers as all parties tried to build their fortunes. Congress had earlier established a federal railroad-regulating agency in 1887, the Interstate Commerce Commission (ICC), but the body's powers and decisions had little impact on the railroads. Although many railroads forged ahead, dozens had already fallen into bankruptcy due to rising costs and low rates (which were based on the value of the goods shipped), little traffic, and plunging security values.

By 1916, the surviving carriers (about 1,200) were working a rail network that added up to more than 250,000 miles (based on line mileage). The railroads employed a force of more than

Action at Hornell, New York, shows train No. 4 pulling into the Erie Railroad depot around 1910. At the turn of the century, America's railroads were the dominant transportation source of people and goods. Railroading was the nation's largest business, and the battle was on to see which railroad would emerge as the biggest and most profitable. *Cal's Classics*

Train No. 101 behind Milwaukee Road's 4-4-2 Atlantic No. 1 is leaving Chicago around Canal and Kinzle streets on February 11, 1936. Surviving the Great Depression during the 1930s was not easy for the railroads, and many declared bankruptcy. Help from the Reconstruction Finance Corporation eased the woes of many carriers. The Milwaukee Road enjoyed better times in the postwar era and survived until 1986. *A. W. Johnson photo, Krambles-Peterson collection*

1.7 million workers making an average annual wage of nearly $900. By comparison, roughly 100,000 miles of track existed in the 1880s with a workforce just over 400,000. The average annual wage was around $560 in 1900.

Within two years, the growing pains of big business eclipsed the sprint to transportation brilliance. With plenty of product to move, the continued rising costs, falling rates, and higher taxes and wages bogged down the railroads. Coupled with a surge of exports to Europe, massive congestion resulted at Eastern ports. Chaos ensued and traffic eventually came to a standstill.

The public became restless. They now had another worry in addition to the fears and uncertainties of World War I. Five days after the United States entered the war (April 1917), railroad executives had formed the Railroad War Board, pledging to help in the war effort and to keep operations from running into a wall. Their efforts weren't good enough, so President Woodrow Wilson appointed William McAdoo (secretary of the treasury and Wilson's son-in-law) as director of the United States Railroad Administration (USRA) on December 26, 1917. The government now controlled nearly all U.S. railroads, and on March 21, 1918, Congress passed the Railroad Control

Act to guarantee a carrier's rental would not exceed its average net operating income for the previous three years.

Under the government's hand, railroad presidents were discharged, rail competition was eliminated, and schedules were unified. In addition, $20 wage increases were given to employees who made less than $46 a month, and 2,000 locomotives and 50,000 cars (all standardized) were ordered for service. Basically, the USRA stepped in to keep the railroads from shipwreck at a critical time. On March 1, 1920, government control ended with the Transportation Act (of 1920), and the railroads were returned to their owners with a law that provided for a fair rate of return on their investment (5.5 percent). The law also expanded the strength of the ICC, which finally gained some understanding of railway finances and granted a rate increase between 25 and 40 percent.

The Railroad Labor Board was formed as a result of the Transportation Act, handling labor disputes over wages and working conditions as well as grievances. Later (in 1926), a new mediation board was established to resolve such issues with the Railway Labor Act.

During this time, railroad employment had peaked with more than 2 million workers, but not everybody was tinkering with drive rods and steam boilers under the roundhouse roof. A more convenient, more personal transportation invention was just beginning to burst onto the scene: the automobile. In 1916, there were 3 million registered vehicles. By 1929, that figure had exploded to 23 million. The railroads were now in for a little battle to keep at least short-haul passengers on board. And as if that weren't enough, another problem had cropped up October 29, 1929, to pick away at both freight and passenger business: a major stock-market crash. Roughly two months after the market had peaked September 3, Wall Street would experience its worst drop in history, crashing nearly 40 points and hitting a new low for the year in a little more than two weeks (November 13).

During the 1930s, the Great Depression had walloped the pocketbooks of the railroads and only the strongest survived. Many of the major roads declared bankruptcy, and as early as 1933, the workforce had fallen to just below 1 million with many working only part time. A bandage for the railroad's woes came in the form of the Reconstruction Finance Corporation (RFC). The federal recovery agency not only loaned money to some railroads to avoid receivership but also extended loans for new equipment and necessary line upgrades.

The silver linings for American railroading during this dark period came first in the form of the new Model 201 Winton diesel engine, which was operated on display at the General Motors exhibit during the 1933–1934 Century of Progress Exposition in Chicago. The diesel engine, which was the brainchild of German engineer Rudolph Diesel, had been around since the 1890s, but early diesel engines were too bulky to fit inside locomotives, so their initial use was as stationary power sources and then also for ships. However, in 1918 the first successful commercial diesel switchers—there were three—made their appearance on the East Coast. Others followed in the 1920s, but their success was limited to switching duties, not moving passenger trains, and certainly not long, heavy freight trains at main-line speeds.

The newly designed engines that showed up at the Century of Progress were smaller and more efficient than Winton's earlier engines, but during the first year of the fair in 1933, they too were used only as stationary power to light the GM exhibit. That changed a year later at the same exposition when a revolutionary new type of train was unveiled in the form of two lightweight, high-speed "streamliners" built of new alloy metals. One of these trains, Burlington's *Zephyr* 9900, was equipped with a Winton 201-A model diesel engine. Thus was born the first truly successful application of diesel-electric power to main-line railroading. At the same time, railroading's streamliner era was now under way. Both of these developments would play a critical role in railroading's Golden Era.

Yet, what the railroads really needed to battle the Depression was a shot to eradicate a crippling virus, and after 12 years of very tough times, a temporary cure came along in December 1941, albeit with great apprehension. On December 8, the United States would officially enter World War II following Japan's attack on Pearl Harbor the previous day, and that would precipitate an exchange of war declarations against Germany and Italy as well.

As the great baseball player Yogi Berra once said, "It's déjà vu all over again." The railroads needed to step up to the aid of the war efforts for the second time in a little more than two decades. This time the railroads were in a better position to perform admirably with equipment refinements and line improvements including a new signaling system (Centralized Traffic Control, or CTC) allowing dispatchers to control train movements from a single, remote location. However, personnel issues had to be worked out. Roughly a third of the railway workforce entered military service, but railroad management recruited replacements—women, minorities, and workers from Mexico—which raised the number of laborers to more than 1.4 million by 1945.

In the end, railroading had shown the nation its importance as a transportation source as well as its potential. The rail network handled unprecedented amounts of traffic moving 97 percent of domestic troops and about 90 percent of army and navy supplies. Freight movements were up 50 percent, and passenger service was up 25 percent from figures posted

The Railroads and World War II

If there was ever a time in U.S. history when railroads should have been awarded a medal of honor for performance, it was during World War II.

Twenty-four years earlier, in 1917, America's railways fell flat on their faces when it became necessary to step up for their country in World War I. Here was the transportation leader—poised to be the mover and shaker of commerce across the land with tracks in place nationwide—hitting the wall with a big "splat," resulting in a governmental rescue.

We can't all wear wings

WE know how you feel, young fellow—that stout heart of yours is breaking because you can't be up there in those army bombers.

You couldn't help it that the medicos turned you down. You wanted to *fight* for your country.

Well, what else do you think you're doing now? You're fighting—even though your uniform is a railroad trackman's overalls.

Every time men of your courage and character apply for work that will help shorten the war, we of The Milwaukee Road learn anew

what makes this nation invincible.

Out on the endless plains of the Dakotas, or in the rugged mountains of Montana or Washington, the sound of heavy war trains rolling over your stretch of track is like the roar of a bomber to your ears.

You don't wear wings. But we thought the country you're serving ought to know about you.

And we can tell you that over 5,000 men and women of The Milwaukee Road in the armed services consider you their kind of man.

★   ★   ★

"They should not have taken a railroad man for the Army unless he, himself, clamored for military service. He is in as fine a military place as he can ever occupy when he is helping run the railroads." Colonel J. Monroe Johnson, Interstate Commerce Commission.

THE MILWAUKEE ROAD
11,000-MILE SUPPLY LINE FOR WAR AND HOME FRONTS

America's railroads played a key part in World War II efforts. In order to move record amounts of traffic, the railways had to work together and maintain their roads, as this advertisement illustrates. Since World War I, the railroads had made significant improvements in trackwork and signaling and were able to move more freight and passenger trains at higher speeds. In the end, the railroads performed near flawlessly. *Les Hammer collection*

Chalk it up to inexperience. The industry didn't have the skill or capacity to process the onslaught. The railroads had serious growing pains, particularly in the financial arena as railroads were entering receivership (thanks to low rates and increased operating costs). The industry's regulating body, the Interstate Commerce Commission, had little knowledge of the business to offer anything helpful. Perhaps it's best said that everyone was trying to "sort out" and "make sense" of what railroading was all about.

The railroads knew the basics of shipping goods and people, but they got hit by a blind-side blitz. During this time frame, export traffic exploded due to British and French requests for aid, coal demands were on the rise, bumper crops were produced, the U.S. Armed Forces experienced growth requiring the movement of soldiers and supplies, and nasty weather halted rail service around the Midwest and East Coast. All this happened at a time when the railroads lacked the equipment and the resources to manage the overload. Add to this the problem of holding valuable cargo ships at port (to avoid being targeted) and curtailing loadings, and the railways suddenly came to a screeching halt.

That prompted government involvement. Under the United States Railroad Administration, headed by President Woodrow Wilson's son-in-law, William McAdoo, the railways experienced a "house cleaning," and order was restored at the most important time in American history. On March 1, 1920, the railroads were returned to their owners with the Transportation Act of 1920.

With no knowledge of what would happen 21 years later, the chaos of World War I rail woes was more than enough motivation to improve traffic flow on the high iron—not just for playing a key role in crisis situations, but for the betterment of the industry. After all, this was big business, and there was money to be made. And the faster refinements and advancements could be implemented, the sooner the nation would be better off.

Within two decades, the railroad had made significant strides in signaling and handling capacity. Automatic block signals were governing more than 65,000 miles of track, and Centralized Traffic Control covered another 2,000 miles. In addition, many routes had been double-tracked, which allowed the roads to move more freight at faster speeds.

In the predawn hours of U.S. involvement in World War II, the railroads were already coordinating the movement of military supplies due to the Lend-Lease Act of March 11, 1941. Eighteen months after the war had started, the United States, which had taken a neutral stance, came to the aid of the Allies with the shipment of tanks, airplanes, trucks, food, and additional goods and equipment. The United States provided Great Britain with $31.4 billion worth of supplies, while the Soviet Union received $11.3 billion. America also contributed $3.2 billion in armaments to France and another $1.6 billion to China.

A funeral train on the Illinois Central makes a short stop at Freeport, Illinois, on April 6, 1948. Those who died in military service would be transported for burial at their homes. From 1941 to 1945, the railways moved 90 percent of supplies and 97 percent of military personnel. They accommodated some 114,000 troop trains carrying nearly 44 million people associated with the armed forces. *Dick Caudle collection*

History records this act as part of what precipitated Germany's war declaration on the United States. The shipment of materials—staggering as it was—served as a pregame warm-up for the record amounts of traffic that would soon follow. And, apparently, the railroads were ready.

During the war years (1941 to 1945), the railways transported 90 percent of military supplies and moved 97 percent of military personnel. In addition, the railroads picked up extra traffic (freight and passenger) that the highways couldn't handle (due to funding cuts and gas rationing), on top of its regular volume.

Alongside its civilian passenger train service, which took on added strain as many more people moved around, the railways accommodated some 114,000 troop trains, which carried nearly 44 million people associated with the armed forces. In four years, passenger-mileage climbed from 23.8 billion to an astronomical 95.6 billion.

As for freight trains, ton-mileage increased from 292 billion before the war to 477 billion, thanks to the Lend-Lease aid shipments. After the United States jumped in, that figure skyrocketed to 740 billion just before war's end.

Fortunately, there were no serious car shortages, and although car capacities had increased, the railroads were able to pull it off with fewer cars and fewer locomotives than they had at the beginning of World War I.

Astounding as the statistics were, the greatest accomplishment for America's railways in this time frame was the ability to perform these important and monumental shipping tasks almost flawlessly. The railroads never came to a standstill, and there was no need for the government to step in and take control, as the roads managed their affairs in commendable style.

In the end, the railroads showed the country just how efficient the leader in transportation could become.

in 1918, and operating revenue was at its highest point since 1930. And, as a final merit badge on their apparel, the railroads never lost control of their affairs.

As much as the public recognized (and still recognizes) this time as the pinnacle of America's railroad success, there was no time to bask in the limelight. Not only was there business at hand, but the railroads were now staring at two very hungry competitors—the automobile and the trucking industry. By 1945, U.S. auto manufacturers hadn't produced a car in four years. Like the railroad explosion at the turn of the century, highways had greatly improved and Americans were ready to invest in their own set of wheels to get from place to place. Distance no longer seemed to be an issue. Further, the new or improved highways were in essence new and improved "tracks" for fledgling trucking companies. Whereas railroads had to raise their own capital to build their own tracks, trucking companies had their roadways financed by federal, state, and local governments.

By 1950, there were 40 million registered automobiles, and the threat of much-improved (again, thanks in part to government assistance) air travel loomed around the corner. Although railroads assumed that the ridership boom they experienced during the war would continue afterward—and accordingly introduced new equipment and new trains—ridership instead began an increasingly steep decline.

On the freight side, the news was a little better. The postwar boom kept the call for the movement of goods and materials at a high, though not as much as during the war itself. In 1939, further benefiting North American railroads, the diesel-electric locomotive finally proved itself as a worthy means of moving high-tonnage freight trains at high speed. Now, with the war out of the way, railroads began to focus on dieselizing their locomotive fleets, which would vastly and positively affect the economies of moving freight. With less than 6,000 diesel units in service in 1947, production boomed to nearly 20,500 units on America's railroad rosters.

Yet no matter what the railroads did to make their transportation mode far more efficient and better than ever before, they weren't able to pull travelers away from their love affair with the automobile. Further, and regardless of newfound economies that came with dieselization, railroads still found it difficult to compete with government-aided competition, expressly the booming highway and aviation systems. With dwindling markets, overbuilt networks, and heavy-handed government regulations, the tone would be set for a tough go in the second half of the century.

The Players

As mentioned in this chapter, there were some 1,200 railroads in North America in 1916, some larger than others, of course.

Before this time, the ICC classified railroads based on operating mileage. After 1911, a revised system was put into place and railroads were classified based on annual revenue, which is still true today, although the figures between the classes have dramatically changed. From 1911 through 1950, railroads with annual revenues exceeding $1 million were categorized as Class 1.

There were 127 Class 1 railroads in 1950—all weathering the storms that battered them in the first half of the century. Of that group, 28 North American railroads (26 U.S., 2 Canadian) laid the groundwork and set the stage for today's successes in rail transportation. Following a multitude of bankruptcies, takeovers, buyouts, and mergers in the century's second half, only four of the seven major railways that now exist have retained their original name (or flag). It should be noted here that the "Super Seven" making up today's Class 1 railroads are based on annual revenues exceeding $346.8 million (2006 figure). See the following chapter for additional information on these new-age railroads.

Recent mergers have created a rail network that has two competing railroads in the West (with equal access) handing off to two competing railroads in the East (also with equal access). The two Canadian railways battle head-to-head across all the provinces, exchange traffic with all U.S. roads at numerous points, and now even pass through the United States and own what had been privately owned, U.S.-based companies. The remaining road is a major north-to-south shipper linking Mexico with the United States.

Just previous to this time, the railroads more or less operated quadrants—Northeast, Southeast, Southwest, Northwest—using the Mississippi River as the primary dividing point between East and West. As we look at the 28 classic railroads that ruled during the Golden Age (surviving the Great Depression and winning World War II), we'll group them by their operating region.

The Northeast

Pennsylvania Railroad: Who hasn't heard of this railway giant? It's easy to figure out why the road made it to the Monopoly board. With an annual revenue just under $900 million (1950), the Pennsylvania was the wealthiest of all the railroads. The Pennsylvania's main route stretched from New York to Chicago with extensions to St. Louis, Detroit, Buffalo, Cincinnati, and Louisville. Its network of lines covered nearly all of New Jersey, Pennsylvania, Ohio, and Indiana. From Philadelphia, the Pennsy also extended southwest to Baltimore and Washington, D.C. The railroad also fielded secondary main lines that ran through Michigan all the way to Mackinaw City and one to the Peoria Gateway in central Illinois. Declaring itself the "standard railroad of the world" (because, internally, it indeed was heavily standardized), the Pennsy owed much of its success to electrification of the New York–Washington line and the Philadelphia–Harrisburg line in the 1920s and 1930s. Record amounts of passenger and freight traffic were handled on these routes—and still are in terms of passengers. On a final note, the company has the longest continuous dividend history, paying out annual dividends to its shareholders for more than 100 consecutive years.

New York Central: The archrival of the PRR was the New York Central. It was second to the Pennsy in terms of revenue (exceeding $700 million), but it was first in track mileage. The NYC main linked New York with Chicago with a more northerly route that followed rivers and lakefronts (the Water Level Route) via Albany, Buffalo, Cleveland, and across to Chicago. The network included legs to Cincinnati and out to St. Louis with additional branches reaching north into Montreal and Ottawa, Canada, and even southward down into West Virginia. The railroad made its mark with efficient freight service and first-rate passenger operations. Pulling these trains was a remarkable fleet of powerful steam locomotives including 4-6-4 Hudson types as well as 2-8-4 Berkshires.

New York, New Haven & Hartford: Also known simply as the New Haven, this railroad built its network and flourished in the heavily populated New England states of Connecticut, Rhode Island, and Massachusetts with its trunk linking New York with Boston via New Haven, Connecticut. The New Haven was a pioneer in electrification between 1905 and 1914 on the New York–New Haven segment, and in a joint venture

New York Central and Hudson River Railroad Depot, Rochester, N. Y.

The New York Central Railroad was first in track mileage and second to the Pennsylvania Railroad in revenue among the early successful carriers. That may explain in part the grandeur of the Hudson River Railroad depot in Rochester, New York, circa 1910. The New York Central linked New York with Chicago using the northerly Water Level Route via Albany, Rochester, Buffalo, Cleveland, and across to Chicago. *Mike Schafer collection*

Hell Gate Bridge, New York City.

In a joint venture with the Pennsylvania Railroad, the New York, New Haven & Hartford Railroad built the impressive Hell Gate Bridge over the East River at New York, completing the project in 1917. The massive structure carried four tracks and still stands as the longest railroad arch ever built. The bridge was a vital link for the Pennsy to New England, and along with tunneling projects under the Hudson and East rivers, the Pennsy and Long Island Rail Road gained access to Manhattan's Penn Station. *Mike Schafer collection*

with the PRR, the two railroads built the Hell Gate Bridge over the East River at New York, which afforded a direct link between New England and PRR lines south from New York to Virginia as well as to the west. Dodging bankruptcy during World War I thanks to USRA control, the debt-burdened New Haven finally fell in 1935, yet made a comeback by World War II after shedding unprofitable branches, upgrading passenger equipment, and purchasing new locomotives.

Erie Railroad: Before the turn of the century, the Erie was a stumbling railroad at best and destined for future failure. But like a good fighter, it kept coming back after a few knockdowns. From 1895 to 1938, the "new" Erie Railroad battled back to respectability only to fall into bankruptcy again during the latter

part of the Great Depression. Brushing itself off once again, the Erie reorganized in time to prosper during World War II, and in 1942 the railroad produced a small dividend for the first time in 69 years, quieting jokesters for the time. Like the PRR and NYC, the Erie's main line linked New York with Chicago. Using a route through the Southern Tier of New York state, the line included legs to Buffalo, Cleveland, and Dayton, Ohio.

Reading Company: In 1923, the Reading became an *operating* company following its *holding* company marriage of the Philadelphia & Reading Railroad and the Coal & Iron Company back in 1896. (Prior to that time, the railroad had purchased over 100,000 acres of coal land.) The Central Railroad of New Jersey—a.k.a. Jersey Central—and the Wilmington Northern were part of Reading's operation, although the railway had sold 40 percent of controlling interests to both the Baltimore & Ohio and the NYC. The Reading merged a group of wholly owned railroads in 1923 as it took on operating company status, and 10 years later, the Reading and the PRR agreed to consolidate operations. With Reading, Pennsylvania, as the hub, the railroad branched out to Philadelphia, Atlantic City, and Jersey City to the east; Wilmington to the south; and to Williamsport and Harrisburg to the west with legs to other eastern Pennsylvania cities.

The five preceding railroads eventually became part of Conrail, which was formed in 1976. Conrail's network was sold off in 1999 with CSX taking half and Norfolk Southern taking the other half of its lines and equipment.

New York, Chicago & St. Louis: Known as the Nickel Plate Road, the formal name is a bit misleading as the line was built to link Buffalo—not New York City—to Chicago and St. Louis. Chesapeake & Ohio management ruled the Nickel Plate for nine years starting in 1933 before the NKP took back control in 1942. There were a few occasions both before and after this time when the two roads tried to tie the knot, but it never materialized. Like its corridor rivals, the Nickel Plate did well during World War II, and up to the 1950s it had developed into a good railroad with positive financial gains.

Wabash Railroad: The Wabash was a high-speed artery running between Buffalo, Detroit, and Kansas City with extensions to Chicago, St. Louis, Omaha, and Des Moines, Iowa, but Detroit was the railroad's major launching point as the automobile industry was centered there. The Wabash carved a straight main from Detroit through the heart of Indiana, Illinois, and Missouri to interchange at Kansas City with its "heart" located at Decatur, Illinois, where the principal routes intersected. While automobile sales initiated the decline of passenger service on the rails, shipping cars benefitted the Wabash as that became a major source of freight traffic. The railroad overcame a multitude of reorganizations through the years to continue to compete with other carriers.

Norfolk & Western: Prior to 1964, the N&W earned its reputation and the lion's share of its profits as a regional coal hauler. From Roanoke, Virginia, the line stretched east to Norfolk and a major ocean port at Portsmouth, Virginia, north to Hagerstown, Maryland, and northwest to Cincinnati and Columbus. The road also had two southward extensions to Winston-Salem and Durham, North Carolina. The N&W eventually became a large and much more diverse railway with the merging of the Nickel Plate and the leasing of the Wabash and the smaller Pittsburgh & West Virginia. The road also purchased the Akron, Canton & Youngstown.

The Norfolk & Western merged with the Southern Railway in 1982 to form today's powerful Norfolk Southern.

Baltimore & Ohio: No railroad, other than perhaps the Pennsylvania, has more notoriety than the B&O. It was the first common-carrier railroad with scheduled freights and passenger service. Just prior to the turn of the century, the B&O was forced into receivership, but the road emerged three years later. Under PRR control in 1901, the B&O regained strength, and in five years, the Pennsy began selling its B&O stock. The B&O avoided going bankrupt during the Great Depression as the RFC provided relief. Linking Baltimore and Washington, D.C., with Chicago and St. Louis, the B&O network covered all the major cities in Maryland, West Virginia, Ohio, Indiana, and western Pennsylvania. The B&O also reached Northeast to Philadelphia and New York via affiliates Reading Company and Jersey Central.

Chesapeake & Ohio: Like the Norfolk & Western, C&O's rise to dominance came as a result of hauling coal to centrally located markets. From the Chesapeake Bay area at Newport News, Virginia, the C&O extended west to Chicago via Richmond, Virginia; Charleston, West Virginia; Cincinnati; and Muncie, Indiana. The C&O also extended north from the Kentucky/Ohio state line to Toledo and Detroit. Part of C&O's fame was derived from its premier passenger train, the *George Washington*. During the Great Depression, the road launched this, the first all-air-conditioned long-distance train from Washington and Newport News to Cincinnati and Louisville. In addition, the railroad introduced one of the industry's most recognized icons—the sleeping "Chessie" kitten in 1933.

The Southeast

Seaboard Air Line: One of the four major players in the Southeast, the SAL connected northern Virginia—specifically Richmond—to Jacksonville, Tampa, and Miami. From Hamlet, North Carolina, the road stretched westward to Atlanta and Birmingham. Thanks to government loans and its new *Silver Meteor* streamliner between New York and Florida, the SAL bounced back strong during and after World War II with traffic-control upgrades, excellent passenger service (especially for vacationers), and valued business in phosphate rock shipments (used in producing fertilizer).

Atlantic Coast Line: The ACL was nearly a duplicate of the SAL on the map, running south from Richmond to Jacksonville and Tampa, though Miami was reached through an affiliation with the Florida East Coast. The ACL also had lines to Atlanta, Birmingham, and Montgomery, though not as direct in its approach. The ACL had its line upgrades in place before the SAL, which made the ACL the preferred route. The ACL was one of the few railroads in North America in 1950

FLORIDA

23⅓ Hours *from* New York

THE Atlantic Coast Line operates 17 passenger trains into Florida every day during the winter tourist season.

It has 2058 miles of standard railroad in Florida—more than a third of the State's total mileage.

Its network of lines reaches and supplies efficient transportation to every important tourist and trade center of Central, South and West Coast of Florida, and through direct connection with the Florida East Coast Railway to all East Coast Points.

The double-track sea-level main line between Richmond, Va., and Jacksonville, Fla., is protected by every proved safety device found anywhere, including automatic signals, and, part of the way, automatic train control. All necessary traffic areas in Florida are double-tracked.

Consult Purple Folder Time Table for Passenger Train Service to Florida.

The splendid transportation facilities of the Atlantic Coast Line and its connections make possible the highest type of freight and passenger service between Florida and the North and West.

Atlantic Coast Line
The Standard Railroad of the South

General Offices:
Wilmington, N. C.

The Atlantic Coast Line covered all the bases of how efficient railroad travel was in the 1930s with this advertisement. Passengers had as many as 17 trains to choose from, and since the railroad was double-tracked and updated with automatic signals and automatic train control, the ACL could get the vacationers from The Big Apple to sunny Florida in just 24 hours. *Kevin EuDaly collection*

that had a double-track main line with a legal passenger-train speed of 100 miles per hour. At the turn of the century, the ACL's network expanded rapidly as a result of owned, leased, or controlled lines.

Louisville & Nashville: As the twentieth century came around, the L&N fell under the control of the ACL, which used "Old Reliable" to connect to New Orleans and Nashville. From the latter, the L&N branched out westward to interchange points at Memphis and St. Louis, and north to Louisville and Cincinnati. The L&N also had access to Chicago via the Chicago & Eastern Illinois. Earning its keep as a coal hauler, the L&N built many of its own steam locomotives including Consolidations, Mikados, Pacifics, and eight-wheel switchers.

The ACL and SAL combined in 1967 to form the Seaboard Coast Line; later, the L&N and the Georgia Railroad Group (Georgia Railroad, Atlanta & West Point, and the Western Railway of Alabama) came into the fold, and together all were known as the Family Lines System. When the Family Lines and the Chessie System (which came from the B&O, C&O, and Western Maryland affiliation that had solidified early in the 1970s) merged in 1982, CSX Transportation was born—CSX ostensibly standing for Chessie Seaboard Inc.). CSX is now Norfolk Southern's principal competitor east of the Mississippi River.

Southern Railway: As its slogan indicated, the "Southern Serves the South." Its network fanned out from Atlanta, serving Jacksonville to the southeast, Washington, D.C., to the northeast, New Orleans to the southwest, Birmingham and Memphis to the west, Cincinnati to the north, and St. Louis to the northwest. As a result of many line acquisitions—many of them, such as Central of Georgia and the Cincinnati, New Orleans & Texas Pacific, operated as subsidiaries—the Southern grew to become one of the South's most prominent and respected railways.

The Southern teamed up with the Norfolk & Western to become Norfolk Southern in 1982, competing with CSX for rail traffic in the East and Southeast.

Illinois Central: If you scooted the L&N over just a bit to the west, you'd have the Illinois Central. Although it paralleled the L&N, the IC had a much stronger, longer, and more extensive north-south main line, parts of which boasted 100-mile-per-hour passenger-train speeds. The IC connected New Orleans to Chicago via Memphis and also had several extensions off the trunk: one southeast to reach Birmingham, Alabama; two northeast, with one ending at Louisville, Kentucky, and the other at Indianapolis, Indiana; a major route west from Chicago to Waterloo and Sioux City, Iowa, and Omaha; two lines into St. Louis; and myriad branch lines all over Illinois and Mississippi. Simply put, the IC was a strong, well-run railroad that met the shipping needs between America's heartland and the Gulf Coast.

The IC became part of the Canadian National family in 1999 to form a very strong north-to-south traffic lane.

The Midwest and Northwest

Chicago & North Western: The C&NW trunk line was primarily a fast main line between Chicago and Omaha and Fremont, Nebraska, that developed into a preferred connection with the Union Pacific. C&NW trackage also reached north and northwest, serving many areas in Wisconsin, Minnesota, Upper Michigan, Iowa, and South Dakota. Later on, through mergers with the Chicago Great Western and other smaller

Travelers riding on Illinois Central's *Panama Limited* gather on the platform of the observation car for a photo taken in the 1930s. This train linked Chicago with the Gulf Coast via Memphis. Introduced in 1911, it became an all-sleeping-car train by 1916 and continued to be one of the most revered overnight runs in the country well into the 1960s. *Illinois Central photo, Al Lind collection*

carriers, the C&NW wound up with connecting points to the south at St. Louis and Kansas City. Beyond Omaha, C&NW had its own lines in northern Nebraska and South Dakota as well as a far-reaching extension to Wyoming all the way to Riverton.

Predictably, the C&NW and Union Pacific merged operations in 1995. Only the Southern Pacific outlasted the C&NW of all the roads that currently reside in the UP family.

Chicago, Milwaukee, St. Paul & Pacific: Better known as The Milwaukee Road, if there was any railroad that had potential to make it to the twenty-first century, it was the Milwaukee. The Milwaukee network was built in nearly all directions out of Milwaukee and Chicago and covered much of Wisconsin, Iowa, northern Illinois, and Minnesota. It had

main lines to the Twin Cities, Omaha, Sioux City, and Kansas City as well as an unremarked main line down into the coal fields of southern Indiana. In 1909, the Milwaukee opened its great Pacific Extension to Seattle and Tacoma, Washington. This line featured electrified segments in Montana, Idaho, and Washington.

Although it was the last to reach the Pacific Northwest, the Milwaukee arguably had the best route. Despite bankruptcies, the Milwaukee experienced better health in the postwar years, although another bankruptcy in the 1970s nearly put it under. But after shedding a number of its lines in 1980, including its Pacific Extension, The Milwaukee Road bounced back and the resulting core system made it an ideal merger partner.

The Milwaukee was merged into the Soo Line in 1986. The Soo Line became part of the Canadian Pacific in 1992.

The *Olympian Hiawatha* running behind one of the Chicago, Milwaukee, St. Paul & Pacific's most beloved electric locomotives, the Little Joe, is pictured at Sixteen Mile Canyon in Montana in the early 1950s. Milwaukee Road's Pacific Extension featured two electrified segments including Harlowton, Montana, westward to Avery, Idaho, across the Bitterroot Mountains; and from Othello, Washington, westward to Tacoma across the Cascade Mountains. *Milwaukee Road photo, Milwaukee Road Historical Association archives*

Chicago, Burlington & Quincy: The CB&Q was a rock-solid railroad between Chicago at the east end and Denver and Billings, Montana, at the west end. The network included lines covering southern Iowa, northern Missouri, southern and central Nebraska, and the northeast section of Wyoming. Key anchor points were Kansas City, Omaha, and Denver with a subsidiary line extending from Denver all the way to Galveston, Texas. Another valuable interchange point was Minneapolis/St. Paul to the

northwest of Chicago. Thanks to James J. Hill's purchase of 98 percent of CB&Q's stock in 1901, that extension gave Great Northern and Northern Pacific easy access to the Windy City.

Great Northern/Northern Pacific: It took 69 years for these two major rivals to officially merge, though their history of trying to cement the relationship is well documented. Before the turn of the twentieth century, "Empire Builder" James J. Hill, who built the GN, gained working control of the NP, which had gone through financial difficulties. Both lines from Minneapolis/St. Paul to the Seattle region are shadows of each other. The GN took a slightly more northerly approach through North Dakota, Montana, and Washington while the NP took the southerly route through the same states except for North Dakota (NP went through South Dakota). After buying CB&Q stock to tie Seattle with Chicago, Hill tapped into the Portland market with his building of the Spokane, Portland & Seattle.

These three major railroads plus the smaller SP&S merged in 1970 to form what was then the largest railroad in the United States (in track mileage), the Burlington Northern.

Union Pacific: Judging from railroad history books, the UP appears to stop just short of declaring itself the modern "standard railroad of the world" as the Pennsylvania Railroad did in the early days. The UP has retained its name and image longer than any other U.S. railway that exists today. From Omaha (its headquarters) and Kansas City, the UP took a central corridor approach to the Pacific with its main line splitting Nebraska and Wyoming to land at Salt Lake City. From there, the UP built a main southwest to Los Angeles as well as an extension northward to connect Salt Lake City to Pocatello, Idaho. The Pacific Northwest main breaks off west of Green River, Wyoming, and runs through Pocatello en route to Portland and Seattle. The UP also tapped into a connection with Canada on a branch line from Hinkle, Oregon, north through Spokane to Eastport, Idaho. Always looking for bigger and better power, the UP ran not only the largest steam engines with the Big Boys (4-8-8-4) and Challengers (4-6-6-4), but also the largest diesel engines including the EMD DDA40Xs.

Racing past the stopped freight train on the left, the Chicago, Burlington & Quincy's westbound *Exposition Flyer* kicks up the dust at Somonauk, Illinois, in October 1943. This train was a precursor to the *California Zephyr*, which was run by three railroads—the CB&Q, Denver & Rio Grande Western, and Western Pacific. The CB&Q stood as a rock-solid freight and passenger railroad until the formation of the Burlington Northern in 1970. *David P. Oroszi collection*

The holidays always generated more freight and passenger traffic on the rails. Just west of Kirkwood, Missouri, a Missouri Pacific Christmas mail Extra was photographed eastbound at Lake Hill Junction on December 23, 1950. The six-car train was powered by MoPac 4-8-2 Mountain 5326 with a friendly engineer at the throttle. The MoPac was a strong Midwestern carrier and was merged into the Union Pacific in 1982. *Joe Collias photo, Kevin EuDaly collection*

The Southwest

Southern Pacific: Like the UP, GN, and NP, the Southern Pacific piled up some impressive long-distance mileage covering a vast portion of the country. With connecting points to eastern railways at St. Louis, Memphis (both through subsidiary St. Louis Southwestern—the Cotton Belt), and New Orleans, the SP moved traffic westward to El Paso on two lines, the first from St. Louis and Kansas City through lower Kansas and Tucumcari, New Mexico, and the second from Memphis and New Orleans through Dallas and Houston, respectively,

hitting San Antonio along the way. Traffic was funneled from El Paso to Southern California, and then the line split to serve both the California coast and the valley. From the Sacramento Valley, the SP extended a main north to Portland and east to Ogden, Utah. In both the steam and diesel eras, the SP found ways to overcome problems running through mountain tunnels. Cab-forward steam locomotives kept the engineer and fireman from being smoked to death, and in modern times, diesel locomotives designed to pull in cooler air from the ground (Tunnel Motor units) kept the engines from overheating.

Missouri Pacific: Many railroads were designed for east-west traffic, while fewer were designed for north-south shipments. The MP built a network of lines in the south-central states designed to do a little of both. Its interchange points to Eastern and Southeastern railroads were the same as SP— New Orleans, Memphis, and St. Louis. All three cities were connected by a north-south main. From Brownsville, Houston, or San Antonio, the "MoPac" built lines through Little Rock, Arkansas, to reach St. Louis and through Dallas/Fort Worth to reach Kansas City and Omaha. From Fort Worth, the MP built west to El Paso, and from Kansas City, another line was sent west to Pueblo, Colorado.

These two railroads, along with two smaller Class 1 railways, the Western Pacific (Salt Lake City–Oakland) and Missouri-Kansas-Texas (Houston–San Antonio to Kansas City and St. Louis) were merged into the Union Pacific. The WP and MP were merged in 1982, the MKT in 1988, and the SP in 1996.

St. Louis-San Francisco: Also known simply as the "Frisco," the original builders of this line envisioned its main reaching San Francisco at some point. It never got close—not by a long shot—and one has to wonder why the name stuck all the way to the railroad's demise in 1980. The Frisco was like a large X, with one main line striking southwest from St. Louis to Oklahoma City via Springfield, Missouri (the operating heart of the railroad), and Tulsa, Oklahoma, and its other principal main line running from Kansas City southeast to Birmingham, Alabama, via Springfield and Memphis, Tennessee. Other lines reached down to Dallas/Fort Worth; Mobile, Alabama; and Pensacola, Florida. The Frisco also covered portions of Oklahoma, Arkansas, the Texas Panhandle, and a small arm in Kansas. The Frisco came out of two receiverships, the last in 1947 following World War II traffic surges. The Frisco went on to operate for 30 more years in its south-central nest.

Swinging around Houlihan's Curve on Edelstein Hill (just west of Chillicothe, Illinois), this Atchison, Topeka & Santa Fe freight is headed westbound in November 1941 on the strength of 2-8-2 Mikado 3258. The Santa Fe was among the most popular railroads in North America, much of which can be attributed to its excellent passenger service. The railroad survived until 1996 and the formation of the Burlington Northern Santa Fe Railway. *Harold K. Vollrath collection*

This brochure advertising Canada's National Transcontinental Railway was released in 1918, four years before the Canadian National was organized. The five railroads that came under the control of CN were experiencing financial problems. In addition to the NTR, the Intercolonial Railway, Canadian Northern, Grand Trunk Railway, and Grand Trunk Pacific all tied the knot, and today, CN remains as one of the seven Class 1 railroads in North America. *Mike Schafer collection*

Atchison, Topeka & Santa Fe: The Santa Fe will be long remembered as one of the classiest and most highly respected freight and passenger railways in North American history. For a long time, it was the only single-carrier rail route between Chicago and California. Running west through Kansas City, its main line split into two principal traffic routes near Emporia, Kansas. Both dipped down into New Mexico, rejoining near Albuquerque, and then headed west through the desert to Southern California where the main line split for the Los Angeles Basin and the San Francisco Bay Area. The Santa Fe also fielded lines into Texas to serve Dallas/Fort Worth, Houston, and, on the Gulf Coast, Galveston. Another main line carried Santa Fe trains up into Denver. Branch lines blanketed the bread belt in Kansas and Oklahoma. Turning to diesels as early as any railroad, the Santa Fe offered fast, reliable freight and passenger service that few of its peers could match. Its passengers were treated to sparkling coaches and sleepers in addition to excellent dining on board thanks to the Harvey House Company, and its *Super Chief* became a world-class train. Among the most popular roads in North America, the Santa Fe adorned its passenger diesels (and later all of its new freight locomotives) with the red and silver warbonnet scheme—perhaps the most recognizable railroad paint scheme in history.

The Burlington Northern, formed in 1970 when the CB&Q, GN, NP, and SP&S merged, absorbed the Frisco in 1980. The BN and Santa Fe merged in 1996, forming the Burlington Northern Santa Fe Railway, later renamed BNSF Railway.

Kansas City Southern: The KCS is the smallest Class 1 railroad featured in this chapter. Using figures from 1950, the KCS had less than half the annual revenue of all the railroads listed here. It is noted because it has survived in the land of giants (both then and now) and is one of just a few North American railroads retaining its original name. In the latter half of the mid-1900s, its main line was a pretty simple trunk from Kansas City to the Gulf Coast (New Orleans, Louisiana, and Port Arthur, Texas) with a branch extending from Shreveport to Dallas. Today's version is much larger, of course, as the railway tapped into a large portion of Mexico traffic following NAFTA (North American Free Trade Alliance, 1994) and also picked up new lines shed by other carriers. The KCS kept itself in pretty good shape through the years, extending BN's coal traffic southward as well as hauling grain and petroleum products.

KCS still stands as the smallest Class 1 railroad among the "Super Seven." It avoided being absorbed in the last round of mergers, primarily due to lack of interest on the part of larger railroads in its route structure.

A long, heavy freight train rolls westward through a pair of semaphore signals at Binghamton, New York, on February 18, 1934, on the Lackawanna Railroad. On rails across North America, thousands of freight trains like this one would be hauling millions of tons of important products that build neighborhoods and communities coast to coast. The groundwork laid in the early half of the twentieth century set the stage for today's railway success. *Erie Lackawanna Historical Society*

Canada

Canadian Pacific and Canadian National: These two long-time powerhouses of North American railroading are now also as much a part of the U.S. railroad scene as any other railway today. On their original Canada maps, both roads paralleled each other from the Atlantic Ocean to the Pacific Ocean—true transcontinental railroads—hitting every major city between the two coasts. Thanks to CP's partnership with Soo Line, the Canadian Pacific is a major player in Chicago, Milwaukee, and St. Paul. Through other acquisitions over the years, CP's presence is now also prominent in Washington, D.C., Philadelphia, and New York in the East and even Kansas City to the west. Similar to the Conrail story in the United States, CN was organized in 1922 to operate five railroads that had come under government control due to financial problems: the Canadian Northern, the National Transcontinental Railway, the Intercolonial Railway, the Grand Trunk Pacific, and the Grand Trunk Railway. Out of

the GTR came CN subsidiary Grand Trunk Western, which links Detroit with Chicago to the west and Cincinnati to the south. CN's network in the United States was greatly enhanced with its more recent takeover of Illinois Central. Both roads have made their living off of huge shipments of grain from the Canadian prairies as well as export coal and sulfur, petroleum and chemicals, forest products, and the growing intermodal market.

Back at the turn of the twentieth century, America's railroad network created great cities as freight and passengers rapidly moved from region to region. There was a time when nearly everyone lived within earshot of a locomotive's whistle. The nation's rail lines have been pruned since that time, and many people have sought quieter confines away from the hustle and bustle of commerce. They may no longer hear the sound of a diesel horn, but if they explore and investigate hard enough, the railroad will have likely played a part in the shipping of the make-up and expansion of their neighborhoods.

✎ 3 ✎

Reversals of Fortunes, 1950–2005

by Steve Glischinski

A s the railroad industry entered the 1950s, it had good reason for optimism. The American railroad industry still transported the majority of intercity travelers and had the largest market share in transporting freight. Passenger trains on major routes had been, or were in the process of being, reequipped with new cars, and the wholesale elimination of steam locomotives and replacement with lower-cost diesel locomotives was well under way. Yet, by 1970, the railroad industry in the United States was teetering on the edge of nationalization, with several roads in bankruptcy and others barely hanging on. How could such a thing happen to this once-proud industry that once was in the forefront of U.S. commerce? The reasons are many.

Two of the major culprits responsible for the reversal of railroad fortune were competition and government regulation. Americans began acquiring automobiles en masse as far back as the 1920s. In 1916, there were only 3 million motor vehicles registered in the United States; by 1929 it was 23 million. As roads improved through the 1920s and 1930s,

Postwar optimism soared in the late 1940s and early 1950s, and passenger trains continued to ply rails across North America. Perhaps no paint scheme ever conceived captured the public imagination like, Santa Fe's red and silver warbonnet scheme. F7A 300 leads train No. 124, one of the two *Grand Canyon* passenger trains between Chicago and Los Angeles, on a sunny day in 1953. *Don Richardson photo*

The rise of automobile traffic in North America throughout the last five decades has caused drastic changes in railroad passenger traffic. The years when travel by train dominated the landscape quickly vanished, along with the associated revenue. This view of a C&NW commuter train among a sea of automobiles was taken in 1969, just as the intercity passenger train crisis was culminating in the formation of Amtrak two years later. *Chicago & North Western Historical Society Archive*

the railroads' passenger traffic began a precipitous decline. Railroads carried 1 billion passengers in 1916—close to 100 percent of the people who made intercity travel; by 1930 this had dropped to 700 million and to 450 million by 1940.

World War II stopped the decline as a flood of war-related passenger and freight traffic flooded the railroads, but with the end of hostilities in 1945, more and more people abandoned the intercity passenger train for the comfort and convenience of the private automobile. However, railroads remained optimistic that people would not want to drive long distances, especially on substandard roads. The airline industry didn't seem to be much of a factor, either, as flying was expensive and not as convenient or as comfortable as the train. But

that would soon change. Between 1946 and 1964, the annual number of passengers carried by the railroads declined from 770 to 298 million.

Private automobile ownership continued its upward trend, going from 40 million in 1950 to over 131 million by 2000. People could now travel any time they wanted, at their convenience. Their only limitation was having a good road to drive on, and the U.S. government found a solution to that problem: the Federal-Aid Highway Act of 1956, popularly known as the National Interstate and Defense Highways Act of 1956. It had been lobbied for by major U.S. auto manufacturers and pushed by President Dwight Eisenhower, who was influenced by his experiences in 1919 as a young soldier crossing the United States and his appreciation of the German autobahn network. In addition to facilitating private and commercial transportation, the Interstate Highway System was sold partly as a way to provide ground transport routes for military supplies and troops in an emergency. Eventually the system would total 46,837 miles and cost a staggering $114 billion, taking 35 years to complete.

The same year the interstate system was born, railroading and its competition (excluding automobiles) were about even in passenger transportation: railroads handled 34.8 percent of passengers, buses 31 percent, and airlines 31.5 percent. Airlines took a huge step toward dominance with the introduction of the first jet service. Within the United States, National Airlines became the first to begin jet service, using leased Boeing 707s, on December 10, 1958. American Airlines offered the first domestic jet service using its own aircraft on January 25, 1959, with a flight from New York to Los Angeles.

As the air and road system grew, passengers deserted the passenger trains. Some railroads, such as Lehigh Valley and Southern Pacific, were quick to throw in the towel on their passenger trains, while others such as Burlington and Santa Fe remained optimistic, buying new cars and promoting their trains. But by the late 1960s, even the optimists had to face reality: passenger trains were hemorrhaging money that the railroads desperately needed as profits turned to deficits. An irony in this was that train passengers were taxed by the federal government, but those tax revenues went into the U.S. General Fund and were never reinvested in the rail industry.

Other reasons for passenger train losses were antiquated work rules and railroads' inflexible relationships with unions. Work rules did not adapt to changes in technology; for example, for several years diesel locomotives still carried firemen, even though they were no longer needed after steam locomotives disappeared. Average train speeds doubled from

Throughout the first half of the twentieth century, railroads offered local passenger service on a plethora of routes. As the automobile and the road systems that carried them improved, the convenience of the family car began a shift away from these local trains. In June 1963, the Rio Grande's *Yampa Valley* was still offering such local service from Denver to Craig and is shown westbound at Granby on the Denver–Grand Junction main line. At Orestod/Bond, the train will head up the branch to Craig. *Alan Bradley photo*

C&NW train No. 482 rolls under the Highway 42 bridge at Rousseau, South Dakota, in August 1977, crossing through Lake Sharp on the North Western's main line to the Black Hills. This set of branches was sold to upstart Dakota, Minnesota & Eastern on September 4, 1986. The sale included 826 miles of owned trackage, along with 139 miles of trackage rights. Many Class 1 roads shed marginal lines during the 1970s and 1980s. *Mike Schafer photo*

1919 to 1959, but unions resisted efforts to modify their 100- to 150-mile workdays established when steam engines could only travel that far in a day. As a result, railroaders' workdays were roughly cut in half, from 5 to 7 ½ hours in 1919, down to 2 ½ to 3 ¾ hours in 1959.

Freight service suffered too. As more highways were completed (except for toll roads, at taxpayer expense), the trucking industry found it easier to compete with railroads for freight traffic. While truckers paid taxes to pay some of the cost of building highways, it wasn't—and still isn't—enough to cover the true costs. Yet railroads continued to pay 100 percent of the cost of maintaining their own rights-of-way and often had to pay taxes on it to boot.

In 1944, at the height of World War II, a record for railroad cargo carried was set at 746 billion ton-miles. In that year, 69 percent of all intercity freight ton-miles were moved by rail. From that high, railroads experienced a low point in freight traffic around 1960 when they carried less than 600 billion ton-miles of freight.

Freight profits were difficult to come by, especially in the East and Midwest. The short distances between cities in these areas left railroads especially vulnerable to strong competition from trucks. Western railroads, with longer distances between cities, were able to bring in more cash by moving freight farther and largely remained profitable. But by the 1960s, Eastern and Midwestern railroads began losing money. One strategy they adopted was to cut costs through deferred maintenance, preserving cash by cutting back on their repair budgets. This was at best a short-term solution, since eventually the trackage would have to be repaired if the company was to stay in business. Nonetheless, many railroads, including the great Pennsylvania Railroad, allowed their track structure to fall into disrepair.

Another problem was too much trackage. Built in the nineteenth century when the railroad industry was dominant, branch lines allowed railroads to serve every nook and cranny of the country. By the 1960s, the railroads still had thousands of miles of branch lines, but their business had been siphoned away by trucks using new or upgraded public highways, causing many branches to lose money and to fall in ill repair. Logically, the railroads should have shed themselves of these lines. One railroad, the Chicago & North Western, pruned its branch-line network aggressively. But management had to be aggressive if it was to cut back its systems, and many managers who were steeped in railroad tradition were reticent to do so.

To abandon a line, management had to face off against the Interstate Commerce Commission, a government agency established in 1887 that tightly regulated railroads. The ICC governed rail-line abandonment cases, the termination of passenger-train services, and railroad mergers. Even more significant, the ICC had the power to determine maximum "reasonable" rail rates and required that rates be published. As railroads lost money, the ICC was frequently an impediment to raising rates or eliminating unprofitable services. Railroads sometimes had to wait years to get a ruling from the ICC, the most memorable case being the proposed merger of the Union Pacific with the Rock Island. In 1964, the Rock Island and Union Pacific applied to the ICC for permission to merge. That application triggered years of intra-industry fighting and bureaucratic stalling that finally ended with the ICC's approval of the merger in late 1974. By that time it was too late: the Rock Island was near collapse and, UP no longer wanted to merge. In 1980, the Rock Island did indeed collapse and shut down overnight.

The railroads, faced with dwindling market share, overbuilt systems, and heavy-handed government regulation, sought to cut costs by merger. It was thought if railroads could merge and eliminate duplicate lines, facilities, and employees, the industry might get back on its feet. In 1960, rivals Erie and Lackawanna merged to form the Erie Lackawanna. In 1962, the ICC approved the Chesapeake & Ohio taking control of the Baltimore & Ohio. Norfolk & Western absorbed the Virginian in 1959 and purchased the Akron, Canton & Youngstown and Pittsburgh & West Virginia in 1964; at the same time it merged with the Nickel Plate Road and leased the Wabash Railroad. In 1967, the Atlantic Coast Line and

Seaboard Air Line became the Seaboard Coast Line. The merger with the greatest long-term impact on the industry was the combination of one-time foes New York Central and Pennsylvania railroads on February 1, 1968, creating the Penn Central.

It's July 16, 1977, and the ICC has been deliberating for over a dozen years on the UP–CRI&P merger. First-generation power has freight rolling southbound across the Harry S. Truman drawbridge in Kansas City, Missouri. Most of this traffic will head west on the route to Tucumcari, New Mexico. While the deliberations continued, the Rock slowly crumbled, and three years later threw in the towel and declared bankruptcy. *Kevin EuDaly photo*

The Pennsylvania Railroad was a conservative Northeastern powerhouse. Long aligned with the Norfolk & Western, observers expected a merger of those two roads but were surprised when their long-time competitor, New York Central, stepped into negotiations. Here a Pennsy FA-2 sits at the engine facility in Columbus, Ohio, in the early 1960s. *Alan Bradley photo*

Most agree today that the PC merger should never have been allowed to happen. The two railroads were historic rivals with parallel systems, heavy passenger- and commuter-train traffic, and excess capacity. Although the Central had trimmed down its plant somewhat under the leadership of Alfred E. Perlman, the Pennsy was more conservative, and the two companies had vastly different operating practices. When the two railroads were still powerful and profitable, the thought was that any merger would pit the Central and Pennsy against each other through the merger of each with other roads and not each other (e.g., Norfolk & Western with PRR and Chesapeake & Ohio with NYC). Thus, the result would be two major, equal systems in the East. Instead, in 1957 the Central and Pennsy announced merger talks with each other. Even though the merger was 10 years in the making, the roads were little prepared for the 1968 merger. Former PRR executives were put in charge of most key areas; the new chairman was PRR head Stuart Saunders, who had come from the N&W. Many former NYC executives headed for the door when they saw that PRR men were being put in charge, which contributed to turmoil in the company. And where NYC and PRR managers remained, internal rivalries developed.

The cost of combining the railroads drove the company into debt, aggravated by an ICC order to purchase the bankrupt New Haven Railroad by the beginning of 1969. Clashing corporate cultures, incompatible computer systems, and inflexible union contracts drove up costs, as did years of deferred track maintenance, which forced trains to run at reduced speeds. Derailments became frequent, causing operating costs to spiral. Saunders and his team used expensive short-term borrowings to finance the company and used its wealth of assets to show that Penn Central was on the right track, but it still reported a $2.8 million loss for 1968. In 1969, the railroad reported a loss of $182 million. In 1970, the railroad's parent holding company, Penn Central Co., had assets of nearly $7 billion, but the bulk of its salable holdings of real estate, securities, and other nonrail property were already pledged to secure $2.6 billion of debt. Penn Central's liquidity crisis forced the railroad to declare bankruptcy on June 21, 1970—the nation's largest corporate bankruptcy at the time. In his bankruptcy petition to the court, Chairman Paul Gorman (Saunders had been pushed out by then) said that the railroad was "virtually without cash, unable to meet its debts, and has no means of borrowing." The petition declared that the company could not repay $9,795,000 in commercial notes and $21,900,000 in debt and rental charges on its equipment, all due by July 1, 1970, according to *Time* magazine.

The PC bankruptcy wasn't the first in the East. The Central Railroad of New Jersey had entered bankruptcy on March 22, 1967. Three days after PC went bankrupt, the Penn Central–owned Lehigh Valley followed. In 1971, the Reading Company was declared insolvent, and the next year the Lehigh & Hudson River went bust as well. Another large

New York Central FA-2 1079 leads three more Alcos on manifest tonnage in November 1964 across the northern plains. New York Central aligned itself with the Chesapeake & Ohio before pairing up with the Pennsy. The formation of Penn Central was an early test of merging parallel systems and one that clearly failed. The rivals couldn't see eye to eye on much, and the resulting turmoil doomed Penn Central. *Kevin EuDaly collection*

By the time this view was taken at Collinwood Yard in Cleveland, Ohio, on October 5, 1970, Penn Central markings appear on nearly everything. The merger between the two giants occurred in February 1968, and the New Haven was added in 1969. Penn Central didn't do much better than its predecessors, and in fact declared bankruptcy on June 21, 1970. After several private-sector failed attempts to operate Penn Central, Congress stepped in and the federal government took over under the Conrail flag in 1976, which included a number of other failed Northeastern roads. *Dennis Schmidt photo*

Eastern road, the Erie Lackawanna, might have stayed out of bankruptcy had it not been devastated by Hurricane Agnes in June 1972. Damage to the railroad was $9.2 million, forcing it into bankruptcy.

Just as the Eastern railroads were coming apart, Congress was addressing the "passenger train problem." With passenger losses mounting, and with the public demanding some form of passenger-train service, Congress in 1970 passed the Rail

In December 1972, when the seasonal New York–Florida *Vacationer* was photographed in Florida, Amtrak was just a year old. Operating with a variety of equipment inherited from the roads that joined, the early era saw trains with equipment from competitors and allies alike. In this view, two E8As lead a B-unit of Union Pacific heritage. *Riley Kinney photo*

Passenger Service Act, which created the National Railroad Passenger Corporation, known better by its marketing name, Amtrak. It is a common misconception that Amtrak is simply another government agency; it's actually a public-private railroad company that receives taxpayer funding to offset any losses (which there have been every year since its formation). Amtrak assumed operation of about half of the remaining intercity passenger trains in the United States on May 1, 1971. Any railroad operating intercity passenger service on that date could contract with Amtrak. Participating railroads bought stock in the NRPC using a formula based on their recent intercity passenger-train losses. The purchase price could be satisfied either by cash or rolling stock and locomotives; in exchange, the railroads received common stock. Railroads that chose not to join Amtrak were required to continue operating their existing passenger service until 1975 and then had to pursue ICC approval to discontinue or alter their service. The Denver & Rio Grande Western, Georgia Railroad, Rock Island, Southern Railway, Long Island Rail Road, Reading Company, and Chicago South Shore & South Bend were eligible but declined to join; eventually the Rio Grande and Southern turned over their passenger services to Amtrak.

A common opinion at the time was that the Nixon administration and many in Congress viewed Amtrak as a way to satisfy the public's demand for passenger trains, but expected it to quietly disappear as public interest declined. But Amtrak turned out to be surprisingly popular and continues in business today, although not at a profit. In fiscal year 2007 the company carried 25,847,531 passengers, marking the fifth straight year of gains and setting a record for the most passengers carried since it started operations, when ridership was just above 15.5 million.

With Amtrak picking up the railroad industry's passenger losses, Congress began to turn its attention to the ills facing the freight side of the business. In 1973, Congress developed a plan to nationalize the bankrupt Northeastern railroads. The Association of American Railroads (AAR), a lobbying and trade organization representing North America's railroads, opposed the plan. The AAR came up with its own plan for a private company using government funds. In January 1974, President Nixon signed the Regional Rail Reorganization Act (3R) into law and provided interim funding to the bankrupt railroads. It also defined a new Consolidated Rail Corporation—Conrail—using the AAR's plan.

The 3R Act formed the United States Railway Association (USRA), a government corporation that took over the abandonment powers of the ICC in regard to line abandonments. The USRA was also to create a Final System Plan to decide which lines should be included in the new Consolidated Rail Corporation. The USRA and its president, Edward G. Jordan (who became Conrail's first CEO), had to come up with a plan to save the railroad system in the Northeast, and they did so extraordinarily well—but not without a struggle. Only the USRA-designated lines were to be taken over, with other lines sold to Amtrak, various state governments, transportation agencies, and other railroads. The USRA plan revealed in 1975 included lines from Penn Central, Erie Lackawanna, Central Railroad of New Jersey, Lehigh Valley, Lehigh & Hudson River, Reading, and Pennsylvania-Reading Seashore Lines. President Ford signed the Railroad Revitalization and Regulatory Reform Act of 1976 on February 5, 1976. To retain some competition in the Northeast, the USRA assigned trackage rights to the Delaware & Hudson Railway, allowing it to reach Philadelphia and Washington, D.C.

At first Conrail continued to lose money, despite more than $3 billion from the government to rebuild infrastructure and rolling stock. By the close of the 1970s, it was close to bankruptcy. In 1981, L. Stanley Crane, who had served as president of the Southern Railway, came to Conrail as its president. Crane moved quickly to reduce costs, eliminating thousands of jobs, cutting lines, and focusing management on competing in the free-market atmosphere brought on by the deregulation of railroads. Also helping Conrail was the Northeast Rail Service Act of 1981, which relieved Conrail of its requirement to provide commuter-train services in the Boston–Washington Northeast Corridor. In 1983, remaining commuter services provided by Conrail were transferred to state or metropolitan transit authorities. Crane did what many deemed impossible: Conrail became profitable. It earned $39.2 million in 1981 and $174.2 million in 1982 on revenues of $3.6 billion.

Two Conrail Geeps, a GP9 and a GP7, pull red and green Penn Central equipment on the Valparaiso, Indiana, local across the lift bridge at 21st Street on September 2, 1976. At the time, Conrail was seven months old and was trying to turn the corner from bankrupt predecessors to a viable and profitable entity. The small "CR" on the long hood is directly over a large black square where the Penn Central logo has been painted over. *Joe Piersen photo*

For the first seven years of its existence, Conrail proved highly unprofitable, to the accumulated tune of $2.2 billion in losses from 1976 to 1982. After exemption from state taxes, the railroad improved, with positive net incomes through 1986. On March 26, 1987, Conrail stock was sold to private investors, and in 1998 NS and CSX each purchased a portion of the railroad. On May 9, 1985, SD40-2 No. 6384 and SD40 No. 6312 are moving through Danville, Indiana. *Kevin EuDaly photo*

Conrail made so much money that the Reagan administration decided to sell it to Norfolk Southern. Crane fought to keep the company independent and was successful: in 1987, Conrail went public with a stock offering. The sale of the government's 85 percent stake brought in $1.65 billion, the largest stock offering in Wall Street history at the time. The company's increasing success attracted the attention of other railroads. On August 22, 1998, Norfolk Southern, along with CSX Transportation, purchased the assets of the 10,797-mile Conrail. The railroad was split up, with NS acquiring 58 percent of Conrail's assets and CSX receiving 42 percent. NS and CSX agreed to pay $115 per share, raising the purchase price of Conrail to $10.2 billion, five times the price the Reagan administration had been willing to sell for. The two railroads began operating their new lines on June 1, 1999. A smaller Conrail, called Conrail Shared Assets, was formed by CSX and NS to run trains in three large metro regions.

Although Conrail brought a solution to the rail problem in the Northeast, in the mid-1970s two Midwestern railroads, the Rock Island and The Milwaukee Road, went bankrupt. The 7,000-mile Chicago, Rock Island & Pacific (Rock Island Lines) declared bankruptcy on March 17, 1975, with the Chicago, Milwaukee, St. Paul & Pacific (The Milwaukee Road) following on December 19, 1977. Both railroads had long and colorful histories, but by the 1970s had fallen on hard times. The Rock Island attempted to reorganize on its own, but on August 28, 1979, its clerks went on strike in a

dispute over wages, followed by the members of the United Transportation Union. President Jimmy Carter appointed an emergency board to settle the dispute and UTU members came back to work, but the Brotherhood of Railway and Airline Clerks stayed off the job. By order of the ICC, the Kansas City Terminal Railway took over operations of the Rock Island on September 26, 1979, under an ICC "directed service" order. In early 1980, the bankruptcy court determined that the Rock Island could not be reorganized and ordered the liquidation of the railroad, the largest such liquidation in U.S. history. On March 31, 1980, the Rock Island operated its last train. However, nearly all of Rock Island's main lines were sold to other railroads and remained in service.

The first reorganization plan put forth by the trustee of The Milwaukee Road in 1979 called for abandonment of all lines between Montana and the Pacific Coast and many branch and secondary main lines in the West and Midwest. By cutting off these lines, management could concentrate on the remaining "core" railroad in the Midwest. Congress passed The Milwaukee Road Restructuring Act on November 2, 1979, which took from the ICC the power of abandoning The Milwaukee Road lines and gave it to the Court, and provided as much as $75 million in funding for employee protection. On March 15, 1980, service ended west of Miles City, Montana, on the scenic Pacific Extension, which at one time included over 600 miles of electrified trackage. In March 1982, the railroad cut back farther, to Ortonville, Minnesota. Although many keenly felt the loss of the Pacific Extension, the strategy

In a surprise move, Rock Island opted for a complete image change in 1974 and went with this blinding blue and white scheme with lettering that was later dubbed "bankruptcy blue." These two GP9s are working a transfer run in Peoria, Illinois, on September 29, 1979. As much as the designers hoped for a solid Rock Island, it crumbled into ruin and the last train ran on March 31, 1980. *Kevin EuDaly collection*

While The Rock slipped into oblivion, The Milwaukee Road was fighting to stay solvent, and with some help from Congress managed to survive, even though the Pacific Extension became a victim and was abandoned west of Miles City, Montana. Four SD40-2s have just come off The Milwaukee Road's line from western Indiana into Bedford, and have swung onto the former Monon line to Louisville on May 14, 1985. The stoplights are green as the units run on tracks that run down the middle of J Street. *Kevin EuDaly photo*

of cutting down to a core railroad worked: in March 1982, the 3,000-mile core system saw its first profit, a net income of $4.2 million. The Soo Line purchased The Milwaukee Road in 1985.

It's possible the Milwaukee's Pacific Extension might have been saved had it hung on a few more years following the partial deregulation of the railroad industry in 1980. President Carter signed landmark rail deregulation legislation into law on October 14, 1980. Named for Rep. Harley O. Staggers of West Virginia, the Staggers Rail Act marked a turning point for the industry that is largely responsible for its good health today. The effects of the Staggers Act were far reaching. The abandonment process was accelerated and streamlined,

resulting in railroads finally being able to shed thousands of miles of underused lines. Railroads were free to set rates and enter into contracts with shippers to set price and service without the interference of the ICC. Merger proceedings were also streamlined and time limits set to prevent the debacle of the Rock Island–Union Pacific 10-year merger proceedings. The ICC itself disappeared in 1995, replaced by the smaller Federal Surface Transportation Board.

The result of deregulation was a leaner, profitable U.S. rail industry. Railroads were now freer than ever to merge, and in the 1980s merger mania struck the industry. Railroad corporate consolidations had been part of the U.S. railroad scene since soon after the first rails were laid, but the final

When Burlington Northern and the Santa Fe merged into the Burlington Northern Santa Fe on the last day of 1996, the result was a route map that blanketed the Midwest and West. This view of an eastbound coal train parked and waiting for a crew at Armour, Missouri, on May 11, 2008, shows the latest paint scheme of what became simply the BNSF Railway in 2005. *Kevin EuDaly photo*

movement toward the seven Class 1 giants of 2008 picked up steam in the early 1980s. (Class 1 is defined as having annual operating revenue exceeding $319.3 million.) A half century ago, any railroad that earned at least $1 million a year was a Class 1, and there were more than 100 of them, from giants like Pennsylvania, New York Central, Santa Fe, and Southern Pacific down to a few that were really "short lines." Today, as a result of mergers, there are just seven Class 1 systems. Two, Canadian National and Canadian Pacific, are based in Canada. Five have their headquarters in the United States. An overview of each follows:

BNSF Railway was the result of the September 22, 1995, merger of Burlington Northern, Inc., with the Santa Fe Pacific Corporation. Their two railroad subsidiaries, the Atchison, Topeka & Santa Fe Railway and Burlington Northern Railroad,

merged on December 31, 1996. Burlington Northern was itself the result of the successful March 1970 merger of the Chicago, Burlington & Quincy; Great Northern; Northern Pacific; and Spokane, Portland & Seattle railways. BN was one of few railroad success stories in the 1970s—unlike the Penn Central merger, the integration of the four railroads that made up BN went smoothly. In 1980, BN merged the St. Louis-San Francisco (Frisco) Railway into its system. Unlike BN, the Santa Fe was one of the most famous names in railroading; its name remained virtually intact since 1863, with only a minor change from "railroad" to "railway" in December 1895. Famous for its fine passenger-train service, in the 1980s and 1990s Santa Fe remade itself as a high-speed intermodal railroad, with its "franchise" route being the Chicago–Los Angeles main line that once hosted several transcontinental streamliners.

Initially named the Burlington Northern & Santa Fe Railway, the name was simplified to BNSF Railway in January 2005. BNSF is based in Fort Worth, Texas, and operates 32,000 miles of track.

CSX Transportation has a convoluted history. It was formed on July 1, 1986, when the Seaboard System Railroad changed its name to CSX. Seaboard System was created on January 1, 1983, when Seaboard Coast Line (itself the result of the 1967 merger of the Seaboard Air Line and Atlantic Coast Line railroads), Louisville & Nashville, and Clinchfield Railroad were merged, along with several smaller subsidiaries. Another company, Chessie System, had been incorporated in 1973 to own the Chesapeake & Ohio, which also owned the Baltimore & Ohio. The C&O/B&O also held more than 90 percent of the stock of the Western Maryland. The three roads operated separately under the Chessie System banner, but in late 1983 B&O merged the WM.

On November 1, 1980, Chessie System, Inc. and Seaboard Coast Line Industries, Inc. merged to form the CSX Corporation. Originally, the subsidiary railroads retained their separate identities within the corporation. On July 1, 1986, the Seaboard System name was changed to CSX Transportation. Still, C&O and B&O continued to exist corporately, but on April 30, 1987, the 160-year-old B&O—the nation's first common-carrier railroad—was formally merged into the C&O. The final step took place on September 2, 1987, when the C&O was merged into CSX Transportation.

CSX locomotives have worn a number of paint schemes, and one of the more uncommon was this handsome blue and gray version that adorns B30-7 5569, shown exiting Willow Valley Tunnel in southern Indiana on May 27, 1988. This location is on the former B&O route headed for St. Louis, the western end of what is now CSX, a system that inhabits every state east of the Mississippi River and south of the Great Lakes. *Kevin EuDaly photo*

The last remaining Class 1 from decades past with little change from a merger viewpoint is Kansas City Southern. CEO Mike Haverty brought back the classic *Southern Belle* paint scheme in the twenty-first century with this trio of F-units used for special trains—this one is at Kansas City Union Station and is headed to Atchison, Kansas, on May 9, 2008, for the dedication of a statue depicting an early railroad builder with a spike-driving maul. *Kevin EuDaly photo*

On June 1, 1999, CSX began operating 42 percent of Conrail's assets (Norfolk Southern got the remaining 58 percent). As a result, CSX grew to include some 3,800 miles of the Conrail system, mainly lines once owned by the New York Central. Based in Jacksonville, Florida, CSX Transportation operates a 21,000-mile network linking 23 states, the District of Columbia, and two Canadian provinces.

The **Kansas City Southern Railway** remains a renegade independent north-south Class 1, while the other Class 1s are largely east-west systems. KCS, which began as the Kansas City, Pittsburg & Gulf in 1890, was completed to the Gulf of Mexico in 1897. The KCS name dates from a turn-of-the-century reorganization in which founder Arthur Stilwell was ousted. KCS acquired Louisiana & Arkansas in 1939 and remained a stable midsized system until the 1990s, when, beset with megamergers all around it, it began expanding under president Mike Haverty by acquiring regional lines and linking up with Mexico, marketing its newly expanded system under the banner the Nafta Railway.

KCS lines head south from Kansas City to Shreveport, Louisiana, where they divide into routes to Meridian, Mississippi (on the former regional railroad Mid-South, ex-Illinois Central lines acquired in 1994); to New Orleans and Lake Charles, Louisiana; and to Beaumont, Texas. From Beaumont, KCS makes its way via trackage rights and over the Texas-Mexican Railway it acquired in 1995 to the Mexican border, where it links up to subsidiary Kansas City Southern de Mexico. KCSM's 2,661-mile network in Mexico has routes from the border cities of Nuevo Laredo and Matamoros that come together at Monterrey and run south to Mexico City, where lines run east to Veracruz on the Gulf of Mexico and west to Lazaro Cardenas on the Pacific Coast. In 1997, KCS acquired the Gateway Western Railway, a 408-mile regional railroad linking East St. Louis, Illinois, with Kansas City. In 1998, KCS invested in the Panama Canal Railway Company, in which it now holds a 50 percent interest. The 47.6-mile line, originally constructed in 1855 and the first transcontinental railroad in the world, was fully restored in 2002 and today provides passenger and freight service from Panama City to Colon, Panama. KCS, based in Kansas City, Missouri, operates 6,476 miles of trackage in 10 U.S. states, Mexico, and Panama.

Norfolk Southern Railway was created on June 1, 1982, with the merger of the Norfolk & Western and Southern Railway. The two railways operated as separate subsidiaries under parent company Norfolk Southern Corporation until December 31, 1990, when Norfolk & Western became a subsidiary of the Southern Railway, and the Southern Railway changed its name to Norfolk Southern Railway. Norfolk &

With the thoroughbred herald on the nose, this Norfolk Southern ES40DC waits its turn on June 15, 2007, at Farm, West Virginia, located on the Pocahontas Subdivision in the southwestern part of the state. The system reaches as far west as Kansas City, and operates 21,500 miles in 22 Eastern states. *Kevin EuDaly photo*

Western's name dates from 1881. It ran west from Norfolk, Virginia, originally to Columbus and Cincinnati, Ohio, but expanded to cities such as Detroit, Chicago, Des Moines, Iowa, St. Louis, and Kansas City, when it acquired the Nickel Plate and Wabash railroads in 1964. N&W was well known for being one of the last Class 1 railroads to operate steam power, not dieselizing 100 percent until 1960. Many of its steam locomotives were built at the company's own shops in Roanoke, Virginia. The Southern Railway, whose first predecessor dates from 1833, covered the Southeast from Washington to New Orleans, and from Cincinnati, Louisville, St. Louis, and Memphis through Birmingham and Atlanta to Savannah and Jacksonville. One of many Southern predecessors was the original Norfolk Southern Railway, which ran from Norfolk, Virginia, to Charlotte, North Carolina, and was absorbed in 1974.

On August 22, 1998, Norfolk Southern, along with CSX Transportation, purchased and divided the assets of Conrail, with NS getting 58 percent of the railroad. The acquisition expanded both NS's track miles and its number of employees by 50 percent. NS began operating its portion of Conrail on June 1, 1999. Today's 21,200-mile Norfolk Southern system, based in Norfolk, serves 22 states, the District of Columbia, and the province of Ontario.

Among the oldest names in railroading is the **Union Pacific**. UP began as the eastern link of the first trans-continental railroad from Omaha, Nebraska, to Promontory, Utah, where it linked up with the Central Pacific on May 10, 1869. The railroad later added lines serving Kansas City, Denver, Los Angeles, Portland, Oregon, and Seattle. UP was known as a pioneer in railroading. In 1934, it introduced the nation's first streamliner, the M-10000. In 1941, UP received the first

The Union Pacific's heritage is among the longest-lived of all North American railroading. The addition of the large wing heralds on the nose of units like AC4400CW 5930 began in 2000. This eastbound coal train was photographed at Lawrence, Kansas, on the way from the connection with the Nebraska main line at Gibbon to Kansas City on May 3, 2008. *Kevin EuDaly photo*

Big Boy, the largest steam locomotive ever built. It was the first railroad to experiment with gas-turbine-powered locomotives, and in 1969 introduced the largest diesel locomotives ever built to that time, the 6,600-horsepower "Centennials" named for UP's 100th anniversary.

The Union Pacific of today is the result of the merger mania that gripped the railroad industry after deregulation. It acquired the Western Pacific in 1981 and the Missouri Pacific in 1982, extending its system to San Francisco and throughout the south-central states. In 1988, it added the Missouri-Kansas-

Texas ("Katy") that linked Kansas City with Houston and San Antonio. In 1995, UP acquired the Chicago & North Western, long its link from Omaha to Chicago. On September 11, 1996, UP merged Southern Pacific Lines into its system, adding over 14,000 miles of trackage. Included in the acquisition were SP's Denver & Rio Grande Western and St. Louis-Southwestern (Cotton Belt).

Based in Omaha, Union Pacific is the largest U.S. railroad, operating a 32,000-mile network serving 23 states. Well aware of its history, UP operates a museum in Council Bluffs, Iowa, and runs two large steam locomotives as part of its Heritage Program, which also includes streamlined E9 diesels and passenger cars used on UP streamliners in the 1950s and 1960s.

In addition to Class 1s, midsized regional railroads popped up in the 1980s and 1990s. The creation of these companies stemmed from two major factors. One was the bankruptcy of the Rock Island and The Milwaukee Road. Several smaller carriers, such as the Iowa Interstate, Iowa, Chicago & Eastern, Twin Cities & Western, and Wisconsin & Southern, rose from the ashes of these bankrupt systems. The other factor was the sale of marginal routes by Class 1s, made easier by deregulation. One Class 1 in particular kick-started the regional movement: the Illinois Central Gulf. A 1972 merger creation when Illinois Central and Gulf, Mobile & Ohio got together, ICG in the 1980s went from a 9,568-mile system to 2,981 miles in just seven years. Seven new regional railroads represented about half the reduced mileage. Others, such as Dakota, Minnesota & Eastern and Wisconsin Central, were created from lines cast off by Chicago & North Western and Soo Line.

Regional railroads were able to operate the routes more efficiently and provide personalized service, since the new startups were not hampered by antiquated work rules on the Class 1s (rules that are largely gone today) and local management could concentrate on service. The regional movement was so successful that Class 1s have bought back many lines. Examples include ICG spin-off Mid-South Rail, acquired by Kansas City Southern in 1994; Chicago Central, repurchased by the Illinois Central (it dropped the "Gulf" from its name in 1988) in 1996; Wisconsin Central, bought by Canadian National in 2001; and Dakota, Minnesota & Eastern/Iowa, Chicago & Eastern, purchased by Canadian Pacific in 2008.

Railroads' portion of intercity commercial freight reached 42 percent by 2007. The U.S. railroad system is in excellent condition, though it now lacks capacity and is virtually overrun by freight traffic—a far cry from the 1960s and 1970s when the industry struggled to survive. Unlike government involvement in the 1970s, twenty-first-century government assistance may be needed to help a healthy rail industry handle a crush of traffic, not to keep a struggling industry alive.

One of many regional railroads is the 1,400-mile Iowa, Chicago & Eastern, which began operations on July 30, 2002. Based in Davenport, Iowa, the regional is owned, along with sister road Dakota, Minnesota & Eastern, by Cedar American Rail Holdings, and reaches as far southwest as Kansas City. This transfer run is on the way into BNSF's Argentine Yard and is about to pass under 12th Street in Argentine, Kansas, on May 11, 2008. Two BNSF trains wait in the distance for their turn into the yard. *Kevin EuDaly photo*

Teakettles to Super Power:
Steam Locomotives

by Jim Boyd

Camden & Amboy No. 1, the *John Bull*, looked like this in revenue service, with a wooden cab and large tender. The brakeman rode under the awning atop the tender and used his legs to apply the brakes with a long lever. The cab, headlight, and cowcatcher with pilot wheels were added to adapt it to U.S. service. The C&A covered the shortest land gap between New York Harbor and the Delaware River connection to Philadelphia. *Jim Boyd photo*

North America has to credit England, that rainy little island, with the creation of both railroads and locomotives. Once the technology made it across the Atlantic Ocean, however, it developed in a manner distinctly American. The British railways were built through already civilized and urbanized countryside for the primary purpose of moving people, while the North American railroads were flung out into the wilderness for the purpose of building a nation.

The first locomotives in North America were imported from England, and they brought with them the "Stephenson gauge" of 4 feet 8 1/2 inches, which was based upon the chariot-wheel grooves in the old Roman roads, which were determined by the centerlines of two horses harnessed side by side, so the wheels would not hit the indentations made by the hooves. Horse-drawn carriages and wagons had the same considerations, so most existing wheel spacings at that time were also 4 feet 8 1/2 inches. It was the carriage-makers and their existing jigs that ultimately determined the track

The first successful steam locomotive was the *Locomotion*, built for the Stockton & Darlington in England in 1825. Its vertical cylinders and maze of walking beams were a function of steam water-pump technology of the time. Like the *John Bull* and *Rocket*, it ran on George Stephenson's 4 foot 8 1/2-inch standard gauge track. Railfan & Railroad Magazine *collection*

In 1829, the idea of railroading was not new in America, however. As early as 1811, Colonel John Stevens had petitioned the New Jersey legislature for a charter to build a railroad from South Amboy to Bordentown, linking New York Harbor and the Delaware River to create a water-rail-water route from New York to Philadelphia; this route would be a quicker and more comfortable ride than the traditional stagecoach route via Princeton and Trenton (today this is the Northeast Corridor, one of the most heavily traveled rail routes in the world). It would be many years, however, before Colonel Stevens' Camden & Amboy would turn a flanged wheel.

gauge. When the early British railroad builders needed cars (still referred to as carriages in the British Isles), they went with the standard wheel spacing and simply added flanges. While some of the earliest horse-drawn industrial tramways used a variety of gauges, ranging upward from 1 foot 11 1/2 inches, it was the most successful locomotive builder of the 1820s, George Stephenson, who created and promoted the 4 feet 8 1/2-inch standard gauge, or Stephenson gauge, for general service.

The first successful steam locomotive was the *Locomotion* of 1825. It was a four-wheel machine with a horizontal boiler and vertical cylinders linked to the driving wheels by a maddening array of rods and beams that looked for all the world like a closet full of coat hangers in the midst of a violent rebellion.

For all practical purposes, however, the birth of the steam locomotive came in October 1829 with a seven-day event in Rainhill, England, where a handful of locomotive builders competed head-to-head for the contract to supply steam locomotives for the Liverpool & Manchester Railway. The winner of the contest was Robert Stephenson & Company of Newcastle with its four-wheel locomotive *Rocket*. It was the nineteenth locomotive built by Stephenson and incorporated a horizontal fire-tube boiler, exhaust-driven forced draft, and horizontal cylinders connected directly to the big front driving wheels. It recorded a speed of 28 miles per hour—the fastest man had ever traveled on land and lived to tell about it.

A seven-day competition was held in October 1829 at Rainhill, England, to see who would get the contract to build locomotives for the Liverpool & Manchester Railway. The winner was Robert Stephenson with his locomotive *Rocket*, which achieved a speed of 28 miles per hour, a world record at the time. This replica from the National Railway Museum at York, England, operated at the Sacramento RailFair in California in 1991. *Jim Boyd photo*

In 1828, Horatio Allen ordered four locomotives from Foster, Rastrick & Company of Stourbridge, England. One of these, the *Stourbridge Lion*, went to the new Delaware & Hudson Canal Company (see Chapter 1), which employed an incline cable railway on the westernmost portion of its transport route to move coal over a mountain. On August 8, 1829, the *Stourbridge Lion* became the first steam locomotive to operate in North America. It was too heavy for the crude wood-and-strap-iron rail of the D&HCC, however, and never entered revenue service.

The great Baltimore & Ohio Railroad had its beginnings in 1830 when Peter Cooper's home-built *Tom Thumb* hauled passengers 13 miles from Baltimore to Ellicott's Mills, Maryland. The *Tom Thumb* went down in history, however, when it lost a race with a horse-drawn rail carriage. The event was restaged here in 1977 at the B&O Railroad Museum in Baltimore. *Jim Boyd photo*

On August 8, 1829, the first steam locomotive to operate in the United States was the *Stourbridge Lion*, built by Foster, Rastrick & Company of Stourbridge, England, for Horatio Allen's Delaware & Hudson Canal Company at Honesdale, Pennsylvania. The locomotive was too heavy for the track, however, and never pulled a revenue load. The replica, displayed today at Honesdale, was on a D&H display train for the canal company's 150th anniversary in April 1973. *Jim Boyd photo*

In 1830, Peter Cooper created the *Tom Thumb*, a vertical-boiler four-wheeler, for the Baltimore & Ohio Railroad, and it made the 13-mile run from downtown Baltimore out to Ellicott's Mills in just under an hour. But the *Tom Thumb* was doomed to go down in history as the steam locomotive that lost a race with a horse.

The next locomotive didn't fare much better. On January 15, 1831, the four-wheel, vertical-boiler *Best Friend of Charleston* became the first steam locomotive in North America to enter regular service. It was built by the West Point Foundry in New York City and operated on the South Carolina Canal & Railroad Company, where it served successfully until June 17, 1831, when the fireman, irritated by the constant hissing sound, tied down the safety valve and shortly thereafter became the first American victim of a boiler explosion.

Getting back to the Camden & Amboy project in New Jersey, Colonel Stevens had gone to England and purchased a four-wheel, horizontal-boiler locomotive from the Stephenson Company. The *John Bull* was built and tested in England and disassembled and loaded into great wooden crates that were then sent by sailing ship to Bordentown, New Jersey, on the Delaware River above Philadelphia.

They arrived in August 1831. Receiving them there was Isaac Dripps, a 21-year-old mechanic who had never seen a steam locomotive and did not know how one operated or what it should look like. And, of course, there were no blueprints

The world's oldest operable self-propelled vehicle, the 150-year-old steam locomotive *John Bull*, built in England in 1831, was restored by the Smithsonian Institution and operated on the B&O's Georgetown Branch in the District of Columbia in September 1981. In an era when all previous locomotives were one-of-a-kind, it was the first that was successful enough to be duplicated. The Camden & Amboy had 16 *John Bull*–class engines. *Jim Boyd photo*

or instructions with the crates, and the boss, Colonel Stevens, was still in England. To everyone's amazement—and probably his own—Dripps had the machine up and running by September 15, 1831.

To make it track better, the *John Bull* was soon modified with the first pilot truck and cowcatcher. The external drive rods were disconnected from the front driver set, leaving only the cylinder-connected rear drivers to power the locomotive. A wooden outrigger with a set of small wheels was hung from

the former-driver axle hubs to help guide the locomotive over track undulations and around curves. The C&A track was made of strap iron on wooden rails laid on stone "sleepers," rather than wooden cross ties. Modern calculations show that even with only the rear drivers powered, the *John Bull* had a perfect "factor of adhesion" and would have pulled as much as if all wheels had been powered.

In spite of the relative crudeness of the engineering, the C&A actually ran quite well and became an immediate economic success. Business boomed, and over the next six years no less than 15 duplicates of the *John Bull* were built and put into service. Up to this point in American locomotive history, all locomotives had been one-of-a-kind designs. The *John Bull* was the first steam locomotive that was successful enough to be duplicated in kind, and it was the fleet of 16 *John Bulls* that eventually powered the Camden & Amboy into the history books as the great Pennsylvania Railroad.

The *John Bull* remained in revenue service until 1866 and was later donated to the Smithsonian Institution for preservation. It had been the first steam locomotive in North America to get the proportions correct. It had the correct-size boiler and firebox for the size of its horizontal direct-drive cylinders. Its exhaust provided an efficient forced draft, and the *John Bull* acted and sounded like a real locomotive.

After borrowing the original for extensive systemwide operation on historical occasions, in 1940 the Pennsylvania Railroad built an exact replica of the *John Bull* for public events. In September 1981, the Smithsonian restored the original to service for its 150th birthday, and it clearly demonstrated the soundness of its design. It also showed that the replica *"Johnny" Bull* very closely duplicated the performance and characteristics of the original—right down to its balky throttle.

As the idea of railroading expanded in the 1830s, it was obvious that the Americans couldn't afford the time or expense of importing all of their equipment from England. A locomotive was basic hardware that was within the technology of the blacksmiths, foundries, and machine shops of the time. In 1827, Matthias Baldwin had built a 5-horsepower stationary steam engine to power his machine shop in Philadelphia, and in 1832 he used that shop to construct *Old Ironsides*, a four-wheel horizontal-boiler steam locomotive roughly similar to the *John Bull*. By the time of his death in 1866, Baldwin's company had constructed more than 1,500 locomotives. In 1928, it opened a huge new industrial complex in Eddystone, Pennsylvania, along the Delaware River just south of Philadelphia and soon became the world's largest manufacturer of steam locomotives.

Baldwin's story was not unique, and in the 1830s and 1840s locomotive builders thrived up and down the Eastern Seaboard. Boston and New England were centers of manufacturing, and at one time Paterson, New Jersey, had more than a dozen locomotive builders within its city limits, including such enduring names as Rodgers and Cooke.

Developing the Designs

A steam locomotive consists of two primary and surprisingly unrelated components: the boiler and the running gear. The boiler generates the steam, and the running gear applies the power to the rails.

One of the first exhibits that a visitor to the California State Railroad Museum in Sacramento encounters is Central Pacific No. 1, *Gov. Stanford*, in a setting representing a tunnel on the first transcontinental railroad in the high Sierra. The classic Civil War–era wood-burning 4-4-0 was built by Norris & Sons in Philadelphia in 1862 and shipped around Cape Horn to Sacramento. It is restored to its appearance in 1899, when it was retired. *Jim Boyd photo*

The boiler required a pressurized container for the water and a firebox in which to burn the fuel. The earliest fuel, of course, was readily available wood, but its heat content was often unpredictable, and under a forced draft it produced a dangerous exhaust of hot embers that could set fires wherever they landed, in lineside grass or on the passengers' clothing. Although wood-burners with oversized cinder-screen smokestacks survived until the 1900s, by the Civil War coal had been recognized as a far superior fuel.

Draft for the fire was provided by the exhaust from the cylinders. The boiler was a horizontal tank with the firebox at the back and a hollow chamber smokebox on the front. Pipes (known as flues) ran through the boiler from the firebox to the smokebox, carrying the fire through the surrounding water and transferring the heat. The exhaust from the cylinders would blow into the smokebox through a focused nozzle and directly out through the stack, creating a partial vacuum in the smokebox that would draw the fire through the flues. Thus,

Duquesne Slag Company 0-6-0 switcher No. 8, in the former DL&W roundhouse at the Steamtown National Historic Site in Scranton, Pennsylvania, has been cut open to show the smokebox, yellow front flue sheet, blue horizontal flues, and radial staybolts around the firebox at the rear flue sheet. Also exposed are the inner workings of the cylinder and slide valve chamber in red and white. This basic arrangement varies only in size and proportions on nearly all steam locomotives. *Jim Boyd photo*

The sizes are different, but the basics are the same between the 1837 Norris 4-2-0 *Lafayette* and brand-new EM-1 2-8-8-4 No. 7800, posed together in 1944. The Norris engine had a rigid pilot truck, and the locomotive rode on the center pivot and the flanges of the one driver on each side. The massive EM-1 had a fully sprung and equalized suspension system and even a hinge in the center to ease it through the curves. *B&O Railroad photo*

the harder the locomotive worked, the more exhaust and draft would be created and the hotter the fire would burn, producing more steam in the boiler. The distinctive chug-chug sound of a steam locomotive is this exhaust at work.

The biggest problem to be overcome by the early designers was how to add water to an already pressurized boiler. You couldn't just open the top and pour in a jug of water. The earliest locomotives used "ram pumps" to force water into the boiler. These were simple piston pumps driven off the moving drive wheels to force water in at a slightly higher pressure than that inside the boiler. The only problem there, of course, was that the locomotive had to be moving to get any water into it.

The problem was soon solved with the injector, a device that used a jet of hot steam from the boiler blown into a small chamber of cold water with a narrow venturi into the boiler feed pipe. The hot steam would make the cold water expand and push itself into the boiler. The secret to the injector was not the pressure of the steam, but the temperature difference between the steam and the fresh water. Even in later years, in hot environments like a desert, injectors would sometimes falter when the water in the tender became too warm.

The running gear consisted of an underframe, the wheels, cylinders, and valve mechanisms. The number and size of the wheels would determine the type of work the locomotive could do in terms of power and speed. Tall drivers with a relatively short cylinder stroke would produce speed, while smaller drivers with a longer stroke would yield greater power. The entire history of the steam locomotive is made up of machines that sought the desired balance between speed and

power, and that is why there were so many different sizes and wheel arrangements.

Just getting a locomotive around a curve was a challenge for the early builders. The simple four-wheel machine was not a problem on curves, but it seriously restricted the overall weight of the locomotive. If you wanted a bigger locomotive, you needed to add more wheels to distribute the weight, but they had to be flexible enough to go around curves.

Among the earliest successful designs were the Norris Singles, with a single set of drivers under the firebox and a smaller four-wheel truck under the front end. The pilot truck kept the four wheels in rigid alignment and supported the smokebox on a fixed center pin. The center pin and the flanges of the two drivers gave the Norris a perfect three-point suspension that could handle almost any curve or vertical undulation in the track. The Baltimore & Ohio Museum's *Lafayette* is an excellent example of a Norris Single.

The next logical development of this was the American type with an additional set of drivers and the rigid pilot truck. On early Americans, to go around the curves, the front set of driving wheels had no flanges! They had wide treads that would stay atop the rails, but they depended on the pilot truck and the rear driver flanges to keep the locomotive on the track, just like the Norris Single.

This soon changed with the development of the swing-hanger pilot truck that would swing side to side but use gravity and the arc of the swing to always try to hold the center. With the swing-hanger pilot truck, they could put flanges on all four drivers and produce a very stable-riding machine.

Baltimore & Ohio 4-4-0 No. 25, built by William Mason in 1856, was renumbered 5 for the 1999 motion picture *Wild, Wild West*. The Civil War–era wood-burner, owned by the B&O Railroad Museum in Baltimore, was restored by the Strasburg Rail Road shop in Pennsylvania for the movie. This was its first test run. The huge stack contains screen baffles to catch sparks from the wood fire—though it burned oil for the filming. *Jim Boyd photo*

As locomotives grew in complexity, there needed to be a simple way of defining them, and Frederick Whyte of the New York Central came up with a system that was generally accepted until the end of steam. Whyte classified the wheels under a locomotive in three groups: lead truck, driving wheels, and trailing truck. He counted wheels (so they were always even numbers) and separated the groups with a hyphen. If there was no lead or trailing truck, a "0" would go in its place. Thus, the Norris Single was a 4-2-0, while the classic American became the 4-4-0. The *John Bull* was built as an 0-4-0 but was modified into a 4-2-0.

Back in the 1820s, the reciprocating water pump, air compressor, and steam engine were all developed by the same group of engineers from a basic cylinder, piston, and valve concept. What you put in and how you took it out determined

In the cab of B&O No. 25, the vertical lever with the notched quadrant is the Johnson bar manual reverse lever in its centered, or neutral, position. Pushing it forward will make the locomotive go forward. The throttle is the angled lever on the backhead above the three "try cocks" that are used to determine the water level in the boiler if the water glass, just in front of them, fails. *Jim Boyd photo*

While the transcontinental railroad was still under construction in 1868, Central Pacific 2-6-0 was passing through Cisco, California, in the Sierra Nevada. This photo typifies the communities and freight loads of the mountain frontier. Were those two loads of hay on one of the earliest double-stack trains? The wood-burning *Hercules* was built by Danforth, Cooke & Company of Paterson, New Jersey, in 1867 and moved by sailing ship around Cape Horn to California. Railfan & Railroad Magazine *collection*

whether you had an "engine" or a "pump." The valve timing on a steam engine was roughly 90 degrees off the crank, and reverse was 90 degrees to the other side. So the earliest valve gears were hook-and-link arrangements with two eccentric discs for each cylinder, one for forward and one for reverse. The *John Bull* has this configuration, and the engineer would use levers to position the valve and then hook its connecting rod into the correct link. It is possible, with such an arrangement, to get one driver wanting to go forward and the other wanting to go into reverse!

Stephenson, in England, soon realized that by connecting the forward and reverse eccentrics together with one common link, you could go from forward to reverse in one smooth movement with a single lever. In addition, the increments between forward, neutral, and reverse would vary the length of the valve stroke and give the engineer much greater control

of his steam usage. Using the full stroke would give maximum power, while "hooking up" near center would permit greater speed and steam economy. After that, all the different types of valve gears used that same concept, allowing the engineer to control even the biggest locomotives with the throttle and reverse lever (usually referred to as the "Johnson bar" or simply "the bar").

The earliest railroads were limited by the track structure, weight of the equipment, and the strength of the couplers. By the Civil War, in the 1860s, railroads were growing rapidly in the Eastern half of the nation, and the 4-4-0 was truly the American standard locomotive for both freight and passenger service, although other more specialized types were emerging, such as 2-6-0s and 0-8-0s for freight service. The metallurgy and quality of iron and steel at the time limited further development.

At the turn of the twentieth century, speed was all the rage with the traveling public. On May 10, 1893, New York Central & Hudson River high-drivered Buchannan 4-4-0 999 was the first locomotive to exceed "the century mark" when it set a world speed record of 112.5 miles per hour on the *Empire State Express* near Crittenden, New York. It is shown here taking water on the fly from track pans. Railfan & Railroad Magazine *collection*

Speed and Tonnage

At the turn of the twentieth century, railroading was at the heart of the American industrial revolution. It combined technology, geography, politics, and banking with an almost unlimited potential for everything from legitimate profit to unlimited corruption. As rail networks spread, locomotive technology grew. The archrivals Pennsylvania Railroad and New York Central had multitrack main lines between New York City and Chicago, and on May 10, 1893, the tall-drivered NYC 4-4-0 999 became the first locomotive to exceed "the century mark" and set a world speed record of 112.5 miles per hour near Buffalo. On June 12, 1905, the Pennsy topped that with 4-4-2 7002 hitting 127.1 miles per hour on the *Pennsylvania Special* in Ohio, a world record for steam that stands to this day (although the more accurately documented 126-mile-per-hour sprint down Stoke Bank on the London & North Eastern in England by streamlined 4-6-2 *Mallard* in 1938 is recognized as the official world steam speed record).

The unofficial steam speed record that stands today was set on June 12, 1905, when Pennsylvania Railroad 4-4-2 7002 hit 127 miles per hour on the *Pennsylvania Special*. When it discovered that it had unceremoniously scrapped the 7002, the PRR restored the nearly identical 8063 to take its place in the historical collection. It was returned to service by the Strasburg Rail Road and was on the old PRR main line at Thorndale, Pennsylvania, in May 1986 with 4-4-0 1223. *Jim Boyd photo*

Florida East Coast lightweight Pacific 148, built by Richmond in 1920, is typical of the early 4-6-2s that quickly became the most popular passenger engines of the early twentieth century. The 148 was brought to New Jersey for tourist service and is on the old Erie main line at Waldwick in September 1975. The 148 closely resembles the slightly older Erie 4-6-2s that were used on this line in commuter service. *Jim Boyd photo*

The first true heavy freight engine was the 2-8-0 Consolidation, named in honor of the recent consolidation of many smaller lines into the Lehigh Valley, for which it was designed and built in 1866. The 734 is actually a Lake Superior & Ishpeming 2-8-0 cosmetically restored by the Western Maryland Scenic Railroad to closely resemble the original Western Maryland Baldwins of 1911. It is on a chartered "photo freight" near Frostburg, Maryland, on October 20, 2003. *Jim Boyd photo*

The development of the trailing truck in the 1890s permitted larger locomotives with bigger fireboxes placed behind the drivers. Thus the workhorse 2-8-0 grew into the much more powerful and usually faster 2-8-2 Mikado (named after the emperor of Japan in 1897, when Baldwin delivered 2-8-2s to the Nippon Railway). Milwaukee Road 512, at Council Bluffs, Iowa, on March 17, 1952, was built by Baldwin in 1920 and is a typical medium-sized "Mike." *William F. Stauss collection*

One of the most important advances in steam technology was the development in 1910 of superheaters. These were tubes that passed saturated "wet" steam from the boiler back through the fire flues to dry it out and drive the temperature dramatically upward, greatly increasing its efficiency. In the PRR shop in Altoona, Pennsylvania, in 1986, the superheaters for K4 4-6-2 No. 1361 were laid out in order, ready for insertion into the boiler through the open smokebox. *Jim Boyd photo*

The Pennsylvania 4-4-2 represented a major advance in steam locomotive design over the nineteenth-century machines that were limited by small fireboxes squeezed between the tall drivers of passenger engines or mounted above the low drivers of freight engines. The two-wheeled trailing truck, introduced in the 1890s, permitted a wide and deep firebox to be placed behind the drivers and made possible much larger boilers. The classic freight 2-8-0 could now become the much larger 2-8-2 with more power and bigger drivers. The 4-6-0 quickly grew into the 4-6-2, and the 4-8-2 soon followed. As a general rule, the four-wheel pilot truck characterized a passenger or dual-service engine, while the two-wheel pilot truck was used on most freight locomotives.

Improved lubrication made the bigger locomotives possible. Remember that petroleum-based lubricants didn't exist before Colonel Edwin Drake opened his oil well in Titusville, Pennsylvania, in 1859. Prior to that, lubricants were mostly made of animal tallow.

Petroleum-based lubricants that could withstand high temperatures made possible the superheater, a major improve-ment in boilers in 1910. Water in a 200-psi boiler boils at about 387 degrees Fahrenheit. This is saturated, or "wet," steam. The superheater takes this wet steam and pipes it back through the firetubes to dry it out and drive itstemperature dramatically upward to about 700 degrees. Since it is heat and not pressure that actually does the work in a steam engine, this boosts the efficiency of the boiler by about 30 percent by making further use of the fire that is already there. Because of lubrication problems, the hot, dry super-heated steam cannot be used in the older slide valves on the cylinders but requires piston spool valves and lubricants that can handle the higher temperatures.

One advantage of superheaters is that they can be retrofitted to older locomotives. Many railroads made these modifications and took advantage of the shop time to refit the older Stephenson valve gear (on the axles inside the frames) with a more modern Walschaertz or Baker external valve gear that was easier to maintain.

The Pennsylvania Railroad did things its own way, but it was devoted to standardization. While the square-topped Belpaire firebox was not common in American railroading, it did have its advantages in construction and maintenance, and the Pennsy used the same boiler on its 425 K4 4-6-2s and 574 L1 2-8-2s. The restored K4 No. 1361, which had been on display for decades at the apex of Horseshoe Curve, is running on the Bald Eagle branch in May 1987. *Jim Boyd photo*

In 1910, Alco's Richmond Works built the first 4-8-2 for heavy passenger service on the Chesapeake & Ohio's Mountain Subdivision, giving the wheel arrangement its name: Mountain type. Among the most handsomely proportioned and typical 4-8-2s were the 1500-class built for the St. Louis-San Francisco by Baldwin between 1923 and 1926. Restored Frisco No. 1522, from the National Museum of Transportation in St. Louis, is working crisply uphill, cresting the top of a grade at New Cambria, Missouri, in September 1996. *Kevin EuDaly photo*

The "Standard Era"

As mentioned earlier, the steam locomotive comprises two basic elements: the boiler and the running gear. It's the running gear that determines the speed and power of the final machine. The PRR had some excellent examples of this. The boiler used on its H-10-class 2-8-0 was also used on the commuter-service G-5 4-6-0 and the very fast 80-inch-drivered E-6 4-4-2. The boiler designed in 1914 and applied to 425 K-4 4-6-2s was also used on 574 L1-class freight 2-8-2s.

In the first 15 years of the twentieth century, the 4-6-2 Pacific and 2-8-2 Mikado became America's most popular road engines. They combined speed and power and could be used on almost any trackage. The next logical development was the 4-8-2 Mountain built for the C&O in 1911 and the 2-10-2 Santa Fe. The 4-8-2 could be used in either passenger or freight service, while the 2-10-2 was definitely a heavy freight hauler.

Each railroad had a mechanical department whose purpose was to develop locomotives and equipment that was suited to its particular operations. Because of the need to tailor running gear and boilers to specific loads and speeds, there was a tremendous

During World War I, the United States Railroad Administration (USRA) created 12 standard-design steam locomotives that represented the best technology of the era. Atlantic Coast Line No. 1691 was one of 165 USRA Light Pacific copies built by Baldwin in the 1920s and used in both passenger and freight service. They differed from the "government engines" most visibly in having cast "Delta" trailing trucks. *Bill Folsom collection*

Cuyahoga Valley USRA Light Mikado No. 4070 was built as a "government engine" by Alco in 1918 as Grand Trunk Western 474. It was renumbered 3734 in the 1920s and became 4070 in 1956. Compared to ACL Pacific 1691, note that 4070 has the standard USRA-fabricated Hodges trailing truck. The USRA built 625 Light Mikados. The 4070 is entering Cleveland with a CVL tourist train on the former B&O Akron branch in September 1981. *Jim Boyd photo*

One of the most popular USRA designs was the 0-8-0 switcher, and New York Central No. 7925 at Paris, Illinois, on September 1, 1955, is a classic example of one. It was one of 50 USRA copies built for the NYC by Alco and Lima in 1924 and 1925. The USRA design was heavier than previous 0-8-0s, and although only 175 originals were built, they influenced the design of nearly every eight-wheel switcher built after 1920. *James F. EuDaly photo*

The 2497 was 1 of 15 USRA Light 2-10-2s built by Baldwin in 1919 and assigned to the Seaboard Air Line. Their 57-inch drivers made them powerful but slow locomotives that were restricted to its Atlanta–Birmingham line, though they outlasted their faster 63-inch drivered 2-10-2 brethren on the SAL. It is under the wooden coaling tower at Birmingham, Alabama, in June 1934. Note again the Hodges trailing truck. *Harold K. Vollrath collection*

variety of different machines in use across the country. Each railroad had its own ideas on use of appliances, headlights, cowcatchers, and infinite other details. As a result, there was no mistaking a Pennsy locomotive for one on the Santa Fe or Northern Pacific or—heaven forbid—the New York Central.

When America entered World War I in April 1917, there was concern that the privately owned and hotly competitive rail system would not be able to perform as a unified system for the war emergency. As a result, in January 1918 the United States Railroad Administration (USRA) was created to take over operation of the nation's railroads. It was a bitter pill in both the boardrooms and mechanical departments.

As a part of its authorizing legislation, the USRA was mandated to simplify and speed up manufacturing by creating a series of standardized locomotives that could be used anywhere in the country. In a rare example of a bureaucracy doing it right, the USRA assembled a committee of the nation's best locomotive designers, headed by Samuel Vauclain of Baldwin, that within four months had submitted 12 superb standard designs (an 0-6-0 and 0-8-0 switcher; light and heavy versions of the 4-6-2, 2-8-2, 4-8-2, and 2-10-2; and a compound 2-6-6-2 and 2-8-8-2). All the designs were superheated and were considered state-of-the-art machines. Not surprisingly, the USRA engines were all quite handsome in appearance with a clean family look. By the time the railroads were returned to private ownership in 1920, 1,856 government engines had been built, but the designs were so successful that 3,251 more copies were ordered by the railroads themselves, and the last steam locomotive built for a U.S. customer by Baldwin in September 1949 was USRA 2-6-6-2 1309 for the Chesapeake & Ohio!

Compounds and Articulateds

C&O USRA 2-6-6-2 1309 was a compound articulated. The terms "compound" and "articulated" actually refer to very different things. The concept of compounding had come first. When steam was exhausted from a locomotive's cylinders, it still possessed considerable heat and pressure. A compound locomotive routed this exhaust into a larger second cylinder that would use its lower pressure to produce an equal power output. With a slight increase in mechanical complexity, the locomotive would gain power and efficiency by using its steam twice. Compounding was just being developed at the turn of the century when it was rendered obsolete on modest-sized locomotives by superheaters.

The influence of the USRA designs lasted until the very end of North American steam. The last steam locomotive built by Baldwin for a U.S. customer was Chesapeake & Ohio No. 1309, now on display at the B&O Railroad Museum in Baltimore. The 1309, outshopped in 1949, was a modern copy of the 1918 USRA compound 2-6-6-2. The C&O had 20 government 2-6-6-2s and 55 copies that were the workhorses of the coalfield mine shifters. *Jim Boyd photo*

Articulation was a concept originated by Anatole Mallet in Switzerland in 1888. In an effort to create a large locomotive that could negotiate sharp curves, Mallet divided the running gear into two engines with a hinge between them. The boiler and firebox were fixed rigidly to the rear engine, while the pivot under the middle of the boiler let the front engine swing from side to side while supporting the smokebox on a sliding bracket.

The first U.S. compound articulated was Baltimore & Ohio's 0-6-6-0 No. 2400, known as *Old Maude*, built by Alco in 1903. Note the external high-pressure steam pipe from the center dome to the rear cylinders, which are fitted with piston valves. The frame is hinged just ahead of those cylinders, and the exhaust steam is fed through a hinged pipe to the larger-diameter low-pressure front cylinders that have the older slide valves, identifiable by the rectangular valve chests on top. *B&O Railroad photo*, Railfan & Railroad Magazine *collection*

Baltimore & Ohio EL3 2-8-8-0 No. 7118, built by Baldwin in 1917, is a classic compound Mallet. The huge 41-inch-diameter low-pressure front cylinders used the steam exhausted from the 26-inch high-pressure rear cylinders. The boiler was affixed to the frame of the rear drivers, while the front engine could swing from side to side on curves and supported the boiler on a sliding plate. It is at Benwood Junction, West Virginia, in May 1944. *J. J. Young Jr. photo*

The Lima Locomotive Works in Ohio was the smallest of the Big Three steam builders (with Baldwin and Alco) but was regarded as the best when it came to craftsmanship and innovation. Among Lima's finest were 65 Nickel Plate 2-8-4s built between 1942 and 1949 (Alco built the first 15 in 1934). The 740, easing through "The Works" in 1944, was the first of 30 S-2 class Berks. Lima's last steam locomotive was NKP 779 in 1949. *Lima photo*, Railfan & Railroad Magazine *collection*

Mallet supplied the rear engine's smaller cylinders with hot steam from the boiler and sent the exhaust through flexible pipes to the larger compound cylinders on the front engine. The exhaust from the front engine was directed into the smokebox and up the stack like a conventional engine. The compound articulated was brought to the United States by the American Locomotive Company in 1903 in the form of an 0-6-6-0 for the Baltimore & Ohio. The compound articulated was ideally suited to heavy-duty American service and quickly grew in size. The compound Mallet (rhymes with "alley") became even more efficient when superheated. Compound articulateds lasted right up to the very end of steam in the coalfields of Appalachia on the C&O and N&W.

The Locomotive Builders

Following World War I, there were three major steam locomotive builders in the United States. In 1901, the Schenectady Locomotive Works near Albany, New York, merged with seven regional builders (among them Richmond Works in Virginia; Brooks in Dunkirk, New York; and Cooke in Paterson, New Jersey) to create the American Locomotive Company (Alco). By 1928, all manufacturing was concentrated in Schenectady. In 1926, the historic Baldwin Locomotive Works had moved into a huge new industrial complex at Eddystone on the south side of Philadelphia. The third of the "Big Three" was the Lima Locomotive Works in Ohio. Lima (pronounced LIE-ma) dated back to 1880 when Michigan logger Ephraim Shay came to the Lima Machine Works to build a strange-looking little geared steam locomotive for use in the woods. The "Shay" locomotive was an immediate success, and Lima ultimately built 2,800 of them over the next 65 years. In 1901, Lima began to add conventional rod locomotives to its product line.

While all of the builders could contract for USRA engines or bid on Pennsylvania-designed orders, they each had their general characteristics. Baldwins were the Fords and Chevys and pickup trucks of the steam locomotive world.

Its engines were simple, rugged, and basic, if sometimes a bit rough around the edges. Baldwin had some fiercely loyal customers, like the Santa Fe. Baldwin also offered an entire catalog of smaller locomotives for use on short lines.

Alco produced somewhat more refined machines that were often cleaner in appearance and neater in detailing. Alco also had its loyal following, such as the hometown NYC and the transcontinental UP. The fast passenger express engine of the 1920s was most likely to be an Alco.

Under the leadership of Will Woodard, Lima soon developed into the Swiss watchmaker of the trio, noted for its fine workmanship and advanced engineering.

In 1922, Lima's Will Woodard created the concept of "super power" when he put a larger firebox on an NYC heavy 2-8-2 and added another set of wheels to the trailing truck, creating the first 2-8-4. It was tested on the Boston & Albany's line in the Berkshire Mountains, giving the wheel arrangement the name Berkshire. The Illinois Central bought the Lima original and 50 duplicates in 1926. The 7008 is at East St. Louis, Illinois, in 1933. *R. J. Foster photo*

Rarely has the first model of a wheel arrangement become as much of an enduring classic as the New York Central 4-6-4 Hudson. Alco built the first NYC 4-6-4, J1a 5200 in February 1927, and followed it with a fleet that ultimately reached 265 engines by 1938. This included the final 50 J3a Super Hudsons, like the less-than-one-year-old No. 5409 on a northbound milk train at Garrison, New York, on June 13, 1938. *R. P. Morris photo*

Working with the Advisory Mechanical Committee of the railroads controlled by the Van Sweringen brothers of Cleveland (Erie, C&O, NKP, W&LE, and Pere Marquette), in 1930 Lima designed a massive 2-10-4 for the C&O. With 69-inch drivers, the T1 was a perfect balance between speed and power, and it was scaled down in 1934 to produce the first Nickel Plate Berkshire. C&O No. 3032 is marching through Fostoria, Ohio, in August 1949. *J. J. Young Jr. photo*

Super Power

The engineering and design of steam locomotives still involved a lot of trial and error in the early twentieth century. Moving the firebox back over a trailing truck had greatly improved boiler capacity, and in 1922 Lima's Will Woodard took it one step further by building an NYC 2-8-2 with an even bigger firebox without enlarging the overall boiler. Increasing the furnace volume with a bigger firebox and combustion chamber between the firebox and flues greatly increased the steaming capacity of the boiler with a surprising reduction in fuel consumption through more thorough combustion.

In February 1925, Lima outshopped the first 2-8-4 with a huge firebox. This Berkshire type (named after its test runs on the Boston & Albany's line through the Berkshire Mountains) dramatically outperformed the B&A's large, modern 2-8-2s by delivering comparable drawbar pull at greater speeds. The secret was horsepower, not just pulling power.

This new concept was soon dubbed "Super Power," and it rapidly led to the development of 2-10-4 heavy freight engines and fast 4-6-4 passenger engines. The most famous and successful of early Super Power machines was the first 4-6-4, designed by the New York Central's Paul W.

Because they were used in precisely the high-speed freight service for which they had been designed, the 80 Nickel Plate Berkshires are regarded as some of America's most successful steam locomotives. In September 1979, the newly restored 765 is making her test runs in an industrial park near Fort Wayne, Indiana, before launching a long career in excursion service. *Jim Boyd photo*

Keifer and completed by Alco on February 4, 1927. The NYC Hudson became an enduring classic, and many 4-6-4s followed on railroads ranging from the New Haven to the Santa Fe.

The most popular design, however, was the 4-8-4; it could be built as either a heavy freight engine or fast passenger engine or dropped into the middle as a dual-service machine. This was accomplished by the proper combination of driver diameter, boiler pressure, and cylinder diameter and stroke.

The rule of thumb was that the top speed would be "driver diameter plus 10 percent." Thus, the 63-inch drivers of the typical 2-8-2 or Lima 2-8-4 would top out at 70 miles per hour. An 80-inch-drivered 4-6-4 would be good for 88 miles per hour. Specific design elements like driver counterbalancing, rod weight, and bearing types could affect this. The 63-inch-drivered USRA Mikado could cruise at 70 miles per hour, while the 2-10-4s with the same drivers but heavier rods were more comfortable as 50-mile-per-hour engines, and many of the 80-inch-drivered engines were good for 100 miles per hour.

Typical of the large Midwestern 4-8-4s were the 36 Chicago, Burlington & Quincy O5s. The first 8 were built by Baldwin in 1930, while the next 28 were assembled in the CB&Q's West Burlington Shop using Baldwin boilers and GSC cast underframes. With 74-inch drivers, they could handle both heavy freight and fast passenger assignments. Home-built oil-burning O5b No. 5632 is on an excursion train on the branch near Prophetstown, Illinois, on May 17, 1964. *Jim Boyd photo*

The last steam locomotive in North America that is still on the active roster of its original owner without ever having been retired is Union Pacific 4-8-4 No. 844. Built by Alco in December 1944, it was the UP's last new steam locomotive. It is a true Western Super Northern with 80-inch drivers, 300-psi boiler pressure, and roller bearings. The superbly maintained veteran oil-burner is at Elvas Tower in Sacramento in June 1999. *Jim Boyd photo*

Another Super Northern entered service after being overhauled in Portland, Oregon, to pull the *American Freedom Train* in 1975. Southern Pacific GS4 *Daylight* 4-8-4 No. 4449 was built by Lima in May 1941 with 80-inch drivers and a 300-psi boiler. Its only shortcoming was the lack of roller bearings on the drivers (the SP had two roller-equipped GS4s but dieselized before converting the fleet). The 4449 eases through San Francisco's Jack London Square in May 1984. *Jim Boyd photo*

Santa Fe No. 3751 was Baldwin's first 4-8-4 and only the thirteenth of its type constructed when it was outshopped by Baldwin in 1927. It looked quite different then, however, with 73-inch drivers. It was heavily rebuilt in 1941 with 80-inch drivers and roller bearings. Restored by the San Bernardino Railroad Historical Society, it is on its debut excursion to Bakersfield as it ascends Cajon Pass at Sullivan's Curve on December 27, 1997. *Jim Boyd*

Lima quickly discovered that its 2-8-4s and 2-10-4s became much more productive machines with 69-inch drivers. Working with the Advisory Mechanical Committee that served the railroads controlled by Cleveland's Van Sweringen brothers (Erie, Nickel Plate, C&O, and Pere Marquette), in 1930 Lima produced an awesome C&O 2-10-4 on 69-inch drivers. They then scaled down the C&O engine to a 2-8-4 that became one of the most successful freight steam locomotive designs of all time. Although the C&O had the largest fleet of Van Sweringen Berkshires, by far the most famous were the 80 engines on the Nickel Plate Road. The Berks could cover an entire division at 70 miles per hour and made the Nickel Plate a fierce contender in the hotly competitive Chicago–Buffalo territory.

The combination of boiler capacity and running gear configuration would produce a locomotive that performed best within certain speed and horsepower ranges. Richard Melvin, an engineer on the restored Nickel Plate 2-8-4 765 in the 1980s, noted that his engine would tend to struggle at low speeds, but once over 50 miles per hour, "she became a whole new machine!" Lima had built the 765 for maximum performance in the 50-to-70-mile-per-hour range.

In 1928, Canadian Pacific's motive power chief, Charles H. Temple, designed and had the Angus Shop build two handsome 4-8-4s that were too heavy for many CP lines. His successor, Henry Blaine Bowen, concluded that the 4-8-4 was not suitable for Canadian service. Meanwhile, in 1927, the neighboring Canadian National was getting its first lightweight dual-service 4-8-4s with 73-inch drivers. The CN went on to acquire 203 4-8-4s, the world's largest fleet! CN 6218 is headed for Stratford, Ontario, in September 1966. *Jim Boyd photo*

The 2-8-4s were perfectly sized for the operating conditions on the Nickel Plate, while elsewhere in the Midwest, 74-inch-drivered 4-8-4s were more ideal. The Chicago, Burlington & Quincy's Baldwin-built dual-service O-5-class 4-8-4s could cruise all day at 80 miles per hour on the *Exposition Flyer* or handle a mile of refrigerator cars at 60. The Milwaukee Road and Rock Island fielded similar machines.

One of the finest steam locomotive designs, the Union Pacific 80-inch-drivered 4-8-4, built by Alco between 1939 and 1944, produced its maximum horsepower output at 90 miles per hour, but its boiler was calculated for sustained operation at 110 miles per hour! In December 1944, Alco outshopped the UP's last new steam locomotive, 4-8-4 No. 844. To this day, the 844 has never left the UP's active roster and is the last North American steam locomotive to remain in service for its original owner without ever having been retired.

Designing steam locomotives, even Super Power, never became a precise art. The Canadian railways adopted U.S. standards and became a seamless part of the North American rail network. Each of Canada's two largest roads, the Canadian Pacific and the Canadian National, had its own distinctive locomotives, with the majority of its engines being utilitarian 2-8-0s, 4-6-0s, 2-8-2s, and 4-6-2s. The CP got into Super Power with two handsome passenger 4-8-4s in 1928. The 3100 and 3101 were too heavy for most of the CP lines, and "the 4-8-4 was not considered suitable for Canadian service." Meanwhile, next door, the CN had gotten its first one in 1927, and by 1944 it had acquired the world's largest fleet of 203 4-8-4s!

It worked the other way, too. CN bought five 4-6-4s in 1930 but concluded that "the 4-6-4 is not suitable for Canadian service." Meanwhile, the CP across the street had a fleet of 65 4-6-4s. The largest locomotives used in Canada were 35 CP streamlined 2-10-4s.

Last of the Giants

The concept of "Super Power" showed tremendous potential, but the locomotives were limited in size by their ability to fit the clearance diagram and get around tight curves. Articulation had been used successfully on low-speed compounds, and it held great promise for faster locomotives. In 1924, Alco built some huge 2-8-8-2s for the Chesapeake & Ohio that piped boiler steam directly to all four cylinders. This "simple articulated" worked very well, though it was still an essentially low-speed machine.

In 1928, a four-wheel trailer truck was added to create the first 2-8-8-4 Yellowstone for the Northern Pacific that was dubbed the "World's Largest Steam Locomotive" at the time. Other Yellowstones soon followed on 63- and 64-inch drivers that were good for 60 miles per hour. The Duluth, Missabe & Iron Range used 18 2-8-8-4s built by Baldwin in 1941 and 1943 to handle its heavy ore trains, while the Baltimore & Ohio had 30 stylish EM-1 2-8-8-4s built by Baldwin in 1944–1945 to handle both coal trains and fast main-line merchandisers.

In 1930, the Canadian National received five big 80-inch-drivered 4-6-4s from the Montreal Locomotive Works. Management concluded that the 4-6-4 was not suitable for Canadian service. Meanwhile, in 1928, the Canadian Pacific acquired the first of 20 Temple-designed 4-6-4s with 75-inch drivers. The locomotives were a great success, and in 1937 45 more semi-streamlined "Royal Hudsons" were added. Royal Hudson No. 2839 had just been restored and fired up at Northampton, Pennsylvania, in February 1979 before heading south for excursion service on the Southern Railway. Note the crown above the cylinder. *Jim Boyd photo*

Northern Pacific owned 12 Yellowstone 2-8-8-4 steam locomotives, Nos. 5000–5011. The first, built by Alco in 1928, was the world's largest steam locomotive at the time. In 1930, NP took delivery of 11 Baldwin-built Yellowstones. No. 5006, is seen here at Livingston, Montana, on June 10, 1941. The type was a "simple articulated" that fed hot steam to all four cylinders. The huge firebox was needed to burn the low-grade local "Rosebud" coal. Operation on the railroad's Yellowstone Division also gave the wheel arrangement its name. *R. V. Nixon photo*

Southern Pacific 4-8-8-2 No. 4101 is at Lancaster, California, in May 1940, and is a Yellowstone that runs backward. Fuel oil and water piped up from the tender permitted it to operate firebox-forward to keep the crew ahead of the exhaust smoke in tunnels. It differs from a conventional 2-8-8-4 in having a guiding lead truck instead of a more passive trailing truck. The 4101 was the second of 195 Cab-Forwards built by Baldwin between 1928 and 1944. *Harold K. Vollrath collection*

Opposite: The longest rigid-wheelbase engines in the United States were the Union Pacific's 88 three-cylinder 4-12-2s, built by Alco between 1926 and 1930. With 67-inch drivers, they were 40-mile-per-hour engines that rode well, but the long wheelbase was a problem on curves and switches. The middle cylinder drove a crank on the second axle, and the arrangement kept the diameters of the cylinders within practical limits. A valve gear invented in England by Sir Nigel Gresley regulated the center cylinder. The No. 9057 is eastbound at Lawrence, Kansas, on January 26, 1953. *Robert P. Olmsted photo*

Trying to get the power of the 4-12-2 into a more flexible and faster locomotive, UP motive power chief Arthur Fetters worked with Alco to develop the 4-6-6-4 simple articulated in 1936. Eliminating any vertical play in the front engine made the locomotive very stable and smooth riding. Otto Jabelmann improved the design to produce 65 Alco Super Challengers during World War II. Challenger No. 3941 takes a spin on the turntable, viewed from inside the roundhouse at Cheyenne, Wyoming, on September 4, 1957. *John Dziobko photo*

The Southern Pacific had a dozen coal-burning 2-8-8-4s built by Lima in 1939, but it was far better known for its "backward Yellowstones," the 195 Cab-Forward 4-8-8-2s built by Baldwin between 1928 and 1944. These were indeed Yellowstones that were simply turned around, and the only significant engineering change was to alter the four-wheel passive trailer truck to a four-wheel lead truck with a different suspension system to make it a better guide truck. It was possible to put the cab up front because the locomotive was oil-fired, and the fuel could be simply piped up front to the firebox—a

feat nearly impossible with a coal-burner. The Cab-Forwards, with their cylinders behind the drivers and running in reverse most of the time, proved conclusively that the rod-driven steam engine was a truly bidirectional mechanism.

Opposite: The coal-hauling Norfolk & Western built many of its modern steam locomotives in its huge backshop in Roanoke, Virginia. The N&W turned the lumbering compound articulated into a truly modern and efficient machine with its 227 Y-class 2-8-8-2s. The brand-new Y4a No. 2091 poses for its portrait in 1930. The N&W's big Mallets were ideal for the low-speed coal trains on both the main-line hauls and mine shifters. *N&W Railway photo*

The queens of the N&W Roanoke-built steam fleet were the 43 high-speed-freight simple articulated Class A 2-6-6-4s and 14 Class J passenger 4-8-4s, built between 1938 and 1950. The sole survivors of each class, A No. 1218 and J No. 611, are side by side near Salem, Virginia, during the NRHS National Convention in August 1987. Both locomotives had modern lubricating systems for rapid servicing and were ideally suited to the N&W's operating needs. *Jim Boyd photo*

Although one would suspect that the hinge on an articulated would make the engine very wiggly at speed, quite the opposite was the case. Steve Lee, steam manager for the Union Pacific, pointed out that on a simple articulated "that lead engine becomes the world's most efficient pilot truck."

Back in 1926, the UP was trying to develop a high-speed freight engine and came up with a three-cylinder 4-12-2 that performed quite well on 67-inch drivers. The third cylinder sat beneath the stack between the outer cylinders and drove a crank on the second driver axle. Outside clearances prevented making the outer cylinders any larger in diameter, and the third cylinder gave the overall running gear the equivalent power of two larger cylinders. Both the UP and neighboring SP had large fleets of three-cylinder engines, along with such an unlikely Easterner as the Delaware, Lackawanna & Western.

Previous pages: The Union Pacific's 25 4-8-8-4 Big Boys, built by Alco in 1941 and 1944, were arguably the world's largest steam locomotives. All coal-burners, they had 68-inch drivers for speed and weighed 772,000 pounds. Because of their size, they were restricted to the main lines out of Cheyenne, while their slightly smaller brethren, the 105 4-6-6-4 Challengers, could roam the system. Big Boy No. 4017 is under the Laramie, Wyoming, coal chute on August 20, 1957. *Jim Shaughnessy photo*

The long rigid wheelbases severely limited the UP's 4-12-2s to prairie main lines. In an effort to create a comparable but more flexible machine, UP General Mechanical Engineer Arthur H. Fetters worked with Alco to take the 4-12-2-sized boiler and put it over a 4-6-6-4 underframe with 69-inch drivers. The first "Challenger" was built in 1936 and proved to be easily capable of 70-mile-per-hour operation in either passenger or freight service. One of the secrets to the Challenger's smooth tracking was a very rigid front boiler support that permitted no vertical motion between the boiler and the lead engine, forcing the equalized spring rigging on the entire locomotive to cushion the ride. The UP took delivery of 40 Fetters Challengers in 1936–1937.

As World War II heated up, the UP needed more power, and Mr. Fetters' successor, Otto Jabelmann, redesigned the 4-6-6-4 with cast engine beds, roller bearings, and 280-psi boilers. Alco built 65 of these "Super Challengers" that became the UP's most useful and versatile locomotives. As local conditions mandated, the Challengers could burn either coal or Bunker C fuel oil, and many were converted back and forth over their careers.

One of the UP's "War Baby" 4-6-6-4s, No. 3985, built by Alco in July 1943, was retired in August 1957 and put on public display at the UP depot in Cheyenne, Wyoming. In 1979, the 3985 was retrieved by the UP and put into the Cheyenne round-house alongside 4-8-4 No. 844 to become the nucleus of the corporate steam program. The 3985 steamed again in March 1981.

There were other Challengers built by both Alco and Baldwin for the Northern Pacific; Great Northern; Spokane, Portland & Seattle; Denver & Rio Grande Western; Western Pacific; Clinchfield; Western Maryland; and Delaware & Hudson. They were probably the most successful simple articulateds used in North America.

One of America's best-known users of articulateds was the Norfolk & Western, which carved its own motive power path through Appalachia. The N&W built most of its own locomotives at its shop in Roanoke, Virginia, and was one of the nation's last operators of steam locomotives. In the 1950s, the N&W workhorses were the N&W-designed "big three" locomotives: the Y-6 compound articulated 2-8-8-2s, the high-speed Class A simple articulated 2-6-6-4s, and the superb streamlined Class J 4-8-4s. The N&W engines all had roller bearings and were set up for high-pressure lubrication. Specialized servicing facilities could clean and lubricate and turn a road engine in less than an hour.

But who had the world's largest steam locomotive? The often cited simple answer to that is the Union Pacific's 25 4-8-8-4 Big Boys built by Alco in 1941 and 1944. They burned coal and rode on 68-inch drivers. Their massive size, however, limited the Big Boys to the main lines around Cheyenne, whereas the Challengers could roam almost systemwide. There was no question that the UP 4000s were the largest steam locomotives ever built.

However, if you measure by weight or boiler horsepower, there were some other contenders. In December 1941, Lima created the 2-6-6-6 Allegheny for the Chesapeake & Ohio. This 67-inch-drivered, high-speed, simple articulated, at 778,000 pounds, was the heaviest reciprocating steam locomotive ever built (the Big Boy topped out at 772,000 pounds). The C&O had 60 of these brutes, while the nearby Virginian had 8 near-duplicates.

The Big Boy's closest rival in the "world's largest" realm would have been the Chesapeake & Ohio's 60 2-6-6-6 Alleghenies, built by Lima between 1941 and 1948. The first 45 Alleghenies, at 778,000 pounds, actually outweighed the Big Boys and were the world's heaviest steam locomotives. Eight nearly identical 2-6-6-6s were built for the Virginian Railway in 1945. Eastbound C&O No. 1624 approaches Thurmond, West Virginia, along the New River with a manifest freight in 1955. *Gene Huddleston photo*

Off the Beaten Path

While the quest for the biggest and fastest dominated steam locomotive technology in the twentieth century, there were other aspects of the business. Around the turn of the twentieth century, the locomotive had grown in size to be a respectable main-line machine. But the country was being webbed with hundreds of smaller railroads that provided local service in the era before highways and trucks.

Since these small railroads didn't need and often couldn't use main-line locomotives, a lucrative market began to grow for

smaller locomotives. Although many short lines simply picked up older, obsolete small engines, there was a real market for new small locomotives.

Baldwin created a line of standard components such as boilers, cylinders, underframes, and drivers that could be assembled in almost any combination to create an engine tailored to almost any customer's needs. These "catalog Baldwins" were distinctive in appearance and found homes all across the country. Similarly, Alco developed a line of smaller engines, and they would often be built for stock and held for

America's small railroads and short lines that didn't have extensive mechanical departments could order custom-built locomotives from the Baldwin catalog by specifing weight, wheel arrangement, valve gear, cylinder size, and boiler style, with or without superheaters. Duluth & Northeastern 2-8-0 No. 16, at the DM&IR interchange in Saginaw, Minnesota, on June 14, 1963, is a typical "catalog" Baldwin, built in November 1913 with saturated steam, Stephenson valve gear, and 51-inch drivers. *Jim Boyd photo*

The smallest common carrier railroads in the United States were the numerous 2-foot-gauge lines in Maine. These were all abandoned by the 1940s, but some significant equipment was preserved by Ellis D. Atwood on his Edaville Railroad in South Carver, Massachusetts. Bridgton & Harrison 2-4-4T No. 7 was historically restored for a railfan weekend in October 1991. The Edaville had 5 miles of tourist line, while the real Bridgton & Harrison was only 15.8 miles long. *Jim Boyd photo*

future off-the-shelf sales. Lima continued to build its Shay geared locomotives right up to 1945, while competitors Heisler and Climax could never match the Shay's success.

While the national rail network was converted to standard gauge following the Civil War, not all railroads were built new or converted to standard gauge. The stalwart 2-footers in Maine hung on with very little change until the Great Depression, and a few survived into the 1940s.

In the mountains of Colorado, a 3-foot-gauge network developed west of Denver because a narrow gauge line could be economically built up canyons and into the highlands where the cost of standard gauge would have been prohibitive. On a system developed with 2-8-0s and 4-6-0s, in 1903 the Denver & Rio Grande bought 15 compound 2-8-2s from Baldwin to handle its 4 percent grades and severe winter conditions. By 1928, it had acquired a fleet of 45 gutsy Mikados to handle everything from cattle to coal. The last Class 1 railroad in North America to operate steam was the D&RGW, with its narrow gauge lines in 1967!

Above: Probably the best-known 3-foot-gauge railroad outside of the Colorado Rockies was the coal-hauling East Broad Top in central Pennsylvania. When the line shut down in 1956, the scrapper did not tear up the railroad and preserved its entire locomotive fleet and most of its rolling stock. It became a tourist operation in 1960 and has since been declared a National Historic Site. Mikado No. 14 powers a chartered "photo freight" in October 2002. *Jim Boyd photo*

Opposite: America's most famous narrow gauge lines were the Colorado 3-footers. The states of Colorado and New Mexico bought the 64-mile Denver & Rio Grande Western line from Chama, New Mexico, to Antonito, Colorado, to operate as a tourist railroad. In October 1987, Cumbres & Toltec Scenic Railroad ex-D&RGW K-36 Mikado No. 487 accelerates away from the Cresco water tank after taking on water for the climb up the 4.5 percent grade of Cumbres Pass. *Jim Boyd photo*

There were numerous 3-foot-gauge lines in the mountains of California and Nevada. The SP had a narrow gauge system in California that operated with 4-6-0s until 1956 and then continued with a lone diesel until 1960.

There were a few 3-foot-gauge railroads east of the Rockies, but most had perished by the Great Depression. The most famous exception, however, was the East Broad Top, a 43-mile coal-hauler in central Pennsylvania with a fleet of six 2-8-2s built between 1911 and 1920 from standard Baldwin catalog components. The EBT ceased revenue service on April 6, 1956, but remained intact and operates today as a tourist attraction. The entire roster of Mikados is still housed in its Orbisonia roundhouse.

Under the Wire:
Electric Locomotives

by Jim Boyd

The last GG1s were in service for NJ Transit on its New York & Long Branch route from Penn Station to South Amboy, with trains forwarded to Bay Head by diesels. The 4877 was repainted into the Pennsy Tuscan red livery by local railfans in June 1981 and used in regular service. It is on a Bay Head train on the Raritan Bay Bridge in April 1983 with the red "subscription" (private commuter) car on the head end. *Jim Boyd photo*

As Robert Stephenson & Company was assembling the *John Bull* in Newcastle, England, in 1831, Michael Faraday was nearby completing 10 years of experimentation that proved that electricity could be generated using rotating magnetic fields. Meanwhile, in Albany, New York, Professor Joseph Henry had developed an electromagnet and produced a rudimentary electric motor. It is ironic that the steam locomotive and the technology that would ultimately replace it had the germs of their creation at the same time.

Interestingly, many of the experiments that followed in the next couple of decades focused on applying motors to locomotive-like moving machines. While steam technology was enabling railroads to spread throughout England, Europe, and North America, electric technology was developing slowly in the background. In 1879, however, Dr. Ernst Werner von Seimens demonstrated a passenger-carrying electric railway at the Berlin Industrial Exhibition with power supplied by a steam-driven generator.

A year later, Thomas Edison laid out 1,400 feet of electric-powered track at Menlo Park, New Jersey, and tested locomotives at speeds up to 40 miles per hour. The experiments showed so much promise that Henry Villard, president of the Northern Pacific, seriously proposed to have Edison electrify 50 miles of his railroad. Unfortunately, construction costs of the Seattle extension bankrupted the NP and cost Villard his job, and no further action was taken on the electrification.

There were numerous experimental machines demonstrated in the next few years, but in 1887 Frank J. Sprague came up with two major breakthroughs, the "nose-hung" traction motor and a multiple-unit (MU) control system. Sprague electrified the Richmond (Virginia) Street Railway in 1888, and the idea of streetcars and electric interurbans soon swept the country with relatively low-voltage direct current (DC) systems. In addition to Sprague's street trolleys, his MU concept made possible heavier, multicar trains for use on elevated and subway systems as well as some heavier interurban railroads. MU control allowed a single operator to operate all of the powered cars in a train.

As the railroads grew and became an integral part of intercity and local transportation, steam locomotive smoke was becoming an overwhelming problem in urban areas. The first major steam-road electrification was the Baltimore & Ohio's 7,339-foot Howard Street Tunnel under downtown Baltimore, opened on June 27, 1895. At a time when fledgling electric locomotives operating elsewhere were about 10 tons, General Electric provided three 96-ton steeple-cabs that were actually made up of two semipermanently coupled units each. The electrics pulled both freight and passenger trains over the 3.6-mile double-track Belt Line with the steam road engines idling behind them. The units used a pantograph to collect the 650-volt DC power from a rigid trough rail suspended above the main line.

The B&O electrification was upgraded over the years and converted to an outside third rail on the ground in 1902. It was rendered obsolete by diesels and discontinued in 1952.

The technology that led directly to electric locomotives was first applied to streetcars, when in 1887 Frank J. Sprague invented the nose-hung traction motor geared to the wheels. Here at the Illinois Railway Museum in 1971, Chicago Surface Lines No. 144 (left), built by Pullman in 1904, meets Milwaukee Electric Railway & Light Company No. 972, built by St. Louis Car Company in 1927. Thousands of cars like these swept across America in the early 1900s. *Jim Boyd photo*

The New York Central's first electric locomotive, S-motor 100, was borrowed from the Mohawk & Hudson Chapter of the National Railway Historical Society in September 1986 and returned to Grand Central Terminal for the filming of *The House on Carroll Street*, starring Kelly McGillis and Jeff Daniels. Originally built as road engines, these third-rail "tunnel rats" were used as switchers in GCT. Note the tiny top pantograph used for the power rail over complex switchwork. *Jim Boyd photo*

Grand Central Terminal

The most enduring monument to electrification was also one of the earliest. By 1900, the open-air Grand Central Station in midtown Manhattan was seeing 700 steam-powered train movements a day with both main-line and suburban service for the New York Central & Hudson River and the New York, New Haven & Hartford. Making the smoke problem even more severe was the 2-mile-long Park Avenue tunnel that trains had to traverse coming into the station from the north. A serious wreck with 15 fatalities caused by smoke-limited visibility in the tunnel on January 2, 1902, prompted both the politicians and railroad to action.

The New York Legislature passed a law banning steam locomotives south of the Harlem River after July 1, 1908. The NYC&HR responded by assembling an engineering team to implement electrification and design a huge new passenger terminal. Instead of electrifying just the terminal and tunnel, the NYC&HR decided to electrify its entire suburban service up 34 miles of its four-track Hudson River Line to Croton, New York, and up the double-track Harlem Line 24 miles to White Plains, New York. The suburban service would use MU cars, while the through trains would change from steam to electric locomotives at Croton and White Plains. The electrification would use 660-volt DC power delivered through an

Big Penn Central 2-C+C-2 motor No. 4627 comes down the third-rail approach to Grand Central Terminal at 125th Street and Park Avenue with an Amtrak intercity train in July 1974. The unit had been built by Alco-GE in 1929 for the New York Central's Cleveland Union Terminal operation and was later moved to New York to handle commuters and through trains south of Croton–Harmon, where the main-line third-rail territory began. *Jim Boyd photo*

underrunning outside third rail. (This system was much safer to work around, since the contact rail faced downward, and the top and off-track side could be covered with insulation.)

The first "T-class" locomotive was built by General Electric and Alco in late 1904. This strange little 37-foot machine had a rigid frame with four gearless bipolar motors and a single two-wheel pilot truck at each end. The unit was configured for bidirectional operation and carried the first MU equipment applied to a locomotive, meaning that two (or more) units could be coupled together and operated by one person from one of the locomotive's cabs. This T-class locomotive could easily make 80 miles per hour, and in power it was roughly equivalent to a typical 4-6-2 steam locomotive of the time. The railroad acquired 34 more T-motors in 1906. On February 17, 1907, there was a fatal derailment attributed to the locomotive "nosing" at speed, and the T-motors were modified with

four-wheel trucks replacing the two-wheel trucks at either end, changing their class designation to S1.

To make use of the electrification, the NYC&HR began construction on the largest public building attempted up to that time. Electric operation permitted the new Grand Central Terminal to keep all of its tracks underground on two levels. Construction began in June 1903, and, most remarkably, the new facility was built on the site of the old Grand Central Station without interrupting its operation! Architect Whitney Warren (the cousin of NYC&HR Chairman William K. Vanderbilt) prevailed in the building's final design, and his concept for the grand Beaux-Arts structure turned out to be one of the architectural masterpieces of all time. The electrification and engineering of Grand Central's trackage allowed it to take advantage of locomotive technology developments over the decades and is as functional today as it ever was.

Grand Central Terminal, at 42nd Street and Park Avenue in New York City, served all lines of the New York Central and most electric suburban and intercity trains of the New Haven. Construction began in 1903, and the building is maintained today in its full magnificence. Approaching from the north on Park Avenue, all tracks are third-rail electrified and duck underground and terminate on two levels beneath the station. At left is NYC's Commodore Hotel. *Jim Boyd photo*

New Haven Electrification

The New York, New Haven & Hartford had little trouble adapting to the Grand Central electrification. As early as 1895, it had been experimenting with DC electrification on some of its branch lines. The New Haven used 12 miles of NYC&HR track from Woodlawn, New York, into Grand Central, and it was logical that the New Haven would adopt the NYC&HR's type of electrification eastward into Connecticut.

During this time, Thomas Edison and GE were strong promoters of direct current (DC), while airbrake inventor George Westinghouse was advocating alternating current (AC) through his Westinghouse Electric & Manufacturing Company. There was room for legitimate disagreement, since DC motors were compact and easy to control, but DC current was difficult to transmit over long distances because its voltage could not be stepped up or down using transformers. Alternating current, on the other hand, was very efficient to transmit using transformers, but AC motors were cumbersome and difficult to control.

The New Haven surprised everyone when it opted for a Westinghouse 11,000-volt, 25-cycle, single-phase AC system to extend from Woodlawn 21 miles to Stamford, Connecticut. Baldwin and Westinghouse teamed up to produce a 41-unit fleet of two-truck, four-motor Boxcab units that could run off of both the 11,000-volt AC overhead catenary and the NYC's 660-volt DC third rails. Subsequent units added a nonpowered guiding axle at each end to improve their tracking qualities.

In addition to the Baldwin-Westinghouse locomotives used on the intercity trains, the New Haven acquired a fleet of MU passenger cars for its suburban service. The electrification was extended east into New Haven, Connecticut, in 1914.

The four-track main line between Woodlawn and Stamford was hung with an interesting triangular catenary, with the single contact wire suspended beneath two catenary suspension wires. Portions of this unique overhead, energized in 1907, survive in service to this day.

Penn Station

Before the turn of the twentieth century, the Pennsylvania Railroad was forced to terminate its main lines approaching New York City at the west bank of the Hudson River in Jersey City and transport its passengers to and from Manhattan by ferryboat. Desperately needing a direct access into Manhattan, as early as 1884 the Pennsy had proposed a huge 14-track bridge over the Hudson River, but the War Department considered it too restrictive to steamship traffic in the harbor.

By 1901, however, electric locomotive technology had made enough advances that it made a Hudson River tunnel a realistic option. The Pennsy had recently gained control of the Long Island Rail Road and was eager to bring both properties into a Manhattan terminal. Thus, in early 1905, the PRR began boring two single-track tunnels from the New Jersey Meadowlands into midtown Manhattan at 34th Street. They also began four tunnels under the East River for the LIRR.

In the center was Penn Station, a massive structure that was intended to outshine the proposed Grand Central Terminal that would replace Grand Central Station. Occupying two full city blocks, Penn Station featured Roman Doric architecture and huge open spaces with soaring internal ironwork and glass ceilings.

The tunnels utilized a 675-volt DC system using an outside third rail. To handle its main-line passenger trains in from Manhattan Transfer, 13 miles from Penn Station in the New Jersey Meadowlands, PRR's Altoona (Pennsylvania) Shops and Westinghouse Electric developed the unique DD1 locomotive. The DD1 was a Boxcab that looked like it had been dropped over a 4-4-0 steam locomotive. Its huge traction motor was mounted on the floor of the carbody and drove steam-style driving wheels through a jackshaft and side rods. Two of the 4-4-0 units were semipermanently coupled back-to-back to create one DD1 locomotive. As strange as it looked, the DD1 was a rugged and reliable locomotive that could sprint at 80 miles per hour.

Penn Station opened for business on November 27, 1910, and its usefulness became even greater when the Hell Gate Bridge over the East River was completed in 1917, permitting through-train operation over the New Haven from Boston to Washington, D.C., on the PRR—and rendering mighty Manhattan just another stop on today's Northeast Corridor.

Unfortunately, land values in midtown Manhattan and the incredible value of "air rights"—the space above ground level—doomed Penn Station. In 1963, its grand spaces were replaced by low ceilings and a tomblike basement existence beneath the Madison Square Garden sports complex.

Milwaukee in the Mountains

At the turn of the twentieth century, far from the tunnels of midtown Manhattan, the Chicago, Milwaukee & St. Paul (or The Milwaukee Road) was feeling the need for its own route from Chicago to the Pacific Coast. Construction of the Pacific Extension from the Missouri River in South Dakota 1,400 miles to Tacoma, Washington, began in 1906 and was completed in 1909.

That year, John D. Ryan, president of Anaconda Copper Mining Company, joined the Milwaukee's board of directors. He raised the idea of electrifying the Pacific Extension as a market for his copper and interests in hydroelectric plants in Montana. In 1911, his electrification of the Butte, Anaconda & Pacific demonstrated—right in the Milwaukee's backyard—what could be done.

On an October morning in 1971, a trio of boxcabs led by the E34B were just getting their eastbound train moving at Avery, Idaho, the west end of the Rocky Mountain Division electrification. Motor E50A was leading this train's midtrain helper set. Inside the immaculate brick Avery substation was the motor-generator equipment to convert commercial AC power to 3,000-volt DC for the trolley wire. Note how the power cables on the back wall lead to the terminal rack outside at the southwest corner of the building. *Jim Boyd photo, top; Mike Schafer photo, bottom*

With steep grades and numerous tunnels, the Pacific Extension could put electrics to good use. The board was convinced, and in April 1914 electrification began on the 438-mile Rocky Mountain Division from Harlowton, Montana, to Avery, Idaho, crossing the Belt, Rocky, and Bitterroot mountain ranges. The Milwaukee would use 3,000-volt DC delivered through a simple overhead trolley wire. Huge motor-generator substations, placed about every 32 miles, converted the commercial 100,000-volt AC from Montana Power to DC for the trolley wire.

In 1915 and 1916, GE and Alco delivered 42 Boxcab locomotives that rode on heavy articulated underframes in a 2-B-B configuration (a nonpowered four-wheel lead truck on the front and two powered axles on each section of the frame). Each locomotive comprised two units semi-permanently coupled back-to-back. Thirty of the loco-motives were geared for 30-mile-per-hour freight service, while a dozen were passenger geared for 60 miles per hour and carried oil-fired steam boilers for train heat and lighting controls.

The Boxcabs also employed regenerative breaking that reversed the polarity in the motors and turned them into generators to act like brakes on a downgrade and feed the generated power back into the overhead trolley. The Boxcabs were powerful and reliable and remained in service until the very end of electric operations in 1974!

The Milwaukee expanded its electrification in 1917 by hanging wire over 207 miles of the Cascade Division between Othello and Tacoma, Washington. This left the Idaho Division, however, as a 216-mile steam-powered gap between the two electrified divisions. Talk of electrifying the gap never translated into action.

The most bizarre locomotives to operate under Milwaukee Road wires were the five bipolar passenger units. These three-segment articulated machines had a 1-B-D+D-B-1 wheel arrangement, with motors on all axles except the one at each end. The bipolars lasted long enough to get the new Union Pacific passenger colors in the late 1950s. The E-1 was at Deer Lodge, Montana, on April 29, 1958. *Monty Powell photo*

Passenger-equipped Little Joe E20 drops off St. Paul Pass at Adair, Idaho, approaching Avery in the early 1950s with No. 17, the *Columbian*. It just passed over the bridge on the other side before curving around the end of the valley. The streamlined 2-D+D-2 5,500-horsepower motors had been built by GE in the late 1940s for the Soviet Union but were embargoed before shipment and sold in the United States and Brazil. *Sandy Goodrick photo*

The Chicago South Shore & South Bend got three of the GE Little Joes (and Brazil got five) before the Milwaukee could buy the remaining 12 units in the lot in 1950. No. 803 works the steel mill complex at Gary, Indiana, in June 1978. These units were built to Russian wide gauge and rebuilt to standard gauge for the South Shore and The Milwaukee Road. *Jim Boyd photo*

The very first Milwaukee Road electric locomotive, General Electric boxcab E50A, built in 1915, was still in service in October 1971, as it was being prepared to be cut in as a mid-train helper over St. Paul Pass, east out of Avery, Idaho. The creation of the Burlington Northern in 1970 had opened new Western interchange gateways for the Milwaukee and nearly doubled its traffic, putting the veteran "Pelicans" back to work. *Jim Boyd photo*

Milwaukee Road *Thunderhawk* 261 is westbound near St. Regis, Montana, in October 1971 with Joe-motor E79 leading a trio of GP40s. The Little Joe would assist the diesels for 440 miles over the numerous mountain ridges between Harlowton, Montana, and Avery, Idaho. The Milwaukee quit the electrification in 1974 and abandoned much of the Pacific Extension shortly thereafter. *Jim Boyd photo*

As its biggest steam locomotives, the 2-6-6-6 Alleghenies, were being retired in the mid-1950s, the Virginian was using four GE streamliner electrics that combined the best of existing electric and diesel technology. They used standard diesel-style DC power trucks fed from the AC overhead by an internal motor-generator set. Each unit had the tractive effort of a Union Pacific 4-8-8-4 Big Boy! The diesel in the background is a Fairbanks-Morse H-16-44. *J. J. Young Jr. photo*

Between 1915 and 1923, the Virginian Railway and neighbor Norfolk & Western electrified their lines in the coalfields of Virginia and West Virginia with 11,000-volt AC systems. Their "Squarehead" locomotives each had huge AC traction motors mounted inside the carbody, connected to the driving wheels with steam-locomotive-style side rods. Virginian Squarehead No. 100 is in the servicing facility at Princeton, West Virginia, in the early 1950s. *John Dziobko photo*

Over the years, The Milwaukee Road was able to take advantage of developments in locomotive technology, and the Boxcabs were soon joined by a variety of other units, including five huge bipolar units that looked like a cross between a tank car and a New York Central S-motor. Suffice it to say, they rode on a 1-B-D+D-B-1 wheel arrangement.

Following World War II, GE accepted an order from the Soviet Union for 20 of the world's most powerful electric locomotives. Designed for the Soviet 5-foot gauge and 3,300-volt DC overhead wire, the 2-D+D-2 double-ended streamlined locomotives were rated at 5,500 continuous horsepower. Deterioration of political relations between the wartime allies caused GE to cancel its shipment to Russia. GE finished construction of the "Little Joes" (nicknamed after Joseph Stalin), with the final five built to standard gauge.

After one of the Joes was sent west to demonstrate, the Milwaukee made an offer for the entire fleet, but three had already been sold to the Chicago South Shore & South Bend and five to Brazil's 5-foot 3-inch gauge Paulista Railway. In 1950, the Milwaukee got the remaining dozen Little Joes as is and put them through the home shops to convert them for domestic service.

The Joes breathed new life into the electrification in the face of rapidly expanding dieselization. The Joe motors were modified to be able to MU with diesels, so that a through freight with four or five diesels could run all the way to the coast over the Idaho Division gap, with one or two Little Joes up front for additional power over the mountains.

Technology was developing rapidly, and in 1956 the Virginian got 12 ignitron rectifier road-switcher electrics from GE. These used huge vacuum tubes in a bridge rectifier circuit to create DC for the traction motors. When the Virginian merged with the N&W in December 1959, the electrification was torn down, and the new 3,300-horsepower rectifiers were sold to the New Haven. Two red "bricks" are westbound at New Haven in August 1966. Note the different pantographs. *Jim Boyd photo*

Facing intensified competition and diminishing traffic and lacking the capital necessary to modernize its electrified system, The Milwaukee Road killed the electrification on the Cascade Division in 1972 and the Rocky Mountain Division in 1974.

The Milwaukee was not the only railroad to employ electrification in mountain territory. In 1909, the nearby Great Northern electrified the 2.63-mile Cascade Tunnel in western Washington with a 6,600-volt AC system and expanded it in 1929 to 73 route-miles between Skykomish and Wenatchee with an 11,000-volt AC system that included the new 7.79-mile Cascade Tunnel. The GN used heavy motor-generator Boxcab units that used the AC overhead to spin a motor attached to a generator that output DC for the traction motors.

Squareheads in Appalachia

Back East, the Norfolk & Western began electrifying its 56-mile heavy eastbound grade from Iaeger to Bluefield, West

Virginia, between 1915 and 1923 with an 11,000-volt AC system. The nearby Virginian Railway electrified its entire 134.5-mile main line from the coalfields at Mullens over the mountain at Clark's Gap and up the New River to Roanoke with a system similar to the N&W's. Both railroads employed Boxcab "Squareheads" that used side rods to connect heavy AC traction motors to the driving wheels. Alternating current motors are difficult to control because they tend to "go synchronous" with the pulses of the alternating current. The N&W Squareheads were designed to go synchronous at 14 and 28 miles per hour.

The N&W dropped its electrification when the new Elkhorn Tunnel was opened up in 1950; the Virginian not only continued operation but went in quest for more modern motive power. Diesel technology had produced very rugged and reliable off-the-shelf DC traction motors, but there was no simple way of converting the AC trolley power to DC

With the AC electrification of the Pennsylvania Railroad main line under way, the railroad turned to Baldwin-Westinghouse, GE, and the company's Altoona Shops to mass-produce 90 2-C-2 P5 locomotives for both freight and passenger service (top). The up-front, exposed cab caused concern, and 26 modified P5s were built with a center-cab configuration, like No. 4744, shown in the New Jersey Meadowlands at the Kearny engine terminal. Each big driving wheel was powered by two traction motors. *Both photos John Dziobko*

"Ol' Rivets," prototype GG1 No. 4800, was in passenger service in the early 1950s as it brought a train from New York Penn Station into South Amboy, New Jersey, where the wire ended and a K4 4-6-2 would forward the train south to Bay Head. The 4800, built in 1935, remained in freight service into the mid-1970s and is preserved today at the Pennsylvania State Railroad Museum in Strasburg. *John Dziobko photo*

for traction. In 1948, the Virginian got four huge streamliner electrics that each consisted of two units riding on four two-motor diesel-style trucks. Inside, however, was the same basic motor-generator arrangement as the Great Northern Boxcabs. These 150-foot, two-unit streamliners were rated at 6,800-horsepower and produced an astounding 260,000 starting tractive effort (a UP Big Boy was rated at 135,375 tractive effort).

Even with the streamliners in service, the Virginian desperately needed to replace the aging Squareheads, and diesels provided an attractive option. To retain the viability of its already intact electric infrastructure, in 1956 the Virginian turned to GE for a dozen new electric road-switchers. These remarkable units used banks of huge ignitron-rectifier vacuum tubes to convert the AC to DC (the technology had been proven

in the New Haven's 10 double-ended EP-5 passenger units of 1955). The 3,300-horsepower Virginian units were laid out like a diesel road-switcher and rode on off-the-shelf three-motor DC power trucks.

The new Virginian units permitted the retirement of the Squareheads and performed up to expectations. However, the Virginian electrification was doomed by the railroad's merger with the N&W on December 1, 1959. The N&W wanted to combine the parallel N&W and Virginian main lines in the New River Gorge to function as a double-track railroad with east-bound loads on the Virginian and returning westbound empties on the N&W. A one-direction electrification was obviously impractical, and the power was cut off in July 1962 as diesels took over. Ironically, the 12 new ignitron rectifiers were sold and joined their technological brethren on the New Haven.

The first GG1 was built with a conventional riveted steel shell, but stylist Raymond Loewy suggested that it be smoothly welded instead. The result was a timeless classic. The Pennsy was not beyond the grand publicity photo, and in the late 1930s it lined up five shiny new GG1s in the Long Island's Sunnyside Yard, the engine terminal for New York Penn Station (top). Aside from the perfect alignment, however, that scene was not unusual, as it was normal to find a dozen GG1s being serviced at Sunnyside at any given time, even in the Amtrak era. In August 1977, No. 4935 (restored to its original Brunswick green and pinstripes) was in that same spot with E60CP No. 952 and a GG1 in Amtrak's rather garish red, blue, and silver (bottom). *Pennsylvania Railroad photo, top; Jim Boyd photo, bottom*

The Pennsylvania Railroad set up a heavy maintenance facility for its electric fleet at Wilmington, Delaware. In August 1977, there were a number of well-weathered Conrail freight and Amtrak passenger GG1s in the bay, along with a power truck from an E60CP. Also note the large driving wheels for the GG1s. Conrail dropped electric freight operations in 1981, but Wilmington continued to be the primary electric shop for Amtrak and the Northeast Corridor. *Jim Boyd photo*

The Greatest Electrification

Penn Station was made possible by a short DC electrification, but it made the Pennsylvania Railroad acutely aware of the potential of electric power. The same smoke and congestion problems that had caused the creation of Grand Central Terminal and Penn Station were plaguing the PRR's Broad Street Station in Center City, Philadelphia. With an eye toward an electrification that would extend beyond the suburban territory, the Pennsy drew upon the New Haven's success and opted for an 11,000-volt, 25-cycle AC system.

The first segments electrified were the 20-mile Main Line (a proper name that prevails today thanks to the Main Line of Public Works described in Chapter 1) to Paoli and the 12-mile Chestnut Hill branch. The Paoli electrification was opened in September 1915, and Chestnut Hill came on line in 1918. Replacing the steam trains in suburban service was a fleet of

steel MP54 MU cars. These venerable "grinders" remained in service into the late 1960s.

With the electric cars easing the congestion at Broad Street, the PRR was eying The Milwaukee Road and considered electrifying the heavy Allegheny grades over Horseshoe Curve between Altoona and Conemaugh, Pennsylvania. But increasing passenger traffic was pushing its four-track New York–Wilmington segment of the Washington main line to near capacity, and management concluded that electrification there would be a more effective use of the money.

On October 13, 1928, PRR President William Wallace Atterbury announced that AC electrification would commence on 325 route-miles from New York to Wilmington, Delaware, and Trenton, New Jersey, to Columbia, Pennsylvania, for a total of 1,300 track-miles. The $100 million project was the

most ambitious electrification in the world. The project soon grew even bigger, with the wires extending to Washington, D.C., and across the river to Potomac Yard in Virginia, where the PRR interchanged with the Richmond, Fredericksburg & Potomac, the Chesapeake & Ohio, and Southern Railway. In 1938, the wires were extended west from Paoli to Harrisburg, and the low-grade Trenton Cut-Off freight line bypassing Philadelphia was electrified.

It is a tribute to the PRR's economic power that the program pressed forward even after the stock-market crash of 1929 and the onset of the Great Depression.

The Depression actually contributed to the project by making skilled labor readily available, and the reduced traffic level permitted easier rebuilding. As the financial strain increased, in 1932 the Reconstruction Finance Corporation granted the railroad a $27.5 million loan, and two years later another $80 million loan was granted by the Public Works Administration. It was public money well placed, as the massive project not only employed local workers but created a heavy demand from nearby industries for construction materials.

Three types of heavy Boxcab units were tested, and the 2-C-2 P5a class got the nod in 1932 for mass production of 90 units by Baldwin-Westinghouse, GE, and Altoona Shops. With the high speed and heavy trains, concern grew about the Boxcab design with the crew compartment exposed at the end of the unit. The final 28 modified P5s were redesigned with a streamlined steeple-cab design that placed the cabs amidships. The versatile P5a locomotives could handle passenger trains at 90 miles per hour, though they demonstrated some tracking problems that soon limited them to 70 miles per hour.

In an effort to come up with a better high-speed unit, the PRR began an extensive testing program. A New Haven EP-3 2-C+C-2 Boxcab demonstrated superior performance, and the PRR ordered a single prototype GG1 built in 1934 by Baldwin, with GE electrical equipment. At the same time, Altoona Shops built a solitary R1-class unit with a 2-D-2 wheel arrangement that was essentially a P5 elongated by one more driving axle. Both the GG1 and R1 had the streamlined styling of the modified P5 and rode on roller bearings throughout. When tested at speed, the articulated frame of the GG1 provided vastly superior performance at speeds up to 115 miles per hour!

The prototype GG1 had typical steam-era construction, with a heavily riveted steel shell. In a stroke of genius, the PRR contracted with industrial designer Raymond Loewy to clean up the appearance of the GG1. In a radical departure for the time, he had the carbody arc-welded into a smooth, solid shell.

The welded GG1s were put into production at Baldwin, GE, and Altoona, with electrical gear supplied by both GE and Westinghouse. In spite of the manufacturing diversity, when delivered in 1935, the 57 new GG1s were effectively identical. More GG1s were produced through 1943, with the final fleet totaling 139 units. The "Old Rivets" prototype 4800, however, remained in regular service into the mid-1970s.

The GG1, geared for 100 miles per hour, was one of the finest electric locomotives of all time. It was equally at home on the *Broadway Limited*, local passenger trains, heavy freight, and New York & Long Branch commuter trains. The GG1s survived to see premier service for Amtrak into the 1970s and lasted in New Jersey Transit commuter service until October 28, 1983. Although most of the GG1s on Conrail and Amtrak had shed their dark Brunswick green or Tuscan red and gold pinstripes for Penn Central black (except for a few rendered in a ghastly Amtrak silver, blue, and red), in 1977, under the sponsorship of a railfan group, the 4935 was restored by Amtrak to its green and pinstripes, and Raymond Loewy was on hand to "autograph" the active service unit. As Amtrak retired its GG1s, a number of them were transferred to NJ Transit for the New York & Long Branch service to South Amboy. On June 1, 1981, NJ Transit rolled 4877 out of its Raritan Shop with the Tuscan red livery, a project sponsored by the Jersey Central Chapter of the NRHS. It was just in time to be loaned to Amtrak on June 6 for the "Farewell to the GG1" Amtrak excursion, because all Amtrak GG1s had been retired by then. The 4877 remained in regular service until October 28, 1983, when the last GG1s were retired by NJ Transit.

Carrying Commuters

Electrification and MU passenger cars were a perfect combination to replace steam on many big-city commuter operations. They eliminated the smoke problem, and the typical high-density but short route operations made the expense of the infrastructure quite justifiable. The MU cars also eliminated the need for back-out and turnaround moves in crowded stub-end terminals. Although MU cars are not true locomotives but, essentially, powered passenger cars, we will touch upon some of them here as they relate to some of the standard railroads (versus subway and similar transit-only systems) that used them.

Direct descendants of the old-fashioned streetcar or trolley, MU cars are self-powered rather than locomotive-hauled. Each

Opposite: The 45-year-old GG1s served Amtrak well with 100-mile-per-hour operation into the 1980s. The Sunnyside car washers kept the black sides shiny, but the noses didn't always get the needed hand scrubbing, as evidenced by No. 4925 southbound at Elizabeth, New Jersey, in September 1980, crossing over the old Jersey Central main line to Jersey City. The GG1s needed replacement because their cast underframes were beginning to suffer metal fatigue that couldn't be repaired. *Jim Boyd photo*

car has axle-mounted traction motors fed by electricity drawn from overhead catenary wire or third rails and is controlled by an operator stationed in a cab at one or both car ends. MU cars can operate singly (except for those semipermanently coupled to a mate car or to a nonpowered trailer) or strung together into multicar trains, and yet the motors on all cars can still be controlled by one operator. MU-type trains are the backbone of commuter-rail systems in metro New York and Philadelphia and to a lesser extent in Montreal and Chicago.

One of the first uses of heavy-rail rapid transit was in a very unlikely place: Sausalito, California. Residents in the growing suburban communities in Marin and Sonoma counties on the north side of San Francisco Bay got to work in San Francisco by riding the narrow gauge North Pacific Coast down to the ferryboat at Sausalito. In 1903, the narrow gauge was replaced by a 12-mile double-track standard gauge electric railway. The new North Shore Railroad used a 550-volt DC outside third rail and had open-platform wooden MU cars that were both built new and rebuilt from existing cars. In 1907, the line became part of the Northwestern Pacific Railroad. The opening of the Golden Gate Bridge spelled the line's demise, and the railroad and ferries made their last run in early 1941.

The next suburban enterprise turned out to be one of the greatest electrifications of all time: the Long Island Rail Road.

By the turn of the twentieth century, the LIRR had already grown into a huge suburban service and permitted the island to become a viable bedroom community for New York City. At that time, the steam-powered LIRR ended at terminals on the East River, where passengers had to transfer to ferryboats or the city elevated rail system. In 1900, the LIRR came under the control of the PRR, and plans got immediately under way for electrification and a tunnel connection to Penn Station in Manhattan. In 1905, the LIRR opened up 38 route-miles of a 650-volt DC outside-third-rail system that employed 134 MU cars. The tunnels into the new Manhattan Penn Station were opened on September 8, 1910, two months before the PRR itself inaugurated service under the Hudson River from New Jersey. Nearly the entire west end of the LIRR was soon electrified, from Babylon on the south and Huntington on the north, and is to this day one of the most intensive electric operations in the world.

Up in Canada, the Canadian Northern was using tunnels to penetrate downtown Montreal and opted for a 2,400-volt DC system using overhead trolley wires. Since the tunnels would handle both suburban service and main-line passenger trains, the railroad purchased MU cars for the former and six Boxcab locomotives for the latter. Two of the Boxcabs, MU'ed together, could handle a 16-car heavyweight passenger

Multiple-unit cars made possible high-density commuter operations in America's biggest cities. In July 1966, a set of vintage multiple-unit cars pulls into the Jamaica station, a major junction point before the trains continued under the East River into New York's Penn Station. The LIRR utilizes a 650-volt DC outside-third-rail system, similar to the one used by the New York Central into Grand Central Terminal. *Jim Boyd photo*

In 1918, the Canadian Northern used a 2,400-volt DC system with overhead trolley wire to get trains through Mount Royal Tunnel into what is today's Montreal Central Station. The intercity trains, as well as some commuters, were handled by boxcab motors. The system became Canadian National in 1925, and on June 17, 1991, two 1926 English Electric boxcabs lead a westbound VIA train out of the tunnel. The line also used MU cars for commuters. *Howard Ande photo*

train. The terminal opened in 1918. The Canadian Northern became part of the Canadian National in 1925, and the railroad continued to expand and receive new MU cars and locomotives. The original 1914 Boxcab motors remained in service until the early 1980s!

The Illinois Central drove its main line right up Chicago's showpiece lakefront in 1856, but by the turn of the twentieth century the pesky steam trains were becoming a smoky nuisance. The IC's suburban line that paralleled the main line for 29 miles from downtown to suburban Richton by 1917 was carrying 18 million passengers a year behind small steam engines. Chicago wanted to enact a law like New York City had that would ban steam locomotives, but the network was far too large and complex to be workable. In 1918, however, the city focused on the IC and mandated electrification by 1927.

The IC began immediate plans to electrify the multitrack suburban main line, as well as the double-track South Chicago branch and the single-track Blue Island branch. The system would use a 1,500-volt DC power supply delivered through overhead catenary. Between 1921 and 1929, Pullman and the Standard Steel Car Company built 280 steel and aluminum MU cars that were semipermanently joined in motor-and-trailer sets. They could be run in trains of up to 10 cars and would balance at 64 miles per hour. The Pullman green cars were introduced to Chicago with festivities on August 7, 1926. As part of the IC project, the interurban Chicago South Shore & South Bend was upgraded from South Bend, Indiana, into Kensington, Illinois, where it then began operations over the IC to the downtown Chicago terminal at Randolph Street. The original green cars served the IC very reliably until they were replaced by new bi-level Highliners beginning in 1971. The new cars had about the same acceleration as the green cars but boosted the top speed to 75 miles per hour.

Shortly after the completion of the IC electrification in Chicago, the Delaware, Lackawanna & Western committed to the electrification of three of its commuter lines in New Jersey totaling 70 route-miles. The DL&W was already carrying 60,000 passengers a day through its Hoboken Terminal across the Hudson River from Manhattan. Passengers got into New York City on DL&W ferry boats or the recently completed Hudson & Manhattan subway tunnels. Congestion at Hoboken Terminal was reaching crisis levels at rush hours with the need to extract and turn steam trains with an army of switch engines.

The DL&W opted for the 3,000-volt DC system that had proven so successful on The Milwaukee Road Pacific Extension. Pullman produced a fleet of 141 motorcars that were similar in appearance to the IC cars, right down to the green paint. The MUs were placed in service as motor-trailer pairs and could be made up into trains of up to 12 cars with speeds up to 71 miles per hour.

On September 3, 1930, the first DL&W MU train departed Hoboken for South Orange with none other than Thomas Edison at the controller. Once operations were established, they continued almost without change into the 1980s—even after DL&W merged with Erie in 1960 to form the Erie Lackawanna Railway—and acquired the nickname "wickerliners" for their wicker seats. In 1967, the New Jersey Department of Transportation began to subsidize the EL suburban service. In 1980, a massive re-electrification program began that would convert the former-DLW lines to 25,000-volt commercial-frequency AC to make them compatible with the ex-PRR Northeast Corridor

lines that were being similarly upgraded. The entire oper-ation was taken over by NJ Transit on January 1, 1983, and the DL&W cars made their last run on August 24, 1984. Because the old, non-air-conditioned cars were completely incompatible with the new system, the DL&W lines were shut down for a week while the changeover to AC operation was engaged, and a fleet of air-conditioned Jersey Arrow cars took over.

In 1990, NJ Transit introduced something never before seen on the DL&W lines: electric locomotive–hauled trains. ALP44-model commuter electrics, built by ASEA Brown Boveri of Sweden, were used to power push-pull trains. The system that began with Thomas Edison at the controller rolled into the twenty-first century with service better than ever.

In November 2001, NJ Transit began taking delivery of 29 ALP46 units built by Bombardier in Kassel, Germany. These sleek, double-ended 7,100-horsepower units have tapered ends and computer-controlled AC traction motors and were based on the highly successful German Railways Class 101 that had been running since 1996.

One of the last major steam commuter networks to be electrified was the Reading Company's service in Philadelphia, and its development was quite similar to that of the DL&W. The Reading had a stub-end terminal in Center City, Philadelphia, that was even more congested than Hoboken, and it served a sprawling network of lines to the north and east. In October 1928, the Reading announced a $20 million project to electrify its commuter routes fanning out from Philadelphia.

The Illinois Central built an excellent 29-mile separate double-track commuter line parallel to its main line south from Chicago's lakefront. Originally steam powered with 2-4-4T Forney steam engines, it was electrified with a 1,500-volt DC overhead in 1926. A set of the original motor-and-trailer "green cars" is southbound near Kensington in 1965 (left). The heavy interurban Chicago South Shore & South Bend used the IC electric line from Kensington up to the lakefront terminal at Randolph Street. In 1970, a modernized South Shore coach is southbound at 23rd Street (right) with a baggage trailer full of *Chicago Tribune* newspapers headed for readers in Indiana. *Both photos Jim Boyd*

The Delaware, Lackawanna & Western electrified its main line with 3,000-volt DC overhead through affluent northern New Jersey from Hoboken Terminal, across the Hudson River from downtown Manhattan. Ferryboats provided the connection into New York City, along with the Port Authority Trans-Hudson subway. Thomas A. Edison was at the controller of the first train out of Hoboken in 1930, and four cars of that vintage are at the Dover, New Jersey, western terminal in August 1976. *Jim Boyd photo*

Unlike the DL&W, however, the Reading selected 11,000-volt single-phase 25-cycle AC power that was already in use by the neighboring Pennsylvania Railroad. In 1930, the Reading placed an order for 70 MU cars with the Wilmington, Delaware, works of Bethlehem Steel. In 1932, another 30 cars were built. The Reading cars made use of an unusual top-mounted 11,000-volt buss to distribute power from a variety of energized pantographs. The overhead buss contacts were quite noticeable on the ends of the car roofs.

The Reading's green—later, blue and white—MUs were a fixture of the Philadelphia scene and provided decades of

reliable service. In 1958, the city began to subsidize the suburban service in a program that developed into the Southeastern Pennsylvania Transportation Authority (SEPTA). In 1963, the Reading service received 17 new Budd Silverliner cars, followed in 1974 by 14 Jersey Arrow cars financed by the State of New Jersey for the West Trenton service.

On November 6, 1984, the magnificent arched trainshed of Reading Terminal was closed down as SEPTA rerouted the former-Reading service through a new tunnel into the nearby former-PRR Suburban Station. The durable Blueliners were there to the end.

The DL&W electrics had run since 1930 with MU cars, but NJ Transit introduced a new concept there with locomotive-hauled push-pull trains. To make the equipment compatible with Amtrak's Northeast Corridor, in 1984 NJ Transit completely rewired the former DL&W lines with 25,000-volt AC. At that time, Amtrak was planning to upgrade its 11,500 volts to 25 Kv, but as of 2008, the change hasn't taken place. Fortunately, the new locomotives can automatically adjust to the voltage change at speed. The first units, acquired in 1990, were the 7,000-horsepower ALP44 versions of Amtrak's AEM7s. In 2001, NJ Transit began taking delivery of 7,100-horsepower German-built ALP46 motors. In March 2008, at North Elizabeth, ALP44 No. 4425 is southbound with a Long Branch train. *Jim Boyd photo*

Replacing the P5 and GG1

By 1950, the PRR was operating its passenger service with high-speed GG1s and handling its tonnage with freight-geared GG1s and the venerable P5s. Diesels were rapidly replacing steam locomotives, and the electrics could potentially meet the same fate. Numerous advances had been made in electric technology, however, and the PRR was eager to explore them before rendering its massive electric infrastructure obsolete.

The AC power system was efficient to transmit, but AC traction motors were cumbersome and difficult to precisely control. Diesels had made DC traction motors efficient, rugged, and "off the shelf." As early as 1913, the PRR, New Haven, and Westinghouse had been experimenting with mercury vapor rectifiers to produce DC for traction motors on an MU car, but the tubes of that era could not withstand the rigors of rail service. The rectifiers were huge vacuum tubes that could block the reverse pulses in the AC current and route it through a simple bridge rectifier circuit to output all the pulses in a smooth direct current.

As the rectifier technology improved, it was used with great success in four experimental freight units built in 1951 by Westinghouse for the PRR. In 1955, GE put that technology in 10 4,000-horsepower double-ended EP-5 passenger units for the New Haven. The howling blowers that cooled the rectifiers gave the colorful units the nickname "Jets." A year later, GE began producing a dozen 3,300-horsepower rectifier units for the Virginian Railway. These units rode on standard six-wheel diesel three-motor trucks and were laid out like a diesel road-switcher.

Opposite: The arched trainshed of Reading Terminal in Center City, Philadelphia, was elevated above street level, and the headhouse looked just like any other office building on the block. A set of 1930 "Blueliners" rolls out of the shed in August 1966 (top). Note the high-voltage buss contact above the headlight to link all cars and pantographs into one circuit. The Reading used an 11,000-volt system on its routes that spread out like an open hand. A few minutes after the Blueliners departed, 1 of the 17 new Budd Silverliners rolls out and meets a Budd RDC (Rail Diesel Car) on the elevated approach (bottom). The elevated terminal was torn down in 1984, and the Reading trains were rerouted through a new tunnel into the nearby former PRR Suburban Station. *Both photos Jim Boyd*

After Westinghouse built four experimental freight motors that looked like big diesel cab units, in 1955 GE adopted their ignitron rectifier technology for 10 4,000-horsepower double-ended EP-5 passenger units for the New Haven. With its cooling blowers howling, EP-5 No. 377 has a New York–bound intercity passenger train well in hand at Bridgeport, Connecticut, in the mid-1950s. The EP-5s had no multiple-unit capability, and that limited their usefulness when they went into Penn Central freight service. *T. J. Donahue photo, Kevin EuDaly collection*

Between 1960 and 1963, the Pennsy took delivery of 60 upgraded versions of the 4,400-horsepower Virginian motors. Before the delivery of the E44s was completed, on the final six units the liquid-cooled ignitron rectifiers were replaced with air-cooled solid-state silicon rectifiers that greatly simplified the machinery and boosted the output to 5,000 horsepower. The rest of the fleet was soon refitted with the silicon rectifiers.

The E44s succeeded in retiring the P5 fleet and immediately dominated the freight lines, although the GG1s continued to soldier on. Having committed to the new motors, the PRR was

studying extending the electrification over Horseshoe Curve to Conway Yard in Pittsburgh. These plans were apparently set aside with the PRR-NYC merger on February 1, 1968, that created the ill-fated Penn Central.

With an interest in exploring some of the new technology developed in Europe, in the early 1970s diesel-builder Electro-Motive Division of General Motors teamed up with ASEA of Sweden to produce two prototype electric demonstrators. The GM6C, road number 1975 (for the year of its debut), strongly resembled the E44, except for having a low short hood. Riding on six-wheel trucks, it was rated at 6,000 horsepower. The next year, EMD outshopped GM10B 1976, packing 10,000 horsepower on three heavy four-wheel trucks with large frame-mounted traction motors. Both units contained solid-state circuitry that would allow them to automatically adapt to various types and voltages of power input. The two stark-white units went to work for Conrail, which had taken over the bankrupt Penn Central in 1976.

The GM6C and GM10B went into revenue Conrail service, usually working between Kearny, New Jersey, and Harrisburg, Pennsylvania, on hot van trains. One Conrail engineer observed about the robust GM10B, "If it wasn't for the rate-of-application circuits, you could skin that baby open and brown out the entire Northeast!"

When the N&W killed the Virginian electrification on June 30, 1962, the 12 Virginian rectifier units were sold to the New Haven, where they were painted red and immediately dubbed "Bricks." When the New Haven became part of the Penn Central and Amtrak took over Northeast Corridor operations in 1971, they both wanted to get freight off the busy passenger lines. Since the PC could easily reroute into New Haven, Connecticut (the east end of the NH's electrification), off the NYC Boston & Albany line, electric freight service soon came to an end. The ex-Virginian motors were transferred to PRR lines where they went to work as E33s alongside the E44s. When the New Haven streamlined Jets were retired from passenger service because they would not MU with anything, two of them were put into local freight service between Baltimore and Newark.

Amtrak assumed ownership of the Northeast Corridor (Boston–New York–Philadelphia-Washington and Philadelphia–Harrisburg) at the creation of Conrail on April 1, 1976. The

General Electric used the ignitron rectifier technology employed in the New Haven EP-5s for a dozen 3,300-horsepower road-switcher motors for the Virginian Railway in 1956 and followed those with a fleet of 60 similar 4,400-horsepower E44 motors for the Pennsylvania Railroad. The E44s continued service for the Penn Central, and in July 1974 a pair with a freight out of Kearny, New Jersey, pulls into the yard at Waverly 5 Tower in Newark. *Jim Boyd photo*

The American Electric Power Company opened up a brand-new 15-mile railroad in southeastern Ohio in 1968 to move coal from the Muskingum Mine to a power plant. The Muskingum Electric Railroad was powered by a 25,000-volt commercial-frequency AC overhead and used two 5,000-horsepower E50C motors that were very similar to the PRR E44s. Muskingum No. 100 is at the north-end coal-loading loop in 1969. The line was later fully automated. *Jim Boyd photo*

numerous railroads included in the merger had given Conrail a number of alternate freight routes around the electrified corridor. As a result, Conrail decided to terminate all electric

Opposite: In the early 1970s, the Penn Central was considering extending its freight electrification west from Harrisburg over the Horseshoe Curve main line to Pittsburgh. With this potential market, the Electro-Motive Division of General Motors built two heavy-duty freight motors based on new computer-controlled solid-state technology. The GM6C 1975 was a 6,000-horsepower unit riding on convential diesel-style six-wheel power trucks (top). Its sister GM10B 1976, rated at 10,000 horsepower, rode on three four-wheel trucks with underframe-mounted traction motors (bottom). The stark-white 1976 stands out in the night at Harrisburg in May 1977, while the 1975 is at the Kearny, New Jersey, engine terminal in August 1976. Although the freight electrification was ultimately abandoned, the technology was used for a new generation of passenger motors. *Both photos Jim Boyd*

freight operations in 1981, and the GG1s, E33s, E44s, and Jets were retired; the white demonstrators went back to EMD, where they were ultimately scrapped.

Although the future of electrified main-line freight service in North America effectively died with Conrail in 1981, electrics continued to thrive on captive industrial operations. Back in the late 1920s, the Kennecott Copper Company had installed a 750-volt DC trolley-wire electrification in its huge Bingham Canyon open-pit mine near Salt Lake City, Utah. More than 100 miles of track ultimately laced the circular terraces of the pit. The pit was actually carved out of a mountaintop, and the steeple-cab freight motors carried the ore downhill to a tunnel at the bottom of the pit that popped out on the lower mountainside. There the cars were handed over

To tap two coal mines in the Canadian wilderness 500 miles north of Vancouver, the British Columbia Railway built a brand-new 86-mile line with a 5,000-volt overhead catenary system. The Tumbler Ridge Subdivision used seven GF6C cowl-carbody motors built by EMD and ASEA based directly on the technology developed in the white GM6C Penn Central demonstrator 1975. The 6004 and 6003 are at Murray, British Columbia, on September 1, 1985. *Kevin EuDaly photo*

to much larger 150-ton road-haul steeple-cabs to be carried 16 miles north to the concentrators and the Garfield smelter on a 3,000-volt DC system that had replaced steam in 1947.

In 1968, the American Electric Power Company opened up a 15-mile line between the coal loader at the Muskingum Mine in southeastern Ohio and the dumper at a power plant. A trolley wire supplied 25,000-volt commercial-frequency AC power for two E50C locomotives. The GE E50Cs were thyristor-controlled silicon diode rectifiers that strongly resembled PRR

E44s. Two coal trains operated on the line, with one train on the road while the other was loading. The operation, effectively bereft of grade crossings, began with manned crews but was ultimately converted to fully automatic unmanned operation.

Another coal-hauling electric was the Black Mesa & Lake Powell in Arizona, which had a 78-mile line from the Black Mesa Mine to the Navajo Generating Station near Page. The isolated line had no connection to the national rail network and was powered by a 50,000-volt commercial-frequency AC trolley wire system. The BM&LP used three GE E60C single-ended Boxcab cowl units that had internal systems similar to the Muskingum E50Cs. The three 5,100-horsepower units MU'ed together handled 10,000-ton coal trains at speeds up to 72 miles per hour.

On November 2, 1983, the British Columbia Railway opened up an 86-mile coal line some 500 miles north of Vancouver, British Columbia, and about 500 miles inland from the Pacific Coast. The Tumbler Ridge Subdivision tapped two major coal mines at the east end and carried the loads over a mountain to the dieselized line at Wakeley. The overhead wire was energized with 50,000 volts of commercial-frequency AC supplied by BC Hydro. The Tumbler Ridge motive power consisted of seven 6,000-horsepower GF6C cowl-carbody units built by EMD and ASEA as a direct result of the 1975 GM6C and GM10B Conrail demonstrator project. In spite of its technological success, the world coal market collapsed in the 1990s, and the mines and railroad closed down in April 2003.

Speeding up Amtrak

As nationalized railroads overseas were making headlines with new high-speed sets like the Japanese "Bullet Train," unveiled in 1965, the Penn Central recognized the potential for faster service on the Northeast Corridor, and with the New Haven now in the family, it controlled the entire line from Washington to Boston. Airlines were setting up hourly Boston–New York–Washington shuttle service, but the distances from downtown to the airports, takeoff and landing delays, and potential of bad weather could make fast train service highly competitive.

The advances in solid-state silicon rectifiers were being applied to a new generation of commuter MU cars, pioneered in 1958 by the Reading Budd-built Silverliners and New Jersey–financed Jersey Arrows built by St. Louis Car Company in 1968 for the PC. The compact rectifiers made MU cars an attractive alternative to locomotive-hauled trains, and tests proved that the Silverliners could equal the performance of the GG1s in high-speed service.

With encouragement from an act of Congress, in 1966 the Penn Central ordered 50 high-performance Metroliner multiple-unit cars capable of 150-plus-mile-per-hour speeds. One of the regularly scheduled Metroliners is southbound at Wilmington, Delaware, in June 1969. The popular Metroliners were normally operated at 125 miles per hour, and with downtown-to-downtown convenience, they competed successfully with the airlines' hourly shuttle flights. They were taken over by Amtrak in 1971. *Jim Boyd photo*

The first new electric locomotives purchased by Amtrak to replace the venerable GG1s were 26 E60C motors from General Electric in 1973 with solid-state rectifier technology. The first six (950–955) were equipped with oil-fired boilers for use with steam-heated passenger cars, while the rest were fitted with electric head-end power for the new Amfleet equipment. The No. 950, northbound near MetroPark in New Jersey, in November 1978, was one of the steam-equipped units. *Jim Boyd photo*

In 1965, Congress authorized the High Speed Ground Transportation Research & Development Act that encouraged the Pennsylvania Railroad to undertake a project to bring 150-mile-per-hour service to the Northeast Corridor. The result in 1966 was an order from the Budd Company for a fleet of 50 high-performance MU cars run in trains dubbed "Metroliners" that could attain speeds up to 167 miles per hour. The Metroliners became a highly successful service with typical speeds of 125 miles per hour. Unlike the utilitarian commuter MUs, the Metroliners featured more comfortable long-distance seating and food service.

When Amtrak took over most of what remained of America's intercity passenger services on May 1, 1971, it inherited the Metroliners and the GG1s that were still handling the long-distance trains that used electrified Northeast Corridor trackage to reach New York. To begin replacing the aging GG1s, in March 1973 Amtrak placed an order for 15 E60C electrics from GE. A few months later, Amtrak ordered 11 more E60Cs. Delivered in 1974 and 1976, the 26 E60Cs—six were given E60CP designations for having steam generators for heating conventional trains and the rest as E60CHs, designating that they had head-end power (HEP) for lighting and climate control on newer, all-electric cars—were intended to be 120-mile-per-hour units, but they proved to be much too heavy and tracked so poorly that they were soon limited to

75 miles per hour. While the new E60s were restricted to the slower long-distance trains, the tireless GG1s still dominated the fast non-Metroliner schedules.

Passenger electric technology was moving much faster in Europe than in the United States, and Amtrak looked across the Atlantic for a replacement for the GG1. Diesel-builder EMD had worked with ASEA of Sweden on the white freight demonstrators, and they turned to the Swedish Railways' Rc4a, a compact four-motor 6,000-horsepower, double-ended Boxcab. An Rc4a demonstrator arrived in July 1976. After initial tests, it was placed in Metroliner service in October 1976 where it performed spectacularly, delivering the power of an E60 from a package half its weight. In January 1977, the French demonstrator X996 arrived at Elizabeth, New Jersey.

When the E60Cs proved too heavy and rough-riding for truly high-speed service, Amtrak went looking overseas for existing powerful but lightweight passenger units. Diesel-builder EMD teamed up with ASEA of Sweden in mid-1976 to test a standard Swedish Railways 6,000-horsepower Rc4a electric. The Amtrak-painted X995 is southbound at MetroPark in regular Metroliner service in November 1978. Amtrak also tested a heavier and much less successful French motor. *Jim Boyd photo*

The locomotive that finally beat the GG1 at its own game was not the hulking E60, but a compact little "toaster." In 1980, EMD and ASEA turned the Swedish Rc4a into the AEM7, a 7,000-horsepower speedster that was a perfect match for the Amfleet equipment. Here in August 1981, AEM7 No. 924 meets a set of inbound Jersey Arrow MU cars at Hunter Tower in Newark. *Jim Boyd photo*

The Alsthom SNCF 21000-class 7,725-horsepower unit rode on six-wheel trucks that each carried a single huge motor. Those big trucks didn't like the corridor track, however, and the French unit was quickly rejected.

The robust little "Swedish meatball," however, was an unqualified success, and on September 28, 1977, Amtrak placed an order for eight units—the American versions would be designated as AEM7s—to be built by EMD at La Grange, Illinois, with ASEA technology. The new 7,000-horsepower units would be based on the Swedish Rc4a but would be slightly longer and capable of higher speed. By the time the first AEM7s were entering service in mid-1980, orders had been placed for 47 additional units! By mid-1981, Amtrak had no more active GG1s.

In 1983, Philadelphia's SEPTA acquired seven AEM7s for trains to Paoli, and Maryland's MARC bought five in 1986 for

Washington–Baltimore commuter service. When NJ Transit wanted AEM7s for push-pull service on its former-DL&W lines, EMD had closed down La Grange and had moved diesel production to the London, Ontario, plant, which was not set up to produce the electrics. As a result, in 1990 NJ Transit took delivery on 15 very similar ALP44 units directly from ASEA Brown Boveri in Sweden. Another 18 arrived in 1995 and 1997.

Although the AEM7s and ALP44s were built as rectifiers with DC traction motors, the technology of computer-

Opposite: Seeking a train that could regularly run 150 miles per hour on existing Northeast Corridor track, in 1993 Amtrak tested the Swedish X2000 and German ICE trainsets that actively leaned into the curves for a smoother ride. The X2000 is in Washington Union Station in May 1993 after running a regular Metroliner schedule from New York. Normally allowed 140, because of wire conditions Amtrak had put a 130-mile-per-hour slow order on it this day. *Jim Boyd photo*

In January 2000, Amtrak completed the electrification of the Northeast Corridor by extending the wire from New Haven to Boston's South Station. To make the Boston service even more competitive with the airline shuttles, Amtrak contracted with Bombardier to adopt French TGV technology into new *Acela* 160-mile-per-hour trainsets. In August 2001, a Boston-bound *Acela* passes over the boat basin at Norwalk, Connecticut. *Jim Boyd photo*

controlled AC motors was proving far superior in reliability, performance, and economy, and the newer versions were built as AC units, while the older ones were subject to conversion as they came up for major shopping.

As the AEM7s took over as the 125-mile-per-hour workhorses of the Corridor, Amtrak was still looking toward its 160-mile-per-hour goal. In the late 1990s, Amtrak had been upgrading its entire electric infrastructure, and the crown jewel of the project was the stringing of 25,000-volt AC catenary from New Haven to Boston's South Station. It was energized for service in late January 2000, completing for the first time the 100 percent electrified 457-mile Northeast Corridor from Boston to Washington, eliminating the locomotive change at New Haven.

Now all Amtrak needed was a truly high-speed train. Since its testing of the Swedish Rc4a had been so successful in creating the AEM7, Amtrak brought over two service-proven European high-speed trainsets in 1993: the Swedish X2000 and the German ICE (Inter City Express). Both trainsets performed well, and Amtrak probably could have gone with the off-the-shelf X2000 and saved a lot of time, money, and trouble. Instead, Amtrak contracted with Bombardier of Canada for a purpose-built train based on the French TGV technology. The new trains would be given the name *Acela*, a Madison Avenue creation based on "acceleration" and "excellence."

While the six-car and two-unit *Acela* trainsets were being engineered, Bombardier began delivery in 1998 of the first of 15 HHP8 locomotives based on the *Acela* power cars. The 8,000-horsepower HHP8s had the same European-style noses as the *Acela* units but were double-ended. These sleek units are rated for 135-mile-per-hour service on trains equipped with Amfleet cars.

The first *Acela* trainsets went into service between Boston and Washington in December 2000. The trains had a 6,000-horsepower power car at each end with four business coaches, a cafe car, and a bistro car. The *Acela*s are authorized to travel at 150 miles per hour where curves don't impose lower speed limits.

The *Acela* service got off to a troubled launch when problems with the brake discs sidelined the entire fleet for a retrofit. Once those problems were sorted out, the *Acela*s became a very popular service, especially after Homeland Security problems and inspections drastically complicated airline travel. With fast, reliable, and effectively weatherproof schedules, the *Acela*s and their kin have become a vital part of the twenty-first-century Northeastern transportation infrastructure.

The 6,000-horsepower single-ended *Acela* power units were also built as 15 free-standing double-ended HHP8 locomotives. These units, delivered in 1998, are rated at 8,000 horsepower and are authorized 135 miles per hour with Amfleet equipment. The 653 is eastbound in the historic curved station at New London, Connecticut, with an Amtrak regional express on June 8, 2002. With the hassles of increased airline security, the Northeast Corridor has become one of Amtrak's true success stories. *Robert A. LeMay photo*

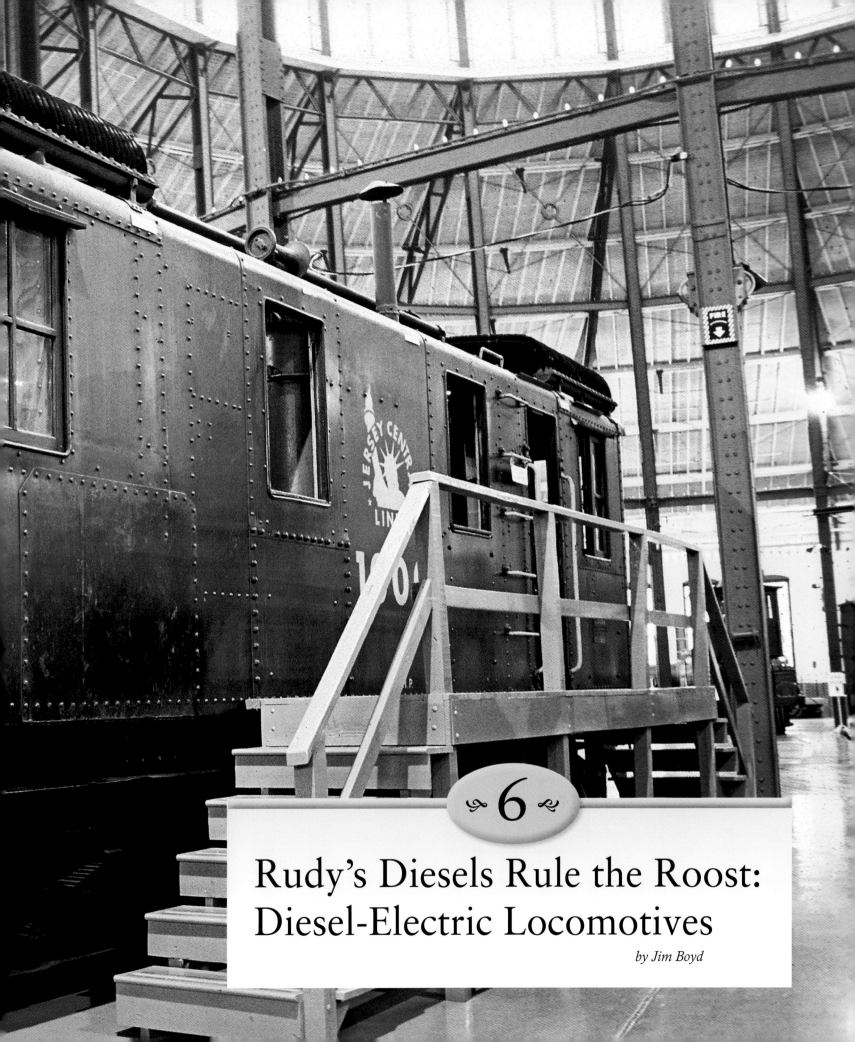

6

Rudy's Diesels Rule the Roost: Diesel-Electric Locomotives

by Jim Boyd

The diesel-electric locomotives that completely replaced steam by 1960 owed their success to the technology developed for main-line electric locomotives in the early twentieth century. Diesel-electrics are essentially electric locomotives that carry the generating station around on their backs. The electric traction motors do the pulling work, while the diesel engine swings the generator that creates the electricity for the motors.

Like trolley cars and main-line electrification, the diesel-electric locomotive owes its origins to Frank J. Sprague and his creation in the late 1880s of the nose-hung geared traction motor and the concept of multiple-unit control. After that, all that was needed was a fuel-burning internal combustion engine with the necessary power output in a package compact and light enough to fit into a locomotive carbody.

Doctor Diesel's Engine

Rudolf Diesel was born in France in 1858 of German parents and educated in Aughsburg, Germany. At age 20 he attended the Polytechnic School in Munich, where he studied thermodynamics. There he was exposed to the concept of compression ignition, where air in a cylinder could be compressed to raise its temperature enough to ignite a spray of injected fuel. He realized that this could be the basis for an internal combustion engine and began experimenting. After trying with pulverized coal, in October 1896 he got it right with a single-cylinder oil-burning engine that produced 25 horsepower.

About this time, Dr. Diesel became acquainted with Adolphus Busch of the Anheuser-Busch beer brewing company in St. Louis. Busch acquired the rights to Dr. Diesel's engine for production in North America. Busch installed the first American-made diesel engine, a 60-horsepower, two-cylinder A-frame, in his St. Louis brewery in January 1899.

In 1906, Dr. Diesel signed a contract with Sulzer Brothers of Winterthur, Switzerland, to develop an internal combustion "thermal" locomotive, and in 1911 Busch and Sulzer set up the Busch-Sulzer Brothers Diesel Engine Company in St. Louis.

Meanwhile, Dr. Diesel was in deteriorating health, and his European ventures were not going well. On September 29, 1913, he departed Antwerp for London on the steamship *Dresden*. When the ship docked in England the next morning, Dr. Diesel was missing. His body was found in the sea 10 days later.

Previous pages: After numerous experiments with turning gas-electric motor cars into freight-hauling locomotives, Alco and General Electric produced a 300-horsepower diesel-electric powered by an Ingersoll-Rand diesel engine. Central Railroad of New Jersey 1000, outshopped in July 1925 and now on display in the B&O Museum in Baltimore, went into the history books as the first commercially successful diesel-electric locomotive. Many similar units went into service over the next four years. *Jim Boyd photo*

But Rudolf Diesel had made his mark, as his name would be forever associated with the compression-ignition engine. Other designers and companies would modify and perfect the engines, but probably the greatest honor to Dr. Diesel was that the name became so generic that the capital "D" was dropped in the English dictionary.

Gas-Electrics

In 1862, Frenchman Alphonse Deau de Rochas came up with the concept for the four-stroke combustion cycle that in the summer of 1877 Nicolaus August Otto of Deutz, Germany, turned into the first successful spark-ignition gasoline engine. Germans Gottlieb Daimler and Karl Benz applied that technology to the first automobile in 1884. Between Daimler-Benz and Rudolf Diesel, the twentieth-century internal combustion revolution was off to a sputtering start.

It was a gasoline engine and not a diesel that was first mated to an electric generator and traction motors in a piece of railroad equipment. At the turn of the century, General Electric was developing self-propelled passenger cars that had a gasoline engine driving a DC generator to supply electricity to a single power truck with two nose-hung traction motors.

In 1910, a 25-year-old self-educated machinist and electrician from Seattle, Richard M. Dilworth, went to work as a field-service man for GE, helping to keep those temperamental gas-electrics generating revenue for the customers. Dilworth was fascinated by the concept of an internal combustion engine turning an electric generator for traction motors, and he was quoted at the time as saying, "I swore a terrible oath that I was going to stay with that kind of motive power until it was pulling the *20th Century Limited*." It was prophetic, indeed.

In the next few years, GE outshopped 85 motor cars before it began to back away from that market to refocus on heavy main-line electrification. By 1915, GE had decided that the gas-electric motor car was a lost cause. The price of gasoline had skyrocketed to 15 cents a gallon, rendering them uneconomical.

Before the bottom dropped out, Dilworth moved back to the plant in Erie, Pennsylvania, and got involved in developing diesel engines for GE. In his typical fashion, he spent his time on the production floor, manufacturing solutions to problems and not theorizing them on paper.

In the GE motor cars, the biggest problem was the complex control system that required a throttle for the gas engine and a separate control to load the generator. In 1916, Dilworth's friend and colleague, GE electrical engineer Hermann Lemp, developed a single-lever control system that put an electro-mechanical governor on the fuel throttle to coordinate the generator field excitation with engine rpm. In its basic form, the

The Secret of the Traction Motor

The key to the success of both electrics and diesel-electrics was the traction motor that was geared to the driving wheels. The secret to the traction motor is found in the most basic of the mathematical formulas for electric power: W=VxA. Watts equal volts times amps. In locomotive practice, watts is the power available from the overhead wire or the capacity of the diesel engine and its generator. In diesel practice, the size of the diesel engine limits the potential watts to a finite number. Volts represent speed, while amps represent pulling power.

When you plug any real number into the watts side of the formula and set the speed (volts) at zero, the resulting pulling power (amps) is infinite. Thus the electric traction motor has its greatest power potential when it's standing still. As the speed begins to increase, the amps drop from infinity to real numbers that combine with the speed to equal the power of the diesel engine.

In real performance, a diesel-electric can exert its greatest pulling power just as soon as it starts moving, and that ability to pull is limited only by the weight and adhesion of the locomotive. Notice that a diesel will start a train with a gradual application of power and then rev the diesel as the speed picks up.

In the cab, the engineer will be watching an ammeter that indicates how hard the locomotive is pulling. A typical road diesel will "peg" at about 1,200 amps. As the speed picks up, the ammeter will begin to drop back as that volts number gets bigger. The engineer will then gradually open the throttle to keep the ammeter around 1,100 amps. When the throttle is wide open and the speed continues to increase, the ammeter will begin to drop down once the maximum output has been reached. Depending on the weight of the train and the power of the locomotive, the speed will ultimately flatten out when the speed and amps combine to match the output of the wide-open diesel engine and generator.

If you want to go faster, you need to increase the watts available, and that is done by adding more locomotives. This is why a 1,200-horsepower switch engine can shove a 100-car train slowly around the yard, but it takes four 3,600-horsepower road units to get it up to 70 miles per hour and keep it moving.

This is where the diesel-electric forever outperformed even the finest steam locomotives. With everything static when standing still, the steam engine could not generate any power until it actually started to move (the standing diesel-electric, by contrast was already thriving with kinetic energy as the diesel engine and generator were creating potential power just waiting to be applied to the rails). The steam locomotive began its power curve at zero and had to climb upward as the machinery began to rotate and move the train.

To overcome this starting problem, steam engineers often had to back up and "take slack" to be able to jerk the train into motion as the steam began to work. As the speed picked up, the steam engine would increase in pulling power until it hit its horsepower range determined by the size of the drivers and cylinders and the capacity of the boiler. Thus the steam engine gained power as its speed increased, while the diesel-electric was losing power as its speed increased. Fortunately for the diesel, the vast majority of railroad work was done in that low speed range where it had the advantage. In the 1940s, a modern steam engine, like a 4-8-4, could often outpull a four-unit 6,000-horsepower diesel set at 60 miles per hour—but at any lower speeds, the diesel could dramatically outperform the steam engine.

The diesel's victory over steam was legitimate for a variety of reasons, but it was that W=VxA formula that ultimately put steam in its grave.

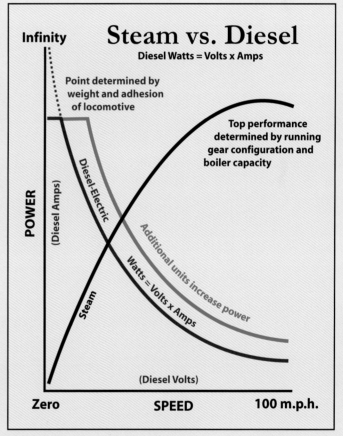

Steam vs. diesel chart drawn by Jim Boyd

Lemp system made possible the automatic performance controls for diesel-electric locomotives.

If the gas-electric system could power a passenger coach, why couldn't it be applied to a free-standing freight locomotive? By 1913, the Minneapolis, St. Paul, Rochester & Dubuque Electric Traction Company (better known as the Dan Patch Line, after its owner's racehorse) was running its passenger service with 15 GE gas-electric motor cars. On July 2, 1913, GE delivered to the Dan Patch the first internal combustion locomotive in America. No. 100, the 36-foot, 57-ton Boxcab, rode on two two-motor trucks and carried two 175-horsepower V-8 gas engines and generators in its carbody, which was built

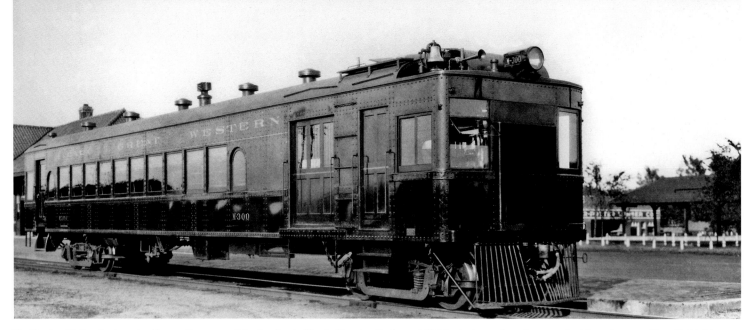

The Electro-Motive Engineering Corporation opened its storefront office in Cleveland in August 1922 to design and service gas-electric motor cars. Since it didn't have a factory, Electro-Motive contracted with a car builder, engine manufacturer, and electrical supplier to build the cars. Its first product was Chicago Great Western M-300 in the summer of 1924. Built by St. Louis Car with a Winton gas engine and GE electrical gear, it was quite successful. *EMD photo*

by the Wason Car Company of Massachusetts. The 100 had a long career, winding up on the Minneapolis, Anoka & Cuyuna Range industrial switching line in the 1960s. Rebuilt with diesels, it is a serviceable museum piece today.

In the next decade, GE pioneered internal combustion locomotive technology, teaming up with the American Locomotive Company for carbodies and engine-builder Ingersoll-Rand. Utilizing straight-electric locomotive technology, in July 1925 the Alco/GE/I-R team delivered Boxcab switcher 1000 to the Central Railroad of New Jersey; it is recognized as America's first production diesel-electric locomotive. Many more of the 300-horsepower switchers were soon working all across the country.

The Legend of Electro-Motive

In the first decades of the twentieth century, gas-electric motor cars had become a big business for GE and a variety of smaller builders. One of those was created on August 21, 1922, by Harold L. Hamilton and Paul Turner in Cleveland, Ohio. Their Electro-Motive Engineering Corporation would design and market gas-electric motor cars without actually manufacturing them. Hamilton would contract with carbuilders (most frequently the St. Louis Car Company) and equipment suppliers (including General Electric) to create the cars that his company would market and service.

Electro-Motive got off to such an auspicious beginning that its first stenographer in the Cleveland office left at lunchtime and never returned, observing that " . . . these blue-sky companies start and fizzle out in no time." She didn't even bother to collect her paycheck and told Hamilton that she would ". . . donate it to the company—they may need it!"

Even without her services, the renamed Electro-Motive Company (EMC) delivered Chicago Great Western motor car M-300 in the summer of 1924. It was built by St. Louis Car Company and was powered by a 175-horsepower gasoline engine from Cleveland neighbor Winton Engine Co. and GE electrical equipment, complete with the simplified Lemp control system that had not been available to the earlier GE cars.

In the 1920s, Henry Ford's automobiles were traveling the nation's rapidly spreading highways, and the railroad industry was ready for the economical "doodlebug" motor cars. Over the next eight years, EMC fielded 400 of its motor cars in a variety of passenger, mail, and baggage car configurations.

Following the lead of GE with its Alco/GE/I-R diesel switchers, between 1927 and 1929 EMC worked with the Rock Island to turn out similarly sized Boxcab freight locomotives powered by twin distillate engines. (Repowered with small diesels, many of these units remained in service into the mid-1960s.)

At this time, the GE liaison with EMC was Dick Dilworth, who liked Hamilton's attitude and dedication to the technology and the product. On January 1, 1928, Dilworth left GE to become chief engineer for Electro-Motive. Dilworth's common-sense engineering and hands-on work style served EMC well as gas-electric motor cars grew in size and popularity, with production hitting 400 units.

With the price of gasoline going up to 15 cents a gallon, the economic advantage of the motor car versus steam had been marginalized. The answer would be an engine that could burn three-cent-a-gallon distillate that was the leftover from gasoline and benzene production. This heavy "waste oil" was hard to atomize and ignite (requiring a carburetor for every two cylinders and four spark plugs per cylinder), but Dilworth and Winton soon worked out a cumbersome but powerful and reliable engine.

In 1931, the Santa Fe wanted a powerful baggage motor car that could pull conventional coaches. Dilworth and EMC went to work on the M-190, powered by a 900-horsepower Winton V-12 distillate engine. They incorporated in it two very significant firsts. The distillate engine was so heavy that it would require its own two-truck 22-foot power unit, but the short length forced them to put the fuel tank under the frame. Up to this time, all doodlebugs had their airbrakes laid out like a boxcar, with its one big actuating cylinder mounted on the underframe and linked to the trucks and brake beams by a system of rods. Putting the fuel tank under the M-190 would not leave room for the brake rigging. Dilworth suggested that they go with a number of smaller cylinders and just "drape them around" the power truck. It was a radical idea, but it worked beautifully and became a standard fixture on nearly all locomotives and passenger cars that would follow.

The second new concept applied to the M-190 was articulation, whereby the rear truck of the power car was moved aft and used to support the rear of the 22-foot power car and the front of the 60-foot baggage car. This eliminated one entire truck under the two-car set. This would lead directly to the articulated streamliners that would follow in the next few years. (In 1949, the M-190 was repowered with a 12-cylinder 567 engine and remained in revenue service until 1968 on passenger runs in New Mexico.)

The stock-market crash of 1929 and the onset of the Great Depression began to have its effect on the railroads and the market for motor cars. In the late 1920s, however, the Cleveland doodlebuggers, EMC and Winton, had attracted the attention of the burgeoning automotive giant General Motors, and on June 20, 1930, Winton was purchased by GM, and EMC joined the family on December 31.

Charles F. "Boss" Kettering of GM Research and his son Eugene began working with Winton to develop a powerful but lightweight diesel engine that would be suitable for marine and rail applications. (Boss Ket had just gone through an experience similar to Winton and EMC 10 years earlier when his Dayton Engineering Laboratory Company [DELCO] had been acquired by GM after he had developed the first electric starter and lighting system for automobiles. It was introduced on the 1912 Cadillac.)

After 397 more cars built since CGW M-300, Electro-Motive went to work on a big motor car for the Santa Fe that included a couple of significant firsts. It was the first articulated car to have the power unit and trailer pivot on a common center truck, and it was the first car to have its brake cylinders mounted directly on the trucks. The M-190 is at the California State Railroad Museum in May 1986. *Jim Boyd photo*

● As a color for the exterior of the new train, canary yellow was selected after exhaustive tests. It was chosen as an additional safety measure. Canary yellow can be seen for a greater distance than any other color and its blended combination with golden brown trim constitutes one of the outstanding features of the train.

SUPER SPEED—WITH SAFETY—AND COMFORT

In a Depression-era quest for a headline-grabbing new train, the Union Pacific, Electro-Motive, and Pullman-Standard teamed up on an articulated trainset, initially known simply as *The Streamliner*. The four-car M-10000, powered by a Winton distillate spark-ignition engine, debuted on February 25, 1934, and sprinted at 111 miles per hour en route to the Century of Progress world's fair in Chicago. It later entered service in Kansas as the *City of Salina. Union Pacific brochure artwork*

The Winton 201 was a welded-block two-stroke-cycle diesel with power assemblies (cylinder cooling jackets, liners, heads, and pistons) that could be removed individually for maintenance, in contrast to the massive cast-iron engine blocks that were standard for the day. But the secret to the 201 was the unit injector, a precision-machined device about the size of a Coke bottle, inserted in the cylinder head that measured the fuel and squirted it under very high pressure into the cylinder at the top of the compression stroke. The 201 was very powerful and smooth-running.

General Motors wanted a high-profile presence at the Century of Progress Exhibition world's fair in Chicago in 1933, and it decided to power its entire exhibit with two Winton 201 600-horsepower inline eight-cylinder engine and generator sets. These engines impressed one very significant future customer, the Chicago, Burlington & Quincy's President Ralph Budd.

Feeling the effects of the Depression, the railroads were looking for novel ways to attract business, and speed became a fixation. With extensive experience with gas-electric motor cars, both the CB&Q and Union Pacific were looking at internal combustion for new lightweight streamlined trains that could be debuted at the Century of Progress fair. Both opted for three-car articulated trains that were to be powered by the 600-horsepower Winton 201A engines. Since neither Winton nor EMC had an assembly plant, the trains were contracted to be constructed by the car builders. The Union Pacific went with an aluminum train built by Pullman Car & Manufacturing, while the CB&Q went with a stainless-steel set built by Edward G. Budd of Philadelphia (distantly related to CB&Q President Ralph Budd). The UP M-10000 and Burlington *Zephyr* were roughly the same size but quite different in appearance. The UP power car had a turret cab perched above a bulbous radiator nose, and the train was painted Armour yellow with brown trim. The *Zephyr*, on the other hand, had a smaller radiator mounted above a sweep of windows, and the whole thing was in gleaming silver stainless steel. Both trains were, of course, air-conditioned.

Eager to be the first on the road, the UP decided not to wait for the first 201A diesel engine and went instead for a readily available distillate engine (history would never forgive this unfortunate decision). The M-10000 rolled out on February 25, 1934, and immediately made headlines by hitting 111 miles per hour on test runs before going on display at the Chicago fair.

Burlington *Zephyr* 9900 came out of the Budd Plant on April 9, 1934, with the intended 600-horsepower Winton 201A inline eight-cylinder diesel engine and entered the history books as America's first diesel-electric passenger train. It easily topped 100 miles per hour heading west on the Pennsylvania Railroad across Indiana. And the 9900 went to the Century of Progress Exposition in style on May 26, 1934, by making a nonstop 1,015.4-mile sprint from Denver to Chicago in 13 hours, 4 minutes and 58 seconds, averaging 77.61 miles per hour (scheduled time for the *Exposition Flyer* behind a 4-6-4 was 27 hours!).

The M-10000 went into service as *The Streamliner* (later the *City of Salina*), shuttling between Kansas City and Salina (187 miles) and Topeka (68 miles), Kansas. It had a relatively short career, however, and was retired on December 16, 1941, and subsequently scrapped. The 9900, later dubbed the *Pioneer*

Zephyr, remained in service on various routes until being retired from the Lincoln–St. Joseph, Nebraska, runs on March 20, 1960, and was subsequently preserved at Chicago's Museum of Science and Industry.

The UP followed the M-10000 with the M-10001 in October 1934. This *City of Portland* articulated train had a 900-horsepower V-12 Winton 201A diesel power unit similar in appearance to the M-10000, plus a baggage/mail car, three Pullman sleeping cars, and a blind round-end coach buffet car. The Burlington got three more trainsets similar to the 9900 that went into service as the Chicago–Minneapolis *Twin Zephyrs* (9901–9902) and the Burlington–St. Louis *Mark Twain Zephyr* (9903). All the trainsets soon had a fourth car added. A fifth copy of the *Pioneer Zephyr* was the *Flying Yankee*, built for the

Boston & Maine and Maine Central in 1935 for daily round trips on the 345-mile run between Boston and Bangor, Maine.

A "Real" Passenger Diesel

Articulated trains were fun and flashy, but Dick Dilworth was still looking for a way to kick New York Central J3 4-6-4s off the *20th Century Limited*. Taking into account the typical weight and desired speed of such a main-line passenger train, Dilworth determined the weight of a locomotive he'd need for sufficient adhesion and then slide-rule calculated the horsepower that would be needed to achieve track speed. It would take 3,600 horsepower to do the job. He could achieve that with four 900-horsepower Winton 201A V-12 engines. Divide those into two 1,800-horsepower units, add

In 1934, EMC's Richard Dilworth built two 1,800-horsepower boxcab passenger units, each powered by two 900-horsepower Winton 201A diesel engines. The 3,600-horsepower pair could match the performance of a modern steam passenger engine. EMC 511 and 512 are at the Milwaukee Road passenger station in Milwaukee on October 8, 1935. The awkward machines led directly to the elegant E-units that followed in the next few years. *Milwaukee Road photo, MRHA archives*

After the B&O got a single duplicate of a Dilworth boxcab, the Santa Fe ordered two for its new all-Pullman *Super Chief*. Santa Fe Nos. 1 and 2 were built by St. Louis Car Company in September 1935 with cast, rather than fabricated, underframes and a modest attempt at streamlining the brow. The colorfully painted diesels were posed with a Santa Fe 4-6-2 shortly after delivery. *AT&SF photo, Kevin EuDaly collection*

multiple-unit control, and Dilworth had his 3,600-horsepower locomotive. General Motors agreed, and in the middle of the Great Depression in 1934, it gave him a half-million dollars to make it a reality.

With a design team consisting of only himself and two draftsmen, Dilworth created the world's first true high-speed diesel-electric passenger locomotive. In his common-sense approach to keeping things simple, Dilworth assembled available and proven components into a plain Boxcab carbody

riding on two four-wheel trucks, each carrying two DC traction motors. There was nothing really new in the locomotive except the overall package. Since neither EMC nor Winton had a shop big enough to produce the carbodies, Boxcabs 511 and 512 (using their EMC construction numbers as road numbers) rolled out of the General Electric plant at Erie, Pennsylvania, in June 1935. GE had supplied the electrical equipment for the units, and not surprisingly, they looked a lot like a typical GE straight-electric Boxcab.

In 1934, EMC's Richard Dilworth built two 1,800-horsepower boxcab passenger units, each powered by two 900-horsepower Winton 201A diesel engines. The 3,600-horsepower pair could match the performance of a modern steam passenger engine. The awkward machines led directly to the elegant E-units that followed. The prototypes were never sold, but the 511 was painted silver and leased to the CB&Q in 1936–1937 to augment the *Twin Zephyrs*. On October 27, 1936, it was with *Denver Zephyr* 9906A, *Silver King*, at the west end of the Aurora, Illinois, passenger station. *L. E. Griffith photo*

In August 1935, GE outshopped a third Dilworth Boxcab that was the first to be delivered to a customer. The Baltimore & Ohio had just completed two new streamlined passenger trains and two new steam locomotives to power them. The 4-4-4 No. 1, *Lady Baltimore*, and 4-6-4 No. 2, *Lord Baltimore*, were modern and distinctive machines. One trainset went into Washington–New York service as the *Royal Blue*, while the other was assigned to the B&O-controlled Alton Route for service between Chicago and St. Louis as the *Abraham Lincoln*. The B&O diesel Boxcab 50 worked both runs and was then permanently assigned to the *Abe*.

In a famous quote, Dilworth summed up the Boxcabs: "The 511 and 512 proved that a diesel locomotive couldn't be built and it wouldn't run—but when it did run, it would pull a train."

Responding to its archrival Union Pacific's vest-pocket articulated trains, the Atchison, Topeka & Santa Fe decided to go big-time with a Chicago–Los Angeles first-class train with Budd-built stainless-steel sleeping cars. To power the new *Super Chief*, in September 1935 the Santa Fe received

In addition to its passenger units, in 1936 EMC introduced a line of standard switchers with Winton 201A engines. The Missouri Pacific was an early sampler of nearly all builders and bought four 201A-powered SC switchers built in July 1937, including No. 9000, pictured in St. Louis, Missouri, on April 20, 1948. This particular locomotive was later re-engined by EMD with a 12-567B and designated as an SCm. *Kevin EuDaly collection*

Between July 1937 and March 1938, the Santa Fe got three E1A–E1B cab-and-booster sets from EMC. The classic red, yellow, and silver warbonnet paint scheme was developed by General Motors artist Leland Knickerbocker and utilized the Southwest Native American motif used throughout the *Super Chief*. The train, with its new stainless-steel consist, is eastbound down Edelstein Hill at Chillicothe, Illinois, in 1937. In 1938, the Santa Fe got six more E1As and one more E1B. *Santa Fe photo*

two semistreamlined Dilworth Boxcabs built by the St. Louis Car Company with cast, rather than welded, underframes. The Super Chief was the first full-sized passenger train to be designed for and operated by diesel power.

The power of the Boxcabs appealed to the Burlington, which ordered four more *Zephyrs* as free-standing locomotives packing the same 1,800-horsepower twin V-12 Winton 201A powerplants. The 9904 and 9905, *Pegasus* and *Zephyrus*, outshopped by Budd in Philadelphia in December 1935, were assigned to the new six-car articulated *Twin Zephyrs*. Meanwhile, Budd was assembling two new 10-car consists for the overnight *Denver Zephyrs* that included sleeping cars. Two more shovel-nosed, twin-engine 1,800-horsepower units, 9906A and 9907A, *Silver King* and *Silver Knight*, were built in December 1936 and were mated with the first booster units, cabless 9906B and 9907B, *Silver Queen* and *Silver Princess*. The boosters were unique in each having a single 1,200-horsepower V-16 201A engine.

The success and potential of the *Zephyrs* and Boxcabs, and the persuasion and salesmanship of Dick Dilworth and Hal Hamilton, got GM to allocate 6 million Depression dollars for the building of a new diesel locomotive factory at La Grange, Illinois, a western suburb of Chicago. Locomotive production commenced at La Grange in late 1935. (Interestingly, while EMC had its post office address in La Grange, the plant itself occupied nearly all of the adjacent suburb of McCook.)

While Dilworth was focusing on his main-line passenger units, EMC had been using the Winton 201A diesel engines in a variety of freight switchers. The first units to come off the La Grange production line were actually EMC's new standard 600-horsepower and 1,000-horsepower end-cab switch engines.

With the new factory at his disposal, Dilworth teamed up with the GM automotive Styling Section in Detroit to make a true marketable locomotive out of the Boxcabs. The 61-foot-long Boxcabs had the power and speed necessary to replace a steam engine on a conventional passenger train, but they had some problems. The four-wheel trucks would tend to "hunt" from side to side at high speed, and the up-front control cab meant that the locomotive crew would be the first to arrive at the scene of any accident. Also, the cross ties in the track passing right under the nose at speed had a hypnotic effect on the engineer.

Dilworth and the Styling team decided to move the cab up and back behind a rounded nose. But moving the cab required a total redesign of the platform, since it would force the front diesel engine back off the truck bolster. This would require a much stronger carbody frame to support the weight amidships. Thus the simple Boxcab-type framing was replaced with an underframe braced with heavy side trusses like a bridge. Since

two units would make up the typical road locomotive, the new EMC design would need only one cab, with the intention that they would usually run back-to-back.

For its power trucks, EMC had looked at existing passenger-car and steam locomotive tender trucks. Engineer Martin Blomberg got his name forever in the history books by adapting the General Steel Castings three-axle outside swing-hanger Commonwealth tender truck to a long-wheelbase A1A power truck with motors on the outer axles and a center idler. The outside swing hanger caused the locomotive to lean into a curve, and the Blomberg passenger truck gave a smooth and stable ride.

With the Boxcab innards spread out in the 68-foot truss frame, the Styling Section team, led by Leland Knickerbocker

In 1937, the Rock Island bought six four-car articulated trainsets for its new *Rocket* fleet. To power the trains, EMC took the 1,200-horsepower *Denver Zephyr* booster unit, with a Winton 201A V-16, and dropped on the nose developed for the E-units. EMC built six of the unique TA units, and one poses here for a heroic publicity portrait. EMC considered these units to be motor cars rather than locomotives. *Kevin EuDaly collection*

The Union Pacific wanted its first E-units to maintain the family look of the M-10000 and its early streamliner brethren, so EMC produced a custom bulbous nose for the two E2 cab units, SF-1 and LA-1, for the *City of San Francisco* and *City of Los Angeles*. The SF-1 is being serviced at West Oakland in 1938. It was jointly owned by the UP, C&NW, and SP. The three railroads handled the train between Chicago and Oakland. Railfan & Railroad Magazine *collection*

and stylist Christopher J. Klein (whose specialty was designing automobile hood ornaments!), wrapped the whole thing in a steel shell highlighted by a smooth slanted nose with a matching pilot. Combined with Blomberg's truck, it was one of the finest pieces of industrial design ever to grace the rails.

The first of the new EMC streamliners went to the Baltimore & Ohio. EA 51 joined pioneer Boxcab 50 on the B&O and the Alton. The EA designation indicated *E*ighteen-hundred horsepower and *A*-unit (cab carbody). The B&O got six cab-and-booster EA/EB sets delivered in 1937. Shortly thereafter,

the Santa Fe got three nearly identical cab-and-booster E1 sets, followed by five E1 cab units in 1938. For the Santa Fe, EMD stylist Leland Knickerbocker created one of the most famous diesel paint schemes of all time: the red, yellow, and silver warbonnet. The B&O and Santa Fe units (and E3 demonstrator 822) were the only slant-noses built with flush headlights.

At this time in 1937, the Rock Island wanted six power cars similar to the *Zephyrs* for its new lightweight *Rocket* fleet of four-car articulated trainsets. EMC took the *Denver Zephyr* 1,200-horsepower booster unit and added the cab and nose designed for the EA. The result was the Rock Island TA *Twelve-hundred-horsepower A*-unit). Three consecutively numbered and same-dated patents over the names of Leland Knickerbocker, Chris Klein, and Harold Hamilton cover the EA nose and cab design, the Santa Fe warbonnet paint scheme, and the RI *Rocket* TA paint scheme.

The next E-units were real oddballs. Back in 1935 and 1936, EMC and Pullman had produced a series of articulated trains for the *City of Los Angeles*, *City of San Francisco*, and *City of Portland*. The turret cabs had rounded bulbous noses with huge radiator grilles like the M-10000 *City of Salina*.

Seeking the new standard 1,800-horsepower E-units but wishing to maintain the image of its turret cabs, the UP took delivery in October 1937 of two A-B-B E2 sets for the *City of San Francisco* and *City of Los Angeles*. The E2 cabs replaced the slant nose with a round, bulbous nose and painted a turret cab on the unit with gray top trim sweeping down behind the cab and extending back (that fake turret cab scheme remains on UP units to this day!). The E2s were the last EMC passenger units built with Winton engines.

The 567 Engine

The Winton 201A was a good performer, but it had some shortcomings. With the new plant in La Grange, the GM Research and EMC engineers, headed by Gene Kettering, redesigned the 201A to make it more suitable for locomotive use and easier to manufacture. The result was the Model 567, reflecting its cubic-inch displacement per cylinder. It incorporated EMC's goals of standardization and parts interchangeability. The new 567 was introduced in three versions: the 600-horsepower V-6, the 1,000-horsepower V-12, and the 1,350-horsepower V-16.

The new 567 engine was tested and proven to be far superior to the Winton 201A. The production line was set up at La Grange, and the new diesel engine was available for placement in locomotives in October 1938. The first unit to get it was the E3 passenger demonstrator 822, with two V-12s yielding a 2,000-horsepower locomotive. In early 1939, EMC introduced its new 600-horsepower SW1 and 1,000-horsepower NW2 standard switchers with 567 engines.

"FT" For Freight

With the robust new 567 engine soon to be available, Dick Dilworth was ready for his ultimate goal: replacing steam in freight service. Just as the passenger unit had to equal the performance of a 4-6-4, Dilworth set out to make a freight locomotive that could outpull a 2-10-2. He calculated that four 1,350-horsepower 567s would give him a 5,400-horsepower package that would do the job.

The diesels were already causing labor unrest by making firemen unnecessary, and Dilworth had to create a locomotive that would not aggravate that situation any more than necessary. As a result, he laid out his freight diesel in two configurations, a two-unit set and a four-unit set.

The basic package would be a 48-foot carbody riding on two four-wheel trucks and carrying one 1,350-horsepower V-16 567 engine and DC generator set. He used a truss carbody similar to the E-units, but he moved the cab farther forward and put it behind a shorter rounded nose with a nearly vertical front. An early advertising campaign boasted that the FT was the "Bulldog of the Rails," and the FT nose became forever known as the "bulldog."

Once again, Martin Blomberg made a major contribution to the project by creating a four-wheel, two-motor freight truck with outside swing hangers that became the standard of the industry for the next 60-plus years.

Dilworth created a cab and booster that he semi-permanently joined together with a drawbar instead of a coupler, and to ensure that the labor unions could not claim it as two locomotives requiring two firemen, he did not put any starting batteries on the booster, so it could not be self-sustaining. The 5,400-horsepower set would be made up of back-to-back A-B sets—and some were even delivered to customers as a single drawbar-linked four-unit package with a single road number.

The unit was dubbed the FT (*Freight, T*wenty-seven-hundred horsepower). The steam railroads were skeptical, and the mechanical departments, accustomed to designing their own locomotives, were reluctant to welcome this diesel machine created by outsiders. To overcome this, in November 1939, La Grange outshopped the A-B-B-A demonstrator set with road number 103. As Dilworth had initially envisioned, it was two A-B sets.

In November 1939, the 103 went to work on the B&O, and in the next 11 months it worked numerous trips from coast to coast, performing on 20 railroads in 35 states and racking up 83,764 miles by October 1940. It outperformed every steam locomotive it encountered and sold to nearly every railroad that tried it. The FT 103 was probably the most successful salesman in railroad history.

Standardizing the Streamliners

Meanwhile, the 567 engine was ushering in a new family of passenger streamliners. After the UP bulb-nosed E2 experience, EMC wanted to standardize the 567 streamliner production on the slant-nosed E3. Demonstrator 822 was rolled out on September 13, 1938, with an eye on a sale to the Kansas City Southern to power the new *Southern Belle*. The 822 was a big

Wanting to maintain the family look ushered in earlier by the shovel-nosed *Zephyrs*, in 1940 the Chicago, Burlington & Quincy began taking delivery of E3s clad in stainless steel. These unique 2,000-horsepower units were designated E5s. Note the shovel-nose-style *Zephyr* "radiators" painted on either side of the headlight. The 9915B, *Silver Clipper*, is on all-stops Chicago–Denver local No. 7 on a dreary winter day in March 1962. *Jim Neubauer photo*

The Seaboard Air Line wanted to divide and combine the Miami and St. Petersburg sections of its trains at Wildwood, Florida, and needed nose doors that were not available in the earlier E-units. Thus the 14 SAL E4s of late 1938 had unique fold-up doors that made an ersatz vestibule with top and sides that was not noticeable when folded back. The 3008 is in Atlanta in 1937 in the GM-styled citrus livery. *David Salter photo, courtesy ACL&SAL Historical Society*

One of the more impressive paint schemes in North America was the Atlantic Coast Line's purple, gold, and silver, created by the General Motors Styling Section and introduced on the *Champion* in late 1939. The ACL had the nation's biggest fleet of 24 E3 and E6 passenger units. The 518, an E6, is southbound out of Atlanta, Georgia, on local 101 to Jacksonville, Florida, over the old Atlanta, Birmingham & Coast. *David Salter photo, courtesy ACL&SAL Historical Society*

hit on the KCS, which quickly bought the 822 and followed up with two more E3s in 1939 and 1940. The 822 was the only 567-powered streamliner to have the flush headlight of the Winton units. The new standard would have the headlight pulled up to make the lens vertical, and the 822 was so modified before being delivered to the KCS.

But before EMC could settle down with the off-the-shelf E3, it had to get a custom order out of the way. The Seaboard Air Line needed to split and combine trains at Wildwood, Florida, so that it could serve both Florida coasts and wanted a door in the nose so the units could be MU'd "elephant-style" nose-to-rear. Thus the E4 had a unique nose door with a top and sides that would swing upward to make an ersatz vestibule. This required a substantial modification, since the area behind the nose contained the water tank for the train-heating steam generator. The E4 cabs 3000–3013 were outshopped between October 1938 and December 1939, along with five boosters.

Production of the standard E3 finally got under way but lasted less than a year, delivering 13 cabs (UP, C&NW, Rock Island, KCS, AT&SF, MoPac, and ACL) and four boosters (UP, C&NW, and AT&SF). The last E3s were actually stainless-steel-clad E5s for the Chicago, Burlington & Quincy. The Burlington got seven cabs and five boosters between

March 1940 and June 1941, and subsidiaries Fort Worth & Denver and Colorado & Southern got one A-B set each in March 1940.

In April 1940, EMC made its first major change in the 567 engine by going from a dry sump to a wet sump oil system. The dry sump stored the lubricating oil outside the crankcase, and while that had its advantages in keeping the oil cleaner, it involved a lot of extra plumbing. The wet sump kept the full lube oil supply right in the bottom of the crankcase. Field research had revealed that the advantages of the dry sump were outweighed by the simplicity of the wet sump. The E3 with wet sump engines was reclassified E6.

The first E6s delivered were three cabs (12L–14L) and a booster (12A) for the Santa Fe in April 1940. The E6 was an immediate success, with orders ranging from two units (such as The Milwaukee Road) to entire fleets like the L&N's 16 cab units or the Atlantic Coast Line's 22 cabs and five boosters.

Meanwhile, on January 1, 1941, EMC and Winton were formally merged into GM to become the Electro-Motive Division of General Motors. With the power of GM's money, salesmanship, and advertising solidly behind it, EMD began to aggressively market and sell its switchers, streamliner locomotives, and FT freight units.

Alco's first twin-engine 2,000-horsepower passenger unit was the unique Rock Island DL-103b 624, built in January 1940. It was on the *Rocky Mountain Rocket* in the summer of 1940. It was powered by the same turbocharged six-cylinder engines as the 1,000-horsepower high-hood switchers. The Otto Kuhler–styled chisel nose and carbody were used on the subsequent Alco prewar passenger units (mostly DL-109s) that differed from the one-of-a-kind 624 in electrical and cooling systems. *Rock Island Technical Society Archives*

Diesels from the Steam Builders

While EMC was cobbling together motor cars in the 1920s using other people's factories, the two biggest builders of steam locomotives (Alco and Baldwin) were not ignoring the internal combustion interlopers—although their finest advances in steam technology were still ahead of them.

The American Locomotive Company (Alco) of Schenectady, New York, had a long relationship with General Electric, building the carbodies for straight electrics and the GE/Ingersoll-Rand Boxcab diesels. In 1927, however, GE set up its own fabricating shop in its plant at Erie, Pennsylvania, and no longer needed Alco.

Recognizing the future potential of the business, Alco began to produce its own diesel-electrics at Schenectady. To

Opposite: Steam builder American Locomotive Company (Alco) had been working with General Electric for many years building carbodies for electric locomotives and early diesels. In 1929, Alco bought engine builder McIntosh & Seymour and in 1931 introduced its own line of high-hood switchers. Kansas City Terminal HH900 No. 50, built in 1938, is at work in 1964 at Union Station beside EMC NW No. 61, built that same year but upgraded with a 567 engine in 1952. *Jim Boyd photo*

secure prime movers (diesel engines), in 1929 Alco bought engine-builder McIntosh & Seymour Corporation of Auburn, New York. After a few experimental units, in June 1931 Alco turned out the first of what would become its standard High-Hood models. For electrical equipment, the customer could specify either GE or Westinghouse gear.

In 1930, Westinghouse and Baldwin had broken away from the Boxcab format and introduced the idea of the high-visibility cab that utilized one cab instead of two and narrowed the carbody to a hood over the machinery to provide a view fore and aft. The Alco High Hoods (HH models) adopted this format with an end cab and running boards atop the frame on either side of the hood and crossover walkways on the end sills.

To power the HH units, Alco used the McIntosh & Seymour 531 engine, a massive cast-iron brute with pistons the size of wastebaskets, producing 600 horsepower from an inline eight-cylinder engine. Unlike the Winton 201A and EMD 567, the Alco engine was a four-stroke-cycle machine like an automobile gasoline engine.

In 1939, steam-builder Baldwin put its 1,000-horsepower De La Vergne eight-cylinder inline Model VO engine in the first of its standard VO 1000 switchers. Baldwin continued to build the nonturbocharged VO 1000s throughout World War II, with production totaling 548 units by 1946. Chicago, Burlington & Quincy No. 9369, working in Clyde Yard in Cicero, Illinois, in 1965, was a "War Baby" built in 1944. *Jim Boyd photo*

The HH units rode on a new truck designed by Alco Engineer James G. Blunt. The Blunt truck was a crude-looking affair, but it was extremely flexible and would perform on even the worst track. The HH Alcos were very successful and sold 78 units in the Depression years between 1931 and 1937 (while Alco was also cranking out 0-6-0 and 0-8-0 steam switchers). In 1937, Alco added an exhaust-driven turbocharger to increase the air-intake pressure and upped the 600-horsepower 531 engine to 900 horsepower. The Alco turbo used the hot exhaust from the cylinders to drive the turbine that compressed the intake air. With this, the engines first exhibited what would become an Alco characteristic: "turbo lag." As the throttle was opened, the 531 would snort to life and pour out an impressive plume of black smoke while the turbo spooled up to speed with a distinctive whistling sound, at which point the exhaust would clean up. At the other end, when idling, the governor

would allow the engine to almost stall before catching with a cough and sputtering back to life. You'd swear it was going to stall on the next stroke.

By the time production of the High Hoods ended, Alco had sold 177 of them. Responding to Baldwin and EMC—both had switchers with relatively low hoods—Alco redesigned its switchers in 1940. To create the new low profile, Alco moved the engine support rails on the engine from the bottom to up on the side, lowering the engine's crankcase down between the beams of the frame. With this new 539 engine, Alco offered the nonturbo 660-horsepower S-1 and the 1,000-horsepower turbocharged S-2 standard switchers, both riding on Blunt trucks.

Watching the dazzling success of the Electro-Motive streamliner locomotives, Alco considered its own 2,000-horsepower twin-engine passenger unit. In the six-cylinder 1,000-horsepower turbocharged 539 engine, Alco had a prime mover with the output of GM's 12-cylinder 567. General Steel Castings had an elegant long-wheelbase three-axle steam locomotive tender truck that could be easily adapted into an A1A power truck.

In 1939, Alco laid out two 1,000-horsepower engines on a 79-foot platform with both sets of cooling radiators grouped at the rear. With electrically driven cooling fans, traction motor blowers, and an air compressor, this DL-103b was a very electrically sophisticated machine. Alco's steam stylist Otto Kuhler was enlisted to design a carbody for the new unit, and he came up with a striking "chisel nose" with some distinctive trim details. The unit hit the road in December 1939 as Rock Island 624.

For the production units, Alco took a technological step backward by going with belt-driven fans and air compressors driven off each diesel engine. The front engine's radiator was moved amidships to facilitate the belt-driven fans. These next two units were delivered to the Gulf, Mobile & Ohio in September 1940. Orders soon followed for the Rock Island, Southern, Santa Fe, C&NW, Milwaukee, and New Haven for the standard model, later designated DL-109.

Over in Eddystone, Pennsylvania, on the south side of Philadelphia, Alco's steam archrival Baldwin had been working since 1925 on a couple of heavy diesel switchers that

looked like electric Boxcabs powered by Knudsen and Krupp engines. In 1928, it had teamed up with Westinghouse Electric to build a few diesel-electric switchers.

Baldwin entered the diesel switcher field on its own in 1937 with units that looked a lot like the Alco High Hoods and were powered by De La Vergne VO-series four-cycle engines yielding 660 horsepower from the inline six-cylinder and 900 horsepower from the inline eight-cylinder versions. In 1939, Baldwin placed the VO engine in what had become the typical end-cab, low-hood format, producing the VO 660 and VO 1000 switchers.

The Road-Switcher and War

In the quest for a switcher that could be equipped with a steam generator for passenger terminal work, in 1940 Alco stretched out the frame of its 1,000-horsepower S-2 switcher and mounted a short hood behind the cab. Instead of Blunt switcher trucks, the new unit rode on two new standard AAR Type B two-motor road trucks. The first RS-1 was shipped to the Rock Island in March 1941, and a production of a dozen units soon followed.

Then the Japanese changed everything when they bombed Pearl Harbor on December 7, 1941.

While the railroads had been nationalized under the USRA during World War I, that was not felt necessary in

In 1940, Alco created the first road-switcher when it extended the frame on its 1,000-horsepower switcher and put a boiler for passenger service in a short hood behind the cab. Road trucks replaced the more flexible switcher trucks. Thirteen RS-1s were built before World War II, and all were drafted by the U.S. Army for conversion into low-profile six-motors for use on Russia's Trans-Iranian Railway. Rock Island 746 and 747 were among the draftees. *Rock Island Technical Society Archives*

The only passenger units permitted to be built during World War II were the 60 New York, New Haven & Hartford Alco DL-109s, outshopped between 1941 and 1945, which were dual-service units. The 2,000-horsepower twin-engine units were used on the passenger fleet during the day and hauled freight overnight, often making a turn between New Haven and Maybrook, New York, over the Poughkeepsie Bridge. *New Haven photo*

1942; but to ensure that no resources would be wasted on unproven experiments, the War Production Board froze product catalogs of all the locomotive builders. The construction of new passenger locomotives, both steam and diesel, was forbidden. Baldwin was assigned to build diesel switchers, as was Alco. The 13 already-sold RS-1s were drafted from their new owners for military service on Russia's Trans-Iranian Railway. With its FTs already in customers' hands, EMD was given the exclusive right to build road freight diesels. Alco won an exemption for its DL-109, when it was recognized as a dual-service machine that could handle freight as well as passenger trains. The New Haven acquired the country's largest fleet of DL-109s by taking delivery of 60 units through April 1945.

New Haven General Superintendent Phillip H. Hatch observed, "They pulled the railroad through the war." The same could have been said of the Santa Fe's huge 320-unit fleet of EMD FTs.

The WPB restrictions didn't forbid research and development of new designs, but it severely limited the allocation of steel and materials to actually build them. This seriously frustrated Alco, which recognized that the future belonged to the road freight diesel. In 1941, the GM&O had signed a letter of intent with Alco to buy 20 1,500-horsepower freight units using the new 16-cylinder 241 engine, and the design work was under way when the war brought it nearly to a halt. In 1943, the WPB authorized Alco to build a three-unit demonstrator set, the A-B-A "Black Marias."

Alco and GE had entered a marketing agreement in 1940, and wartime technology changed things dramatically when GE developed a powerful turbocharger for the Lockheed P38 Lightning twin-engine fighter plane. The new turbo would let Alco get 1,500 horsepower out of a 12-cylinder instead of a 16-cylinder engine. The 241 was modified to handle the temperatures and pressures of the turbo and turned out in 1944 as the 244 engine.

The Black Marias, looking like small DL-109s with the Otto Kuhler chisel nose, hit the road in September 1945 with modified 241 engines, since the new 244s were not yet available. The units proved the platform layout and electrical design before the turbos fried the inadequate 241 engines.

Things were happening quickly at Schenectady and Erie, however, as the turbocharged 244 could get 2,000 horsepower out of one 16-cylinder engine, instead of needing two V-12s like EMD. At this time, GE was assembling 2,000-horsepower passenger units for newcomer Fairbanks-Morse, using its opposed-piston engine. General Electric home-appliance designer Ray Patten restyled the F-M unit with a squared-off nose to create the Alco 2,000-horsepower passenger PA.

This carbody was scaled down for the 1,500-horsepower FA developed from the Black Marias. Production on the GM&O order commenced in late 1945, and the first FA unit rolled out of the plant on January 9, 1946.

There was just one problem. The 244 engine, which was already installed in a customer's units, was only 81 days old! The first 244 had been completed on October 20, 1945, and had just finished its first 600-hour test period three weeks earlier (the normal test period for a new diesel engine is usually three *years*, not three weeks). The railroads, having seen the FTs during the war, wanted diesels as fast as they could get them, and Alco quickly filled its order books for the FAs. The units performed well for about three years before serious aging problems began to arise with the 244 engine (these would have shown up in a normal testing period).

Meanwhile, Alco burst onto the passenger diesel scene in October 1946 with its magnificent 2,000-horsepower PAs in the stunning Santa Fe warbonnet scheme (ironically, designed in 1938 by GM's Leland Knickerbocker). Like the FAs, the PAs found plenty of eager buyers from coast to coast, but they, too, began to get "244-itis" after a few years of service.

Eager to get into the freight business after the war, in 1943 Alco got permission to build an A-B-A set of 1,500-horsepower freight units. The "Black Marias" used obsolete 241 engines while Alco was rapidly developing the new 244 engine that could handle the powerful GE aircraft turbocharger. Planned for a 16-cylinder engine, the Black Marias got the same 1,500 horsepower from 12 cylinders with the turbocharger, though the turbochargers fried the inadequate 241 engines. *George Jepson photo,* Railfan & Railroad Magazine *collection*

The Black Marias had been prompted by an order placed by the Gulf, Mobile & Ohio before the war for 1,500-horsepower freight units. As soon as restrictions were lifted, Alco began production of FA-1s for the GM&O, although testing was far from complete on the new 244 engine. The 1,500-horsepower FAs performed well for the first few years, until some inherent flaws in the 244 began to show up as they racked up service mileage. *Kevin EuDaly collection*

The Diesel Sales Philosophy

Electro-Motive had made rapid progress in developing a line of off-the-shelf locomotives that could be used anywhere, because it had no history with its customers. The steam builders, on the other hand, were accustomed to working with the different railroads' mechanical departments in designing locomotives. And most of these mechanical departments had their own ideas on how locomotives, diesel or otherwise, should be built. Dick Dilworth dug in his heels and simply ignored the input, confident that he could design a better locomotive than any bickering committee.

Baldwin, on the other hand, in the shadow of one of the country's most powerful mechanical departments—the Pennsylvania Railroad—was led astray by too many steam-oriented men who were trying to buy diesels. The steam men couldn't get used to 1,350- or 1,500-horsepower "building blocks" but wanted really big locomotives like their prize steam monsters. Baldwin lost some valuable market time trying to make the Pennsy happy with a giant 6,000-horsepower passenger unit powered by eight V-8 engines and culminating in the 3,000-horsepower "Centipedes," packing two 1,500-horsepower engines and riding on a heavy articulated underframe like the GG1 electric but with eight driving wheels in a 2-D+D-2 wheel arrangement. The Pennsy bought 20 Centipedes, but they had rather short service lives. The Seaboard Air Line and National Railways of Mexico each bought 14 Centipedes, as well.

Trying to settle down to more conventional formats, Baldwin had more success with 2,000-horsepower twin-engine "Baby Face" passenger and 1,500-horsepower freight units after the war. But even here they got diverted. Unique in American railroading were the six double-ended Baby Face 2,000-horsepower passenger units used in commuter service by the Jersey Central.

When Alco presented GE with the 2,000-horsepower V-16 244 engine, it was in a hurry to replace the twin-engine DL-109. At that time, 1946, newcomer Fairbanks-Morse had its 2,000-horsepower "Erie-Built" passenger units on GE's Erie, Pennsylvania, erecting floor. Alco-GE designer Ray Patten adopted the F-M carbody for the similar-sized 244 engine and modified the nose and a few details to create the stunning PA-1. Santa Fe Erie-Built No. 90 (top) is at San Diego in the 1960s, while a set of PAs is in Kansas City in 1964 with Kansas City Terminal Alco S-2 switcher No. 59 and a whole fleet of yellow cab units (bottom). Note the similarity between the Erie-Built and PA in nose construction and the curved trim behind the cab doors. Ironically, both units wear the warbonnet livery designed for the EMC *Super Chief* E-1As by GM stylist Leland Knickerbocker. *J. R. Quinn collection, top; Jim Boyd photo, bottom*

The "Baby Face" carbody, introduced on the Centipedes in 1945, was applied to a variety of Baldwin passenger and freight units until 1949. The Central Railroad of New Jersey got five A-B-A sets of Baby Face DR-4-4-15 freight units in 1947. A pair of cab units is eastbound near Bloomsbury, New Jersey, in July 1965, headed for the High Bridge Branch. The CNJ also had four unique twin-engine, double-ended Baby Face passenger units on A1A trucks. *Jim Boyd photo*

Adopting heavy electric articulated running gear technology, in 1945 Baldwin produced the first of 54 2-D+D-2 twin-engined 3,000-horsepower Centipedes. The first 24 were built as passenger units for the Pennsylvania Railroad, though they were soon demoted to helpers on Horseshoe Curve. In 1945 and 1947, the Seaboard Air Line acquired a 14-unit fleet of Centipedes that fared reasonably well when assigned to Atlanta–Birmingham freight service. The new 4500 is in Jacksonville, Florida, in January 1946. *Harold K. Volkmer collection*

In 1948, Baldwin adopted the "Sharknose" styling of the Pennsy's T1 4-4-4-4 duplex steam engines to its twin-engine 2,000-horsepower passenger units. Only the Pennsy acquired these truly impressive units. Shortly thereafter, Baldwin scaled down the Shark carbody for its 1,500- and 1,600-horsepower freight units. The freight Sharks sold only to the Pennsy, New York Central, Baltimore & Ohio, and Elgin, Joliet & Eastern. (Many of the NYC units ended up on the Monon-gahela Railway, and the only survivors were two NYC/Monongahela units that went to the Delaware & Hudson in August 1974.)

Baldwin's real success, however, was in enlarging its switchers into 1,500-horsepower road-switchers, based on the general layout of the Alco RS-1. The Baldwin 1,500-horsepower DRS-6-4-1500, built in 1946 and riding on A1A trucks, was the first true road-switcher. It was soon followed with four-motor and six-motor versions, powered by four-cycle diesel engines.

The most impressive and successful Baldwin passenger units were the Pennsylvania Railroad's DR-6-4-20 "Sharks," shown here at Bay Head, New Jersey. The styling was based on the Pennsy's T1 4-4-4-4 duplex steam engines. The Pennsy had nine A-B-A sets, with each unit powered by two 606SC turbocharged 1,000-horsepower inline eight-cylinder engines. The Pennsy had the only passenger Sharks, but Baldwin also condensed the styling for a series of four-motor 1,500- and 1,600-horsepower freight Sharks. *Jim Boyd collection*

Following the format laid down by Alco's 1,000-horsepower RS-1, Baldwin produced the first full-sized road-switchers with the 1,500-horsepower DRS-6-4-15 in 1946. Norfolk Southern No. 1609, at Lillington, Virginia, in April 1973, has A1A trucks with center idler wheel sets to distribute weight on light rail, but Baldwin also built similar units with three- and four-motor trucks. The gutsy Baldwins were known for the pulling power of their rugged Westinghouse traction motors. *Jim Boyd photo*

Fairbanks-Morse and the "OP"

Fairbanks-Morse & Company was not a new name in railroading. Dating back to 1830, it was a manufacturer of heavy-duty mechanical platform scales. In 1885, the company diversified by marketing windmills to pump water for railroad water tanks, and over the years it replaced the windmills with internal combustion engines and electric motors but remained in the pump business. Already supplying the water for steam locomotives, it was logical that F-M would get into the business of building coaling towers. Seeking diesel engines for its pumps and coaling towers, in 1922 F-M hired an expert from De La Vergne and within a decade had developed a line of engines of various sizes.

During the 1930s, F-M had developed a lightweight two-cycle opposed-piston engine for the U.S. Navy to use in submarines. The OP engine had vertical cylinders with a crankshaft at both top and bottom and pistons from each that were timed to meet in the center, where the fuel was injected to ignite and drive them outward. The design completely eliminated cylinder heads and valves and used side ports (like the EMD 567) for both intake and exhaust.

In 1939, F-M produced 800-horsepower, five-cylinder, two-cycle opposed-piston engines for six motor cars for the Southern Railway that were quite successful. During the war, the navy took all the OP engines that F-M could produce at its plant in Beloit, Wisconsin. Based on the success

During World War II, Fairbanks-Morse of Beloit, Wisconsin, produced a lightweight and powerful two-cycle engine with opposed pistons for American submarines. In 1943, the War Production Board authorized F-M to apply its 1,000-horsepower OP engine to a locomotive. The first unit was Milwaukee Road H-10-44 1802, later renumbered 760. That unit is parked in Janesville, Wisconsin, with protective cardboard over the windows on June 26, 1993. The historic unit is preserved today at the Illinois Railway Museum. *Andy Smith photo*

Fairbanks-Morse produced a successful line of switchers, and after the war it offered the Consolidation Line of freight and passenger units in a variety of engine sizes. The Canadian National had six CPA-16-5s with an unusual B-A1A wheel arrangement. In September 1965, the 6703, built in 1954 under license by the Canadian Locomotive Company in Kingston, Ontario, is teamed up with a Montreal Locomotive Works Alco FPA-4 on Windsor to Toronto No. 106 at London, Ontario. *Jim Boyd photo*

of the submarine engines, in 1943 the WPB gave F-M permission to apply the OP to a switching locomotive. Using a GSC cast underframe, Westinghouse electrical gear, and a 1,000-horsepower six-cylinder OP engine, F-M outshopped The Milwaukee Road 1802 (later renumbered 760) on August 8, 1944, in a handsome carbody styled by Raymond Loewy.

With the 10-cylinder OP yielding 2,000 horsepower, F-M was eager to compete with EMD and Alco in the passenger diesel market. It teamed up with General Electric to build a big unit riding on A1A trucks, like its rivals. Since the Beloit plant could not accommodate such a large carbody, the units

were constructed at the GE plant in Erie, Pennsylvania, and the units became known simply as Erie-Builts.

With their units on the floor in Erie, F-M unsuspectingly provided archrival (and GE marketing partner) Alco with the basic package for its new turbocharged 2,000-horsepower Model 244 engine. GE stylist Ray Patten retained the basic carbody of the Erie-Built and made some relatively minor styling changes to create Alco's best-selling PA. Over the next few years, F-M would market a full line of switchers, road-switchers, and Consolidation Line freight cab units (C-Liners), in addition to the Erie-Built.

When production of passenger units resumed in February 1945, EMD resolved some of the issues with the slant-noses with the 2,000-horsepower E7 that sported the FT-style "bulldog" nose. Although it retained the belt-and-pulley internal cooling fans and auxiliaries, the E7 became EMD's best-selling E-unit, with 428 cabs and 82 boosters produced. Milwaukee Road No.19B is at the Milwaukee diesel shop in July 1965. Note the venting boiler for steam-heated and air-conditioned passenger cars. *Jim Boyd photo*

Postwar Prosperity

Wartime service proved the value of the diesel-electric to even the most skeptical steam operators, and orders flooded all the builders. EMD cleaned up the machinery inside the FT by replacing the mechanical belt-driven cooling fans with "drop-in and wire-up" electric fans to create the new F3 at 1,500 horsepower. The E6 lost its long slanted nose as the cab was moved forward and placed behind an FT-style "bulldog" nose on the new E7. The primary reason for that change was to move the train-heating steam boiler water from the nose tank to a new position amidships by the fuel tank. In the slant-noses, the front truck would lose adhesion and get slippery as the boiler water was used up, lightening the nose. Also, this permitted an inward-opening nose door to become standard.

Over at Alco, the GE P38 aircraft turbocharger and 244 engine put the 1,500-horsepower freight FA and 2,000-horsepower PA solidly on the market. Alco also extrapolated its 1,000-horsepower RS-1 into a true road-switcher by replacing the 539 engine with the 1,500-horsepower 244 in the new RS-2 of 1946, with road trucks and full track speed capability. Baldwin and Fairbanks-Morse marketed similar catalogs.

182   Chapter 6

In October 1946, Alco created the grown-up version of the 1,000-horsepower RS-1 when it put the 1,500-horsepower 244 engine on a road-switcher format. In 1950, the horsepower was bumped up to 1,600 in the RS-3 that ultimately sold 1,363 units. Two Monon RS-3s are in charge of northbound train 40 at Harrodsburg, Indiana, on April 20, 1963. The RS-3s were most commonly set up long-hood forward. *James F. EuDaly photo*

Six-Motors

During the war, both Alco and EMD got involved in developing military road-switchers with low profiles and light axle loadings that could be used almost anywhere in the world. The 13 prewar Alco RS-1s were drafted for military service on Russia's Trans-Iranian Railway and were converted to six-wheel trucks to spread their weight out.

These units had traction motors on each axle, and it was a controversial concept at the time. According to laws of physics laid down by no less than Leonardo da Vinci, the third motor per truck should have no advantage in pulling power, though common sense and practical observation proved the contrary. (Da Vinci's law says that the total weight, not the area of contact, affects the friction in moving an object.) The six-motor locomotive had 40 percent more pulling power than a four-motor of equivalent weight.

In 1947 and 1948, Dilworth went to Australia to help EMD-partner Clyde Engineering develop a main-line dual-service unit for the 1,100-mile Commonwealth Railroad. The Australian ML2 was essentially a standard EMD F-unit with a cab on each end and riding on six-wheel trucks. Taking the military three-motor truck, Martin Blomberg scaled it up into a robust three-motor, six-wheel FlexiCoil truck with even wheel spacing that became EMD's standard for the next half century.

In 1947, EMD's Dick Dilworth was in Australia helping subsidiary Clyde Engineering develop a double-ended road locomotive for the Commonwealth Railroad. For the Australian ML2, Martin Blomberg scaled up the military MRS-1 six-wheel, three-motor truck into a heavy-duty FlexiCoil truck that was used with great success on EMD's six-motor road-switchers. Chicago & North Western 1,750-horsepower SD9 1723, riding on Blomberg's truck, is eastbound at Nelson, Illinois, on September 26, 1963. *Jim Boyd photo*

While the Cat's Away...

Following the war, the "covered-wagon" freight units were EMD's big money-makers, and the sales force promoted them heavily. By 1947, however, it was becoming obvious that the company needed a road-switcher in its catalog. With Dick Dilworth in Australia, the design team in La Grange set out to fill that need—"While the cat's away, the mice will play." Only these guys were more like the three blind mice.

Instead of starting with the 1,000-horsepower NW5 and building it up into a full-sized 1,500-horsepower road-switcher, they started with the F3 cab unit and tried to carve some visibility into it. In the "Branch Line" unit (a prototype BL1 and 58 production BL2s), they kept the high cab and bridge truss frame but narrowed the hood top to provide rearward visibility and added crossover walkways on the ends. The pinched hood top made for a very claustrophobic engine room. As one veteran mechanic at a BL2-owning railroad observed, "It's just an F3 with all the working space taken out of it."

Not only that, but it was a bear to manufacture. During the intense production crush of the war, EMD had worked out ways to modularize the F-units into subassemblies that were fabricated elsewhere and quickly put together on the High Bay erecting floor. The BL2 had to be "stick-built" on the floor, taking about six times longer than an F-unit. As one retired EMD exec put it, "A couple of BL2s on the floor could tie up the High Bay for weeks." Production of the BL2 began April 1948 and lasted only a year. The BL2 was actually a pretty good locomotive and saw both freight and passenger (B&M and C&O) service. The Rock Island used it in Chicago commuter service into the mid-1960s.

In the winter of 1946–1947, EMD produced 13 1,000-horsepower NW5 units, but for some reason the company was reluctant to promote it as a road-switcher like the highly successful Alco RS-1. The Great Northern had 10 NW5s, all of which made it onto the Burlington Northern roster after the merger in 1970. In November 1967, GN No. 186 is eastbound on the Hutchinson Branch, east of Minneapolis, Minnesota. *Jim Boyd photo*

In 1947, EMD tried to create a road-switcher by carving front and rear visibility into an F3 cab unit. The result was the disaster called the BL2 (*Branch Line*). It contained the same 1,500-horsepower 567 engine and electrical equipment but narrowed the hood above the engine, creating a very cramped engine room. End walkways made switching easier. Chesapeake & Ohio BL2 No. 82 is on the Pere Marquette at Grand Ledge, Michigan, on April 1, 1961. *Gene Huddleston photo*

Dilworth's Geep

As the BL2 fiasco was being played out, Dick Dilworth returned to La Grange, took one look at the BL2, and decided to "Do it right." Looking at the Alco and Baldwin road-switchers, he laid out the F3 machinery on a heavy fish-belly girder rather than truss underframe. He basically made a mid-cab switcher out of the F3. Steam men, accustomed to riding behind the "protection" of a long boiler, liked the idea of a high hood at each end of the cab, and the limited visibility of the high short hood almost mandated keeping the fireman to watch the left side, a serious labor consideration at the time.

Dilworth wanted his general-purpose unit to be at home "out where the real work was being done." He said that he wanted "to make a locomotive so ugly in appearance that no railroad would want it on the main line or anywhere near headquarters." Form followed function, and Dilworth's ugly unit turned out to be another simple masterpiece of industrial design.

Unlike the F-unit, where the diesel engine and heavy electrical equipment were trapped inside the truss sides and had to be removed through the top by a crane, the road-switcher platform had no side barriers. The hood was just a lightweight

When Dick Dilworth returned from Australia and discovered the BL2, he decided to "fix it" and set about designing the GP7. Instead of the truss carbody, he laid out the machinery on a flat fishbelly frame and covered it with a hood full of access doors. The 1,500-horsepower "Geep" was an overwhelming success. In September 1989, the very first GP7, C&NW 1518, a Monon BL2, and FT 103 are lined up in La Grange, Illinois. *Jim Boyd photo*

The last steam builder to get into the diesel business was the Lima Locomotive Works, which merged with engine-maker Hamilton in 1947 and began producing diesel switchers and road-switchers in 1949. New York Central the subsidiary Chicago River & Indiana had six Lima-Hamilton 1,200-horsepower switchers, built in 1951. The No. 8410 is at Western Avenue Junction in Chicago on June 16, 1964. The CR&I also had 21 800-horsepower Lima switchers. *Jim Boyd photo*

shell to keep the rain out, and it could be simply lifted out of the way for heavy maintenance.

One of F-unit's problems was that the engineer had to stick his head out the window to see backward, and in doing that he could often not reach the controls. To resolve this, Dilworth laid out a full-size cab in La Grange and brought in locomotive engineers to show him how they needed to work in both directions. As a result, he moved the controls from beneath the front window to a rectangular stand near the center, parallel to the side wall. Essentially, the engineer could ride with his back to the side window, facing the control stand, and look out either front or back with equal ease. For normal forward running, he'd simply turn his seat and run the locomotive with his left hand. The Association of American Railroads adopted Dilworth's design as the "AAR Standard Control Stand." The new GP (*General Purpose*) unit could be

Opposite: By the time Dick Dilworth retired as EMD's chief design engineer in 1952, his "terrible oath" of 1910 to see internal combustion engines replace steam on the *20th Century Limited* had been fulfilled, largely through his efforts. In 1964, the *Century* departs Chicago's La Salle Street Station behind E7s built in 1947. EMD Styling Section artwork shows proposed NYC E6s, but apparently the war postponed them until the E7 era. *Jim Boyd photo*

set up to consider either the long engine-room hood or short hood as forward, although the EMD demonstrator was set up short-hood forward.

By the time the GP was ready for production in October 1949, the F3 had been upgraded to the F7 in February 1949, thus Dilworth's road-switcher was introduced as the GP7. It has become universally known as the Geep (pronounced "Jeep"). Within a few years, the road-switcher format completely replaced cab units.

Dick Dilworth retired to his home in Hinsdale, Illinois, in 1952 at the age of 67. And every afternoon at 4:00, a dozen or so miles to the east, a set of his E7 diesels would accelerate out of La Salle Street Station with the *20th Century Limited*. His "terrible oath" from 1910 had been fulfilled.

The End of Steam

The Geep was the final nail in the coffin for steam. The last steam holdout, Lima Locomotive Works, merged with engine-maker Hamilton to become Lima-Hamilton in 1947. In 1949, it introduced a line of switchers and road-switchers using four-cycle six- and eight-cylinder turbocharged inline Hamilton engines and Westinghouse electrical equipment. The Pennsy was still making mischief, and the biggest units produced by Lima were twin-engine 2,500-horsepower six-motor center-cab "transfer" units in 1950, similar to those introduced by Baldwin back in 1946. As one would expect of the craftsmen at Lima, they were good units, but they were too few and too late. Lima was merged into Baldwin in October 1950, creating the Baldwin-Lima-Hamilton Corporation, and the Lima catalog was discontinued after a production run of only 174 units. Ironically, the last steam locomotives outshopped at Lima carried Lima-Hamilton builder's plates. The last was Nickel Plate 2-8-4 No. 779 on May 13, 1949, and Lima-Hamilton's first diesel was Nickel Plate 1,000-horsepower switcher No. 305 on June 29.

Alco terminated steam production in June 1948 with Pittsburgh & Lake Erie 2-8-4 No. 9406, and Baldwin wrapped it up with a World War I throwback Chesapeake & Ohio USRA compound 2-6-6-2, No. 1309, in September 1948. Interestingly, the last steam locomotive built new for a U.S. railroad was USRA copy 0-8-0 switcher No. 244 built by the Norfolk & Western's Roanoke Shop in December 1953.

The Frantic Fifties

The diesel builders—EMD, Alco, Baldwin, and F-M—spent the 1950s cranking out covered-wagon freight and passenger units, switchers, and road-switchers as fast as the erecting floors could satisfy the order books. Eager to replace steam, many customers took whatever they could get, resulting in some pretty chaotic rosters of mixed models and builders. Railroads that remained loyal to steam, such as the coal-hauling Norfolk & Western and Illinois Central, held off dieselization of freight service until the late 1950s and were able to build uniform and efficient diesel rosters. The IC, which had dieselized its passenger service early with EMD E-units, killed steam with EMD Geeps, while the N&W went with Geeps and Alco road-switchers. Keeping the models and makers to a minimum reduced maintenance by reducing the number of replacement parts in the shop stores. It was this parts problem that killed off most of the smaller builders as dieselization matured.

The diesel's primary advantage over steam was in vastly reduced manpower to keep them in service. A simple fuel

In the fall of 1945, Pennsylvania Railroad locomotive mechanic Bill Gardner was disappointed to learn that the new passenger engines that he was to care for at Harrisburg, Pennsylvania, were not the T1 4-4-4-4 duplex steam engines but an almost-orphan pair of E7 diesels. These were the Pennsy's first passenger diesels. Over the next six months, each racked up nearly as many miles as the entire 30-engine T1 fleet! Bill left the Pennsy and went to work for EMD. Pennsy E7s are at South Amboy, New Jersey, in August 1966. *Jim Boyd photo*

In 1953, Fairbanks-Morse introduced its 2,400-horsepower Train Master six-motor road-switcher, powered by its 12-cylinder opposed-piston engine. It set a new power threshold for a single-engine unit and found great success in the Appalachian coalfields on the Virginian Railway, in commuter service on the DL&W and Jersey Central in New Jersey, and on the Southern Pacific working out of San Francisco. Four Train Masters are lined up at the San Francisco terminal in October 1971. *Jim Boyd photo*

pump and a water hose could replace the huge coal chutes and water tanks every 20 or so miles. The bidirectional diesels could minimize the need for turntables and wyes.

And diesels could be run 24 hours a day without the need for roundhouse time to lubricate them and clean the fires. The term was availability. EMD service department executive Bill Gardner had started his railroad career as a mechanic with the Pennsylvania Railroad in the early 1940s, and he was very disappointed to learn that the new passenger engines he'd been assigned to in the fall of 1945 were not the T1 4-4-4-4 duplex steam engines but the first pair of EMD E7s. The diesels were assigned to the *Red Arrow* between Harrisburg, Pennsylvania, and Detroit. At that time, the Pennsy had no permanent diesel facilities. He could use the electric locomotive facility at Harrisburg that supplied diesel fuel for the GG1 electrics' steam boilers, and he set up a fuel tank car and pump at Mansfield, Ohio. The *Arrow* would make a night run to Mansfield, take fuel, and go to Detroit. The next night it would return to Mansfield, fuel again, and run to Harrisburg, a 1,266-mile round trip. After six months, the two E7s had each racked up 69,000 service miles, while in the same time period the highest-mileage 4-4-4-4 had logged only 2,800 miles—that's right, 2,800! Bill left the Pennsy and went to work for EMD.

The Second Generation

By the late 1950s, steam was dead or dying, and many of the older diesels were nearing their 12- to 15-year economic service lives. Also, the newer models were more efficient and easier to maintain. For the first time, it was becoming economical to replace diesels with new diesels. At this time, EMD had 85 percent of the domestic diesel-electric locomotive market.

Back in 1953, Fairbanks-Morse had introduced its massive 2,400-horsepower Train Master six-motor road-switcher powered by a 12-cylinder OP engine. Generally acknowledged as being ahead of its time, the H-24-66 sold 127 units for both freight and passenger service, but it gained lasting fame in commuter service on the Central Railroad of New Jersey and Southern Pacific. In the process, F-M boosted the threshold for six-motor units to 2,400 horsepower and four-motors to 2,000-horsepower.

In 1954, Alco responded with the DL-600 six-motor road-switcher pulling 2,250 and then 2,400 horsepower out of a 16-cylinder 244 engine. Only 17 units were built (for Santa Fe and Pennsy). Unfortunately, Alco was still plagued by "244-itis." The postwar engine had been rushed into service and was proving troublesome as it aged in the PAs, FAs, and RS-2 and RS-3 road-switchers. To resolve this, Alco went back to

After General Electric terminated its marketing agreement with Alco in 1953, it began to develop its own line of road locomotives. The first step was an A-B-B-A testbed set of stylish covered wagons in 1954. The Erie 750 set had four Cooper-Bessemer eight-cylinder engines, two rated at 1,200 horsepower and two at 1,800 horsepower. They are at Salamanca, New York, on July 2, 1956. They were repowered with 12-cylinder 2,000-horsepower engines and sold to the Union Pacific. *John D. Bartley photo, J. R. Quinn collection*

the drawing boards with a completely different engine, the 251, that solved most of the 244's problems of mechanical difficulties and water and oil leaks. The 251 was extensively tested and finally introduced as a production V-12 model in the 1,800-horsepower RS-11 in early 1956. The 251 would give Alco the engine it needed for future growth. The first step was to replace the 244 in the DL-600 with a 2,400-horsepower V-16 251, to produce the DL-600B in early 1956. In the next four years, Alco sold 87 DL-600Bs.

Alco and GE had been partners in the road locomotive business since 1940, but in 1953 they terminated the agreement. However, GE remained the exclusive supplier of Alco's electrical equipment.

In the 1950s, GE was setting its sights on building its own road units using the Cooper-Bessemer four-cycle engine. In 1954, GE produced a four-unit covered-wagon A-B-B-A test set that went to work on the Erie and Union Pacific. By starting with a clean slate, GE was able to make some significant advances in the layout of the equipment on the locomotive frame. One of GE's most significant improvements was a pressurized

The end result of GE's testing was the revolutionary 2,500-horsepower U25B, introduced with a high short hood in 1959. Powered by a turbocharged four-cycle Cooper-Bessemer FDL V-16 engine, the new "U-Boat" had a pressurized engine room and inertial air filters. Both EMD and Alco had to scramble to match those innovations. A demonstrator set with low-hood No. 2501 leading high-hood No. 2502 on June 5, 1962, shows off GE's new red and white demonstrator paint scheme, later adopted by the Frisco. *Kevin EuDaly collection*

EMD entered the second generation of diesel power when it introduced the turbocharged 2,400-horsepower SD24 in July 1958. The high-nosed six-motor unit carried a 16-cylinder 567 engine. The CB&Q got 16 SD24s delivered in the new Chinese Red livery. The 502 and 500 are bracketing a newer GP30 as they cross the Rock River at Oregon, Illinois, with westbound hotshot No. 97 in the summer of 1965. *Jim Boyd photo*

carbody to keep dirt out and the incorporation of a separate clean compartment for engine-breathing air. Inertial filters would clean the incoming air, whereas EMD and Alco units at that time used oil-bath filters in the carbody sides, and the engines inhaled their combustion air from within the often-dirty engine room. GE put all of its new engineering into the U25B "Universal" 2,500-horsepower road switcher in May 1959. The high-nosed unit sent shock waves through the industry. And the U25B quickly acquired the enduring nickname "U-Boat."

Meanwhile, EMD had been experimenting with turbocharging its 567 engine to boost the horsepower on its V-16 from 1,750 to 2,400. In July 1958, EMD applied the turbocharged 2,400-horsepower 567 engine to the standard six-motor 1,750-horsepower SD9 and created an immediate success. While the first of both models had high short hoods, the Alco DL-600B and EMD SD24 introduced the low short hood on units delivered within days of each other to the Santa Fe in May 1959.

The four-motor mate to the SD24 was the 2,000-horsepower turbocharged GP20 that hit the road in November 1959. Though a few were delivered with high short hoods, the standard GP20 was a low-nose unit. EMD was marketing the GP20 as a replacement unit for early F-units and pressed the concept of unit reduction, with three GP20s doing the work of four F-units. The U25B, SD24, and GP20 are generally regarded as the first second-generation units.

The GP20, SD24 and Alco DL-600Bs retained the older equipment layout with oil-bath carbody filters, while the new GE U25B was quickly proving the superiority of inertial filters. Responding to this, EMD redesigned the GP20 with a new air system, placing an inertial-filtered clean air compartment (the "cave of the winds") around the main generator and consolidating the cooling radiators at the rear of the unit. The engineers also moved all the electrical gear into one electrical cabinet immediately behind the cab. There was just one problem: all that gear required an electrical cabinet that was too tall for the GP20 carbody. The EMD stylists went to work and gave the GP30 a unique humped cab that gave the unit a very distinctive appearance that over the years has become a classic. The 2,250-horsepower GP30 had a production run of 948 units in only two years.

Scrambling to match the 2,500 horsepower of the increasingly popular GE U25B, EMD pushed the V-16 567 engine one step too far. The GP35 of October 1963, in a cleaned-up cab carbody, hit the 2,500-horsepower goal, but at

The Alco 2,400-horsepower DL-600B, like the EMD SD24, had been introduced as a high-nosed unit in February 1956, but in May 1959 the Santa Fe took delivery within days of each other the first low-nose SD24s and DL-600Bs. The long snout got the Alcos immediately dubbed "Alligators." On March 13, 1971, Alligator 9837 leads a Santa Fe eastbound at Emporia, Kansas, trailed by Alligators 9807 and 9817, and finally, SD24 4570. *Lee Berglund photo, Kevin EuDaly collection*

EMD followed up the SD24 with the 2,000-horsepower turbocharged GP20 in November 1959, putting an elegantly sloped low nose on the production units. The Santa Fe bought 75 GP20s in 1960 and 1961 that dominated the Chicago–Kansas City line because they were the only new units equipped with the Automatic Train Stop (ATS) equipment required at the time. Four GP20s are making 60 miles per hour on the bridge over the CB&Q at Cameron, Illinois, in October 1965. *Jim Boyd photo*

To compete with the GE U25B, EMD produced the 2,250-horsepower GP30 and 2,500-horsepower GP35 in 1961 and 1963, but they were not up to the job. In 1965, EMD introduced its new bored-out 645 engine and AC/DC electrical system on the 3,000-horsepower GP40. Wearing the brilliant Chessie System paint scheme, ex-B&O GP40 4207 leads a westbound freight at Prince, West Virginia, approaching Stretcher's Neck Tunnel in October 1981. *Wayne Carman photo, Kevin EuDaly collection*

the cost of mechanical and electrical complexity. To protect the DC electrical systems and still get a full speed range of performance, the GP35 had a 16-stage stepping relay driven by a bicycle chain. It was a mechanical and electrical monstrosity! The GP35 was an immediate popular seller (1,333 units in two years), but it soon became the unit EMD wished it had never built.

The 567 engine and DC generator had reached their limit in the GP35, and EMD was already working on a new engine and AC/DC alternator system to replace it. Wishing to keep the general dimensions and parts interchangeability of the 567 engine, EMD bored it out, increasing the piston diameter but retaining the stroke, crankshaft, and auxiliaries.

The new engine had a displacement of 645 cubic inches per cylinder and became known as the 645. The increased cylinder diameter was accomplished by narrowing the water jacket and keeping the outside dimensions exactly the same as the 567. As a result, a 645 power assembly could be dropped into any 567 engine. The smaller water jacket volume was compensated for by increasing the speed of the water flow and the size of the radiators.

The electrical problems were resolved in the new 645-powered 3,000-horsepower GP40 in November 1965 with an AC/DC electrical system based around the new AR10 main alternator that generated AC current. The alternator eliminated the DC generator's fragile commutator, and its slip rings could

Opposite and above: The primary sales point for the second generation of diesels was unit reduction, with fewer, more powerful units doing the same work as a greater number of older units. That concept was graphically illustrated on the Chicago Great Western in the 1960s with its eastbound mid-day freight No. 192 across northern Illinois. In September 1964, No. 192 is east of Holcomb with a perfect A-B-B-B-B-A set of F-units, totaling 9,000 horsepower (opposite top). In late summer 1963, the CGW bought eight GP30s, and four GP30s would often replace the six F-units, such as this set crossing The Milwaukee Road at Byron in 1964 (opposite bottom). The four 2,250-horsepower GP30s totaled 9,000 horsepower. In mid-1966, the CGW bought nine SD40s, and soon three SD40s, totaling 9,000 horsepower, replaced the four GP30s, as shown at Stillman Valley in September 1966 (above). Six F-units to three SD40s in three years: unit reduction at work! *All photos Jim Boyd*

handle a much higher current. Recent developments had produced solid-state high-current diodes that were not much bigger than an automobile spark plug. A series of diode bridge rectifiers mounted in the AR10 housing output the same DC current for the traction motors as a DC generator. This was a major step over the U25B, which had the rugged GE generator and traction motors but was still a pure DC machine.

The Horsepower Race

GE and Alco were quick to pick up the AC/DC systems, and the horsepower race was off and running. Baldwin had quit the race in 1956, and Fairbanks-Morse gave up in 1963, just as everyone else was beginning to match its 2,400-horsepower

Train Master. Steam was gone, and EMD, Alco, and GE were fighting each other to replace the first-generation diesels.

Alco had set the horsepower pace in 1963 with its 2,750-horsepower six-motor C-628 and had responded to the U25B with a series of new "Century" four-motor and six-motor units. Alco's disadvantage, however, was that it still depended on GE for its electrical equipment, and GE would never give Alco the newest gear that it was putting in its own locomotives. Alco had to make do with the previous year's models.

GE adopted the AC/DC systems and began marketing four-motor U30B and six-motor U30C units in the 3,000-horsepower range. The early GEs had their teething troubles, but the folks at Erie were quick learners and began producing

Above: Electro-Motive's ultimate weapon in the horsepower race was the 3,600-horsepower 20-cylinder 645 engine in the new SD45. The big SD45 was just what the industry was looking for, and sales were brisk, with 1,280 sold from December 1965 to December 1971, not including passenger, cowl, and Dash-2 versions. On September 7, 1985, Santa Fe SD45 No. 5401, wearing the brand-new "Kodachrome" paint scheme from the failed Santa Fe–Southern Pacific merger, pulls a priority train eastbound through Sullivan's Curve on Cajon Pass. A second SD45 trails the 5401, and the third unit is the cowled version—the F45. *James R. Doughty photo*

Opposite top: Alco jumped into the lead in the horsepower race in December 1963 when it introduced its 2,750-horsepower "Century 628," with its V-16 Model 251 engine and all the refinements encouraged by the U25B and rival EMD. Lehigh Valley "Snowbird" C-628 No. 625 is at the Lehighton, Pennsylvania, roundhouse in January 1973 in the company of 2,000-horsepower C-420s in Cornell red, yellow, and gray. The LV had quite a variety of diesel paint schemes. *Jim Boyd photo*

Opposite bottom: In spite of the modern 251 engine and all the other improvements, Alco could never seem to get rid of turbo lag when revving up the engine. The black smoke of raw fuel belches from a pair of Belt Railway of Chicago C-424s working at Clearing Yard in September 1987. As the hot exhaust gas caused the turbo to spool up, the smoke would clear up. *Jim Boyd photo*

more and more reliable and economical units. While EMD built its business around the two-stroke-cycle 645 engine, GE and Alco stayed with their lusty four-stroke-cycle FDL and 251 machines.

But EMD had one final trick up its sleeve: the 3,600-horsepower 20-cylinder 645 engine. In February 1965, EMD outshopped its first 3,600-horsepower SD45. This big baby was just what the railroads were looking for, and sales were brisk, especially to the Southern Pacific, which bought 356 of them! Even more popular, though, were the 3,000-horsepower V-16 four-motor GP40 and six-motor SD40, which were becoming the universal workhorses of American railroads in the late 1960s. For the railroads that wanted a simpler unit more akin to the reliable GP9, EMD offered the 2,000-horsepower nonturbocharged V-16 GP38 with either pure DC or AC/DC electricals. By this time, though, six-motors were outselling four-motor units.

In its insatiable quest for more powerful locomotives, the Union Pacific's decades of experimenting with turbines culminated in 1958 with 30 GE 8,500-horsepower "Big Blow" gas-turbine-electrics. In 1964, their horsepower was boosted to 10,000. In July 1965, turbine No. 7 and the only Alco C-855 booster howl uphill, westbound out of Omaha. *Jim Boyd photo*

Diesel Big Boys

While the Pennsy had been able to mess with Baldwin's mind and divert it into building custom big units, nobody could approach the Union Pacific in its desire for unlimited power. The UP and Alco had created the world's largest steam locomotive, the 4-8-8-4 Big Boy, in the 1940s, and UP wanted the same thing with traction motors.

Back in 1939, GE had produced two diesel-looking 2,500-horsepower steam-turbine-electrics for the UP, and in 1948 it turned to the jet engine to create a 4,500-horsepower gas-turbine-electric that rode on four two-motor trucks. In 1952, the UP ordered 10 similar units and followed in 1954 with 15 more. These turbines worked side by side with the steam Big Boys for a few years.

In 1958, just before the end of steam, the UP received from GE the first of 30 huge two-unit 8,500-horsepower gas-turbine-electrics. The "Big Blows" spread the horsepower out over four three-motor trucks. In 1964, the turbines were upped to 10,000 horsepower. These monsters could even be operated in multiple with diesels.

In 1963, the UP's chief mechanical officer, David Neuhart, outlined his desire for a 15,000-horsepower "locomotive" consisting of two or three units. And Neuhart had the authority to buy 'em!

In response, EMD, GE, and Alco packaged their existing locomotives into twin-engine freight units with eight traction motors. Alco and GE used the four-truck span bolsters like the earlier turbines, while EMD took a drastically different approach

The diesel horsepower pinnacle for Alco was a three-unit A-B-A C-855 set built in June 1964, each unit of which generated 5,500 horsepower from two 251C 16-cylinder engines, for a three-unit total of 16,500 horsepower. The units employed truck and span bolster assemblies from retired 4,500-horsepower gas-turbine electric locomotives. C-855 A-unit No. 60 sits with the only C-855 B-unit, No. 60B, awaiting the next assignment from Omaha in November 1966. The other A-unit was numbered 61, and all three units were retired in August 1970 and subsequently scrapped. *Kevin EuDaly collection*

Although GE and EMD built their 5,000-horsepower twin-engine U50s and DD35s in 1963 at the behest of the Union Pacific, the Southern Pacific came aboard for three of each as well. The U50 had a B+B-B+B wheel arrangement, and the UP bought 23; thus, with the additional three for the SP, the production total for the U50 was 26. There was no cabless version. SP U50 No. 9551 sits in glowing sunshine in Los Angeles on May 19, 1969. *Alan Miller photo, Kevin EuDaly collection*

The Union Pacific was sufficiently impressed with its 27 cabless DD35s that it returned to EMD in 1965 for 15 DD35As with cabs. To make room for the cabs, the radiators were shortened and flared outward on the DD35As. No. 75 leads this eastbound freight train at Lenwood, California, just outside of Barstow in January 1980. The Union Pacific yard at Yermo is where this train will stop for a crew change. *Kevin EuDaly collection*

In 1969, GE took the advances made in its conventional units to get 5,000 horsepower out of two V-12 engines instead of two V-16s, and the span bolsters were forsaken for two heavy six-wheel trucks on the new U50C. The noisy radiator fans were placed in the center of the unit, away from the cab. On May 6, 1975, U50C No. 5038 leads an N&W GP38 and a U30C on 91 cars leaving Kansas City, Kansas, at West Yard Junction westbound headed for the connection to the Nebraska main line at Gibbon, Nebraska. *Kevin EuDaly photo*

In May 1969, just in time to debut at the 100th anniversary ceremonies of the driving of the golden spike on May 10, 1869, EMD delivered to the Union Pacific the world's largest diesel-electric locomotive: the 6,600-horsepower DDA40X Centennial 6900. The UP got 47 of these twin-engined monsters in the next two years. Centennial No. 6910 heads east on August 16, 1984, with an auto train at Reno Junction, California, on the former Western Pacific main to Salt Lake City. *Alan Miller photo, Kevin EuDaly collection*

with a huge four-motor FlexiCoil truck. GE and EMD put two of their 2,500-horsepower U25B and GP35 V-16 powerplants on the frame, while Alco topped the horsepower chart at 5,500 horsepower with two of its 2,750-horsepower V-16s.

The Alco C-855 had a typical road-switcher cab and hood, while the GE U50 had a cab perched above an almost-vertical full-width nose. Again, EMD was the oddball, with its DD35 available only as a 5,000-horsepower booster unit with no cab. In the end, by 1965, Alco had sold the UP two C-855 cabs and one booster, and GE had sold 26 U50s. EMD sold the UP 30 boosters and an additional 15 units with cabs. The only double-diesels sold elsewhere were three DD35Bs and three U50s to the Southern Pacific.

Neuhart and the UP liked the big new units, and in 1969 GE followed up with the U50C, placing two 2,500-horsepower V-12s on a carbody riding on a pair of three-motor trucks. Then EMD upped the ante again in April 1969 with the 6,600-horsepower

The last steam builder left in the diesel business, Alco finally gave up the ghost in 1969, leaving its Canadian subsidiary MLW-Worthington to supply replacement parts and support for its existing products. The end was in sight at the historic American Locomotive Company plant at Schenectady, New York, in June 1968, with two ex-C&NW DL-640s and a wrecked Tennessee Central unit in the yard. The plant is used today by Super Steel to build locomotive carbodies. *Jim Boyd photo*

DDA40X, packing a pair of 3,300-horsepower 645 V-16s atop the four-motor trucks. The 47 DDA40X Centennials (named after the anniversary of the May 10, 1869, completion of the transcontinental railroad) were and are likely to remain the world's largest diesel-electric locomotives.

With the big GE and EMD diesels in revenue service, the fuel-hungry gas turbines were all retired by January 1970.

Refocusing on Economy

Alco dropped out of the locomotive business in 1969, and the Montreal Locomotive Works successor MLW-Worthington took over supporting and supplying parts for the existing Alco fleets. This left just EMD and GE to fight it out for the U.S. market.

Diesel-electric technology has always been a balancing act among cost, power, reliability, efficiency, and maintenance. In the early days, the extreme contrast with steam made almost any diesel look good, but as technology got better and time went on, different factors became more or less important.

EMD's all-time most popular locomotive was the SD40-2, with more than 4,000 units produced in a number of variations between 1971 and 1986. Among the largest fleets of SD40-2s was the Burlington Northern at 835 units. A solid set of four BN SD40-2s are seen here powering a westbound freight at Easton, Washington, climbing the Stampede Pass main line in March 1997. The Union Pacific had the second largest fleet, rostering 654 SD40-2s, and the Canadian Pacific was third, with 484. *Steve Jessup photo*

One of General Electric's most popular four-motor models was the B23-7, with 535 units built between 1977 and 1984. Conrail rostered 134 of them, such as the No. 2800, working a local freight at Danbury, Connecticut, in April 1986. The B23-7 had modular control systems and pulled 2,250 horsepower out of the V-12 FDL four-cycle engine and had AC/DC alternator-rectifier electrical equipment with DC traction motors. *Jim Boyd photo*

The next step in GE B-B development was to boost horsepower even further per cylinder, and GE and the MoPac did just that with an experimental set of three B23-7s that were pushed to 3,000 horsepower in the V-12 FDL engine. The test set was captured at Guion, Arkansas, on March 31, 1981, rolling southbound along the shores of the scenic White River. These units were the basis of MoPac's later order for 55 B30-7As, which were 12-cylinder, 3,000-horsepower locomotives. *Kevin EuDaly photo*

In the 1960s, the railroads wanted powerful units that required little maintenance. High availability and "gas-and-go" reliability were the dominant factors. In the late 1970s, EMD replaced the traditional mechanical relays in its units with new solid-state modular Dash-2 electrical systems, and the GP40-2 and SD40-2, while staying at 3,000 horsepower and the SD45-2 at 3,600 horsepower, gained efficiency and reliability. Only a few SD45-2s were built, but the SD40-2 ultimately sold more than 4,000 units!

General Electric was on the same path with its XR e*X*tra *R*eliability program that resulted in the modular "Dash-7" series in 1976. Surprisingly, the 2,300-horsepower four-motor B23-7 became a customer favorite, while the six-motor C30-7 found an immediate home on Western unit coal train service (the Burlington Northern had a 200-unit fleet).

The top-mounted radiators had served EMD units very well since the first Geeps, but with the bigger modern units, they began having problems with overheating while inside tunnels. The hot exhaust from units ahead would accumulate near the tunnel roofs and be blown through the radiators, seriously affecting their cooling capacity. To resolve this, EMD redesigned its radiators to draw in cool air from down near the frame and blow it upward through the radiators. These "tunnel motors" sold in great numbers to the Southern Pacific and Rio Grande in SD45T-2 and SD40T-2 versions.

And then came the energy crisis of the 1970s and the rapidly rising cost of fuel. Suddenly those wonderful, gutsy 20-cylinder SD45s were simply unacceptable fuel hogs. Now the industry wanted fuel economy, but that comes at the cost of complexity and reduced reliability. Diesels are at their

As locomotives got bigger, EMD's traditional top-mounted radiators began overheating in tunnels, since the intakes were high on the carbody where the hot exhaust gasses accumulated in the tunnels. To resolve this, EMD put the intakes down near the frame and put the fans beneath the radiators. It used this "tunnel motor" configuration on the 16-cylinder 3,000-horsepower SD40T-2s and 20-cylinder 3,600-horsepower SD45T-2s. Two Southern Pacific SD40T-2s, Nos. 8572 and 8281, lead an eastbound freight near Alray, California, on May 2, 1987. The SP and Rio Grande ordered tunnel motors. *James R. Doughty photo*

best when worked hard, so squeezing more horsepower out of fewer cylinders gained fuel economy. Drag from air compressors, cooling fans, and other auxiliaries that were mechanically linked and always on in older units now had to be reduced by disconnecting them to save fuel when not in active use.

By now, both EMD and GE were using electronic modules in their control systems, and the next logical step was to unite these modules in a computer. Reliable microprocessors that could handle the rigors of railroad service were now available, and the computer could monitor operation in real time and maximize performance and efficiency. Such auxiliaries as the air compressors and cooling fans were activated only when they were actually needed.

In 1980, EMD was outselling GE on a roughly two-to-one basis. That year, it boosted the output of the V-16 645 engine to

3,500 horsepower and introduced the GP50 and SD50. But these were the GP35s of the 1980s—the units that pushed the capacity of the 645 to its limit. Fully aware of this, General Electric took advantage of the situation by boosting its FDL16 engine to 3,900 horsepower in 1984 in its computer-equipped Dash-8 series units. In 1983, for the first time, GE sold more units than EMD.

To boost the capacity and put some growing room into its prime mover, EMD made a significant change in the 645 engine by adding a new crankshaft and 1 inch to the piston stroke, producing a new engine with 710 cubic inches per cylinder. The new 710 engine was introduced on the computerized "60-Series" units in 1984, pulling 3,800 horsepower out of the 16-cylinder engine.

The SD60 was a good seller, and the Burlington Northern acquired a 100-unit coal train fleet that was owned

In 1980, GE began developing its Dash-8 computerized systems to improve locomotive efficiency and performance. The four-motor B39-8, introduced in 1987, pulled 3,900 horsepower from the V-16 FDL engine. The Burlington Northern had contracted with LMX Leasing for 100 B39-8s on a power-by-the-hour arrangement. Two LMX units—Nos. 8545 and 8523—and two BN units pull a combined auto and stack train westbound through Edmonds, Washington, in the spring of 1994. The gray leasers became known as Rent-A-Wrecks around the BN. *Steve Jessup photo*

EMD's GP60 carried the new long-stroke 710 engine and computerized control system. The GP60 demonstrators were unique in having rounded edges on the nose and cab, clearly visible in this shot. All three demonstrator GP60s were being tested on the Burlington Northern in the spring of 1986, pulling a southbound priority train at South Seattle. Note the Southern Pacific–style light package with dual headlights and the red mars light on the nose. That package did not come on production units. *Steve Jessup photo*

Burlington Northern's second power-by-the-hour fleet consisted of 100 SD60s from Oakway Leasing wearing EMD's demonstrator colors. While the LMX B39-8s were in general main-line freight service, the Oakways were typically assigned to unit coal trains. Popping out of Cascade Tunnel at Scenic, Washington, is Oakway No. 9086 leading a westbound freight in the spring of 1987. In addition to pulling priority container trains and general manifests, the Oakways also found themselves on BN's heavy grain trains. Eventually, the majority of the SD60s were displaced in coal service and put back on general freight trains systemwide. *Steve Jessup photo*

by Oakway Leasing and paid for on a "power-by-the-hour" basis. The Oakway fleet was painted in EMD's blue and white demonstrator colors.

Farewell, La Grange

The magnificent EMD locomotive factory in La Grange that had given birth to the streamliner locomotives and vanquished steam was falling upon hard times in the 1980s. The sprawling facility had grown during the war and the postwar boom and was not laid out particularly well for efficient handling of parts and subassemblies.

Its biggest problem, however, was the General Motors labor contracts with the United Auto Workers Union. The mighty UAW applied the same basic contract demands on

EMD as it did in the Detroit auto plants. GE at Erie had no such problems and had much more realistic labor agreements.

Since 1950, EMD had a well-equipped factory in London, Ontario, operated by its subsidiary General Motors Diesel Division. And London's Canadian Auto Workers Union was not burdened by the U.S. UAW contracts. With production down to about 400 units per year, the UAW refused to rationalize the La Grange labor contracts, so between 1987 and 1992, EMD transferred its total locomotive production to London. Within a few years, the manufacturing buildings of the La Grange plant were demolished, and today a truck terminal occupies the ground that was once the High Bay. Nearby, EMD still maintains its corporate headquarters in a former engineering office building.

From Caboose to Cab

A lot of the advances in locomotive technology were invisible from the outside. Matters of computers, traction motors, and engines were all hidden inside the hood and under the frame. One change, however, was strikingly evident: the super cab.

Since the days of steam and hand brakes, a train needed a crew consisting of the conductor, the engineer, a fireman, and a gaggle of brakemen. Even with airbrakes, the brakemen were needed to pass signals by hand and line-of-sight around curves and in yards when switching.

Steam locomotives and diesels needed three seats to accommodate the engineer, fireman, and head brakeman, while the rest of the crew rode the caboose at the end of the train. The general use of handset radios in the 1960s permitted the reduction in the number of brakemen, and rationalization of union rules in the 1980s managed to get rid of the fireman.

Replacing the caboose, the end-of-train (EOT) device was an electronic device that could be locked into the rear coupler knuckle and connected to the airbrake trainline to give the engineer radio telemetry feedback on brake pressure and whether or not the last car was moving (and in which direction). Although the industry officially refers to the hardware as an EOT device, workaday railroaders almost universally call it a FRED—flashing rear-end device, although that first word was initially a less polite one that reflected the crew's opinion of the job-eliminating contraption.

The elimination of the caboose required the conductor to move up to the locomotive, and not many of the older units had

The use of radios allowed trains to operate safely with fewer crew members, and the end-of-train (EOT) device equipped with telemetry to the cab permitted the elimination of the caboose. However, the conductor still had his paperwork, and a diesel locomotive cab of the 1970s had no convenient place to work. The Canadian Comfort Cab was introduced on the Canadian National in 1973 to resolve this. The first such cabs purchased by a U.S. railroad were on the Providence & Worcester's two Montreal-Alco M420s. Brand-new No. P&W 2001 is at Valley Falls, Rhode Island, in July 1974. *Jim Boyd photo*

The Burlington Northern whiteface SD60Ms of 1990 had the first version of EMD's new Super Cab, which provided working space for the conductor. The next units had a slightly different two-piece windshield. The full-width nose covered some very hefty collision posts inside to protect the crew. BN SD60Ms Nos. 9221 and 9219 power a coal train leaving Neff Yard in Kansas City, Missouri, on March 30, 1991. Neff Yard was originally a MoPac facility. *Kevin EuDaly photo*

General Electric's version of the Super Cab featured two rectangular windows and sloping triangular nose panels. This Santa Fe 4,000-horsepower Dash 8-40CW 826 is leading a westbound grain train south of Matfield Green, Kansas, June 27, 1992. The 826 clearly shows the "York Canyon pinch" cab roof with gull-wing top edges to clear the coal loader. Many six-axle versions wound up in coal service while the four-axle models powered Santa Fe's high-priority trains. *Kevin EuDaly photo*

EMD's SD70 in all configurations has been a very popular line, with over 3,000 units produced, most of which are SD70Ms and SD70MACs. The class demonstrator unit for the SD70M, 7000, which became part of a lease fleet that later went to CSX, was still relatively clean in the KCS engine facility in Knoche Yard in Kansas City, Missouri, on November 21, 1993. *Kevin EuDaly photo*

room for him and a place for all his paperwork. The first units to specifically handle this were those built for the Canadian National in 1973 with the "Canadian Comfort Cab." These units had full-width noses and a spread of front windows with an entrance through the nose door and behind the cab. The first such units in the United States were a pair of MLW M420s built for the little Providence & Worcester in Massachusetts in 1974. (The full-width nose was actually introduced in 1963 on the GE U50 and the EMD FP45 cowl units in 1967.)

Following a national labor agreement in 1978, GE made a serious attempt to put the caboose up front with 10 BQ23-7 road-switchers for the Seaboard Coast Line with a big, boxy "Crew Quarters" cab that incorporated a work desk for the conductor and extra seats.

In 1989, both EMD and GE offered the North American Safety Cab on their big six-motors, and it quickly became a standard fixture on the new generation of units. These super cab units were computer equipped and had desktop controls and computer screens to monitor operations.

But the computer geeks had blown it. A freight train isn't a PC with a mouse. All the visibility problems the engineers had switching with F-units back in the 1940s had returned with the desktop controls. They'd forgotten everything Dick Dilworth had taught them in 1949. By the first decade of the twenty-first century, however, the builders were back to offering Dilworth's conventional control stand in their super cabs, while adding the computer screens.

The super cabs went immediately into production on EMD's six-motor SD70Ms and GE's Dash 8-40CWs, as well as the AC traction versions. Because they pushed the weight limits, the only four-motor super cabs were EMD's GP60Ms and GE's Dash 8-40BWs built for the Santa Fe in 1990.

The EMD SD70M went through a number of carbody modifications while outputting the same basic 4,000-horsepower power package with DC traction motors carried in the new HTCR-II self-steering radial truck. Union Pacific No. 5088 and 5140, built in 2002 and 2003, respectively, race westward through the Columbia River Gorge near Celilo Park, Oregon, with an auto train March 17, 2007. Wearing the patriotic livery, the units clearly show the radial truck, the two-piece windshield, and the newer flared radiators. *Steve Jessup photo*

AC Traction

Alternating current traction motors are as old as electric railroading, and they are highly regarded for their tremendous capacity. The AC motors, however, are very difficult to control, since they will "go synchronous" with the generator's current frequencies. Computer technology solved this problem by using solid-state devices to create and carefully control variable artificial frequencies.

A new "straight AC" unit uses an alternator to generate AC current, but it then immediately uses the standard diodes and bridge rectifiers to create a DC power flow. This DC current is then fed into a solid-state inverter that converts it into precisely controlled AC waves for the traction motors.

The motors themselves are essentially inside-out with the rotating fields fixed rigidly on the outside. The computer controls advance the waves from one field magnet to the next, creating a rotating field inside the unmoving magnets. The pulsing AC current uses induction to excite the rotating magnets on the inside, completely eliminating the troublesome commutators of a DC motor or slip rings of an AC alternator.

With this design, the AC traction motor has tremendous power capacity and can be loaded to a stall without overheating. The biggest drawback of the DC traction motor is its tendency to overheat when overloaded, and DC units all have posted short time ratings to prevent motor damage under heavy amperage loads.

Alternating current technology continued to be of interest, and the SD70MAC was an AC version of the 4,000-horsepower SD70M. Later versions were rated at 4,300 horsepower. In a one-of-a-kind test paint scheme, BNSF SD70MAC No. 9647 was one of a large group of 496 units numbered from 9504–9999. It leads a southbound manifest south of St. Joseph, Missouri, on August 24, 1995, heading toward Murray Yard on Kansas City's north side. *Kevin EuDaly photo*

The most powerful 16-cylinder locomotives EMD produced were the SD90MACs, which carried the new four-cycle 265H engine. While more than 400 "convertibles" were built with 4,300-horsepower two-cycle 710 engines, capable of being refitted with the more powerful 265H engines, about three dozen hit the rails with the 6,000-horsepower four-cycle engines. By May 2008, all the H-engine units had been retired, and many of them were at Mid-America Car in Kansas City for rebuilding with 710s. *Kevin EuDaly photo*

The AC systems are more expensive to build than DC systems, but they are more economical in service. EMD and GE had developed their AC systems from European companies, and the significant difference between them is that EMD uses one inverter per truck and GE uses one inverter per motor. Both systems seem to work quite well, and neither has proven superior to the other.

Computer controls and AC motors permitted the horsepower race to actually exceed its practical limits. In the 1980s, the goal was a 6,000-horsepower single-engine unit, and considerable engineering was expended on the quest. EMD even developed a completely new four-cycle 265H engine that could output 6,000 horsepower and put it in the SD90MAC in 1996. GE developed a new HDL engine with 958.6-cubic-inch displacement that could be bumped up to 6,250 horsepower in 16 cylinders and 7,030 horsepower in an 18-cylinder version.

As this was going on in the late 1990s, the railroads came to the realization that anything more than 4,400 horsepower would cause more problems than it would solve. Few trains could utilize a single 6,000-horsepower unit, and 12,000 horsepower was optimum for most heavy-duty service such as unit coal trains. However, if a coal train had two 6,000-horsepower units and one would fail for any reason, the other unit probably couldn't move the train by itself. But if that coal train had three 4,000-horsepower units and one failed, the other two could probably keep things moving.

There were other factors, too. The Norfolk Southern's old N&W main line had passing sidings that limited its coal trains to 140 cars. Instead of the 4,400-horsepower AC units, the NS opted for a more economical fleet of 4,000-horsepower DC units. As a result, the horsepower race was won at 4,400 horsepower in the 1990s, and the 6,000-horsepower mania just faded away in the early twenty-first century. The 6,000-horsepower SD90MACs were soon retired or de-rated by the Union Pacific.

Five slant-nosed E-units (opposite) were lined up in the Ivy City engine terminal in Washington, D.C., for a 1941 General Motors color advertisement with units from the Atlantic Coast Line, Florida East Coast, Seaboard Air Line, Southern Railway, and Baltimore & Ohio. In January 1968, at precisely the same spot, are a C&O E8; an SCL/ACL E6; a Richmond, Fredericksburg & Potomac E8; a Southern Railway E8; and another SCL/ACL E6. All of these units had one thing in common: their paint schemes were designed by the General Motors Styling Section when the customers bought the locomotives. The GM/EMD stylists had a uniform sense of art deco style and color that gave the entire postwar generation of diesel railroading a colorful and tasteful appearance. By 1968, the RF&P and Southern had stopped using the round nose medallions like those on the SCL that had originally made the noses look more complete. The early 1950s view (above) shows the Styling Section artists in their office with typical examples of their work. *Jim Boyd photo, opposite; EMD photo, above*

What about Passenger Units?

The diesel engine had gotten into the railroad business hauling passengers, but World War II interrupted things. EMD went into the wartime hiatus with its slant-nosed 2,000-horsepower E6, which in 1945 was replaced in the catalog with the bulldog-nose E7. Even though the E7 retained the prewar units' belt-driven cooling fans and auxiliaries, it became the bestselling E-unit (510 cabs and boosters). In the summer of 1949, EMD introduced the E8, with two 1,125-horsepower V-12 567B engines and a completely rearranged internal platform with electric fans on the roof and the provision for dynamic brakes. The E8's exterior was cleaned up with sleek Farr air grilles replacing the three open air intakes and portholes replacing the side windows. There were 457 E8s produced before they were

One of the prettiest sights from the streamliner era was a perfectly matched set of Santa Fe warbonnet F-units on a stainless-steel train. Here, on June 16, 1964, train No. 19, *The Chief*, was outbound for Los Angeles at 21st Street Tower in Chicago behind F7 38L and four B-units. Many railroads, like the Great Northern and Northern Pacific, preferred the compact power and flexibility of the F-units for their passenger trains. *Jim Boyd photo*

replaced in the catalog with the 2,400-horsepower E9 in May 1954. But by now the passenger business was on the decline, and only 144 were produced before Illinois Central No. 4043 went into the books in May 1961 as the last E-unit and the last EMD truss-body covered wagon of any configuration.

Ironically, Alco had gotten itself into trouble by rushing into production with the 244-powered PA, feeling that the single 2,000-horsepower V-16 engine would give it a competitive advantage. The PA had replaced the twin-engine DL-109 that had some early teething problems but by 1945 was proving to be a rugged and reliable machine with an impressive wartime record. The single-engine PA (312 units between 1946 and 1953) was overwhelmed in the market by the old-fashioned twin-engine EMD E-units. The railroads liked the reliability of the twin engines, because if one prime mover failed on the road, the other could usually get the train home. By the late

1950s, there were a lot of passenger trains that didn't need more than one unit.

In the mid-1950s, Alco was tempted to produce a PA with the new 251 engine, but it concluded that the market just wasn't there and never built one. In Canada, however, the Alco subsidiary Montreal Locomotive Works put an 1,800-horsepower V-12 251 engine into the FA carbody to produce 36 FPA-4 passenger cabs and 14 FPB-4 boosters for the Canadian National that were very successful.

When diesels took over general passenger service after the war, they had to be compatible with the existing car fleet that was equipped with trainline steam heat from the locomotive. Thus the diesels were equipped with Vapor-Clarkson oil-burning flash boilers for train heat, and they were temperamental beasts! The boilers required a space-consuming water tank on the locomotive, and in very cold weather under heavy loads, they would consume the fuel oil faster than the diesel engines!

The New Haven Railroad had to deal with two different electrification systems getting into New York. Grand Central used DC third rail, while Penn Station used AC overhead, with the wires ending in New Haven. In 1956, EMD took an elongated F9 carbody with a three-axle rear truck to create the 1,750-horsepower FL9 that could run from Boston and go into Grand Central as an electric with the diesel shut down. Two FL9s running on their diesel engines are moving at high speed at Greens Farms, Connecticut, headed for New York in April 1968. *T. J. Donahue photo, Kevin EuDaly collection*

Although Dick Dilworth intentionally designed the GP7 to be "so ugly nobody would want it anywhere around the general office," it turned out to be an excellent passenger engine. Baltimore & Ohio GP7 No. 6694 makes its Cumberland, Maryland, station stop in November 1967 with No. 8, the *Diplomat*, from Chicago to Washington. It carried a steam generator in the short hood, and like all B&O high-nose Geeps was set up to run long-hood forward. *Jim Boyd photo*

Many railroads used boiler-equipped road-switchers in passenger service. In 1966, the Monon replaced its aging RS-2s and F-units on the Chicago–Louisville *Thoroughbred* with two new Alco C-420s with steam boilers in their high short hoods. The 502 makes a station stop in Bloomington, Indiana, in May 1967. The Monon also bought 16 low-nosed freight C-420s at the same time. *Jim Neubauer photo*

In the 1960s, the Santa Fe wanted to replace its aging F-units with more modern passenger power, and its first acquisitions were 10 2,800-horsepower GE U28CGs, painted in the warbonnet livery. Three of them are bringing the *Texas Chief* across 21st Street in 1967. The U28CG had its boiler in a compartment behind the cab. In 1967, the Santa Fe got six 3,000-horsepower cowl-carbody U30CGs with fluted sides and 14 EMD 3,600-horsepower cowl-carbody FP45s. *Jim Boyd photo*

Some railroads preferred the F-unit for passenger service. The Santa Fe had a huge fleet of passenger F-units that were unique in having their steam boilers only in the booster units. You'd always see at least one B-unit on any Santa Fe train with F-units. The Northern Pacific and Great Northern also preferred the pulling power of the F-units for their mountain-climbing passenger trains. To promote this market, EMD offered the FP7 with a 4-foot-longer carbody for a larger boiler water capacity.

In 1956, the New Haven was looking for a dual-mode unit that could run as a diesel in the open air but work as an electric off the 650-volt DC third rail into Grand Central Terminal (with the diesel engine shut off in the Park Avenue tunnel and station itself). EMD took its existing FL9 carbody design and made a dual-mode unit out of it. The long-distance FL9 was the standard 1,750-horsepower FP9 with an even longer carbody to accommodate large internal water tanks and an A1A rear truck to handle the increased weight. No conventional FL9s were ever built, but the big carbody was perfect for the New Haven dual-mode electrical equipment, and 60 units were produced between 1956 and 1960. The prototype FL9 had a conventional Blomberg front truck, but when it welded itself to the track when the swing hanger shorted out to the third rail in the Grand Central Terminal turning loop, the front truck was replaced by a high-speed FlexiCoil switcher truck that made the FL9s notoriously rough-riding. The FL9 was a great operational success, however, and served very well (some were still in service in 2008 when this book was being prepared), eliminating the electric-to-diesel engine change at the east end of the wires at New Haven. FL9 No. 2059, built in 1960, was the last EMC/EMD F-unit, capping a production since the 1939 demonstrator 103 of 7,612 units.

The high short hood of Dilworth's Geep was a natural space for a steam boiler, and many GP7s and GP9s were passenger-equipped and fitted with high-speed gearing. Alco responded with short-hood boilers in its RS-2 and RS-3 road-switchers. Those units that were equipped with dynamic brakes had them in the short hoods; an interesting variant was the Alco "hammerhead" with a cab-height short hood to accommodate both the dynamics and a steam boiler. Alco even sold boiler-equipped 2,000-horsepower high-nose C-420s to the Monon and Long Island for passenger service in the mid-1960s.

The unit reduction concept of the second generation crept into the passenger business, and in 1964 EMD replaced the E9 in its passenger catalog with the 2,500-horsepower turbocharged SDP35, with a squared-off rear end of the long hood that held the steam boiler. The Seaboard Air Line bought 20 units, the Union Pacific got 10, the L&N bought 4, and the ACL got 1.

General Electric got into the passenger road-switcher field in 1966 with 10 low-nose U28CG units with steam generators in a compartment behind the cab. The 2,800-horsepower units were usually assigned to the *Texas Chief*.

In 1966, the SDP35 was replaced by the 3,000-horsepower SDP40, which sold only 20 units (6 Great Northern and 14 National Railways of Mexico) and the 3,600-horsepower SDP45 that sold 10 to the Southern Pacific in the spring of 1967, permitting the retirement of the SP's last E-units. (As main-line passenger service diminished and Amtrak took over in 1971, the SDP45s were transferred to the San Francisco Peninsula commuter service before being assimilated into the freight fleet.)

Meanwhile, in the summer of 1967, the Great Northern got eight SDP45s in the new Big Sky Blue colors that bumped F-units off the *Empire Builder* and *Western Star*.

The biggest fleet of SDP45s, however, were not passenger units. To avoid the complications of introducing a new model, EMD sold the Erie Lackawanna 34 SDP45s with large fuel tanks and modified with no boilers.

The Santa Fe, which was still pulling its premier passenger trains with five and six aging F-units, wanted the economy and reliability of new power but didn't want to put a road-switcher

The Southern Pacific had used GP9s in passenger service for years, but in 1967 it bought 10 3,600-horsepower SDP45s, primarily to replace multiple F-units. They had EMD's 20-cylinder 645 engine, and their long underframe accommodated a squared-off boiler compartment on the rear and a larger-than-usual underbelly tank for fuel and boiler water. SP 3207 is in charge of an eastbound director's special at Dover, Missouri, on January 26, 1984. This unit saw plenty of action on SP passenger trains before being used in freight service. *Kevin EuDaly photo*

The last new passenger diesels bought by any U.S. railroad before Amtrak were The Milwaukee Road's six FP45s in December 1968. These cowl-carbodies were like those built for the Santa Fe and had two huge steam generators inside the rear of the hood. Already weathered by severe winter conditions, month-old No. 1 and a mate back into Chicago's Union Station in January 1969. The Milwaukee reassigned them to freight service before Amtrak could get them. *Jim Boyd photo*

on the *Super Chief*. To accommodate such a good customer, EMD modified the SDP45 with a full-width cowl carbody. Unlike an E-unit or F-unit where the carbody was a structural part of the frame, the cowl was just a full-width shell, just like the hood of a road-switcher. The angular-faced FP45 was an impressive unit in the classic warbonnet colors. The Santa Fe got nine of the boiler-equipped units in 1967 and liked the carbody so well that it acquired 40 F45 freight cowl units. The only other customer for the F45 was the Great Northern, which bought 10. The last 2 were delivered as Burlington Northern units in green and white, and the BN followed up with 30 more in 1970 and 1971.

While EMD was delivering the FP45s, GE got a piece of the cowl-carbody pie in late 1967 with six big U30GCs with fluted sides and stylish rounded noses reminiscent of the New Haven EP-5 electrics.

The Milwaukee Road was ready for new power for its Chicago–Minneapolis *Hiawathas* and Chicago–Omaha Union Pacific *City* streamliners. In the winter of 1968–1969, the Milwaukee took delivery of five FP45s in UP Armour Yellow, wearing the distinctive numbers 1–5 of the original streamlined *Hiawatha* 4-4-2s (1–4) of 1935. The Milwaukee FP45s were the last main-line passenger units purchased by an American railroad prior to Amtrak in 1971.

In the 1950s, railroads were required to operate money-losing passenger service as part of their civic responsibility. Commuter service was vital, but rush hours caused very inefficient use of equipment and drove up the costs. As a result, much of the commuter equipment was old and powered by hand-me-down road locomotives. By the 1960s, local governments were beginning to step in and help subsidize those civic necessities. In 1968, the Central Railroad of New Jersey purchased 13 new GP40Ps with dual controls and steam generators. No. 3673 accelerates out of Newark, New Jersey, in May 1972 with a string of veteran coaches. *Jim Boyd photo*

In 1970, the New Jersey Department of Transportation financed 32 GE U34CH locomotives for push-pull service on the Erie and Lackawanna lines with new all-electric Comet coaches. The head-end-power alternator required the FDL-16 diesel to run at a constant high speed to maintain correct power frequency. In December 1978, six U34CHs line up, ready to back into Hoboken Terminal to handle the evening commuter rush. *Jim Boyd photo*

Commuter Road-Switchers

The big six-motors were not the only second-generation passenger units, though. Road-switchers had a long tradition in commuter service, from BL2s and Geeps to Train Masters to Alco RS-3s. In 1966, the government of Ontario bought eight GP40TCs on a lengthened frame that carried an auxiliary GM 12V-149 engine and 500-kw alternator for electric head-end power (HEP) for the new cars in the Toronto GO Transit commuter service.

The Central Railroad of New Jersey got 13 similar GP40Ps in 1968 that were equipped with steam boilers for use with the older CNJ commuter cars. The GP40Ps carried their boilers in squared-off rear ends and also had dynamic brakes and large fuel tanks. To avoid having to be turned, the GP40Ps had dual controls and ran half the time long-hood forward. When the steam-heated cars were replaced with modern push-pull Comet cars, the GP40Ps were refitted with HEP generator sets and Dash-2 electrical systems and lost their dual controls.

Since the last new passenger locomotives were the Santa Fe and Milwaukee Road FP45s, when Amtrak needed new power in 1973, it went in the same direction with the SDP40F, a cowl-carbody version of the SDP40 with the 3,000-horsepower 16-cylinder engine. Since the passenger car fleet was mostly steam-heated, the SDP40Fs carried a pair of big skid-mounted steam generators. Three new SDP40Fs have Amtrak's *Southwest Chief* dropping down Edelstein Hill in Illinois in 1974. *Jim Boyd photo*

In the first decade of the twenty-first century, the GP40Ps are favorites of the New Jersey Transit and are the oldest intact passenger fleet in the country.

In New Jersey, the neighboring Erie Lackawanna was eager to replace its aging Alco RS-3s, Geeps, and E-units on its former-Erie commuter lines. It, too, was getting the new all-electric Comet push-pull cars, and in late 1970 it began taking delivery of the first of a fleet of 32 GE U34CH commuter units, financed by the New Jersey Department of Transportation. These were basically U36C units that tapped 170 horsepower from the prime mover for train HEP. To maintain constant voltage in the HEP system, the FDL-16 engines ran at a constant high rpm, regardless of throttle position and load. In service, the U34CHs produced a magnificent plume of flame and smoke out the stack as they loaded during acceleration.

Over in Chicago, the Northwestern Suburban Mass Transit District had taken over The Milwaukee Road commuter service and in 1974 ordered 15 F40C 3,200-horsepower cowl units, similar to the FP45s. The Milwaukee units tapped 700 horsepower from the V-16 diesel for HEP. The F40Cs had unusual fluted panels on the carbody sides that gave them the appearance of rolling pizza ovens.

Powering up Amtrak

Amtrak was created by Congress and reluctantly approved by the Nixon administration in 1970 to relieve the private railroads of the financial burden of intercity passenger service. The affected railroads could get out of the passenger business by buying into the National Railroad Passenger Corporation with equipment and/or money equivalent to half of their 1970 passenger operating losses.

When Amtrak took over on May 1, 1971, it inherited a chaotic collection of equipment and motive power. It made the arbitrary decision to accept only stainless-steel or all-aluminum passenger cars, eliminating several fine fleets like the Illinois Central. And it quickly discovered that not all passenger-car heating, lighting, and air-conditioning systems are compatible.

Railroads with the newest power (the Santa Fe, The Milwaukee Road, Southern Pacific, Burlington Northern, and Seaboard Coast Line) pulled their FP45s, U30CGs, U28CGs, SDP45s, SDP40s, and SDP35s back into freight service while contributing their E-unit and F-unit fleets to Amtrak. Thus,

the new system was immediately faced with a crisis of 247 aging diesels.

Amtrak's solution in 1972 was to order 150 SDP40Fs from EMD. These 3,000-horsepower cowl units were essentially FP45s with the 16-cylinder instead of 20-cylinder 645 engines. They each carried two big steam boilers and rode on EMD's new high-traction HTC truck. It was a poorly kept secret that the government and management had little faith in the future, and part of the logic behind the SDP40Fs was that they could be resold as freight units when Amtrak failed. The SDP40Fs arrived in 1973 and 1974 and went into nationwide service.

When Amtrak began to acquire all-electric Amfleet and Superliner passenger cars, its first new head-end-power-equipped locomotives were 25 GE P30CHs built in late 1975. The "Pooches" had skid-mounted HEP units with auxiliary diesel engines. No. 720 hits the TP&W diamond at Gilman, Illinois, in May 1980 with a southbound Superliner consist on the Illinois Central Gulf. Unfortunately, the heavy six-motor P30CHs and SDF40Fs had tracking issues at high speed. *Jim Boyd photo*

With its SDP40Fs being banned by some railroads, Amtrak had to do something in a hurry. By 1976, the HEP-equipped passenger car fleet was big enough to eliminate the heavy boilers and water supply from new locomotives. Amtrak acquired 213 F40PHs with a 3,200-horsepower 16-cylinder 645 engine that had an 800-kW alternator for HEP. The F40PHs packed the power of an SDP40F in a much more compact unit. Amtrak No. 233 leads the southbound *Coast Starlight* through Steilacoom, Washington, on March 21, 1992. *Steve Jessup photo*

Meanwhile, Amtrak was purchasing new Amfleet passenger cars for delivery in 1975 that used electric HEP instead of steam, and to power them it ordered 25 General Electric P30CHs with HEP units instead of steam boilers. The squarish brutes immediately gained thenickname "Pooches."

Unfortunately, Amtrak discovered that heavy six-motor units (SDP40Fs and P30CHs as well as electric E60s) were not really suitable for universal high-speed service. After some derail-ments of questionable cause, a few railroads refused to operate the big six-motors or slapped speed restrictions on them.

Amtrak had to do something fast. In response, EMD scaled down the SDP40F's 3,000-horsepower powerplant into a compact four-motor unit, the F40PH, that reduced weight by eliminating the steam boilers and water tanks in favor of

a HEP unit. The first 30 F40PHs were delivered in the spring of 1976.

The next 70 units were F40PHRs that were defined as "rebuilt" SDP40Fs to avoid financial and legal entanglements from using public money on a failed design. In effect, the SDP40Fs were simply normal trade-ins on the new units. The SDP40F fleet was rapidly disposed of, with 18 going to the Santa Fe for freight service in trade for much-needed yard switchers.

The F40PH was everything the SDP40F wasn't. It was an excellent universal locomotive that not only served Amtrak but was picked up by many commuter agencies, as well. By the early 1980s, Amtrak was able to completely retire the old F-units and E-units. In an interesting side note,

By the 1990s, Amtrak's F40s were at the end of their 15-year economic life. GE responded with the revolutionary Genesis. With aircraft-style monocoque construction, it packed more power into a lighter-weight unit. After building a 4,000-horsepower DC version and a 3,200-horsepower AC dual-mode that could run off New York's 650-volt third rail, in 1996 GE began delivering 207 4,200-horsepower P42DC units. On November 2, 2002, Nos. P42DCs 118 and 120 are assigned to the *Coast Starlight*, ready to leave Seattle's King Street Station—at exactly 11 a.m. *Kevin EuDaly photo*

before it bought the ill-fated SDP40Fs, Amtrak had asked EMD to built new E-units, but the factory was simply no longer set up to build truss-sided carbody units at a reasonable cost.

The last traditional road units left on Amtrak by 1990 were a dozen ex–New Haven FL9s that handled the regional trains out of New York's Grand Central Terminal. Ironically, while it was getting shiny new road units and retiring its E-unit classics, Amtrak was acquiring a fascinating fleet of even older secondhand switchers and road-switchers for yard work, including Geeps and Alco RS-3s.

In 1992, Amtrak got something completely different in the form of 20 GE wide-nose Dash 8-32BWH passenger road-switchers. These HEP-equipped 3,200-horsepower units came painted in a dramatic "Pepsi can" livery unlike anything else on the roster.

As the Pepsis were entering service in California, GE was putting the final touches on "the first new passenger unit designed from the ground up," the Dash 8-40BP Genesis. This unit weighed less than an F40 while delivering 1,000 more horsepower in a longer but more compact carbody. The first unit rolled out in mid-1993. The model was soon upgraded to 4,200 horsepower as the P42DC, and the 207 of them that were delivered over the next few years completely displaced the 15-year-old and high-mileage F40s from Amtrak service. One special version was the P32AC-DM dual-mode unit that can operate off the third rail into Grand Central Terminal. Metro-North and ConnDOT also got the dual-mode units.

With the influx of Genesis units, a few F40s remained on the roster with their diesel engines removed and replaced with baggage compartments. These non-powered control units are used as unpowered cab control cars for push-pull consists. Some old Metroliner MU cars were also converted into push-pull cab cars without the baggage compartments.

When Amtrak needed more power in 1992, it opted for a pure road-switcher for the first time, with 20 GE Dash 8-32BWHs. They were delivered in a dramatic new "Pepsi can" livery that seemed appropriate for their California assignments, though the units were not exclusive to West Coast service. Here, Amtrak No. 503 is at Carbondale, Illinois, between runs on the *Illini* on April 30, 1999. It's unfortunate that Amtrak's award-winning paint scheme applied to these GE units was short-lived. *Kevin EuDaly photo*

Compact jet engines developed for helicopters prompted United Aircraft to develop the TurboTrain in 1967. The Canadian National and VIA Rail Canada put a fleet of TurboTrains into service on the Montreal–Toronto–Windsor corridor. A VIA TurboTrain whooses nonstop through Brockville, Ontario, in October 1978. *Jim Boyd photo*

Lightweights and Turbos

Back in 1955–1956, when Chevys had bat wings and Chryslers had tailfins, EMD resurrected the concept of the ultra-lightweight streamliner by slapping GM bus bodies on flanged wheels behind an Edsel-looking 1,200-horsepower locomotive designated as an LWT12 (*L*ightweight *1,2*00 horsepower) and calling it the *Aerotrain*. Two LWT12s were built and went on a flashy cross-country demonstration tour; a third LWT12 was built expressly for the Rock Island to power its new, articulated *Jet Rocket* train. No other railroads wanted the *Aerotrains*, so the Rock Island bought them, too. All three trains wound up in commuter service. In 1966, the Rock Island donated both *Aerotrains*, including their locomotives, to museums; the *Jet Rocket* and its LWT12 was scrapped.

Like the completely impractical monorail, the industry and public simply couldn't dismiss the idea of a lightweight jet train. Advances in compact jet engines for helicopters gave United Aircraft a convenient turbine package to power its TurboTrain in 1967 that was sold to the U.S. Department of Transportation. The Canadian National liked the concept and bought 10 trainsets. In 1969, the three-car DOT TurboTrain went into service on the New Haven between Grand Central Terminal and Boston, and Amtrak inherited it in 1971. Amtrak bought two Canadian National sets and expanded its service to two five-car trains. The TurboTrains had hydraulic transmissions, and the turbines shut down in the tunnels, with power being picked up from the third rail for electric motors on the drive and auxiliary systems. The TurboTrains were fun to ride, since passengers in the front dome looked right over the engineer's shoulder with a great forward view, but the UA trains were retired in 1976.

But Amtrak wasn't done with turbos. In 1972, it had purchased two off-the-shelf ANF-Frangeco five-car Turboliners from France for Midwest corridor services. In the era of cobbled-together secondhand streamliners, the Turboliners gave Amtrak something shiny and new to promote. In 1975, it returned to ANF for four more trainsets.

The turbos appeared to be ideal for the former New York Central Empire Corridor between New York and Buffalo/ Niagara Falls, and in late 1976 Amtrak got seven five-car trainsets manufactured by Rohr Industries of Chula Vista, California, under license from France (and after delivering the units, Rohr immediately exited the car-building business). Like the UA TurboTrains, the Rohr Turboliners could operate off the third rail in the tunnels.

Amtrak set up a dedicated turbo maintenance facility in Rensselaer, New York, across the Hudson River from Albany. As more Amfleet and F40s arrived, the ANF Turboliners were retired from the St. Louis service in September 1981, but in the late 1980s three of them were rebuilt at Amtrak's Beech Grove Shop in Indiana and put into service out of Rensselaer alongside the Rohr trains.

Amtrak had one strange little nonturbo turbotrain in the form of the Canadian "LRC" (*L*ight-*R*apid-*C*omfortable) lightweight trainset manufactured by Bombardier and powered by 2,700-horsepower Montreal Locomotive Works "Alco" 251 diesels fore and aft. VIA Rail Canada had a fleet of LRCs, and Amtrak borrowed a 10-car set for testing in 1982. The train was returned without generating any further interest.

The turbos' careers had numerous ups and downs as newer equipment rendered them expensive oddballs. One final Turboliner made it into the twenty-first century before joining the rest in storage, their fate still undetermined.

Amtrak embraced the TurboTrain concept with French-built turbos in the Midwest and California-built Rohr Turboliners on New York's Empire Corridor. In October 1986, a Turboliner is northbound along the Hudson River approaching Breakneck Mountain. The New York Turboliners could shut down the turbines and run off the third rail into Grand Central Terminal. *Jim Boyd photo*

Locomotive Rebuilders

In the steam era, almost any big backshop that could maintain a fleet of road locomotives could probably build its own engines new. The Norfolk & Western built nearly all of its modern power in its Roanoke shops, and the Illinois Central shops in Paducah, Kentucky, rebuilt and upgraded nearly its entire steam fleet and cranked out 20 brand-new 4-8-2s. Paducah followed this tradition into the diesel era.

The IC had dieselized its freight service very quickly in the mid-1950s with a huge fleet of GP7s and GP9s. Unfortunately, by the mid-1960s this entire fleet was coming of age at the same time. The medium-horsepower Geeps were perfect for the flatland IC, so rather than trade them in for expensive new power, Paducah began a program of remanufacturing them

to like-new specs, while incorporating many of the newer electrical control components. The rebuilt Geeps got chopped noses, improved air filters, and fresh orange paint, and hit the road with another dozen years of life put back into them. The "Paducah Geeps" were excellent, reliable machines, and soon the IC was seeking foreign units for rebuilding. In later years, Paducah became an independent company that got into the rebuilding and unit-leasing business. Numerous other companies, such as Precision National, GATX, and LMX, got into the locomotive-leasing business, and their colorful fleets could be seen all over the country.

Out in Boise, Idaho, industrial contractor Morrison-Knudsen set up a locomotive rebuild shop in 1971 and began doing a brisk business in refurbishing vintage units. In 1973,

With its steam-killing Geeps all hitting the end of their 15-year economic life in the 1960s, the Illinois Central set up its Paducah Shop in Kentucky as a state-of-the-art rebuild facility. At Mays Yard in New Orleans in August 1969, GP9 No. 9331 is beside rebuilt Paducah Geep 7957, the former GP7 8957. The 7957 had a remanufactured engine and electrical equipment, a chopped nose, and new paper engine air intake filters atop the hood. *Jim Boyd photo*

In 1967, Delaware & Hudson President Bruce Sterzing bought four Santa Fe PA-1s for his Albany–Montreal service. For the New York state-funded Amtrak *Adirondack*, Morrison-Knudsen of Boise, Idaho, rebuilt the units in 1975 and replaced their 2,000-horsepower 16-cylinder 244 engines with 2,000-horsepower 12-cylinder 251s, fulfilling an Alco proposal from the 1950s that until this time had gone unfulfilled. Prior to the four units being leased to Boston's MBTA in September 1977, D&H No. 17 is captured at Montreal in *Adirondack* service. *Alan Bradley photo*

M-K got the job of rebuilding the Burlington Northern E-unit fleet with HEP for push-pull service for Chicago's West Suburban Mass Transit District. M-K's most famous alumni, however, were probably the four Santa Fe PA-1s from the Delaware & Hudson, which were rebuilt in 1975 with 251 engines, fulfilling the Alco PA-4 ambition that had not been realized back in the 1950s.

M-K tried rather unsuccessfully to market rebuilt units with Caterpillar diesel engines, and it got involved in the 6,000-horsepower race in 1994 by fielding six 5,000-horsepower units built new with Caterpillar four-cycle 3612 engines and DC traction motors. The 6,000-horsepower AC version was never built.

The last units produced before EMD shut down its La Grange manufacturing plant and moved to London, Ontario, were Chicago Metra's 30 F40PHM-2s built between October 1991 and December 1992. These 3,200-horsepower F40s were modified with sloping front windows that won them the nickname "Winnebagos," after the popular highway motor home. No. 198 is operating in push mode with the red marker lights on, shoving an eastbound toward Chicago at Western Springs on September 28, 2007. *Kevin EuDaly photo*

New Commuter Power

Ever since the Rock Island bumped its Pacifics with RS-3s and the Burlington used its main-line E-units between road trips, commuter trains had been running with modified freight units or conventional passenger units.

The heavy acceleration and stop-and-start service was rough duty, but the relatively light consists were ideal for single-unit operation. In the 1960s, most suburban services were using E-units, F-units, Geeps, or Alcos, with some notable exceptions like the SP and CNJ F-M Train Masters.

The same political pressures that produced Amtrak were creating regional commuter agencies to relieve the private companies of the financial burden of providing the increasingly critical commuter service. And most of them were ready to use public money to replace the aging rolling stock and motive power with new equipment. In the Chicago area, new bi-level gallery cars were entering

service even before steam locomotives were gone, and by the 1980s the concept of push-pull trains with HEP was gaining wide acceptance.

In the mid-1960s, the Jersey Central and Toronto's GO Transit began powering their trains with modified freight GP40s, and The Milwaukee Road service in Chicago got its purpose-built F40Cs in 1974. In 1979, the Illinois Central's Paducah Shop rebuilt a fleet of vintage GM&O F3s into HEP-equipped FP10s for Boston's Massachusetts Bay Transportation Authority.

Amtrak's 3,000-horsepower workhorse F40 began to find a place on commuter agency rosters in variants with engine-driven HEP or with Caterpillar auxiliary HEP engine packages. In 1992, the last units built at the EMD plant in La Grange were Metra commuter F40PHM-2s modified with sloping noses that looked so much like highway motor homes that they acquired the nickname "Winnebagos." Production

In 1988, EMD had packed a 12-cylinder 710 engine into the F40 carbody to produce the 3,000-horsepower F59PH. In 1994, the carbody was streamlined with a European-style rounded nose around the isolated WhisperCab. The nine state-financed F59s were styled to match the Amtrak California bi-levels, ordered at the same time. On October 3, 2002, an Amtrak California *San Joaquin* train is southbound at Modesto with the matching F59PHI and bi-level set. *Steve Jessup photo*

of the F40 was not continued at the General Motors Diesel Division (GMDD) plant in London, Ontario, however.

In the 1990s, new safety and exhaust emissions regulations began to squeeze older units out of suburban service, increasing the demand for new compliant locomotives. Only a few commuter agencies could handle the expense of the big new GE Genesis units of 1993, and Amtrak also had the need for a smaller and more economical unit for developing markets. In response, GMDD downsized the F40 with a 12-cylinder 710 engine that matched its 3,000-horsepower output in the new F59PH that carried the new computerized control systems. The F59PHs were nearly identical in appearance to the boxy F40s, but with customers seeking something more stylish, GMDD responded by wrapping the F59PH in a rounded cowl over an isolated "WhisperCab" to produce the F59PHI in 1994. These units went immediately to work in Amtrak California service.

In January 1997, M-K was reorganized as MotivePower Industries, a division of Westinghouse Air Brake & Technologies (Wabtec), and it began to carve out a niche market in commuter units. Working in cooperation with Electro-Motive, MPI created the F40PH-2C stretched F40 with the 16-645 engine and Caterpillar HEP pallet units that was sold to Boston's MBTA and California's Altamont Commuter Express and San Diego Coaster services.

When the EPA upped its emission standards and the feds imposed new crew safety requirements at the turn of the millennium, GMDD decided to exit the passenger business and focus its London facility on freight units. This left a wide-open market for MotivePower, and Boise responded with an all-new commuter locomotive using proven and respected EMD/GMDD components.

Since the end of steam, EMD had fiercely resisted supplying parts to rebuilders, but with MPI, GMDD decided

To meet the increasing demand for specialty passenger locomotives, the MotivePower Industries division of Wabtec, at the former Morrison-Knudsen plant in Boise, Idaho, developed a European-styled carbon-fiber carbody that could handle a wide variety of off-the-shelf power plant and HEP equipment. San Francisco's Caltrain got six MP36PH-3Cs with EMD 710 engines, microprocessor controls, and a Caterpillar HEP package. Two MP36s are at the former-SP San Francisco terminal alongside a veteran Caltrain F40 in 2006. *Jim Boyd photo*

In 2004, the French company Alstom began building 33 new commuter units for NJ Transit at the old Erie Railroad shop in Hornell, New York. The PL42AC units, in a rakish carbody, carry 4,200-horsepower EMD 16-cylinder 710 engines and an all-AC traction system with an 800-kW engine-driven HEP system. The 4017 is laying over at Port Jervis, New York, in October 2007. *Jim Boyd photo*

to take advantage of the market, rather than deny it. In addition to the passenger units, GMDD put a 1,500- and 2,000-horsepower light road-switcher into its catalog, but the GP15D and GP20D were built at Boise, rather than London.

In response to Chicago Metra's request for units to replace the Milwaukee F40Cs, MPI developed a new unit based on the idea of a versatile carbody that could accommodate a variety of engines and airbrake, control, and HEP packages. The 70-foot frame with a rounded cab and nose could accommodate either a 16-cylinder 645 or 710 engine. The nose has a massive steel collision baffle hidden beneath a mostly fiberglass nose cowl that is designed to be fireproof in case of a gasoline truck collision. The semimonocoque carbody above the frame is covered with the same fiberglass and carbon-fiber composite laminate that is now used in airplane wings. The HEP package can be either a static AC inverter driven by the prime mover or a separate Caterpillar engine HEP pallet. When using the inverter, the main engine idles at Run-3, rather than the Run-8 speed required by earlier constant-speed HEP units (constant speed does not mean "full throttle," but a high rpm with only a light load to maintain the AC frequency requirements). The unit would ride on a long-wheelbase version of the time-proven EMD Blomberg truck with standard EMD DC traction motors. The MPI units can meet all present and future emission and safety regulations and can save customers money by incorporating remanufactured parts, where appropriate.

The 27 Metra units, outshopped beginning in 2003, were classified MP36PH-3S, indicating *MotivePower*, 3,600-horsepower, *Passenger*, *HEP*, three microprocessor controls, and *Static* inverter. The six Caltrain units that immediately followed were MP36PH-3Cs, reflecting the Caterpillar HEP unit. In 2007, Toronto's GO Transit began receiving the first of its 27 MP40PH-3C units, pulling 4,000 horsepower out of the EMD 16-710 engine. The new MPXpress line of locomotives by 2008 had sold 93 units to eight customers.

Although GE has cataloged a commuter version of its Genesis unit, none has sold to date, and in the twenty-first century the only new commuter units to hit the rails other than MPI were 33 PL42AC units built for New Jersey Transit by Alstom at the old Erie Railroad shop in Hornell, New York, beginning in 2004. These rakish units with angular noses, designed by Cesar Vergara (who styled the GE Genesis), pack an EMD 16-cylinder 710 engine and a full AC transmission. The engine is rated at 4,200 horsepower, though 800 kW is tapped off for HEP. The carbodies for these units were manufactured by SuperSteel in the old Alco plant in Schenectady, New York.

These "most advanced commuter units ever built" got off to a rocky start, however, when the exhaust muffler turned out to be too efficient and raised too much back pressure, resulting in overheating the turbocharger and burning up the cylinders. They sure looked impressive, though.

While all this was taking place, the unthinkable occurred: General Motors sold EMD. In April 2005, the Greenbriar Equity Group and Berkshire Partners purchased the General Motors Diesel Division and reincorporated it as Electro-Motive Diesel, retaining the familiar EMD brand. It is supremely ironic that the company that killed the steam engine is now owned by two companies, Greenbriar and Berkshire, that share the names of C&O 4-8-4s and Nickel Plate 2-8-4s!

Yard Goats

Most of the very first diesel-electrics were yard switchers, and while the streamliner locomotives and A-B-B-A road freighters got the glory, it was usually a 1,000-horsepower switcher that broke the steam barrier on America's railroads. In the 1940s, Alco, EMD, Baldwin, Lima, and F-M fielded end-cab switchers in the 600- to 1,200-horsepower range. General Electric specialized more in smaller switchers, like its center-cab 44-tonner that dodged the need for a fireman by staying under the minimum weight rule. Its end-cab 70-tonner was a favorite of short lines. Both models were full-fledged diesel-electrics and could be set up with MU capability. Numerous other small companies built a variety of switchers with all sorts of engines and transmissions, often referred to as "critters."

EMD's little 600-horsepower SW1, powered by a V-6 567, was in production from 1939 to 1953 for a total of 661 units. The horsepower was so low that it didn't need traction motor cooling blowers, and it can still be found on short lines today.

Alco continued to build its standard switchers with 539 engines until 1959, when they were replaced by similar models with 251 engines (Alco never put its 244 engine into a classic switcher). Alco's answer to the EMD BL2 in the white-elephant category was the center-cab Century 415, of which 26 were built between 1966 and 1968. These chronic leakers were powered by an eight-cylinder, 1,500-horsepower 251 engine. The high-visibility center cab design gained nothing in the front and severely limited rearward visibility compared to an end-cab switcher.

When EMD moved from its traditional prewar switcher design laid down in the Winton 201A units and carried through the entire 567 era, it stayed with the end cab for its 645-powered SW1000 and SW1500 switchers. For applications where the new, taller cabs would be a problem, EMD offered a low-profile cab in the SW1001. And the SW1500 was available in a semiroad version with FlexiCoil or Blomberg road trucks. Switcher production dropped markedly in the

1980s and dwindled to nothing by the 1990s. The rebuilders, however, got considerable work modernizing the hordes of 1950s-era switchers.

In the early twenty-first century, new emission requirements, particularly in California, forced the development of a new generation of "green" switchers. One of the first on the scene in 2001 was the 2,000-horsepower "Green Goat" hybrid unit that adopted World War I submarine technology to drive the conventional traction motors from a bank of heavy-duty lead-acid batteries. Since switchers spend a majority of their time standing still, the Green Goats constantly trickle-charge the batteries from a small 300- or 667-horsepower diesel engine and generator. Manufactured by RailPower of Vancouver, British Columbia, the Green Goats can be built on the trade-in chassis of a variety of older four-motor units.

A more popular green option, however, was the GenSet concept unit that mounted two or three 600- to 700-horsepower

Above: One of Alco's more unfortunate offerings was the C-415 center-cab switcher, 26 of which were built between 1966 and 1968. The 1,500-horsepower eight-cylinder 251 engine was in the long hood, while the auxiliaries were in the short one. The driveshaft that linked them beneath the cab was troublesome. The only two big fleets were the 10 each owned by the Rock Island and Southern Pacific. Rock Island No. 621 is at Pullman Junction, Illinois, in 1968. *Jim Boyd photo*

Opposite top: EMD's SW1500 switch engine was a great success. Powered by a 1,500-horsepower V-12 645 engine, it was a powerful and quick-responding switcher. Over a thousand were built in a number of variations that included road trucks. Its little brothers, the SW1000 and low-profile SW1001, were powered by 1,000-horsepower V-8 engines. Four of 10 new Great Northern SW1500s with dual controls are being set up for service at the Minneapolis Junction roundhouse in October 1967. *Jim Boyd photo*

Opposite bottom: Federally imposed exhaust emission requirements will be changing the face of motive power in the twenty-first century, forcing the retirement of many older models that might have become hand-me-down switchers and local engines. To meet these needs, a whole generation of new "green" locomotives is being produced. Among the first was RailPower's "Green Goat" that runs off trickle-charged batteries from a small diesel engine-generator set. RPRX 2401 is in service at Long Beach, California, in March 2006. *Jim Boyd photo*

engine/generator/radiator pallets in place of one big engine. These diesel-truck-sized engines yield 1,800 to 2,100 horsepower, but when the work load is light, two of the three GenSets simply shut down, drastically cutting down on emissions and fuel consumption. The self-contained GenSet pallets can be easily swapped out for maintenance while keeping the unit in service. The concept was developed in 2005 by National Railway Equipment of Mount Vernon, Illinois, for the Union Pacific to use in the Los Angeles area. Though the first two-GenSet unit was built on the frame of an SP MP15DC switcher, it ended up looking for all the world like an Alco C-415 on Blomberg trucks.

Subsequent units carrying three GenSets looks like long end-cab switchers riding on road trucks. Like the Green Goats, they can be built on the frames of a variety of trade-in units. RailPower got into the GenSet market, in addition to its hybrid Green Goats.

The Evolution Revolution

As we approach the second decade of the twenty-first century, the two major builders are each offering essentially one model of heavy-haul locomotives. The 4,300/4,400-horsepower super cab six-motors meet the EPA Tier II emission standards and boast vastly improved fuel economy. The customer has

When the horsepower race showed that 6,000 horsepower was impractical in service, the industry settled on the 4,300-horsepower range and refocused on fuel economy and cleaner emissions. EMD used onboard computers to squeeze maximum performance from its reliable 710 engine and AC traction motors in its SD70ACe. In 2007, the Kansas City Southern applied its historic *Southern Belle* livery to its new SD70ACe locomotives. SD70ACe 4039 is northbound arriving at the north end of Knoche Yard in Kansas City, Missouri, on May 9, 2008. *Kevin EuDaly photo*

By the twenty-first century, General Electric was leading the industry in locomotive sales, and in 2002 it introduced its Evolution Series ES44AC with a big new four-cycle GEVO-12 engine that can produce 4,400 horsepower out of 12 cylinders instead of 16. Some things in railroading are slow to change, though. In January 2008, the conductor of a Canadian Pacific freight snags train orders from the hoop at Rondout Tower on the old Milwaukee Road at Rondout, Illinois. *Jim Boyd photo*

the option of AC or DC traction systems and a few minor variations, such as the HiAd or steerable truck, but that's about it. The standardization that Dick Dilworth was dreaming of in the 1940s has become a reality.

In early 2002, General Electric built its first Evolution Series ES44AC prototype, using the completely new GEVO-12 engine. This brawny four-cycle prime mover, with 950-cubic-inch displacement per cylinder, gets 4,400 horsepower from 12 cylinders instead of the 16 required by GE's previously standard FDL engine.

All of the locomotive's systems are monitored and controlled by a hefty new computer system that can even communicate with the shop for problem diagnosis in real time while it's on the road.

Across Lake Erie in London, Ontario, EMD placed its bets on the proven and reliable 710 engine in the AC SD70ACe and DC SD70M-2, both rated at 4,300 horsepower. Although they retained the turbocharged 16-cylinder engines, EMD was able to tweak the performance to give improved fuel economy and to meet the Tier II emission regulations. Like the GE EVOs,

the new SD70s have full computer-management systems and self-testing capabilities. And they, too, can phone home for help if needed.

The EPA emission standards have already banished older units from the rails, especially in environmentally sensitive areas such as the smog-prone Los Angeles Basin. Since EMD still has thousands of older units such as GP38s and SD40s out there, it has offered its 710ECO Replacement program to repower nonturbocharged 2,000-horsepower 16-cylinder 645s with an eight-cylinder 710 and the turbocharged 16-cylinder 645 with a 12-cylinder 3,150-horsepower turbocharged 710. All of these would be microprocessor controlled and would greatly increase fuel economy; they would also meet the Tier II emission requirements, giving new life to the veteran units.

It's a brave new world, but a few time-honored railroad traditions survive. Doug Bailey of Minneapolis has a son in his early twenties who is a Canadian Pacific engineer on the old Soo Line. Son David summed up today's railroading pretty well: "Y'know, Dad, a couple of EVOs and a thermos of hot coffee on the Glenwood Job—it doesn't get much better than that."

Moving Freight

by Steve Jessup

Four sparkling CP Rail SD40-2s led by No. 5989 head up the Thompson River Canyon between Thompson and Drynoch, British Columbia, on May 7, 1989. The SD40s were among the most reliable diesel locomotives ever built by the Electro-Motive Division of General Motors. This quartet is pulling CP Rail's highest-priority eastbound Vancouver–Toronto freight with new automobiles and time-sensitive merchandise loaded into containers and truck trailers. Intermodal trains dominate today's North American rail scene. *Steve Jessup photo*

Anyone who has lugged a heavy suitcase around airport terminals can appreciate the folks who developed the idea of putting *wheels* on one side and a handle on the other side. What a novel concept to effortlessly pull your cargo around. Why didn't they think of that earlier? They could have saved travelers a lot of strain, particularly those who stuff their suitcases so full they can hardly get the zipper closed.

It makes you wonder if the invention was inspired by the transportation industry. The foundation for moving freight across the land wasn't rocket science. All it required were two simple elements found in this suitcase analogy. First, something had to safely hold the cargo, and second, something had to provide the energy to transport the wheel-based receptacle. Once the wheels were in place, it was a matter of enhancing the containers and the power that brought us to the two modes that provide surface transportation: trucks and trains.

A heavy-tonnage freight on the Pittsburgh & Lake Erie Railroad makes its way through downtown Pittsburgh behind three General Electric–built U28Bs in September 1968. Led by P&LE No. 2800, this northbound train has a variety of rolling stock including boxcars, tank cars, gondolas, and open hoppers carrying bulk commodities. The growth of the industry in the last 40 years has necessitated railcar upgrades to efficiently move the extra tonnage. *Jim Boyd photo*

The whole idea of railroading, which came long before trucks (unless you consider horse-drawn wagons as the precursor to trucks), was to connect regions for the sake of moving and trading goods (as well as ferrying passengers). It was basic commerce. Goods had varying values, and the railroads provided the services to move the items between the sellers and the buyers. As common carriers, the railroads were required to accept just about anything that was presented to them for transport as long as it didn't exceed established height, width, and weight restrictions.

There were basic rates the shippers paid the railways based on the value of the freight. One thing shippers may not have known during the earliest times was just how big the railroad industry would become. As the rail network expanded, the railroads spent monumental sums of money to finance their undertaking. Even before the turn of the century, the railways were no longer mom-and-pop outfits. They were America's largest business dealing with serious shippers—a far cry from a donkey toting a backpack around, or even a horse pulling a loaded wagon. This was an industry dealing in tons of commodities to be transported.

To support the growing demands of both the shipper and the railways, it was necessary to build better equipment so that freight would move in a safe and efficient manner. And there was no better time for that to become the hallmark of the industry than during the war years when America fully relied on the railways to come through for the country.

The traffic surges during and after World War II necessitated improved trackwork and signaling, and as trains continued to get heavier and longer, upgrades in rolling stock capacity and reliability were imperative. Steel-sided cars bumped outdated wooden cars out of service, and before too long, America's freight trains had a colorful mix of rolling stock—many designed to handle specific types of commodities.

Rolling Stock Review

Boxcar: Picture your suitcase on a mammoth scale. The boxcar, basically a box on wheels and the universal piece of rolling stock, was designed to haul anything and everything. As long as the commodity could be packaged in some way, it could be shipped on a boxcar. For instance, coal could be bagged, and oil and other liquids could be put in a barrel, and then loaded into the car. Because cars were loaded by hand, the weight of such freight packages was typically less than 200 pounds. Although they actually weren't the first type of freight car—that honor goes to the lowly flatcar and gondola—boxcars made up pretty much the entire consist of freight trains of the last half of the nineteenth century. Thirty-foot boxcars ruled in the late nineteenth century, and then 40-foot cars became standard for a majority of the twentieth

century, hauling up to 50 tons. They were displaced by 50-foot, 77-ton cars by the 1970s, although 50-footers began appearing just before World War II. Fifty-foot-long High-Cube (also spelled Hi-Cube) boxcars with a little extra height, and even 60-foot High-Cube cars, can be seen today. High-Cube cars as long as 89 feet first appeared in the early 1960s, mostly to accommodate large auto parts that are now transported in the smaller versions or containers. Again, the classic boxcar hauled just about anything, notably paper, furniture, appliances, non-temperature-controlled foodstuffs, and many other manufactured goods. They could also be quickly modified with special doors to create what was in effect an ersatz covered gondola to carry loose (unbagged) grain—a practice that went out of favor in the 1970s with the evolution of grain hopper cars.

Four different modern boxcars are seen on this eastbound Union Pacific train at Cascade Locks, Oregon. At the far right just behind the locomotive is a 50-foot single-door boxcar followed by a double-door version. The Milwaukee Road car is a 50-foot "High-Cube" plug-door box that has a little more capacity. At left, the CP Rail box also has a plug door but has smooth sides instead of ribs. It's not uncommon for empty boxcars to ride with the doors open—likely more to air them out than simple crew neglect. *Steve Jessup photo*

An A-B-B set of F7s pulls a string of Santa Fe ice refrigerator cars westbound at McCook, Illinois, in July 1966. At various stops along the line, ice blocks would be loaded into the bunkers through hatches located on the rooftops of the cars. Note that a couple of cars on this train have hatches that are open, indicating this train has empty cars and is headed back to the West Coast for more perishables. These cars eventually gave way to larger mechanical reefers. *Jim Boyd photo*

Modern reefers lettered for Cryo-Trans are on the move at Scribner, Washington, on BNSF rails outside of Spokane in the summer of 2004. The refrigeration unit is mounted on the ends of the cars. The reefers are monitored by satellite for temperature fluctuations, low fuel, and the need for maintenance. Inside, the temperatures are well below freezing; these cars are likely carrying frozen French fries. *Steve Jessup photo*

At Martinsdale, Montana, a Milwaukee Road train of cattle is headed east in October 1971. The majority of stock cars built were 40 and 50 feet in length, but later some railroads had 60-foot and even 91-foot stock cars. Livestock moves required stopping at regular intervals for watering and feeding. Conrail and Union Pacific were among the last two railroads to transport livestock to slaughterhouses and then finished products to the consumer. *Jim Boyd photo*

Refrigerator car: Known as "reefers," these cars replicated the boxcar design except they incorporated heavy insulation, internal ice bunkers, and sealed doors. They also had hatches on the roof that allowed for ice loading to keep the contents—mostly food items—cool. Companies shipping such items as fruits, vegetables, or meats required reefers to keep their products fresh during transit. Forty and 50-foot cars were standard, and later mechanical reefers displaced the ice versions, thus eliminating ice station stops en route to their destinations. Each car had a modular diesel driven compressor installed that lowered the temperature well below freezing to accommodate the growing frozen food and juice market. These reefers, which carried their own fuel supplies, grew to 56 feet, some of which are still used today. The most modern reefer cars, which began circulating on the BNSF and Union Pacific in the past few years, are 72 feet in length and are satellite monitored for temperature fluctuations, low fuel, and the need for maintenance.

Stock car: Another derivative of the boxcar, the stock car was developed in the latter half of the 1800s to transport livestock. Instead of solid sides, the cars had slats, allowing air to circulate through. Cars were typically 40 feet long with others at 50 feet, although two of the nation's last livestock movements—one on Union Pacific, the other on Conrail in the 1980s—involved updated car designs, which measured 60 feet and 91 feet, respectively. Moving cattle from their ranch homes or feedlots to slaughterhouses required care, and getting them on and off the train wasn't easy. At trackside stock pens, they were unloaded, fed, watered, exercised, and reloaded—a very time-consuming process. The cattle had to be monitored for sickness or injury which, of course, would substantially devalue the stock. Livestock no longer moves on trains; however, the finished product often does before it hits your local market.

Covered hoppers can haul a variety of bulk commodities including grain, plastic pellets, soda ash, and in this case, potash. This Canpotex covered hopper is pictured at Bonneville, Washington, on BNSF rails moving westward to Portland on May 31, 2003. The contents of the cars are loaded through hatches located on the roof and are designed for rapid discharge through the bays underneath the hopper. *Julie Jessup photo*

Chicago, Burlington & Quincy twin-bay hoppers are lined up in a train at Mendota, Illinois, in the mid-1960s, showing the wood sides on these 50-ton composite hoppers. After the war years, steel-sided hoppers replaced the wood types, and these cars often hauled coal and crushed rock. Today's open hoppers are longer to accommodate much larger loads, although a smaller, single-bay hopper is still used to haul iron ore and taconite. *Jim Boyd photo*

Tank cars carrying corn syrup are eastbound on the Dixon Switch Job at Dixon, Illinois, in December 1979. The insulated, nonpressurized tanks are lettered for the Clinton Corn Processing Company of Clinton, Iowa. Outside of the agricultural market, such liquid products as oil, propane, chlorine, and ammonia fertilizer are transported in tank cars. Although the cars are similar, most are dedicated to one specific commodity. *Jim Boyd photo*

Covered hopper: Prior to the covered hopper, grain was moved in small boxcars even without being sacked. It was particularly difficult to unload, which led to the design of the hopper car. Whether smooth-sided or ribbed, these 50- to 55-foot, 110-ton cars have hatches on the rooftop where grains such as wheat, corn, and soybeans can be loaded. Underneath the cars are bays that are opened for expedited unloading. Other commodities such as plastic pellets, soda ash, potash, and flour utilize these types of hoppers. Smaller 35-foot versions of the same hopper with two bays underneath (instead of three or four) might carry cement or limestone. Another type of hopper, similar in concept, is the air-slide hopper, which has been used to transport such items as flour or sugar.

Tank car: The development of the tank car meant the end of loading barrels of liquid substances into boxcars and gondolas. If you turned a barrel on its side and put in on a table that rode on wheels, you'd have the basics of the original tank cars. Like all cars, tankers were redesigned and improved to meet growing demands. Early upgraded versions were around 36 to 40 feet rolling on 50-ton trucks with a capacity of about 12,000 gallons. In time these cars, built pressurized and nonpressurized, insulated and noninsulated, grew to lengths greater than 60 feet, holding 33,000 gallons. Tank cars handled crude oil and finished gasoline, which was big business for the railroads as automobiles started rolling off assembly lines. Other tank-car products include propane, chlorine, ammonia fertilizer, ethanol, and petroleum derivatives such as propylene, used in making plastics. From the agricultural market, corn syrup and vegetable oil ride in 40- and 56-foot tank cars. All tanks are generally assigned to one specific commodity and are not universal in service regardless of whether they get steam cleaned.

Open hopper: The open hopper is similar to the covered version in that it has bays (hoppers) underneath for rapid discharge. It is often smaller than its covered counterpart, and the loads don't require enclosed protection. On the smallest scale, 24-foot single-bay hoppers are still used to carry iron ore and taconite (a slightly lower grade of ore). Larger twin-bay hoppers were used for crushed rock or coal, and as the coal market exploded in the latter part of the twentieth century, the hoppers grew to the 50-foot range with three and four bays, accommodating 90 tons. (Also see gondolas, next page.)

Gondolas filled with steel trail the power of Reading's *Bethlehem Star* moving out of Saucon Yard in Bethlehem, Pennsylvania, in June 1975, returning to Reading after serving the steel mill. To the left of the train is a long string of gondolas that can carry just about anything from steel (including steel coils) to scrap, dirt, and debris. *Jim Boyd photo*

Gondola: Most gondolas (the exception being the covered gondola) are nonenclosed, open-top cars without bays. They must be unloaded the same way they're loaded—from the top. Like a boxcar, a gondola can carry just about anything as long as the product can't be spoiled from exposure to the elements. (A covered gondola, however, would offer protection of certain loads.) There are three main varieties of gondolas, distinguishable by the height of the sides (other than length). The more universal gondola has low sides and carries mostly scrap and debris, railroad ties, dirt, and occasionally coils of steel. Coal and crushed rock were sometimes hauled in this version measuring 50 to 66 feet. Also related to this version are drop-bottom and side-dump gondolas that make dumping rock debris a little easier. Many of today's coal cars are similar to the open hoppers in length and tonnage, but, without the bays,

they are technically open gondolas. Instead of dumping from the bottom, the cars are equipped with rotary couplers that allow the car to be turned upside down (without disengaging) and unloaded from the top over a massive pit. Also, many of the cars have "bathtub" bottoms for extra capacity. A third variety has even higher sides and is approximately 61 feet in length. It's often used for carrying woodchips. A much shorter version of this type served the sugar beet industry before trucks eventually took the business away.

Opposite: A British Columbia Railway freight snakes its way southbound at Tisdall, British Columbia, on August 26, 1985. Eight woodchip cars are seen behind the locomotives. The cars measure a little more than 60 feet long. Although not evident in this photo, a net is often secured on top of the car to keep the wind from blowing the woodchips away. *Kevin EuDaly photo*

The common flatcar can haul just about anything as long as the load can be tied down. These flatcars are assigned army tanks at Fort Knox, Kentucky, in May 1979 on Illinois Central trackage. Flatcars date back to the earliest days of railroading, and on some versions, stakes along the sides help to secure loads and keep them from shifting. *Jim Boyd photo*

The modern center-beam flatcar is used to haul much of today's lumber loads. This center-beam flat is coming around Horseshoe Curve in Pennsylvania on a westbound Conrail freight in October 1987. The car has bulkheads at both ends and a divider down the middle. To keep the car balanced, the loads must be evenly distributed on both sides. *Jim Boyd photo*

Two Santa Fe Alco S-4 switchers are assigned duty at the auto loading facility at Hobart Yard in Los Angeles. This 1960s photograph shows the use of open autoracks, which replaced auto boxcars. These auto carriers transported far more vehicles than the boxcars, but the automobiles were not protected and unfortunately drew the attention of vandals. Later, the railroads took another step to install protective side panels. *Santa Fe collection, Kansas State Historical Society*

Flatcar: Yet another car wearing the "all-purpose" label is the flatcar, which dates to the earliest railroading days. Like the basic gondola without the sides, many items can ride on a flat provided the loads can be tied down. Sometimes stakes along the sides kept loads from shifting overboard and could also be used as a prop for securing items. Lumber, farm machinery, and generators and transformers can all be seen on flatcars, although the latter two typically ride on a depressed-center flatcar that is designed for extra-heavy loads and has an extra or larger set of trucks on each end. Lumber frequently moves on another type of flatcar called a center-beam, which has bulkheads at both ends and a divider down the middle. To keep the car balanced, the loads must be evenly distributed on both sides. Flats with only bulkheads (to prevent loads shifting end to end) serve similar shipments and sometimes pulpwood.

Autorack: Nobody had to worry about shipping automobiles until the 1920s, when car manufacturing began to soar. Then, after World War II, the industry surged to astronomical heights. Initially, the railroads used 50-foot boxcars to transport vehicles, which turned out to be a good-news/bad news situation. The good news was that the boxcars, built with wider doors, provided protection. The bad news was that too much space was wasted. A new auto carrier was designed in the 1960s to transport cars in larger groupings. The 89-foot autoracks contained two or three decks and could haul up to 15 vehicles. This also turned out to be a good-news/bad-news issue. They carried more but were open and unprotected, which led to vandalism. The railroads countered with enclosed autoracks, which are in use today along with newer, longer, articulated versions to haul even more cars per unit. Another railcar worth noting here is

Shortly after the Frisco was merged into BN, train No. 33 was renumbered to 31. Here, it rips through Brookline, Missouri, at 70 miles per hour on May 14, 1981. On the head end is a semi-enclosed autorack with side panels, and behind that are open autoracks. Before the enclosed autoracks came on the scene, auto trains were frequently inspected at various points along the way by railroad police. Articulated autoracks with greater capacity are now common on North American rails. *Kevin EuDaly photo*

Led by five shiny Santa Fe GP60Ms, an eastbound piggyback train races toward Kansas City at Holliday, Kansas, on September 17, 1994. The truck trailers are riding on articulated spine cars, which are very common on lightweight intermodal trains. The spine cars are mixed with the more traditional 89-foot flatcars that were designed to carry a pair of 40- or 45-foot trailers, three 28-foot pup trailers, or one modern 53-foot trailer. *Kevin EuDaly photo*

a canopy car, which is similar to an autorack. It's a long flatcar with a large canopy over the top, enabling it to accommodate and protect oversized loads such as Boeing aircraft parts.

Piggyback flatcar: Soon to follow automobiles off the assembly line were trucks and trailers, a mode of transportation that would compete with the railways. Yet not all trucks would cover the entire distance of a freight run. In the 1920s, a

few railroads experimented with hauling truck trailers, thus eliminating the need to transfer contents from the truck into a railcar and then back into a truck at the other end of the run. Later, the railroads began to market this "piggyback" service in a big way, combining the virtues of both forms of transport. The trains handled—very economically—the long-haul part of the trip (eliminating the need for a truck driver for

Union Pacific's dedicated container, or stack train, for American President Lines is westbound near Memaloose State Park on the Oregon side of the Columbia River on August 10, 1996. The first two cars are single well cars followed by slightly different types of articulated "five-packs." The train is loaded with a combination of 40-, 45-, and 48-foot containers. These containers come and go through the Port of Seattle. *Steve Jessup photo*

each truck during that haul), and the trucks did the short hauls at either end. The railroads even developed their own trucking network with their names on the equipment. Flatcars designed specifically for truck trailers were built between 50 and 89 feet, with the 89-footer becoming the standard as it accommodated a pair of 40- or 45-foot trailers. Later, articulated spine cars were developed to reduce excess weight. Coupler to coupler, these "10-packs" (which could be reduced to just two units) contained a hitch and two longer wheel platforms—one on each side of the spine—to accommodate 28-foot "pup" trailers all the way up to today's 53-foot trailers. The conventional 89-foot flat can also carry two 40- or 45-foot containers with right-angle notches at each corner and another four at the center sides of the car. Spine cars can be set up for containers with notches located on the wheel platforms and on a crossbar at the hitch end.

Well car: Increasing trade with foreign countries brought on the need to efficiently move the countless number of ocean-going containers. Add to that the soaring numbers of domestic containers that are also stuffed full of merchandise. In the 1980s, five-unit well cars were designed to handle 10 containers, two per unit with one stacked on top of another. Single well cars were also built, and today the wells can handle 40-, 45-, and 53-foot containers. Some of the earlier versions could handle only 40-footers on the bottom. The well car is essentially a type of flatcar with a perfect rectangular compartment carved into it with the frames serving as the sides to the lower container. The bottom is not solid, but it has cross supports underneath and allows the container to sit at a lower center of gravity. Another container can be stacked on top, and the containers are made to interlock with each other at the corners. Larger containers have interlocks at the corners as well as the 40-foot measurements so they can be stacked on the smaller ones. Because virtually anything that's not perishable can be handled in a container, and containers have become so prolific, the container-loaded well car has become today's boxcar.

Steel coil car: One other specifically designed car worth mentioning is the steel coil car. It's basically a 50-foot flat that contains a type of cradle for the steel coil loads with a pair of canopies on each half of the car for protection from the elements—steel being subject to rusting from moisture. This car type was developed back in the 1960s, although some coils of steel are occasionally loaded in gondolas.

Moving Freight   251

Well cars on a BNSF westbound intermodal train pass by Kansas City's Union Station March 1, 2008. The lower portion of this well car can accommodate two 20-foot containers, as seen here, or one 40-, 45-, or 48-foot container. The photo shows 53-foot domestic containers on top lettered for trucking companies, which now use these "cubes" in addition to the more traditional trailers. Longer well cars have been built to accommodate the growing number of 53-foot containers. *Steve Jessup photo*

A BNSF unit train of coiled steel rolls through the curve at Hart, Missouri, headed westbound on September 5, 1998. The railcars, similar to flat cars, were designed with a cradle to hold the coils in place. Other cars for these loads are built with a canopy over the top to help protect the steel from damage. Occasionally, the loads are hauled in the traditional low-sided gondolas. *Kevin EuDaly photo*

Canadian Pacific and Pacific Great Eastern boxcars take on timber "pit prop" loads being shipped on the PGE from Quesnel, British Columbia, in the early 1950s. Pit props are used as mine roof supports. The forest-rich areas of western Canada have long provided building materials, especially lumber products, for the United States. It's not uncommon today to see huge blocks of lumber streaming down the West Coast from the Pacific shores of British Columbia. Railfan & Railroad Magazine *collection*

Freight Cars on the Move

Once freight cars are loaded with goods, they are ready to be sent to their destinations, but that can be a rather complex process in railroading—although it pays off in incredibly economical transport costs, particularly when bulk commodities such as coal, steel, grain, and aggregate are being moved. A CSX television ad released in 2007 said it all: A gallon of fuel can move a ton of freight 423 miles (when that freight is moving as part of an assembled freight train). The extreme efficiency of steel wheels on rails is the key, since so little friction is involved. With a typical freight train, the contact area between each wheel tread and the rail surface is less than a dime, so the amount of contact for an entire train is perhaps about the size of a dinner plate. Once the inertia is overcome in starting a train, the amount of power necessary to maintain momentum is a fraction of what it takes for a rubber-tired truck to do the same. And when one considers that the average railcar can carry at least the equivalent of a semitruck, if not twice as

much, the economies of scale begin to really come into play. And whereas each truck requires a driver, a two-person crew can handle a train of 70 cars, drastically lowering the cost of movement in terms of both wages and fuel.

How are trains assembled? Once the finished products are safely packed into the appropriate freight cars and are ready to be picked up on the loading/unloading track or industry spur of the producer or manufacturer, they are picked up by a local train or switcher whose job it is to work a particular region or commercial district. The switch job may include distributing empty cars and dropping off loads to various businesses, as well as picking up loads and transferring them back to the yard where they will be placed on a holding track. Cars from other locals and regional inbound trains will be added to the holding track or tracks.

Basically, once cars are gathered at a principal yard, outbound over-the-road trains are built or inbound trains disassembled. When a train is built, its cars are "blocked"

A worker on the Southern Pacific Railroad loads a refrigerator car with ice in this photo from 1952. The SP sent tons of vegetables out of the coastal and valley regions of California to Midwest and East Coast markets. The reefers had to be iced at different points along the way to keep the perishables fresh and cool. Once this worker jams the ice into the bunkers, the hatch will be closed and the car will be on its way. Railfan & Railroad Magazine *collection*

Using a forklift, this worker is loading cotton into a Missouri Pacific outside-braced boxcar in Houston sometime in the 1950s. Whether it be manufactured goods from the East, petroleum or cotton from the South, perishables from the West, or forest products from the Northwest, freight is loaded, moving, and unloaded every hour of the day, every day of the year. Railfan & Railroad Magazine *collection*

or grouped by destination or at least a general direction of travel. The collection of cars picked up from one business may all have different final destinations since each shipper often has multiple accounts. Therefore, they might ride together initially to a common intermediate or interchange point before being broken up or sorted out—classified or reclassified, in railroad terms.

More often than not, some cars are relayed from point of origin to point of destination over more than one carrier. At interchange points, the next railroad in the link takes the exchange of cars and may begin the switching process again, grouping new destination blocks. Now the cars may be on different trains headed to their ultimate destination. And once

they arrive at the destination yard, the cars will be sorted into smaller groupings or blocks for local train service to their drop-off point—the same way it all started.

Railroads have meticulous data on all their equipment all the time. A car's origin, destination, contents, and whereabouts are immediately available through the railway's database and can be tracked 24 hours a day by the shipper and recipient.

Railroad Yards

A railroad yard is a very large area of property with a network of side-by-side trackage to hold and sort rail cars. There are different types of yards: some are for storage while others are active, being continuously used for car sorting or classification.

Maine Central GP7R No. 572 picks up home-road boxcars on the Lewiston Lower Branch in Lewiston, Maine, in September 1981. The load will soon be taken to a large yard for blocking and eventually on the way to its ultimate destination. If possible, the boxcar will return home with loads so that revenue is not lost on the backhaul. *Jim Boyd photo*

The Santa Fe yard at Pueblo, Colorado, is active on October 9, 1950, as a Baldwin DS-4-4-1000 pushes a cut of boxcars and one visible gondola past the tower and over the hump. Steam engines to the left and right can also be seen switching cars. One by one, the railcars will find their way to the appropriate track in the background, where cars with similar destinations have already been "blocked." *Santa Fe collection, Kansas State Historical Society*

Santa Fe and United Parcel Service trailers are being loaded on 89-foot piggyback flatcars in this scene at Corwith Yard in Chicago on October 7, 1980. The view is taken looking toward the northwest. The soaring container and trailer traffic has turned nearly all of these tracks into an intermodal yard today. In addition to the scores of Santa Fe rolling stock present, a string of Santa Fe locomotives can be seen in the background on the left. *Santa Fe collection, Kansas State Historical Society*

Yards may be as small as two tracks or may be dozens of tracks wide. Generally, the most important yards are those used for sorting cars and breaking down or building trains. Taking a closer look at large classification yards at interchange points (where railroads exchange traffic), inbound trains originating from different cities will enter the yard area designated as the receiving tracks. Each train typically has cars with a variety of destinations beyond this point.

We'll describe two traditional methods of car classification within a yard. The longtime traditional method is known as "flat switching" is where the yard switcher and its crew, including one person on the ground, takes a string, or "cut,"

A 50-foot Santa Fe boxcar rolls down the hump through the main retarder (to the right of the signal post) at Santa Fe's Argentine Yard in Kansas City in late 1969. The yard tower is on the right, and the pin puller's building can be seen at left. Gravity will send the car into a bowl of tracks, and once it's automatically switched to the right track, the car will slowly roll and couple into the car ahead of it. *Santa Fe collection, Kansas State Historical Society*

of cars onto the yard lead and sorts them into their respective yard tracks, each track having an assigned destination. The person on the ground must uncouple or couple a car or cars as the locomotive pulls and shoves them to and from different tracks. Together, the switchman and the engineer must coordinate these movements, usually through two-way radios, but in earlier days, hand or lantern signals were used. More and more flat switching today is done using remote-control locomotives operated by a person on the ground who may also be operating couplers and switches.

A second method became widely embraced by North American railroads after World War II: hump switching. It is a faster and often more automated approach to handling a large amount of classification. From the receiving tracks, an engine (or engines, often remotely controlled) will shove an inbound train's cars up an incline to the crest. A switchman there can uncouple the cars one at a time or in groups, depending on the instructions provided by the yardmaster. Each passing car's number can be scanned or read and, based on computer data, its destination is confirmed, which sets the automated routing into motion. The computer will throw a series of switches on the opposite side of the crest, and gravity will send the car rolling down the hump toward a vast bowl or area of tracks. As it's guided through switches, the car moves at controlled speeds thanks to air-operated retarders (like clamps) that squeeze

Union Pacific freight trains are lined up and ready to depart the yard at Ogden, Utah, in July 1969. A variety of motive power is displayed here, including 10,000-horsepower gas-turbine-electric locomotives (center), an SD24 (far left), SD45s (right), and some Southern Pacific SD45s. Trailing the main gas-turbine-electric power consist is a string of mechanical reefers loaded with fruits and vegetables from California. The freights are headed eastward through the Wahsatch Mountains. *Jim Boyd photo*

A BNSF loaded auto train is seen westbound at Hart, Missouri, on October 20, 1997, powered by C44-9W 625 and GP60M 138. This train originated on eastern carriers out of Michigan and was interchanged with the BNSF Railway in Chicago. The cars will likely haul import automobiles from the West Coast on the return trip to Midwestern and East Coast destinations. As cars are freely interchanged, each railroad takes responsibility for the equipment and its contents. *Kevin EuDaly photo*

against the wheels to regulate the movement. Once it navigates to the right track, it slowly glides toward the group of cars ahead of it and couples onto the rear. When each destination block is complete, a yard switcher transfers it to another area designated as the departing tracks.

Yards often have bypass mains that skirt the switching areas. Run-through trains, or those that don't require sorting, use this main line to avoid yard congestion. In addition, most large yards have locomotive-servicing facilities. The facilities usually are equipped with fueling stations, sanding towers, wash racks, and an engine house for light or running repairs.

Car Accountability/Interchange

Don't be deceived. Rail competition is still fierce. It's just that it has a tendency to reside underneath the three-piece suits of the railroad executives rather than being worn on the sleeves like those who built these empires. These railroad pioneers originally envisioned *their* line as a monopoly. They were going to handle all the freight on their line, and the idea of handing off freight to another railroad—a potential rival—was hardly envisioned. But when America's rail network was firmly established coast to coast, the breadth and power of the shipping industry demanded the cooperation of railroads. The game was all about customer care from the shipper's door to the receiver's door.

Prior to the second big merger era—which started in the 1960s and continued to the 2000s—a large Class 1 railroad may have had around 70,000 freight cars, while smaller Class 1s had somewhere between 5,000 and 10,000 pieces of rolling stock. Since trains do long-haul best, freight car statistics become a little irrelevant since so much traffic is interchanged between the railroads.

Although railroads still buy cars, the trend of pooling or sharing cars is a little more visible. An example is the Trailer Train Corporation (TTX), which is owned by North American

Heading westbound through Bingen, Washington, on March 19, 2006, this BNSF freight has three Trailer Train Corporation (TTX) boxcars behind the first grain hopper. TTX is owned by North America's major railroads and lends visibility to the concept of pooling or sharing rolling stock. The CSX unit running on BNSF rails also illustrates locomotive pooling. Calculated by horsepower hours, the amount of time the unit spends on the BNSF will be owed to CSX in a similar power exchange. *Steve Jessup photo*

Some of the newest grain hoppers in use today run on the Kansas City Southern. Two KCS SD70ACe locomotives are seen powering a southbound loaded grain train out of Knoche Yard in Kansas City on May 4, 2008. Each grain car is priced at around $75,000, and rather than coat the cars in basic gray, the KCS spent some extra money in the paint shop with this striking scheme, which also matches the railroad's fleet of executive passenger cars. *Jim Boyd photo*

railroads as a whole. Common cars such as trailer flats, well cars, boxcars, autoracks, and gondolas are bought and then pressed into service, piling up mileage for all the railroads. Also, leasing companies or large shippers will acquire cars to lease or furnish to the railroads.

Part of running an efficient railroad is making sure all cars are generating revenue miles. Boxcars, well cars, trailer flats, gondolas, reefers, and autoracks are all examples of cars that can be sent long distances with loads, short hauled from that point to nearby businesses that need an empty car to load, and shipped back cross-country. The idea is to keep the car from running empty on long hauls, since it's not making money for the railroad while in empty mode. Coal cars, grain hoppers, and tank cars are the main exceptions, as they must be returned to specific areas where bulk loads are generated (that is, the Wyoming coal fields, the heartlands for grain, or the Gulf Coast for petroleum). In some instances, well cars and trailer flats will run empty (also called bare-table trains) so that they can be repositioned to areas that need them (that is, an overflow of containers at a location where enough equipment is immediately available).

As you can imagine, freight cars take a pounding in addition to being exposed to the elements. Parts are frequently replaced, and they eventually wear out. There's always a market for new cars, and the cost varies, depending on the car. Grain hoppers, cement hoppers, center-beams, and gondolas typically run between $50,000 and $80,000. Coal cars and steel coil cars are priced in the $75,000 to $90,000 range. A good 60-foot boxcar rates around $100,000, with an autorack selling for about $130,000. The most expensive cars are the three-unit and five-unit well cars, for obvious reasons, which run between $175,000 and $275,000.

Among today's builders include National Steel Car (all types), Trinity Industries (different types, yet noted for modern grain hoppers), Greenbrier (intermodal market—well cars), FreightCar America (coal cars), American Railcar Industries (tanks and covered hoppers), and Union Tank Car.

Unit Trains

A unit train is one of any length carrying the same cars. Some may go a step further and define it as a train of any length carrying one commodity that is often loaded from one location and delivered to a single customer. However, that's not always true. For example, unit grain trains delivering to one location might collect a group of cars from different elevators in the same region. Also, container trains might be loaded at a port or piggyback facility but then broken up at an intermediate point based on the destination of each container. Besides that, containers carry all sorts of goods.

Bathtub gondolas are being reloaded with coal at the York Canyon Mine in New Mexico on September 18, 1992. These cars are limited to coal service and return to the mines empty as they do not generate revenue on the backhaul. However, due to the millions of tons of coal that must be transported from the mines to power plants across the United States, these cars have no idle time because they're constantly running on the circuit from mine to power plant and return. *Kevin EuDaly photo*

Railroads have operated unit trains or dedicated trains for years, but they weren't as prominent as they have been over the last 25 years or so. The majority of the freights were general or mixed manifest trains carrying a variety of cars and commodities. Unit trains have at least one advantage in that they rarely require switching at intermediate points, which slightly improves their running time and makes unit trains a much more economical operation.

Intermodal trains, such as this eastbound stack train west of Mescal, Arizona, make up nearly half of all the Class 1 railroads' gross revenue. Trade with countries such as China has put millions of these ocean-going containers on the rails and has significantly increased freight traffic. Two Cotton Belt–lettered GP60s and a pair of SP SD40T-2s power this unit train up a slight grade in November 1994. *Steve Jessup photo*

Included in the intermodal unit class are unique military trains that transport tanks, trucks, and related equipment on piggyback flatcars to various bases around the United States. As they did back in World War II, the railroads stand ready to ship necessary supplies for the nation's armed forces in the event of war. South of Nisqually, Washington, four BN units power a long southbound military train through the forests of the Washington coast on January 17, 1993. *Kevin EuDaly photo*

On July 14, 1987, Katy's *Texas Special*, train No. 10, wheels 11 cars of piggyback traffic from Texas into Kansas City at 67th Street. The lead trailer is UPS and represents a shipping company that has partnered with the railroads in an effort to provide customers with fast, efficient, and affordable service. Such trucking companies include Roadway, ABF, J. B. Hunt, Schneider, and Swift, and they headline an increasing number of large trucking firms hopping on board the piggyback bandwagon with not only trailers, but also 53-foot domestic containers. *Kevin EuDaly photo*

An extension of the piggyback idea came to fruition in the form of RoadRailer service, where truck trailers are outfitted with specialized wheel dollies that allow long strings of truck trailers to be pulled without putting them on flatcars. This southbound BNSF RoadRailer is headed for Texas on May 3, 2008, rolling past the Old Union Depot interlocking tower in Kansas City's West Bottoms. *Kevin EuDaly photo*

Another loaded coal train from the Powder River Basin rounds the corner at Ulm, Wyoming, on May 18, 1998. The train is powered by five Burlington Northern 3,000-horsepower C30-7s up front, plus a set of helpers to move the tonnage. The three largest mines alone produce enough coal to load 25 trains per day, each with more than 100 cars. In 2006, the Powder River Basin shipped out more than 431 million tons of coal! *Kevin EuDaly photo*

Burlington Northern SD40-2s shove on the rear of the coal train at Ulm, Wyoming, on May 18, 1998. The entire coal train can be seen in the picture. Spliced between the two units is a fuel tender, which supplies the locomotives with diesel fuel, thus eliminating extra stops on long hauls. On heavy-tonnage freights on steep grades, helper locomotives are needed to assist in pushing the train as well as braking on downhill sections. The helpers also greatly reduce drawbar tension. *Kevin EuDaly photo*

To show how the North American freight train has changed, here's an interesting statistic. According to the American Association of Railroads, the three most common unit train types—intermodal (containers and trailers), coal, and grain—make up nearly *half* of all the Class 1 railroads' gross revenue.

Coal used to be king, accounting for a fifth of the income, but in 2003, the rapidly growing intermodal market surpassed coal, taking in approximately 22 percent of the overall revenue. The intermodal industry has become a traffic gold mine for railroads as America's largest ports continue to off-load (and send out) millions of containers year after year. The downside is that the profit margin on intermodal transport can be thin for railroads. Oddly enough, it's a business where everything is in place for trucks to do all the surface transportation. You'd expect trains to win in the coal and grain commodities, but the staggering financial gains and shipping efficiency that the intermodal market has linked with the railroads has truly dropped transportation jaws.

Unlock an international or ocean-going container, or a 53-foot domestic container, and you'll find all sorts of consumer goods: electronics, toys, bikes, lawn mowers, clothes, auto parts—if it's on the shelves of your local Wal-Mart, K-Mart, or Target stores, it may have spent some time on the high iron in one of these unit trains. And it's not just containers. The railroads are shipping increasing numbers of highway truck trailers, which have now grown to 53 feet in length—pretty much the standard today for trucking giants. In addition to serving the needs of priority shipping firms such as United Parcel Service, Roadway, Yellow Freight, and ABF to name a few, the railroads have entered into partnerships with the likes of J. B. Hunt, Schneider, Swift, Alliance, and Market Transport—just a handful of names regularly riding the rails. The goal between the trucking firms and railways is to maximize customer service—essentially providing the fastest, most efficient shipping solutions for businesses.

Then there's the coal industry. Coal is probably the one commodity most associated with unit trains, and it has the distinction of being first in the unit-train concept. Most people connect coal to the Appalachian region and the original big-time haulers such as the Norfolk & Western, the Chesapeake & Ohio, and the Louisville & Nashville. Few people recognize the one region that forever transformed the coal industry into a massive revenue-maker: Wyoming's Powder River Basin. It was once described like this: If you took a postcard and pretended it was the state of Wyoming, then placed a large stamp in the upper right-hand corner, that would roughly represent the total area mined in this region. And, evidence suggests that a quarter to a third of the state has this low-sulfur coal beneath it.

Normally reserved for excursion trains, Reading & Northern's 4-8-4 steam locomotive No. 2102 works in revenue service, hauling 30 loads of high-grade anthracite coal through Port Clinton, Pennsylvania, on April 6, 1991. This high-grade metallurgical coal from the anthracite region at Tamaqua is excellent for making paint pigment. This shipment is bound for the Quebec Iron & Titanium company on the St. Lawrence River. *Mike Del Vecchio photo*

Three of the largest mines in the region are producing between 100 and 138 million tons of coal per year—enough to load 5,900 cars per day and 9,200 trains a year, which is more than 25 trains a day. Again, that's only from three mines. In 1998, the entire Powder River Basin area, which is served by the Union Pacific and the BNSF Railway, produced more than 293 million tons. In 2006, that figure jumped to more than 431 million tons! Needless to say, Wyoming is the nation's largest coal-producing state. Prior to 1990, that title bounced between West Virginia and Kentucky. Eighty percent of coal burned at U.S. power plants comes from the Powder River Basin, and while most of the plants are located in the center of the country, shipments from this region have gone to both the Atlantic and Pacific coasts.

Although Wyoming headlines the coal industry, the Appalachian region and Colorado and Utah produce their share of unit coal trains. In addition to serving Eastern markets, the

Appalachian region caters to Europe with export coal. On the West Coast, Canadian Pacific and Canadian National deliver many coal trains to Roberts Bank, British Columbia, for export to the Pacific Rim countries, particularly China.

The third most common unit train is grain, and like coal, it doesn't generate revenue on the backhaul. But during the peak of the shipping season in fall and winter, the railroads can hardly return the cars fast enough to handle the tons waiting to be shipped back at the elevators. Grain provides the railroads with about 8 percent of the yearly gross revenue with commodities including wheat, corn, and soybeans. In addition to serving food-production plants and processing facilities, grain trains also serve major ports where the product is loaded into large ships for export to a growing world market. There was a time when the most common method of handling large volumes of grain was for it to be loaded into railcars at trackside elevators,

One of the Western Maryland's two hammerhead RS-3s shoves a cut of grain hoppers toward the export grain elevator at Port Covington, Maryland, in July 1976. Grain provides today's railroads with about 8 percent of their yearly gross revenue. Export grain is big business for the railroads as foreign countries hunger for what's grown in America's heartland. *Jim Boyd photo*

with the cars then retrieved by local trains and hauled back to major yards where the cars were assembled into grain trains. But as North American railroads began to shun the car-by-car operations in an effort to cut costs, the method of handling grain has changed. Now, the trend is for a railroad to consort with an elevator company to build gargantuan elevators at central locations. Grain is trucked in from all over the region and loaded into the elevator. Then, in comes an empty unit grain train that circles through the elevator, with cars loaded one at a time as the train moves through it.

Less common than the three types of unit trains just described are those carrying automobiles, iron ore (and the lower-grade taconite), soda ash, potash, and sulfur. Nearly all the major railroads run unit auto trains, although blocks of autoracks frequently move in both intermodal and mixed-manifest

freights. The iron ore trains that serve steel mills around the Great Lakes region are seen frequently in the upper Midwest loading onto boats before being delivered. Among the Class 1 railroads handling the bulk of ore shipments are Canadian National (much through its recently acquired Duluth, Missabe & Iron Range and Wisconsin Central railroads), Union Pacific, and BNSF. Concerning soda ash, UP sends out unit trains to Portland, Oregon, and Port Arthur, Texas, for export to foreign countries. Rounding out the list, unit potash and sulfur (also spelled sulphur) trains are seen on CP and CN rails. CP and CN will hand off the Canpotex potash trains to either UP or BNSF for the run to Portland, where it is exported to Australia. (Canpotex is an export and marketing company.) The two railways transport sulfur for export with 23 shippers using the Canadian company Sultran.

A unit potash train is westbound on Union Pacific rails at Dodson, Oregon, on March 19, 2006. The potash, which is used in fertilizer, comes from Saskatchewan and is bound for Portland, where it will be exported to Australia. Like other high-tonnage unit trains, this freight requires ample horsepower, and three CEFX SD90/43MACs are assigned to today's movement. These units are leased to both Union Pacific and the originating road, CP Rail. *Steve Jessup photo*

One of the most intriguing unit trains to ride the rails in the West was the Shell Oil tank train from Bakersfield, California, to Wilmington (Long Beach) on the Southern Pacific. This scene shows the "oil cans" coming out of Tehachapi Loop grinding upgrade toward the summit on March 13, 1994, with four SP units on the point. After the SP–UP merger, the Union Pacific ran similar unit trains to the Los Angeles area—though not as long—from San Ardo (on the central coast) as well as Mojave. *Kevin EuDaly photo*

One of Santa Fe's higher-priority intermodal trains between Los Angeles and Chicago was the 881, seen here cruising upgrade at Blue Cut, California, on the west side of Cajon Pass on July 21, 1985. These time-sensitive freights were not to be delayed as shippers expected premium service. Two SD60 demonstrator units, EMD 4 and EMD 1, were being tested by the railroad and are assisting the Santa Fe SD45s on the point. *James R. Doughty photo*

A Burlington Northern local freight works at Leadville, Colorado, in August 1977. The ex–Colorado & Southern branch line from Leadville to Climax is higher in altitude than any other North American standard gauge railroad, reaching more than 11,300 feet in elevation. BN SD9 No. 828 is ready for work with four basic freight cars trailing—a flatcar, gondola, hopper, and boxcar, plus a caboose. This local job worked the branch daily, connecting with the Denver & Rio Grande Western at Leadville. *Jim Boyd photo*

Many of the commodities shipped by rail have likely moved in a unit train on local runs. We won't cover those here, but as trains get longer and heavier, as cars are upgraded, and as switching consumes increasingly valuable time, North American railroads may be rolling out unit trains we haven't seen before, or, at least, haven't seen for awhile.

Freight Categories and Priority

In earlier railroading days, freight trains ran on schedules much like passenger trains, but such is not generally the case today. Movements are assigned varying degrees of priority, all the way from high-priority to low- or nonpriority, as opposed to being run by the clock.

However, that's not to say that time doesn't play a role in freight operations. For example, the highest-priority trains are usually intermodal freights carrying time-sensitive freight, which often involves package-service shippers such as United Parcel Service, or perhaps auto manufacturers shipping parts that have to arrive at their destinations quicker than other goods. Even perishables fall into this category so they won't spoil. As these products are loaded into truck trailers, they must make their way to the intermodal loading facility before certain cut-off times.

After the flatcars and well cars are loaded in an expeditious manner, the railroads will try to set these trains into motion immediately, keeping a fairly regular schedule. Depending on the hauling distance and how the railroads are performing in getting freight over their road, the shippers can calculate a general or broad window of time when the packages are likely to arrive on the receiving end. Both the railroads and the shippers will offer guaranteed service to their respective customers, and if the railroads are unable to come through on time, they are subject to certain monetary penalties.

In an effort to satisfy the world of retail, railroads generally place a priority on their merchandise trains as they try to keep them from being overly delayed on their routes. Ditto for auto trains as dealers try to stock their lots with the latest models.

Drag freights, usually a term for trains with heavy, non-time-sensitive tonnage that are restricted to slower speeds, will fall under the low-priority category. Mixed-manifest trains that usually wear this label may be hauling lumber, paper, chemicals, or other bulk commodities. Loaded coal and grain trains and their empty counterparts typically move over the road in a nonexpedited fashion, although there are exceptions to the rule that may relate to revenue issues.

The local freight may be the one train that actually does run by the clock, as railroads set specific times for crews to be called to these jobs. Other than that, as the old Operation Lifesaver slogan goes, "Anytime Is Train Time!"

Struggling uphill at Scenic, Washington, a Burlington Northern eastbound freight is about to enter Cascade Tunnel at the summit of Stevens Pass in August 1984. The heavy train is loaded with lumber and paper products as well as other non-expedited bulk commodities from the Pacific Northwest. As a slow drag freight, the train is classified as low priority and will typically take the siding for all higher-priority traffic along the way. *Steve Jessup photo*

Perhaps the most interesting unit train since the days of the SP–UP *Salad Bowl Express* is CSX's dedicated "juice train" carrying Tropicana products from Bradenton, Florida, to the New York City area as well as Cincinnati.

In the West, Shell contracted with Southern Pacific to haul an oil train from a loading facility in the lower San Joaquin Valley (Bakersfield, California) to a refinery in the Los Angeles Harbor region. And Montana Rail Link still hauls the "gas train" from Missoula to Thompson Falls, bridging an Indian reservation where pipeline shipments have ceased.

Cabooses

Considering the variety of goods on board general manifests, freight trains have often been described as "rolling warehouses." Every warehouse contains an office somewhere, and trains are no different. In days gone by, that office was tagged onto the rear of each freight.

Known in slang terms as a "hack," "crummy," "shanty," or the more polite "way car," the caboose was invented as a place for half the train's crewmen to ride. At times, it took as many as five people to handle a train over the road, and in the steam days, the cab of the locomotive wasn't exactly designed for more than two people: the engineer and the fireman.

The caboose gave the conductor, who is in charge of the train, a place to do all his paperwork—shuffling through car waybills, switchlists, and train orders. Riding with him was a brakeman or flagman who assisted with switching duties, safely coupling and uncoupling cars, throwing switches, setting car brakes, protecting train movements (his train and others that might be approaching from the rear in unsignaled territory), and anything else the conductor ordered him to do.

From the mid-1800s (when the end cars came on the scene) to the mid-1900s, cabooses were refined and upgraded to better accommodate workers as well as provide maximum visibility for train safety. Early versions were little more than modified boxcars with windows, ladder steps, a side door, and a stove. By comparison, modern cabooses were more like rolling hotels. Inside, they contained a conductor's desk, a coal or oil stove, an icebox, storage lockers, radios (for communication), beds, and a toilet that would flush right onto the track (something that would *not* happen today). Heat and refrigeration were added luxuries.

On the exterior, wooden sides and frames gave way to steel. Narrow platforms were built on both ends, and Pullman-style steps made stepping aboard easier. While early cabooses had cupolas built on the rooftops, these were also modified to enhance sightlines. Sitting on a high-mounted seat, the conductor could look out the cupola (basically a square with windows) and inspect his train as it negotiated curves and tight clearances. The better visibility allowed him to spot potential problems on passing trains as well.

In time, freight cars were built longer and higher for greater capacity. Consider, for example, autoracks, piggyback trailers, and double-stack containers. If these cars brought up the rear of any modern-day freight, the view from the cupola would be blocked. The railroads countered this issue with the development of bay windows on each side of the caboose. Now the conductor could monitor his train from the sides of

Crew men on the platform and steps of this Missouri Pacific caboose prepare to do a roll-by inspection of the approaching mail and express train led by steam locomotive No. 5326 thundering through California, Missouri, in August 1949. This wooden caboose carries the old kerosene marker lamps (just above the flagman's head), which were gone by the early 1960s. In front of the caboose is a "camp car" for laborers who were out on the job for an extended time. *Kevin EuDaly collection*

Brilliant red and white paint adorns this Frisco cupola caboose parked in the shop area of the yard in Springfield, Missouri, on April 3, 1982. This is an extended vision caboose with the cupola having a little extra width for better vision. Cabooses came with a high price tag, and since they didn't generate revenue, the railroads replaced them with modern technology just as soon as state laws would allow it. *Kevin EuDaly photo*

In the early 1980s, the MoPac launched a project to home-build what became known as their shorty bay-window cabooses. This view, taken in October 1981 by the Mechanical Department engineer who oversaw the project, shows the prototype version in fresh paint, and so new the build date on the AAR plate hasn't been stenciled on yet. The MoPac eventually built hundreds of these in its carshops in Sedalia, Missouri. *Ray Curl photo, Kevin EuDaly collection*

The flashing rear-end device, or "FRED," takes its seat on the coupler of the train's last car. This telemetry device can transmit data on airbrake trainline pressure as well as train movement and direction to the locomotive, alerting the crew to changes and potential defects. The hose from the EOT (end-of-train) device attaches to the airbrake hose, and the unit is locked onto the coupler. This particular FRED is riding on a Delaware–Lackawanna grain train at Scranton, Pennsylvania, in October 2000. *Jim Boyd photo*

the caboose. One of the last developments in caboose design was the "extended vision" caboose which retained the height of the cupola and incorporated a little extra width borrowed from the bay-window version.

Even though the caboose was born out of necessity, it was an expense that did not generate revenue. With the improvements came a price tag of some $80,000 per unit by the 1980s, and major railroads had caboose counts in the 1,000 range. By then, the railroads had improved radio and airbrake technology such that they could send cabooses packing.

An end-of-train telemetry device (EOT, ETD, or FRED—flashing rear-end device) was developed to monitor air pressure in the airbraking system, train integrity and direction, and the battery powering the mechanism. Placed on the rear coupler,

the EOT can transmit a radio signal to the lead locomotive, alerting the crew to any changes and potential defects.

The device originated on the Florida East Coast Railway in the early 1970s, and by the mid-1980s, most railroads eliminated cabooses on main-line freights. By then, most diesel locomotives had three seats for the crew (additional crewmembers would ride in the trailing units).

The greatest drawback of EOT devices is that they remove an important set of eyes in back of the train, which has generated much discussion on train safety. To eliminate additional expenses, railroads now operate with "standard" two-man crews: an engineer and a conductor who also does the work of a brakeman and flagman.

Today, you might find cabooses working on local freights, where extra switching is involved. Otherwise, most have gone to the scrap heap if they haven't made their way to a museum, public display, or someone's backyard as an extra bedroom or play house. It's almost a crime to see parents and their children standing trackside, watching a train pass by, and no one to return a friendly wave on the backside.

Moving People

by Mike Schafer with Kevin J. Holland

Looking more like a scene out of the late 1950s, the elegance of the streamliner era is brought to life on this Union Pacific passenger excursion through the Deschutes River Canyon near Sherar, Oregon, on September 30, 1995. Such publicity runs have fueled rail travel interests, and the public is just beginning to catch a glimpse of the importance and success of today's passenger trains. Automobiles chased trains away, and now they're helping to bring back an increase in rail service. *Steve Jessup photo*

In the new millennium, North America is a continent blanketed by roads of all magnitude, from dusty one-laners to high-speed, multilaned superhighways—and everything in between, of course. Roads are the preferred choice for moving people and freight between cities—so much so that about 85 percent of intercity passenger travel today is done in a private automobile. That leaves airlines, bus companies, and railroads to fight over the remaining 15 percent of the population that needs or wants to go somewhere within the confines of the United States, Canada, and Mexico via public transport. Obviously, then, in terms of market share garnered, the automobile must be the most successful means of passenger transport of all time.

Close, but no cigar. The American passenger train won that distinction nearly a century ago and has yet to be unseated. In the years leading up to World War I, about 98 percent of all intercity travel in North America was done on

Amtrak's *Southwest Chief* rolls to a stop at La Plata, Missouri, on July 24, 2006, while passengers wait to board. This stop serves students traveling to and from Northeast Missouri State University in Kirksville, plus those staying at the nearby railroad-themed Depot Inn. Amtrak carried more passengers in 2008—approximately 28 million—than any other year since it began in 1971. Three General Electric Genesis-series locomotives have the train well in hand. *Kevin EuDaly photo*

Formed in 1978—seven years after Amtrak was established in the United States—VIA Rail Canada serves as its country's national passenger-train carrier. VIA's much smaller network includes 8,700 route-miles. VIA transported more than 4 million riders in 2007, with the majority moving between Eastern cities. Long-distance service between Vancouver and Toronto is offered on *The Canadian* three times a week. Here, the westbound *Canadian* rolls past the east switch at Field, British Columbia, on August 9, 1983, with a classic A-B-B-B FP9 set. *Kevin EuDaly photo*

Metrolink commuter trains provide valuable service throughout the Los Angeles area for those tired of sitting on Southern California's congested freeways. Operating in bidirectional, push-pull fashion, this Metrolink train is at San Bernardino on June 1, 2006. Long before Metrolink, passengers could ride Pacific Electric interurban trains, but they were eventually trampled out of existence by highway interests that had taken over L.A.'s transit system by 1960. *Stephen M. Priest photo*

a passenger train—98 percent. Think about that for a moment. For that to be the case, nearly every village, town, and city in North America that was on a railroad—and a vast majority were—had to have some form of daily passenger-train service. And they did.

In North America today, a vast majority of towns and cities no longer have rail passenger service, and only about a thousand locations in the United States and Canada (roughly 500 in each country) are served by a bare-bones network of scheduled intercity (versus commuter, which is a separate story within this chapter) passenger trains operated largely by Amtrak and VIA, respectively.

But the good news is that the darkest hours of rail passenger service in North America have come and gone. In 2007, Amtrak carried more passengers—about 26 million—than ever in its sometimes-bumpy 35-year history. VIA has likewise enjoyed increasing popularity. And at the other end

of the rail passenger spectrum—commuter rail and transit—there have been a record number of upstarts of brand-new systems in places that hadn't had such service for decades, if at all: Albuquerque, New Mexico; Minneapolis, Minnesota; Salt Lake City, Utah; Miami, Florida; Nashville, Tennessee; Houston, Texas . . . .

The biggest miracle of them all may well be in car-hungry Los Angeles, a city that, early in the twentieth century, had one of the most successful, comprehensive, and endearing electric railway transit systems in the world, the famous Pacific Electric Route of the Big Red Cars (at its zenith, PE had 575 route-miles with 2,160 scheduled interurban trains daily according to a 1937 ad). But by 1962, highway interests had bought up the PE and wiped it entirely out, replacing it with fuming buses while local, state, and federal governments built endless freeways. L.A. wound up being the largest city in North America without any urban or suburban rail transit. But

L.A. has seen the light. The Pacific Electric is back. No, not exactly as it was in its heyday. In its new incarnation, the PE is an interconnecting network of transit systems—commuter rail, light rail (the modern term for streetcar), and subway—linking downtown Los Angeles with its countless suburbs and satellite cities. Now, when you arrive in L.A. on an Amtrak intercity train from Chicago, Seattle, or New Orleans, chances are good that you will not need a car to get to your ultimate destination in the L.A. Basin.

As this book was being assembled, rail passenger transport was enjoying a reversal of fortunes. Herein is the story of the rise and fall and rise again of the North American passenger train.

From Novelty to Necessity

In 1827, the Summit Hill–Mauch Chunk Railroad opened. It was a Pennsylvania coal-hauling concern with railcars moved about by a combination of gravity and mule. In 1828, the Delaware & Hudson Canal Company was born (see Chapter 1), also in Pennsylvania. In 1829, both of these companies began carrying paying passengers, and are cited as the first railway companies to do so in the United States. Granted, the passengers were riding more for pleasure than to get from here to there, but they were paying passengers nonetheless. And, by the way, as of 2008, the D&H, although owned by Canadian Pacific, was still in business and still hosting passenger trains,

Amtrak's *Adirondack* and *Ethan Allen Express*, in Upstate New York.

Another railroad company to play prominently in America's development was the Baltimore & Ohio. It would carry its first passengers (aboard horse-drawn carriages) in January 1830, and later that same year become the first carrier to operate scheduled passenger service, between Baltimore and Ellicott's Mills, Maryland. The storied B&O would continuously operate passenger trains in one form or another into the 1980s, when it was merged into CSX Transportation, which today hosts a number of Amtrak trains.

Toward the end of 1830, the South Carolina Canal & Transportation Company operated the first locomotive-hauled passenger train, which was carrying 141 passengers—at that time probably the most passengers any form of land transportation had ever carried on American soil. The evolution of the passenger train was quickly accelerating.

In 1833, folks along the 80-mile-long Camden & Amboy Railroad & Transportation Company in New Jersey had their choice of several scheduled passenger trains. Overall running time, apparently including en-route stops, was about seven hours for an average speed of a little over 11 miles per hour—a phenomenal rate compared to stagecoach or canal boat. The fare was a whopping $3—a princely sum in the early 1800s, but even back then, passengers were willing to pay extra for speed, convenience, and comfort.

As the first half of the 1800s drew to a close, new railways had mushroomed all over the Eastern United States. North of the border, meanwhile, Canada's first railway, the 14-mile Champlain & St. Lawrence, opened for business in 1836 when the locomotive *Dorchester* led Canada's first steam-powered passenger train. Contemporaries of this Quebec line soon began operating in Ontario and in the Maritimes provinces of New Brunswick and Nova Scotia. In 1853, North America's first international railway was completed, linking Montreal with the ice-free harbor at Portland, Maine. Then, as now, Canada's population was concentrated in the southern portions of Ontario and Quebec, and this is where most of the country's new railways were built through the mid-nineteenth century, often connecting with U.S. lines at the border.

It's interesting to note that improved roads, the future nemesis of the American passenger train, predated the

Passengers enjoy a ride up the Jefferson Plane on the Summit Hill–Mauch Chunk Railroad in Pennsylvania in the late 1800s. The railroad opened in 1827 to haul coal, but later it also became a tourist attraction, transporting thousands of people. The cars were pushed uphill by a "barney" car (at right) pulled by cables extending to the enginehouse at the top of the climb. The cars returned on the gentle-grade route (shown passing under the incline) via gravity. *Mike Schafer collection*

Opposite: The Delaware & Hudson Canal Company catered to tourists with open and enclosed coaches for the ride up Plane 13 across from the canal basin station at Honesdale, Pennsylvania. The down track or back track was not as steep, but passengers moved at nearly 60 miles per hour in some cases. These tracks were originally built to lower coal cars down from the mines to the canal for transloading. *D&H photo, Jim Shaughnessy collection*

Coupled to a Little Schuylkill Navigation Railroad & Coal Company coach, this early 0-4-0 steam engine was ordered from Liverpool, England, and delivered to Philadelphia in February 1833. Named the *Catawissa*, this steamer made its first trip shortly thereafter from Tamaqua to Port Clinton, Pennsylvania. The LSNRR&CC was the first railroad to use steam engines in anthracite coal transport service. Prior to the steam engine, the railroad used real horses to transport coal and passengers. *L&N Historical Society collection*

passenger train by almost a quarter of a century. In 1806, the U.S. Congress mandated construction of the National Road, the foundation of today's U.S. 40. Improved roads, usually in the form of turnpikes, wherein users had to pay a fee, boomed after the War of 1812. As infant railways popped up in the 1820s, the states of Pennsylvania and New York together already had some 5,000 miles of improved roadways and turnpikes. Nonetheless, roads of this era were subject to weather conditions, more so than railways, with mud and washouts an all-too-common malady.

To illustrate the impact of the railway on early 1800s passenger transportation, consider the 394-mile Main Line of Public Works linking Philadelphia and Pittsburgh, also covered in Chapter 1. When this transportation artery, comprising a series of connecting canals and railways, opened in 1834, travel time between the two cities was slashed from 20 days to 5 days. The MLofPW would give way to an all-rail route of the mighty Pennsylvania Railroad in the 1850s, which eventually would further reduce Philadelphia–Pittsburgh travel times to

less than eight hours. Similarly, with the completion of the first transcontinental railroad in 1869, a coast-to-coast trip was reduced from months to a few days. Clearly, nothing came close to the passenger train in terms of speed.

By the mid-nineteenth century, there were close to 10,000 route-miles of railway line in the United States and its territories, and by the start of the Civil War in 1861 there were already some 30,000 miles. Following the Civil War, westward expansion resumed with a vengeance, and railroads began proliferating at a breakneck pace—as did competition for freight and passengers.

The Passenger Train Comes of Age

Not having a monopoly on a particular travel corridor was good, of course, for it spawned competition for market share. So, the late 1800s—and the 1880s in particular—brought with it a marked shift in the era of the passenger train. It was about to go from being a fast albeit utilitarian (and often uncomfortable) travel mode to the grand conveyance of all forms of travel.

Until then, trains were trains, and the distinction between a freight or a passenger train was often blurred. But with the explosive growth of both freight and passenger traffic, railroads increasingly segregated the two forms of traffic onto their own trains. (Because of their time-sensitive nature, mail and express traffic continued to be handled by passenger trains.)

Into the 1870s, passenger cars were not much more than wooden boxes on wheels, with minimal appointments: wooden bench-type seats, open windows for "air-conditioning," and wood-burning stoves for heat. These were the trains so popularly depicted in Wild West movies, with opulence—such as it was back then—usually restricted to those cars handling railroad officials.

An important change came in the late 1850s when rudimentary sleeping-car service was introduced. The 1870s and 1880s ushered in dining and lounge cars as well as several technological advances critical to passenger-train comfort and operation: electric lighting, steam heating, automatic airbrakes, enclosed vestibules for car-to-car passage, and coil-spring wheel assemblies. Similarly, heavier steel rail was replacing brittle iron rail, allowing for heavier passenger cars and higher train speeds. Improved methods of train dispatching—notably manual block control and the telegraph—also ramped up overall train running times and safety.

Maximizing on these innovations and infrastructure improvements, railroads began promoting their passenger trains to gain a greater share of the passenger market. Rail had become an unrivaled form of passenger transport. It wasn't a matter of "Shall I take a train, bus, plane, or my Chrysler Le Baron from A to B?" Rather, it was, "I must take the train, of course, but which railroad and which train?"

At that point, you'd likely look at what each railroad offered in the way of departure times and fastest trains. Accommodations would probably play a close second in choosing a train. A train carrying one of those newfangled dining cars—imagine eating while rolling!—would eliminate extended station meal stops (and their chaos as passengers vied for service at the crowded counters) and speed the trip. Overnight trains carrying new Pullman Palace sleeping cars were particularly inviting.

But as the 1800s wound down, and the West was no longer a frontier but a settled and prospering region, North America had become a rich and powerful continent. Many of what would be America's most powerful and long-standing railroad companies would be established in the late 1800s, and the passenger train had become not only a stable revenue source, but a strategic advertising tool for individual railroads. Since nearly all business travel was by train, shippers and other business personnel could see firsthand how well a railroad

operated. Rough ride on the B&O? Next time, ride the Erie Railroad and see if that would be a better bet for your next boxcar load of hotel china.

Wealth abounded in late nineteenth-century America, and increased discretionary spending in upper society meant that a whole new legion of travelers was willing to pay extra in exchange for the very best in transportation. Often, this pertained to whole trains and not just specific accommodations. Also in the late 1800s, railroads began to tailor their passenger trains to specific duties. Though hard evidence may no longer exist, the Pennsylvania Railroad supposedly first applied the term "limited" to some of its passenger trains in 1876. "Limited" implied a fast train that made only selected (limited) scheduled stops. Then, in 1881, PRR used "Limited" as part of the name of its new Jersey City–Chicago service, the *Pennsylvania Limited*. This is also one of the earliest instances of giving trains formal names, a practice that remains to this day on both Amtrak and VIA. Names gave trains individuality, and the name could also be used to underscore a train's service (as in Santa Fe's *de Luxe*), route (the Canadian Pacific's *Trans-Canada Limited*), regionality (California Amtrak's Surfliners), destination (Union Pacific's *City of Los Angeles*), or even to honor a famous individual (Chesapeake & Ohio's *George Washington*).

Today in North America, there is much banter about developing new high-speed passenger train routes, but this is hardly a new concept. Although America has seriously fallen behind in the high-speed rail passenger arena since the 1960s, it was a pioneer in the field in the nineteenth century. The first generation of U.S. high-speed trains came on line in 1875 when New York Central System began fielding fast runs on its newly formed New York–Albany–Buffalo–Cleveland–Chicago Water Level Route main line. The speed limit then was 75 miles per hour—only 4 miles per hour less than the legal speed limit for Amtrak trains today over most of this very same route.

In 1893, the Central's *Empire State Express* between New York and Buffalo reached 112 miles per hour behind 4-4-0 steam locomotive No. 999 (now held by Chicago's Museum of Science and Industry). Also that year, NYC debuted the *Exposition Flyer* between New York and Chicago for the World's Columbian Exposition at the latter. Running time for this new flyer was 20 hours—virtually the same as today's Amtrak *Lake Shore Limited*, which runs on the same route.

New deluxe trains were being established with unprecedented fervor in the 1880s and 1890s as railroads vied for the passenger dollar. Here is a sampling of notable trains that came on line during that time:

California Limited: The storied Atchison, Topeka & Santa Fe Railway inaugurated this Chicago–Los Angeles train on November 7, 1892. Known for its top-of-the-line equipment and stellar service, this train made the 2,228-mile run in 68 hours. It became so popular that it often had to be operated in sections—as many as seven—to accommodate all passengers. Free boutonnieres for men and fresh roses for women passengers were just one of the many service perks.

Black Diamond: The Lehigh Valley Railroad created this deluxe daytime train for its New York–Buffalo/Niagara Falls route in 1896. Originally, the train—also known as the "Honeymoon Express" and "The Handsomest Train in the World"—was a first-class-only parlor car run with dining service. Eventually, through sleeping cars to and from Chicago were added, as was a Philadelphia section. The *Black Diamond* was discontinued in 1959.

Overland: Also known as the *Overland Flyer*, *Overland Limited*, and *San Francisco Overland*, this Chicago–San Francisco train debuted in 1887 and quickly became one of the most well-known Western transcontinental trains in America. Jointly operated by Chicago & North Western (Chicago–Omaha), Union Pacific (Omaha–Ogden, Utah), and Southern Pacific (Ogden–Oakland/San Francisco), the first incarnation of the *Overland* arrived in 1887 and would become the premier train from the Midwest to the Bay Area for turn-of-the-century travelers.

Congressional Limited: This New York–Philadelphia–Washington train, initially named the *Congressional Limited Express* when launched in 1885, quickly became the esteemed first-choice train for businessmen and politicians along the Pennsylvania Railroad's 225-mile route linking those cities. The train would outlive the PRR itself when Pennsy merged with New York Central in 1968 to form Penn Central.

Florida Special: This first-class-only train began speeding passengers out of the cold winter climes of the Northeast to summery Florida on January 9, 1888. Though principally a train of the Atlantic Coast Line Railroad, the *Special* was jointly operated with the Pennsylvania Railroad (Jersey City/New York–Washington) and the Richmond, Fredericksburg & Potomac (Washington–Richmond, Virginia) so that it could seamlessly operate through between New York and Jacksonville. When the Florida East Coast Railway was completed early in the 1900s, the *Special* was extended southward over FEC tracks, eventually to Miami. This seasonal train became so popular that it survived into the early 1970s, of course having gone through many equipment upgrades over the decades.

The Golden Age

The arrival of the twentieth century also brought what is often known as the "Golden Age" of the passenger train, a period that would last until the Great Depression. From the 1880s to about 1910, American railroads experienced exceptional growth, with route-miles booming from 93,000 to 240,000—and nearly all of the new mileage would be served by new passenger trains. As in the late 1800s, nearly 100 percent of intercity travel was done by passenger train in the early years of the twentieth century. Trains served the whole cross section of the public. Commuter trains brought people into city centers to work, catering to those who could not afford to live graciously in the city itself or preferred a more sedate place to live. Accommodation trains, also known as "milk runs," ran on workhorse schedules to facilitate the handling of considerable amounts of mail, express, milk, and local passenger traffic at smaller towns. The majority of people rode standard trains of a democratic nature that carried coaches, basic dining and lounge cars, and "section" sleeping cars if it were an overnight train. Premier luxury trains, catering to an upper-level class of travelers, might have commodious chair seating (coach seating, but of a higher comfort level), parlor cars with individual swiveling seats, stately private-room sleeping cars for first-class passengers, elegant dining cars with four-star cuisine, and amenity rolling stock such as lounge-observation cars.

In fact, the new century began with the launching of what many travel historians consider to be the world's ultimate passenger train, heretofore unmatched in terms of service, speed, and luxury: the *20th Century Limited*. The brainchild of George Henry Daniels, New York Central System's general-passenger agent, the first eastbound and westbound *20th Centurys* rolled forth from Chicago and New York, respectively, on June 15, 1902. Twenty hours and 920 miles later, the following morning, both trains arrived at their opposite terminals. In between was an unparalleled travel experience.

Each of the two initial 1902 trainsets (two were required so that daily service could be offered from both Chicago and New York) comprised a baggage-buffet-smoker-library car; two sleeping cars, each containing 12 sections; a drawing room; a stateroom; a dining car; and a compartment-lounge open-platform observation car. There were no coaches. Capacity was but 42 (well-heeled) passengers.

The amenities provided in these highly varnished, elegantly pinstriped wood cars—with stained-glass windows and electric lighting—were beyond all other trains: The train carried a barber and valet attendant, maid, and stenographer. The *Century* captured public attention and became an extraordinarily successful endeavor—its name being held in high regard right up to its final runs in December 1967.

But the *Century* was anything but a loner. NYC rival Pennsylvania Railroad launched its version of the epitome of New York–Chicago travel conveyances on the very same day: June 15, 1902. The *Pennsylvania Special*, as it was initially

Eastbound Chicago & North Western passenger train No. 91 enters Eau Claire, Wisconsin, behind Class I-2 Pacific 374. The locomotive was built in 1903, and the wooden Railway Post Office car was likely replaced by a steel car by 1912, dating this image somewhere between the two years. The arrival of the twentieth century ushered in the beginning of the Golden Age of passenger trains that lasted until the Great Depression. *Chicago & North Western Historical Society Archives*

named, also had a 20-hour timing and carried equally prestigious accommodations and advertised equally attentive services. In 1912, this train was rechristened *Broad-Way Limited*. Though less successful than the *Century* in terms of patronage, the *Broadway* would survive, albeit in greatly altered form, into the 1990s under Amtrak. In many ways, both of these trains serve as barometers for the fate of the passenger train in North America, as we shall see throughout this chapter.

The Golden Age of the passenger train yielded a number of benchmarks in terms of equipment and infrastructure. A particularly important epoch in this Golden Age was the "standard era," which in essence marked the switch from wood

cars to all-steel cars. This was not an easy switch for railroads, but once it started, the evolution happened quickly.

Metal passenger cars date from the late 1840s, but they were made of iron—steel not yet having been perfected—and therefore were heavy, clumsy, uncomfortable, and expensive. Wood was plentiful and cheap and did have some virtues: wooden passenger cars were more comfortable because of the insulating nature of wood. They were easier to fabricate; they were lighter and therefore more economical to operate. But, although wooden cars may be lovely to behold, in an accident— especially one in a confined area—the resulting conflagration (due to wood- or coal-fired stoves) could be devastating.

This image represents a classic turn-of-the-century passenger train with its short consist of wooden cars and a 4-6-0 (Ten-Wheeler) locomotive with a cowcatcher pilot that swept wayward livestock and other obstacles aside. Wooden cars were more comfortable, lighter, and more economical to operate than the first metal cars that came on the scene early in the twentieth century, but fire, maintenance, and limited capacity proved to be the downfall of wooden cars, whether passenger or freight. *Kevin EuDaly collection*

The steel-making process was refined in the late nineteenth century and would be a boon to railroading. Steel was tougher than iron, yet lighter and easier to fabricate. Steel rails quickly replaced brittle iron rails and at the same time allowed railroads to operate passenger trains faster and with larger, heavier locomotives and rolling stock. Yet, railroads hesitated to invest in steel passenger cars until well after the turn of the twentieth century, as they had too much invested in wooden rolling stock.

It took a tragic subway fire in Paris, France, in 1901 to change those ways of thinking. About this time, the PRR was facing construction of its herculean Hudson River tunnels project to carry trains into Manhattan to what would be one of the great railway terminals of all time: Pennsylvania Station. The Pennsy wisely insisted that all equipment entering the station be of all-steel construction, so it built an experimental all-steel car for New York's Interborough Rapid Transit subway

system, which was already under construction. That car's success led the PRR to design an all-steel car for intercity steam passenger trains.

When Penn Station opened in 1910, the PRR had taken delivery of over 300 all-steel cars for trains using the new station, and this provided the impetus for other railroads to follow suit. At this time, some 45,000 wood passenger cars still moved people all across America, while only about 2,000 passenger cars employed all-steel or at least steel-framed construction. By about 1915, railroads boasted some 16,000 steel passenger cars, and orders for new, wood passenger cars were nil. In many cases, wood cars were being upgraded with steel sheathing.

Along with steel construction came two more important developments: steam heating and electric lighting. Going, going, gone were cars heated by stoves at car ends; instead, steam heat piped from the train's locomotive kept cars toasty warm in frigid weather. Fading, too, was gas lighting, replaced by electric lighting run off of a battery/alternator arrangement under the car whereby the car generated its own electricity when running and drew from batteries when standing. Steel passenger cars made this possible; their inherent strength allowed then-huge batteries and alternator/generator equip-ment to be carried beneath the car. For the same reason, steel-car construction paved the way to air-conditioning, which would require additional underbody mechanical equipment and ice compartments.

A few trains in the late 1800s and early 1900s employed a format known as head-end power (HEP) whereby electricity for lighting the whole train came from a dynamo mount-ed in one of the head-end cars. Initially, this practice looked better on paper than it actually worked and was largely abandoned, only to be revived—successfully this time—after World War II.

Now the Golden Age was known both as the standard era (because of increasing standardization of rolling stock regardless of builder) and the heavyweight era (all-steel construction). The benefits of all-steel cars now became so compelling that railroads began another round of new-train starts. It was during this period that some of the most popular and well-remembered trains of the twentieth century were born.

Pan-American: Louisville & Nashville unveiled this Cincinnati–Louisville–Nashville–Birmingham–New Orleans train on December 5, 1921. The "Pan" catered to all travelers but did so with up-to-date, stylish equipment that included a baggage-club car, chair cars, diner, Pullman-operated sleepers, and a parlor-observation car for first-class passengers. This train would survive until the start of Amtrak on May 1, 1971.

Scenic Limited: This train, jointly operated by the Missouri Pacific, Denver & Rio Grande Western, and Western Pacific, was inspired by the 1915 Panama-Pacific Exposition at San Francisco. It operated between St. Louis, Missouri, and Oakland, California, via Kansas City, Denver, and—via Colorado's remarkable Royal Gorge—Salt Lake City.

Pulling into the State Center, Iowa, depot is this Chicago & North Western passenger train in a 1912 scene. With plenty of people on hand to greet the train, steam engine No. 26 is pulling a consist of three cars behind its tender. About this time, 45,000 wooden cars were rolling across the United States, while only 2,000 were made of steel. By 1915, that figure jumped to roughly 16,000. *James L. Rueber collection, Chicago & North Western Historical Society Archives*

Feeling a little competition from the automobile industry, the Chicago & Alton Railroad gives the public a firsthand look at the benefits of rail travel with the display of its newest train, the *Alton Limited*, at Chicago Union Depot in 1924. Visitors could check out the interior and exterior makeup of the rolling stock and be assured that the railroads were still the preferred choice for short-haul and long-distance travel. *A. W. Johnson photo, Ken Donnelly collection*

Daylight Limited: This train was inaugurated by the Southern Pacific on April 28, 1922, and ran on a day schedule linking San Francisco and Los Angeles, 470 miles. It began as a 13-hour nonstop run with coaches and a dining car, but its popularity prompted the addition of lounge-observation cars in 1923 and lunch-counter cars in 1924. This train inspired the SP to create a whole fleet of *Daylight* trains, some of which would last into Amtrak early in the 1970s.

Erie Limited: Although the NYC and PRR dominated the Chicago–New York market, that did not deter the Erie Railroad from introducing a respectable (if slower) heavyweight flagship train in 1929 between Jersey City and Chicago, with a section

to Buffalo. The *Erie Limited* featured Pullman sleepers, salon coaches, diner, and parlor-buffet car. Its descendant would survive until 1966.

Orange Blossom Special: When Seaboard Air Line Railroad's line from Richmond opened all the way to West Palm Beach, Florida, in 1925, it inaugurated this famous seasonal train, made ever more popular by a song of the same name. The *Orange Blossom Special* was an all-sleeping-car run that featured barber and maid service and even shower baths.

Empire Builder: This train has been continuously operated since its 1929 debut—Amtrak still runs it today—and thus has become one of the most famous and durable name trains in

North American history. Named for James J. "Empire Builder" Hill, founder of the Great Northern Railway, the *Empire Builder* has long been the first choice for travel between Chicago and Seattle, Washington, and Portland, Oregon.

Panama Limited: Linking Chicago and St. Louis with the Gulf of Mexico, Illinois Central introduced its *Panama Limited* between those points in 1911. In 1916, it became a very posh, all-sleeping-car train. It continued to be one of the most revered, luxurious overnight runs in the country well into the 1960s, and for a short time was operated by Amtrak.

Ocean Limited: When it debuted as an all-sleeping-car train between Montreal and Halifax, Nova Scotia, in 1904, the *Ocean Limited* was operated by the Canadian National and its predecessors. The *Ocean Limited* was CNR's premier train between central Canada and the Atlantic coast, even after coaches were added in 1958. Renamed the *Ocean* in 1966, the train's operation was taken over by VIA in 1978 and continues today.

Trans-Canada Limited: The Canadian Pacific had been operating passenger trains across Canada since about 1885, and travelers could ride from Montreal to Vancouver (2,881 miles) without having to change trains. In 1919, the CPR unveiled a luxurious new summer-season all-sleeping-car train on this cross-country route. Billed as the fastest passenger train to cross the continent, the *Trans-Canada Limited* was undone by the Great Depression and made its last run in 1931. Thereafter, CPR timetables of the heavyweight era featured the more egalitarian *Dominion*, a coach-and-sleeper operation that persisted until 1965.

The passenger train played a critical role in transportation, particularly during the late 1910s when World War I raged overseas, as rail was the only truly effective way to move massive numbers of troops to training camps and then to the coasts for deployment "over there."

Following the war, America entered the Roaring Twenties with much fervor and optimism—and still more new passenger trains. That was the good news; the not-so-good news for the passenger train was that, during the 1920s, the popularity of the automobile surged, thanks in part to the 1921 Federal Highway Act, declaring the goal of linking every county seat in the country with a paved road. For the first time, railroads began to feel the brunt of competition—publicly funded, no less.

Initially, interurbans took the blow the hardest. The automobile quickly became the mode of choice for localized travel—intercity U.S. highways still being in their infancy in the 1920s—and since local service was what interurbans had done best, most were doomed early on. The same held true for commuter trains, and then for short-haul or regional intercity passenger trains. As government-sponsored roads on the federal, state, and county levels proliferated throughout the 1920s, the automobile eroded passenger-train revenues commensurately, eventually nipping at the heels of the long-distance intercity train.

And then it came. The stock-market crash of 1929 changed everything for everybody, ushering in the Great Depression. Discretionary income vanished on a wide scale, travel plummeted, and railroads' infrastructure, locomotive, and rolling-stock investments were severely curtailed.

The Streamliner Era

The emergence of the automobile, coupled to the Depression, ended the Golden Age of the passenger train in North America. The peak years of the passenger train had passed—although some surprise developments would surface in the impending years. We can credit the Great Depression for one of these developments: the lightweight streamliner, a modernistic, aerodynamically styled train with flowing contours to minimize wind resistance. The Depression prompted railroads to look at cutting the costs of passenger-train operation, particularly on secondary, local routes where the automobile had made great inroads on traffic. The result was the development of the lightweight, diesel-powered streamliner—"lightweight" and "diesel-powered" being the key words here.

The Milwaukee Road took the first widespread step in lightweight technology, building an experimental lightweight (35 percent lighter than a heavyweight) coach in 1933–1934. Quickly deemed successful, the railroad built a fleet of over 70 cars based on the experimental lightweight prototype, all of them entering service on nearly all of The Milwaukee Road's principal steam- and electric-powered passenger trains by late 1934.

Meanwhile, Chicago, Burlington & Quincy and Union Pacific, separately working with the Edward G. Budd Manufacturing Company and Pullman Car & Manufacturing, developed a whole different streamlining concept. These companies were designing and building two entirely self-contained, articulated, ultralightweight passenger trains that would be powered by internal combustion engines housed in each train's power car.

UP's train, code-named M-10000, had four cars (power-baggage-mail car, coach, sleeper, coach-buffet) fabricated out of aluminum by PC&M. Burlington's three-unit (power-mail car, baggage-coach, coach-parlor observation car) train, dubbed *Zephyr* 9900, was built out of the tough, new "miracle metal" stainless steel, using a new fabrication process known as shotwelding developed by Budd. Electro-Motive Corporation, a fledgling builder of gas-electric motorcar trains ("doodlebugs") that had been the staple of many branch-line

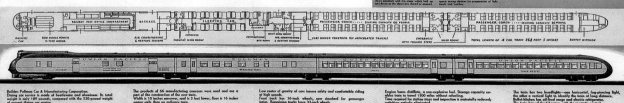

Chicago, Burlington & Quincy's answer to UP's M-10000 was its stainless-steel *Zephyr* 9900, the world's first main-line train to successfully utilize diesel-electric power. The brochure preceded the train's 1934 unveiling; the photo shows the 9900 in 1997 following complete restoration for display at Chicago's Museum of Science & Industry. The train was pulled from the shops by a group of men to illustrate its lightweight construction, mimicking a similar publicity stunt dating from the *Zephyr*'s outshopping in 1934. *Mike Schafer photo*

passenger operations since the 1920s, provided powerplants for both the M-10000 and *Zephyr* 9900. However, UP opted for a tried-and-true spark-ignition engine fueled by distillate (crude petroleum), while Burlington boldly took a chance on a diesel engine that had been developed for transportation.

The M-10000 hit the rails in February 1934, embarking on a 12,625-mile exhibition tour through 22 states and Washington, D.C. Burlington's *Zephyr* came to life in April 1934 and similarly set about the country on publicity tours, one of which included a nonstop, dawn-to-dusk, Denver–Chicago run that ended at the Century of Progress exhibition on Chicago's lakefront.

Public and industry response to both trains was nothing short of phenomenal. UP's yellow-and-brown M-10000 and Burlington's shimmering *Zephyr* brought a breath of fresh air and new hope to a continent in the throes of its worst depression ever. But more than that, it opened the eyes of the ultraconservative railroad industry to new possibilities

in rail transport. (The success of diesel-electric propulsion demonstrated by *Zephyr* 9900 would actually have a greater impact on future rail freight transport in North America than it would on passenger travel.)

Zephyr 9900 went into revenue public service on November 11, 1934, replacing a pair of money-losing, expensive-to-operate, steam-powered local trains running between Kansas City and Lincoln, Nebraska, which had experienced declining patronage. Because of its inherent efficiency, the *Zephyr* replaced two sets of equipment that normally would have been necessary to protect schedules on the 250-mile run.

To the astonishment of railroad officials, the new *Zephyr* began turning a profit on the run while drawing increased patronage. Had things gone unchanged, the steam locals

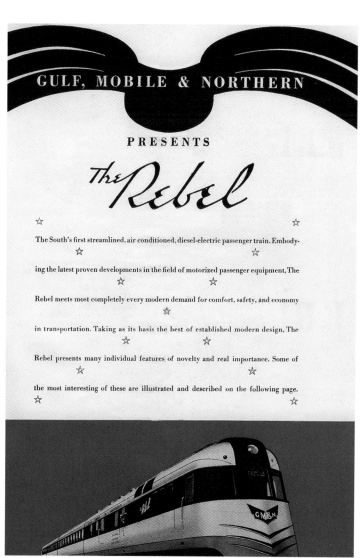

Union Pacific and Chicago, Burlington & Quincy weren't the only railroads hopping on the streamliner bandwagon. The Gulf, Mobile & Northern's *Rebel*, built by American Car & Foundry, entered service with a three-car, conventionally coupled set that made it possible to easily add or subtract cars to accommodate varying travel demands—something that couldn't be done with articulated trains such as *Zephyr* 9900 or the M-10000. *Ken Donnelly collection*

Opposite: In an effort to modernize passenger trains and cut operational costs, railroads began experimenting with lightweight and diesel-powered equipment in the early 1930s. Union Pacific's M-10000, an articulated four-unit set powered by a cranky distillate engine, debuted in 1934. The railroad planned to operate the train at sustained speeds of 100 miles per hour, but this dream was never realized because the Depression-weary railroad was unable to invest in associated track and signaling improvements. *Mike Schafer collection*

Atchison, Topeka & Santa Fe's San Bernardino local with three cars is pictured in the Los Angeles area in February 1935. The 4-6-0 Ten-Wheeler 493 has plenty of power to handle the light movement. This was one of only a handful of steam engines built for the Santa Fe from the Rhode Island Locomotive Works. The plant produced steamers through 1908. *Harold K. Vollrath collection*

likely would have soon been discontinued. Now, however, the railroad had to consider adding cars to the *Zephyr*—and maybe even adding more *Zephyr*s to its passenger network.

The M-10000 had originally been slated to provide 100-mile-per-hour, virtually nonstop service on a 24-hour timing between Chicago and Los Angeles, but, as it turned out, UP was not in a position to invest in necessary track and signaling improvements for sustained high-speed running. The M-10000 thus wound up in a more mundane role of local service between Kansas City, Topeka, and Salina, Kansas, acquiring the name *The Streamliner* in passenger timetables.

Regardless of their less-than-high-profile assignments, the M-10000 and *Zephyr* 9900 were heroes in the now increasingly depressing story of the North American passenger train. The population embraced the new little speedsters, so much so that they begat additional trains. For example, in 1935, UP took delivery of another trainset styled after the M-10000. The M-10001 entered service between Chicago and Portland, Oregon (with Chicago & North Western handling the train between Chicago and Omaha), as the *City of Portland*. The following year, UP took delivery of the M-10002 trainset, christened it the *City of Los Angeles*, and placed it

in Chicago–Los Angeles service. By the summer of 1936, the streamliners *City of Denver* and *City of San Francisco* had joined the ranks.

The same story held true for Burlington, which had the Budd Company building additional *Zephyr*-style streamliners as quickly as it could. In 1935, the *Twin Zephyrs* began their speedy runs between Chicago and Minneapolis/St. Paul, and the Chicago–Denver *Denver Zephyr* premiered in 1936. Several more new *Zephyr*s followed suit.

Burlington and Union Pacific weren't alone in the new streamliner movement, as railroads across North America raced to introduce their own streamliners. Some pre–World War II notables:

- The *Hiawatha* (1935; The Milwaukee Road; Chicago–Minneapolis/St. Paul)
- The *Comet* (1935; New York, New Haven & Hartford; Boston–Providence, Rhode Island)
- *Abraham Lincoln* (1935; Alton Railroad; Chicago–St. Louis)
- The *Rebel* (1935; Gulf, Mobile & Northern; Jackson, Tennessee–Mobile, Alabama/New Orleans, Louisiana)
- The *Green Diamond* (1936; Illinois Central; Chicago–St. Louis)
- The *Mercury* (1936; New York Central; Cleveland–Detroit)

Running on the Texas & Pacific main line is AT&SF subsidiary Gulf, Colorado & Santa Fe with this passenger train arriving at Dallas in May 1936. This train combined cars from the northbound and southbound *Fast 15* at Fort Worth for the last leg of their respective trips over to Dallas. On top of the GC&SF 4-6-2 Pacific No. 1228, the bell is clanging away, announcing the train's morning arrival. *Harold K. Vollrath collection*

- *Capitol Limited* (1938; Baltimore & Ohio/Jersey Central; Jersey City–Washington–Chicago)
- *Super Chief* (1937; Santa Fe Railway; Chicago–Los Angeles)
- The *John Wilkes* (1939; Lehigh Valley Railroad; New York–Pittston, Pennsylvania)
- *City of Miami* (1940; Illinois Central/Central of Georgia/Atlantic Coast Line/Florida East Coast; Chicago–Miami)
- *Empire State Express* (1941; New York Central; New York–Cleveland)

Not all of these streamliners were of the format introduced by the M-10000 and *Zephyr* 9900; that is, short, articulated (the cars semipermanently coupled and sharing trucks), diesel-powered trains. Some railroads elected not to subscribe to this inflexible format because it prevented train size from being adjusted to accommodate demand. Rather, they opted for conventional-format cars (individual cars that had their own batteries and generating equipment and rode on a pair of traditional four-wheel truck assemblies) built with lightweight alloy metals and smooth, welded sides. Similarly, some railroads, such as The Milwaukee Road, New York Central, and Canadian Pacific, used good old-fashioned steam power (though usually dressed up in streamstyle shrouding) to power their streamliners.

By this time, NYC's world-class *20th Century Limited* and rival PRR's revered *Broadway Limited* had gone through several upgradings, transforming both trains from all-wood Palace car runs to steel-sheathed and then all-steel trains between 1902 and the late 1930s. Then, simultaneously in 1938, the NYC and PRR unveiled their new, streamlined versions of the *Century* and the *Broadway*, further upping the ante on the hotly contested Chicago–New York travel market. These two trains, though still steam-powered, thus emerged as arguably the epitome of elegant, pre–World War II streamlining.

The aforementioned streamliners represent only a cross section of a multitude of new, streamlined trains placed in service on both long runs and short throughout North America. Their dazzle and comfort helped revive sagging passenger revenues and in some cases brought profitability back to a railroad's passenger department. In 1939, for example, Seaboard Air Line placed its first streamliner, the *Meteor*, in service between New York and Florida. The bankrupt SAL had only enough capital to purchase one *Meteor* trainset, limiting *Meteor* departures from New York and Miami or St. Petersburg to every third day. Yet demand was so great that the railroad was able to finance additional equipment to provide for daily

Cars from an eastbound New York Central Albany–New York City train form a perfect line as the train speeds through Peekskill, New York, circa 1940. The passenger local is powered by NYC 4-6-4 Hudson No. 5253. Schenectady Locomotive Works turned out 145 Hudsons in this particular class between 1927 and 1931. NYC's steam roster sported more than half of all the Hudsons built for service in North America. *H. W. Pontin photo,* Railfan & Railroad Magazine *collection*

departures from both New York and Miami, and eventually the *Meteor*—a service that Amtrak still runs—helped lift the Seaboard back into the black.

The dedication of NYC's new Budd-built, steam-powered *Empire State Express* between New York and Cleveland in 1941 was especially poignant. The first run was on December 7, and news of the new train was greatly overshadowed by the tragic events in Pearl Harbor. Now, the United States would officially and formally be drawn into World War II, an event that would forever change the world. This war would also change

the face of railroading in North America, especially for the passenger train.

The war effort changed all sorts of priorities, and restrictions on raw materials forced railroads to curtail new equipment purchases and refocus their efforts to handling an explosive volume of passengers (read, troops) and freight. The last major new train put in service as these restrictions came down on the railroads was Illinois Central's newly streamlined *Panama Limited*, then in its thirty-first year of service.

Fall from Grace

World War II pushed North American railroads to their limit—and then some. Record volumes of freight and passengers, including troops, were transported. The slow decline in ridership that began in the 1920s bottomed out in 1932, and then stabilized and even climbed for some carriers thanks to the influx of new streamliners. But with the war came a dramatic increase in rail ridership: six times what it was in 1932! Almost a million troops a month moved on troop trains made up of just about any equipment that would roll.

Because of wartime restrictions on gas and tires, civilians returned to the rails in increasing numbers, although the government encouraged people to avoid discretionary travel so as not to occupy space needed to move military people. Still, standing-room-only situations were the norm on passenger trains, and delays were routine owing to crowds and special troop movements.

Metals were especially in demand for the war effort, effectively curtailing nearly all production of new passenger cars that hadn't been on the assembly line when America became entrenched in the war. In an ironic twist of fate, Union Pacific's M-10000 train—North America's first lightweight streamlined train—was scrapped for its aluminum content.

And so, in 1944–1945, as the war ended and postwar movement of troops wound down, North American railroads carried more passengers than ever before in their history. In 1945 alone, more travelers passed through New York's Pennsylvania Station than resided in the United States. But it was downhill from here for the passenger train, only the railroads didn't know it yet.

The war left North American railroads in shambles, but it was worth the price, as some historians feel the Allies would not have won the war without the tenacity and service of U.S. railroads. Nonetheless, the United States was about to

Missouri Pacific's southbound *Southern Scenic* train makes a station stop at Branson, Missouri, on September 10, 1947. By this time, MoPac's 4-6-2 Pacific No. 6444 was likely putting in her last miles as diesel locomotives began to displace these classic steamers in passenger and freight service. As baggage and boxes are loaded and unloaded, the engineer leaning out the cab window patiently waits for a highball from the conductor to depart. *Kevin EuDaly collection*

SNACK IN THE *Buffet-Lounge* CAR

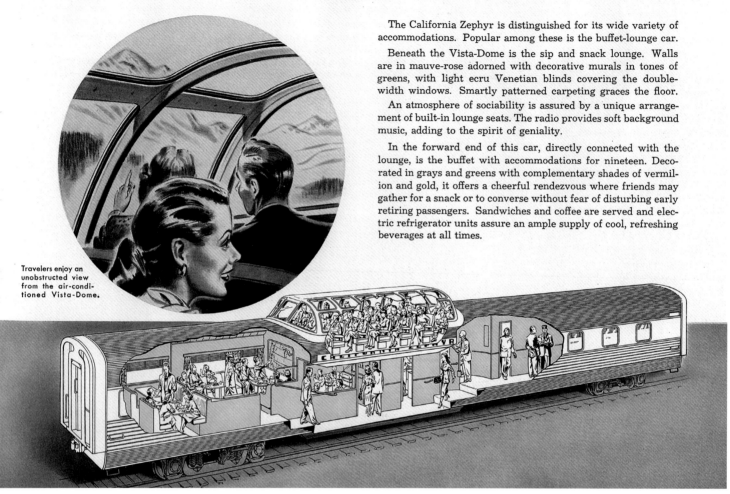

The California Zephyr is distinguished for its wide variety of accommodations. Popular among these is the buffet-lounge car.

Beneath the Vista-Dome is the sip and snack lounge. Walls are in mauve-rose adorned with decorative murals in tones of greens, with light ecru Venetian blinds covering the double-width windows. Smartly patterned carpeting graces the floor.

An atmosphere of sociability is assured by a unique arrangement of built-in lounge seats. The radio provides soft background music, adding to the spirit of geniality.

In the forward end of this car, directly connected with the lounge, is the buffet with accommodations for nineteen. Decorated in grays and greens with complementary shades of vermilion and gold, it offers a cheerful rendezvous where friends may gather for a snack or to converse without fear of disturbing early retiring passengers. Sandwiches and coffee are served and electric refrigerator units assure an ample supply of cool, refreshing beverages at all times.

Travelers enjoy an unobstructed view from the air-conditioned Vista-Dome.

Hoping to keep passengers on board after the war years, railroads went to great lengths to advertise their trains and provide new, innovative equipment. This ad publicizes the new Vista-Dome cars, developed in 1945, on the new (1949) *California Zephyr*. Travelers could enjoy stunning views in the glass-enclosed, upper-level seating area. Three railroads handled the *CZ* between Chicago and Oakland, California: Chicago, Burlington & Quincy, Denver & Rio Grande Western, and Western Pacific. *Kevin J. Holland collection*

turn its back on its railways, embracing instead the airways and highways.

Railroads were blindsided by this shift in priorities. Though battle-weary, North American railroads had reaped huge revenues from war-era operations, and now they were to ready to invest these monies in new locomotives, rolling stock, and infrastructure. Prior to the war, the streamliner had been riding high on a wave of post-Depression hope; now that trip would resume on the postwar wave of euphoria that was sweeping throughout a victorious North America. Surely, Americans would continue riding the rails in the impending new era.

Orders for new passenger cars and locomotives—and even all-new streamliners—that had been placed prior to the war but unfulfilled were now being addressed as locomotive and car builders returned to their normal production routines. Meanwhile, other railroads placed new orders for equipment, including diesel-electric locomotives that would replace the steam locomotive.

It was in this scenario we find the railroad construction field glutted for the remainder of the 1940s. But the railroad industry wasn't alone with feverish activity. In Detroit, Michigan, automobile manufacturers were equally pressed to keep up with a burgeoning demand for new automobiles.

And for those millions of new autos, the federal government was in the throes of planning a new way to accommodate them. During the war, the United States had been startled by the success of Hitler's limited-access, high-speed highway network, the *autobahn*. In the name of national defense, the U.S. government planned a similar national highway system of freeways, as they were misnamed (they aren't free by any means), better known today as the interstate.

New cars, state roads, and interstate limited-access highways were exactly what Americans wanted. The automobile represented the ultimate freedom of being able to go anywhere, anytime for cheap, and now following the Depression and war, the average American was in the best position ever to afford the luxury of owning an automobile. And the government spared no expense in making this dream come true. By 1954, the United States had spent $20 billion of taxpayer money on highway construction. Bus operators such as Greyhound and Trailways benefited as well, for now they had new "tracks" on which to compete with the railroads with no need for capital investment on their part.

Similarly, the airlines stood poised to take a great leap forward. New passenger aircraft were coming on line as many new passenger air routes opened up. Meanwhile, local, state, and federal governments began funding the development of new or improved airports. Early in the 1950s, for example, a little country airstrip known as Old Orchard 16 miles outside of downtown Chicago was being transformed into a state-of-the-art international airport. Today, O'Hare, city code ORD (for Old Orchard), is the second-busiest airport in North America.

Through all this, North American railroads, with the exception of Canadian National, which at the time was operated by the Canadian government, remained steadfastly private in their operations, freight or passenger. American railroads as a whole have a long and noble history of operating independent of government help, so in effect, the post–World War II climate more than ever had railroads competing with government-subsidized or sponsored movement of passengers.

Introduced by The Milwaukee Road in 1948, the Skytop Lounge parlor-observation car was another innovation to lure passengers back to rail travel. This interior view shows the end of the car with its under-glass seating. The rest of the car was equipped with swivel parlor seats. There were also Skytop sleepers built to this format, with private rooms instead of parlor seating. *Jim Neubauer collection*

The Kansas City Southern Railway's *Southern Belle* pulls away from Shreveport, Louisiana, in April 1968. The optimistic KCS was one of two railroads purchasing brand-new cars for its passenger fleet as late as the mid-1960s, even as service nationwide was sliding fast. The handsomely painted cars would transport KCS riders for little more than another year before the railroad changed its mind and bowed out of the passenger business altogether. *Jim Boyd photo*

The Illinois Central garnered the attention of Midwesterners with its attractive rust brown and orange colors on such trains as the *Land O' Corn* seen here near Rockford, Illinois, in the mid-1960s. Following the E-units are four Flexi-Van cars with intermodal containers carrying pouched mail. By 1968, the U.S. Postal Service had ended nearly all of its business on railroads, a devastating move for U.S. intercity passenger trains, which relied heavily on mail revenues. *Jim Boyd photo*

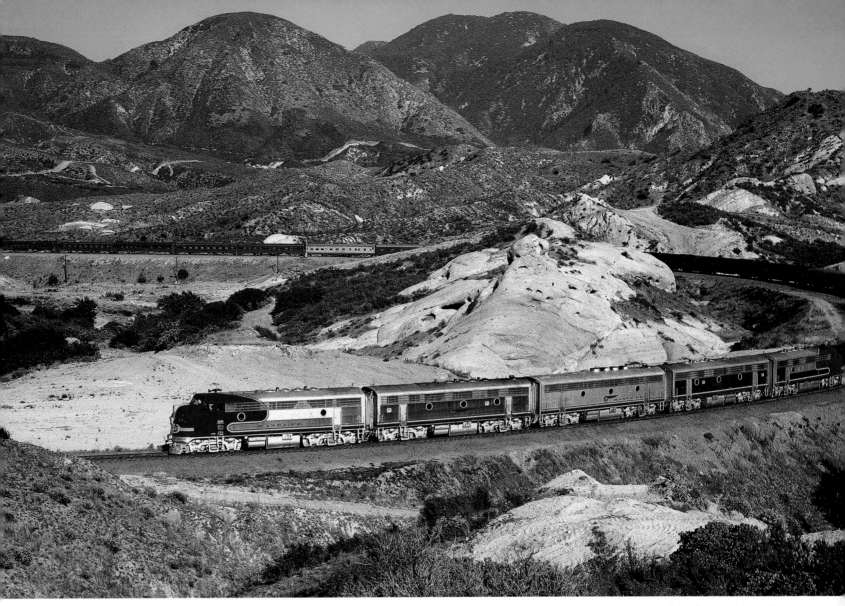

This spectacular image of Santa Fe's eastbound *Grand Canyon*, train No. 24, is captured at Sullivan's Curve west of the summit of California's Cajon Pass on July 4, 1964. The railroad has assigned an A-B-B-B-A set of F3 units to keep the 21-car Los Angeles–Chicago train moving at a good pace upgrade. Santa Fe trains were among the most popular in the nation with a well-earned reputation for excellent service. *Chard Walker photo*

It would be a no-win situation, for government pockets are almost always deeper than those of private companies. As it was, American railroads invested an enormous amount of capital in new and improved rail passenger services following the close of the war, but it would still not be enough to compete effectively with emerging airlines and an interstate highway system that would begin its sprawl across North America in 1955. If U.S. and Canadian governments had a truly pragmatic transportation policy, with investment funding distributed more democratically among all transport modes, postwar railroads might well have developed a nationwide system of truly high-speed passenger trains, just as Japan did, unveiling its world-class Shinkensan bullet-train system in 1965.

But that's not at all what happened. Most major American railroads—and some minor players as well—made a valiant effort on their own to keep passengers after the war. At best,

innovations such as the streamliner and, in 1945, the dome car would only slow the overall decline, not reverse it. Examples abound. The little Illinois Terminal Railroad, an electric interurban carrier linking several semimajor central Illinois cities with St. Louis, placed brand-new, all-streamlined electric streamliners into service in 1948–1949. Within a year, one was discontinued altogether, and by the summer of 1956 all IT intercity passenger trains, heavyweight and streamlined, were gone. That's how fast the decline was happening. By 1948, U.S. passenger train operations had lost some $500 million, and alarm bells were spreading through the industry. In 1951, the passenger side of the nation's largest and most powerful railroad, the Pennsylvania, lost $71 million. These losses were attributed not only to a decline in ridership, but a sharp increase in costs that followed the war, especially in terms of labor.

Moving People   295

There were hopeful moments, though. In 1952, Pleasure Dome lounge cars were added to Santa Fe's all-Pullman *Super Chief*, one of the finest passenger trains in all of North America. In 1954–1955, Santa Fe began introducing innovative Hi-Level cars to *El Capitan*, the all-coach companion train to the *Super Chief*. Also in the mid-1950s, Union Pacific did a wholesale upgrading of all the trains in its *City* train fleet—the *City of Los Angeles*, *City of Portland*, *City of San Francisco*, *City of Denver*, and *City of St. Louis*—with brand-new rolling stock and locomotives. Dome coaches, dome lounges, and dome diners brought the *City* trains to their apex. Similarly, Great Northern, Northern Pacific, Burlington Route, and Spokane, Portland & Seattle—joint operators of the famed *Empire Builder*, *North Coast Limited*, and other northern-tier transcons—did a massive upgrade of those trains. Also in 1955–1956, CN took delivery of 359 new lightweight, streamlined passenger cars to upgrade its services nationwide. CN rival Canadian Pacific did

likewise during the same period, bringing trans-Canada service to its pinnacle with the introduction of the all-stainless-steel, Vista-Dome *Canadian* in 1955.

Between 1946 and 1958, American railroads and the Pullman Company spent $1.3 billion in new equipment. Although these upgrades did result in increased patronage on some routes, overall the decline in passenger-miles continued. An innovation in the airline industry in the late 1950s, the jet airliner, had broadsided rail passenger service, particularly in the realm of long-distance travel. By the end of the 1950s, airlines were now handling more intercity passengers than were railroads, and losses on passenger operations were nearing a billion dollars per year. Train-discontinuances or the consolidation of selected trains to reduce operating costs increased markedly in the late 1950s, hastened by a recession. Signs of the times were evident in the *20th Century Limited*, which lost its all-Pullman status

Running long-hood forward, a pair of Grand Trunk Western passenger GP9s—freight locomotives equipped with boilers for train heat and high-speed gearing—powers the eastbound *Inter-City Limited* through London, Ontario, in September 1966. GTW was a U.S. subsidiary of Canadian National. At a time when America was consumed with highway and air travel, Canadian railroads kept moving along with comfortable, convenient, and attractive train service. *Jim Boyd photo*

Maintaining a high standard of service on its trains, Canadian Pacific held its own against government-controlled rival Canadian National in transporting people as well as hauling freight. Seen at Montreal in June 1968 is one of only three E8A units in all of Canada (all three on CP's roster) and the railroad's classic silver and maroon passenger fleet. It is pulling the *Viger* from Windsor Station to Quebec City. *Jim Boyd photo*

in 1958 when it was consolidated with the coach-and-Pullman *Commodore Vanderbilt*.

This downward spiral continued into the 1960s, resulting in the loss of passenger service on many lines. For example, in 1961, the Lehigh Valley had exited the passenger market altogether, becoming the first (of many) major North American railroads to go freight-only. Ongoing discontinuances began disintegrating the passenger-train network as a whole in North America, though more so in the United States than Canada and Mexico, affecting even the healthier passenger routes that were dependant on interline connections. The loss of passenger trains also adversely affected mail and express traffic being handled by trains, and finally, in 1967–1968, the United States Postal Service ended nearly all Railway Post Office service. Since this had been a lucrative source of revenue for many passenger trains, the number of train-discontinuances increased markedly as the 1960s drew to a

close. Even on the Santa Fe, whose marketing and handling of passenger traffic was among the best in North America and its train well patronized even at this late date, the loss of mail contracts forced the company to discontinue several of its esteemed trains.

When one of the United States' most well-loved trains, the *California Zephyr*, was discontinued in late winter 1970 with much high-profile fanfare, it was a sign that the end of U.S. passenger train service was near.

Interestingly, across the border in Canada, things had fared considerably better. At the end of the 1950s, CN resolutely adopted a pro-passenger stance that would carry Canada past much of the collapse and blight experienced by the United States during the 1960s. Armed with a bright new image—one that, in essence, survives to this day—and out-of-the-box thinking, CN made rail passenger travel hip again. Admittedly, Canada had not become as entrenched in the highway mentality

Two Massachusetts Bay Transportation Authority commuter trains with Delaware & Hudson locomotives meet outside of Boston's South Station in the early 1970s. Power-short MBTA was borrowing locomotives from the D&H until new ones were delivered. These two Alco PA units had put in years of work pulling Santa Fe passenger trains before being sold to the D&H in 1968. Revered for their timeless styling, these locomotives spent their last years in Mexico. *Jim Boyd photo*

as had its neighbor, partially due to the vast, remote, and rural expanses that separated its major urban centers.

CN's plan was pretty simple: Give the passenger what he or she wanted: smart, comfortable, reliable trains; convenient schedules; attractive new innovations; and price-conscious fares. One of the ironies of these tactics was that CN purchased a number of cars that had been cast aside by U.S. railroads in the throes of dismantling their rail passenger networks. Surplus U.S. sleepers bolstered CN train consists swelled by successful marketing and ticket-pricing campaigns, such as the Red, White, and Blue fare system.

Later in the 1960s, CN introduced brand-new corridor-type trains, the *Tempos* and the *Rapidos*.

Canadian Pacific, being a private company with very limited capital, was less enthusiastic about maintaining passenger service, but it managed to maintain a skeletal network of runs, including its revered transcon, *The Canadian*, which never lacked for high service standards.

Further, the Government of Ontario pioneered an experiment that proved there was at least one bright spot in the future of rail passenger transport: the commuter train. In 1966, the province created GO Transit, a regional/suburban operation designed to serve the needs of a booming Toronto. As was the case in so many large cities throughout North America, the automobile was becoming a victim of its own success, making freeway traffic unbearable during rush hours. Suddenly, the commuter train didn't seem so antiquated after all. Ontario was among the first to see this and decided to provide a comprehensive system for moving people between suburbs and downtown Toronto. By the 1980s, GO Transit had set the pace for the rest of the continent in terms of dealing with growing traffic problems in major areas.

Not that the commuter train had gone ignored in the United States. Beginning in the 1950s, Chicago-area railroads that operated suburban services noted a demand for increased and improved services. Burlington and Chicago & North

The Great Northern's Big Sky Blue paint scheme lasted a short time as the GN, Northern Pacific, Chicago, Burlington & Quincy, and Spokane, Portland & Seattle would form the Burlington Northern in 1970. In the fall of 1968, the eastbound *Western Star* leaves the Twin Cities area with two of GN's eight SDP45 locomotives. The train's equipment was used on early Amtrak trains between Chicago and Seattle following its inception in 1971. *Jim Boyd photo*

Western were the pioneers here, investing heavily in efficient new bi-level equipment that would become the standard-bearer for suburban services throughout North America. At one point, early in the 1960s, C&NW even declared that it made money on its eye-catching, yellow-and-green commuter streamliners. By the end of the 1960s, Chicago, San Francisco, and Toronto could boast of up-to-date commuter-rail operations that were flourishing.

But the end of the 1960s would also end the era of the streamliner and the intercity passenger train as it had been known since the late 1930s.

The Renaissance

As 1970 unfolded, the U.S. intercity passenger-train network—what was left of it—was in shambles, brought to its knees by many forces, not the least of which was the disastrous 1968 merger of the NYC and PRR into Penn Central Corp. PC wound up operating a majority of U.S. intercity trains, but it had no intention of keeping them going.

Meanwhile, the passenger-train situation overall in the United States had become desperate, with most railroads wanting out of the passenger business altogether. In 1967, a grass-roots organization known as the National Association of Railroad Passengers headed by Anthony Haswell set out with a formidable goal: save the passenger train.

And it worked. NARP convinced Congress that U.S. railroads had been drained of their earnings trying to keep a seemingly hopeless thing going against the odds. For the United States to have a world-class rail passenger system that would rival the successful systems that flourished overseas (thanks largely to governments dedicated to the task), the federal government would have to somehow intervene.

And so, on October 30, 1970, President Richard M. Nixon reluctantly signed a bill that created the National

Railroad Passenger Corporation, whose marketing name later became Amtrak.

Although often (and incorrectly) referred to as a "government agency," Amtrak was and is in many ways simply just another railroad mandated or chartered by the U.S. government. The stockholders, however, were those railroads who wished to exit the passenger business, and their entrance fee would be in the form of cash and/or locomotives and rolling stock. The unique twist was that the federal government would supply start-up capital and make up for losses, if any, at the end of the fiscal year.

There are some to this day who believe that Amtrak really was created to turn the tide for the American passenger train, while others insist it was merely a means of giving the U.S. passenger train a dignified funeral. The paltry startup capital—$40 million—could certainly be interpreted that the latter viewpoint had more truth. The $40 *billion* that the highways got right after World War II would have had a much greater impact.

The Amtrak law obligated all passenger-carrying railroads—whether they joined Amtrak or not—to maintain the status quo until Amtrak actually began operation. That happened on May 1, 1971, and the significance of that date would grow ever more poignant as the years rolled on toward the new millennium. Alas, with such meager startup funds, Amtrak could only afford to continue operating about half of the intercity trains still running as of that date, so on April 30, 1971, there came a transportation bloodbath the likes of which have never been witnessed before or since. The final trips of such famed liners as the *City of Los Angeles*, *North Coast Limited*, *City of Miami*, *Midnight Special*, and *Pennsylvania Limited* garnered newspaper and TV news headlines from coast to coast. A few railroads—notably Southern, Rock Island, and Rio Grande—opted not to join Amtrak initially and thus were obligated to continue operating their passenger trains for another five years minimum.

With an eclectic array of passenger equipment—all of it still owned by stockholder railroads—a small band of

Amtrak's southbound train 85, the *Champion*, between New York and St. Petersburg is at Auburndale, Florida, near the end of its trip on August 15, 1974. The carrier was a little more than three years old at the time, and most of the equipment—including its big, new SDP40F locomotives—sported Amtrak's red, blue, and silver livery. *Kevin EuDaly collection*

Capitalizing on VIA Rail's unpopular decision in rerouting its premier train, *The Canadian*, from the Canadian Pacific route through the Rockies to that of Canadian National, private operator Great Canadian Railtour Company has greatly profited running the *Rocky Mountaineer* on the CP between Vancouver, British Columbia, and Calgary/Jasper, Alberta, since 1990. The train is seen here working up the Thompson River Canyon near Pitqua, British Columbia, in the summer of 1994. Prospective private operators have kept a close eye on Amtrak routes as well. *Steve Jessup photo*

pro-passenger warriors who worked for NRPC, and 10 tons of hope, Amtrak was off and running May 1, 1971, on a skeletal system that involved operating over the tracks of host railroads, mostly those that had joined Amtrak. Although it reached from coast to coast, the system was severely lacking in many respects. It didn't even include service over the population-dense Chicago–Toledo–Cleveland–Buffalo portion of the once-passenger-heavy former NYC main line. Rail passenger ridership in the United States bottomed out in the last half of 1971. There was nowhere to go but up—unless it was out of business.

The story of Amtrak since those meager beginnings is worthy of a book unto itself, and several have been written. Overall, Amtrak grew systematically, experimenting with its

services, adding new trains (sometimes with the help of state governments that wished to exercise a provision in the Amtrak law allowing states to participate in providing additions to the basic Amtrak route structure), and amassing more employees and gaining ever greater power as a railroad. Amtrak went right to work advertising to make Americans more train-aware. It worked, for ridership increased 13 percent in the first half of 1972.

Amtrak acquired its first new equipment—turbine-powered trains from France—in 1973, and then went on to purchase its own new cars and locomotives in 1975 to replace equipment that had been purchased by Amtrak-member railroads years earlier, some prior to World War II.

The first few years were especially tenuous, but an unexpected oil crisis early in the 1970s prompted government and public alike to rethink the consequences of America's grossly unbalanced transportation system. Suddenly, Americans became a little more train-aware, and Amtrak ridership took another climb—one that would save the railroad. Years later, some Amtrak insiders admitted that, had it not been for the gasoline crisis, the company probably would not have survived past its first five years.

Not that survival was ever easy for the beleaguered carrier. Amtrak critics have always been plentiful, mainly because of ongoing subsidies. While it was generally agreed that the goal for Amtrak was to at least eventually break even (never mind that the reason railroads wanted out of the passenger business in the first place was because it had become virtually impossible to make money moving passengers), that never happened. Every year, Congress was obliged to provide monies

to both offset losses and provide operating capital. Since these subsidies were pretty much out in the open as transportation budget line items, unlike the routing of taxpayer monies—usually shrouded as "investments"—into highway, air, and even water transportation, they were easy targets for anti-rail forces (largely highway lobbyists) and certain segments of the political world that view rail passenger service as a form of welfare.

In the ideal world, at least from a North American perspective, all forms of transportation would make a decent profit, but in the last half of the twentieth century, that was rarely the case with moving passengers, regardless of mode. After World War II, this thinking began to change—albeit slowly—to big-picture mode as more people began to view subsidies as being a necessary evil if they were for the good of the country as a whole. Though certainly not embraced by everybody, this viewpoint would eventually fuel the rail

Amtrak train No. 5, the westbound *California Zephyr*, cruises through Boca, California, June 16, 1998, with a trio of Genesis units and bi-level Superliner cars. Unveiled in the late 1970s, the Superliners featured increased passenger comfort as well as operational efficiencies. At the throttle of the lead unit is veteran Amtrak engineer and railroad author/photographer Phil Gosney, who has experienced Amtrak's uncertainties and successes through the years. *Steve Jessup photo*

In the year 2000, Amtrak introduced the *Acela Express* trains running up and down the Northeast Corridor between Washington and Boston. Though slower than high-speed trains in other countries, the high-tech, high-speed electric *Acelas* can reach speeds up to 150 miles per hour. This *Acela Express* was captured speeding northward through Bowie, Maryland, in January 2006. *Alex Mayes photo*

passenger renaissance that took hold in the 1970s and would boom in the late 1980s and well into the twenty-first century.

Regardless, Amtrak continued to be at the mercy of the whims of the presidential administration at hand, as well as an often mercurial Congress, and Amtrak's budget invariably became a hotly contested and controversial item every year. As a result, to this day, Amtrak has never had the proper funding and capitalization that might have made it a truly world-class passenger carrier. Yet, Amtrak has somehow performed miracles with whatever it could get in terms of financing. In 1976, it took ownership of most of the Northeast Corridor between Washington, New York, Boston, and Harrisburg,

Pennsylvania. Late in the 1970s, Amtrak unveiled a new generation of long-distance passenger cars in the form of bi-level rolling stock—the Superliners—that featured both greater operational efficiencies and increased comfort. Working with selected states, Amtrak has developed popular travel corridors that have bolstered its overall ridership: San Diego–Los Angeles–Santa Barbara and Sacramento–Oakland–San Jose in California, for example; Vancouver, British Columbia–Seattle–Portland–Eugene, Oregon, in the Pacific Northwest; and Boston–Portland in the Northeast. As of 2008, the majority of its fleet of locomotives and rolling stock had been purchased new, including a stable of high-tech, high-speed

In addition to Coaster commuter trains (seen at right), San Diego is one of several cities operating light-rail equipment. Metropolitan Transit Systems has a 53-mile light-rail network around town with 53 stations. Advantages of electric light rail are numerous: most people prefer them over buses for comfort; they are emission-free; they can climb steep grades; and they are extremely quiet. The MTS is captured next to the Coaster train on January 7, 2002. *George W. Hamlin photo*

electric trains, the *Acelas*, introduced in 2000 on the Northeast Corridor. Amtrak now has all its own locomotive and train crews and no longer pays host railroads for these positions; aside from Northeast Corridor right-of-way and track, it owns additional real estate in the form of a portion of the Chicago–Detroit route and numerous depots and terminals, including Penn Station in New York City and Union Station in Chicago.

At the very least, Amtrak has served to make North Americans more rail-aware, even if it hasn't always been flattering. The formation of the NRPC, to some degree, served as a model for Canada, which in the mid-1970s opted to form a similar corporation to take over, market, and operate the intercity passenger operations of CN and CP. In short order, VIA became a respected, innovative carrier that many industry-

watchers feel should serve as an example for Amtrak and the United States.

Perhaps the brightest spot in the rail passenger front in North America has been the boom in the commuter- and rail-transit arena. Automobile congestion, coupled to an increase in public awareness about the virtues of rail transport, has prompted most major North American cities to give more attention to the rail mode. In cities that historically have always had strong ties with rail transit (e.g., New York, Chicago, Toronto, Philadelphia, Boston, Montreal, San Francisco, and Cleveland), there has been a step up in improvements and service expansions. In nearly all these cases, railroads have turned over their commuter operations to new, public-funded agencies that, in turn, have been in a better position to acquire new equipment, revamp or build new stations, add new lines,

Thirty-two North American cities now have commuter rail systems in place—28 in the United States—helping workers avoid increasing traffic congestion on highways and freeways. The Altamont Commuter Express operates from Stockton to San Jose, California, serving a large number of residents who cannot afford to live in the Bay Area and must find housing in valley locations. The ACE is pictured here at Stockton in June 1999. *Jim Boyd photo*

and otherwise unify operations that had been handled by several private carriers.

But the most amazing transformations have come from cities that have not previously had commuter systems (Albuquerque, New Mexico; Nashville, Tennessee; Miami, Florida; Seattle, Washington; Dallas/Fort Worth, Texas; Vancouver, British Columbia; Salt Lake City, Utah; and Houston, Texas), or whose systems were largely and mistakenly dismantled in favor of road mode only (Los Angeles; Minneapolis, Minnesota; St. Louis, Missouri; Denver, Colorado; Washington, D.C.; Atlanta, Georgia; and Portland, Oregon). New systems, be they commuter rail, light rail, or both, have been implemented in all of them and others with a remarkable success rate.

As the first decade of the new millennium closes out, the fate of the intercity passenger train in North America still rides in limbo. Divided by factions who insist that trains must entirely pay for themselves (but look askance at highway and airline subsidies) and those who insist the government should provide a dedicated funding for wholesale improvements and development, Amtrak bumps along on a day-to-day basis with only a vague vision of its future. Yet Amtrak ridership reached its highest point ever—about 26 million passengers annually—in the mid-2000s, and as this book first went to press the United States was in the throes of another traffic congestion and oil crisis. This was a certain indication that there existed a growing demand for intercity passenger service. A secure future for the same would seem to be in the cards, but the hand that's dealt to public transportation in America is anything but consistent. However, things such as global warming, energy issues, and increasing demand for greater transportation options appear to be providing a stronger guiding role in making the right decision, which the writers of this book hope will be the rail mode.

Following pages: Reminiscent of pre-Amtrak days, at least one freight railroad still operating passenger service in North America is the Alaska Railroad. Along with its own equipment, the ARR pulls cars owned by cruise-line companies that serve the region during the summer. Note the silver and blue cars toward the end of the train. On May 24, 2003, the *Denali Star* is pictured in Healy Canyon approaching Moody Tunnel. *Alex Mayes photo*

9

Infrastructure

by Andrew McBride

At the root of railroading is the flanged steel wheel on rail, and this view of a loaded taconite train at Biwabik, Minnesota, on the Duluth, Missabe & Iron Range on May 4, 2007, reveals track at its basic level. The eastbound train is on the main line, the next track over is a long passing siding, and the next two are yard tracks left from what was once a significant yard at this location. In the lower left corner is milepost 59—the distance from the port facilities at Two Harbors. *Kevin EuDaly photo*

The average person thinks of the railroad as a train pulled by a locomotive rushing about with cars of passengers or freight in tow. Much like a Hollywood movie, though, little thought is given to all of the other aspects of the play that make this train the star.

A train requires a large supporting cast to make its run possible. Dispatchers and yard offices, maintenance facilities, signals, stations, bridges, tunnels, corporate headquarters—all these things and more bring a train to life. In the early days of railroading, much of this had yet to be invented. Everything from red and green signals to Standard Time had yet to be created or even considered.

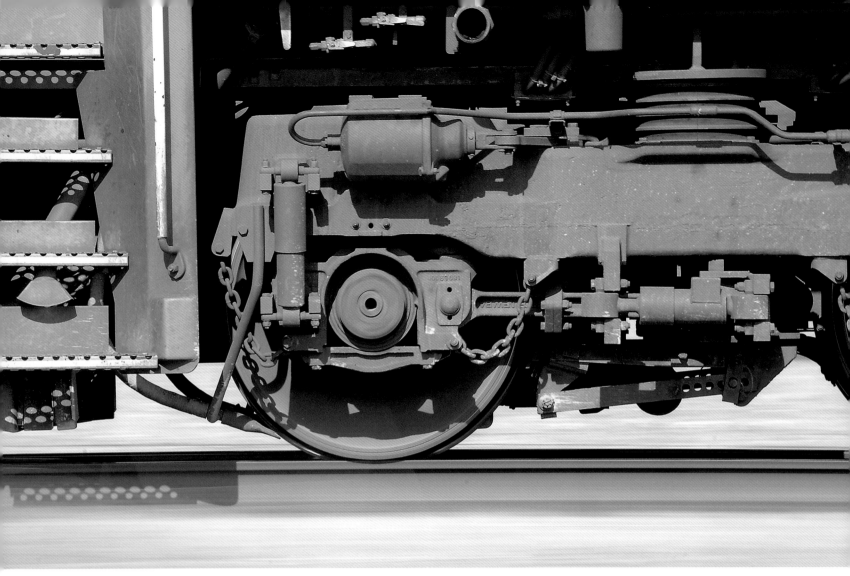

The flange that keeps trains on the track appears minimalistic at first glance; however, with the beveled contour of modern wheels and the rolled shape of the rail head, the flanges don't spend a lot of time in contact with the rail. With the extreme weight of locomotives and cars, less than 2 inches of flange suffices. In this view, a Union Pacific northbound at Mondamin, Iowa, rolls smoothly along the rails on May 20, 2007. *Kevin EuDaly photo*

Track

The most fundamental aspect to railroading is the flanged steel wheel on a steel rail. This system allows for trains to be self-steering and vastly reduces the friction of the rolling wheels, giving a railway the ability to operate mile-long trains with individual cars weighing on average between 100 to 125 tons.

Long before the railroad locomotive was even dreamed of, the Romans discovered it was easier to move horse-drawn wagons along paths made of oblong blocks of cut stone with grooves chiseled in them to guide the wheels. Over time, perhaps 500 years after the Roman Empire, this gave way to "stringer" track consisting of oak stringers (rails) laid upon wooden beams, called ties or sleepers, set crosswise beneath the oak rails that carts rode on. Loaded with coal or aggregate, the cars could be easily rolled along this crude track by man or beast. In Europe and on the British Isles, these became known as tramways.

When Britain gave birth to the locomotive early in the 1800s, inventors and builders also began to experiment with

new track designs to carry the new steam-powered contraption. The next step in the evolution of stringer rail was to fasten straps or narrow plates of iron along the top surface so the weight of the locomotive wouldn't gouge the wood; this also further smoothed the ride and reduced friction. But strap rail was unstable. Extreme temperature changes could cause longer straps to curl up, ripping themselves from the wood beam and projecting up through car floors and causing injury.

Stringers and strap rail went from being wooden beams laid end to end to iron rails of various shapes and sizes, from upside-down *U*-shapes to a trough profile (to obviate the need for flanges) to variations of today's familiar T-shaped rail. Borrowing ideas from the British, Americans in 1828 began to use cast-iron rails set on stone blocks. The familiar T-rail, a variation of which is used today, was first applied in 1830 on the Camden & Amboy in New Jersey by its chief engineer, Robert Stevens. Over the years, the shape of the rail overall has changed little in appearance, but that is where the similarities end. The brittle iron has given way to the more durable and flexible rolled steel rail, and the weight of the rail has dramatically increased as well. In the time of Robert Stevens, rail weighed as little as 36 pounds per yard. Today, rail may weigh as much as 155 pounds per yard with the average main-line rail weighing 126 pounds per yard.

Rail length has also varied a great deal in the last 175 years. In the early days of T-rail, lengths were generally around 15 feet, although there was no standard. This was often determined by how many men it would require to handle the rail when assembling the track. As rolling stock increased in size, so did rail lengths, and eventually the steel mills were producing rail in a standardized length of 39 feet to fit the average 40-foot gondola or flat car. These 39-foot sections were laid so that the joints between the opposite rails were staggered, created the familiar "clickety-clack" and harmonic "rock-and-roll" motion that we still associate with moving trains today. In England and her colonies, however, they preferred the joints to be lined up opposite each other, giving their trains a distinctively different rolling sound.

Well over a century has passed since the completion of the transcontinental railroad on May 10, 1869, and the track that trains roll on today continues to change. Thirty-nine-foot sections of jointed (bolted together) rail, though still prevalent in North America, are constantly being replaced by quarter-mile sections of continuous welded rail (CWR). Welded rail provides for a smoother ride, reduces maintenance by eliminating multiple rail joints, and makes derailments less likely.

Welded rail resolves the temperature expansion problems in an unexpected way. As the rail is laid down, it is fitted with rail anchors on either side of the ties that resist longitudinal movement, and the heat expansion takes place in the rail's cross section that has a minimal effect on the track gauge.

Rails aren't much good for trains to roll on unless they're resting on something, and that's where the tie comes in. Not only do ties provide support for the rail, but they keep the track in gauge. In early days, ties were merely split logs from trees felled along the right-of-way during construction. The rails were then spiked directly into this hewn timber. It got trains running quickly, but it didn't last long. With the rail lying directly on the tie, the rail tended to cut into the timber, a situation remedied by a steel tie plate, which in essence was a seat for the rail that spread the weight over a wider area of a tie's top surface.

The tie itself also has changed. Today, most rail traffic still rolls on wooden ties, but the lumber used now has little in common with its predecessors. Contemporary hardwood ties are larger and treated with creosote to prevent deterioration from moisture as well as insect infestation. Creosoting extends the life of a tie manyfold—up to 25 or 30 years versus just a couple of years for nontreated ties.

New ideas in the manufacture of ties continue to be applied as well. In 1930, the Philadelphia & Reading experimented with ties made from concrete, but it met with limited success. As the technology of cement-making has improved, so has the concrete tie, and its use has now become widespread. Theoretically, concrete ties can last for at least 50 years, which offsets their initial higher cost. Because of the hardness of concrete, however, tie plates used with them usually sit on rubber cushions to soften the ride. Since you can't drive spikes into concrete ties, the rails are held in place with Pandrol clips that are shaped like huge paper clips and anchor into holes in the tie plates. Steel, composite, and even plastic ties are also being used and tested in the railroads' continuous quest to reduce maintenance and lower operating costs.

This museum display shows early strap rail, where iron straps were nailed or screwed down to wooden beams. Unfortunately, the straps had a tendency to come loose, and often wreaked havoc on operations when the straps would come through the bottoms of cars. In the early years, rail developed quickly and through several phases, ending with the standardized T-shaped rail in use today. *Jim Boyd photo*

As rail developed, a standardized 39-foot rail length was employed so the rail could be loaded on standard-length 40-foot gondolas. This view of a BNSF branch line in Virgil, South Dakota, on May 19, 2007, reveals staggered jointed rail typical of early railroading. The general condition of this line limits train speeds to 10 miles per hour, and the grain train in the far distance won't reach the photographer for several minutes. *Kevin EuDaly photo*

Track has developed into a rugged system, employing a variety of design characteristics. Chicago & North Western C-628 No. 6701 is on the lead of a trio of former Norfolk & Western Alcos, crossing a switch at Baldwin Siding on C&NW's ore lines in Upper Michigan on June 1, 1982. Note the heavy angled braces against the outside rail, which provide lateral support as the wheels pass through the frog of the switch. At the frog, the wheels pass from one route to another, and there is a brief interval where the braced outside rail must withstand the lateral force to keep the wheels on the rails. *Kevin EuDaly photo*

Basic Track

A tie clip is used to hold the rail to the tie plate instead of the traditional railroad spike. This tie plate has a much higher brace to keep the rail in place than a traditional tie plate. This system is employed on Union Pacific's main line through Lawrence, Kansas, where this particular curve in front of the depot is laid with 140-pound rail. *Kevin EuDaly photo*

Before rails and ties could be laid, a railroad first had to determine the route for the line. An important aspect to this was the lay of the land and how best to run tracks through it. A line with steep grades and sharp curves might have been cheaper to build, but in the long run it would cost the railroad much more in operating and maintenance costs.

One way to compensate for the variable topography was to build a series of cuts and fills. Excavating through a hill and then using the displaced earth to fill in the valley allowed lines to level out their roadbeds.

While early tracks were just laid on the ground, a more permanent and weatherproof track structure was needed. The ideal solution proved to be a 3- or 4-foot-deep bed of crushed rock ballast. The sharp-edged stone held itself in place but left space inside for water to penetrate and drain out. Railroad track is subject to the weather: heat, cold, rain, snow, freeze, and thaw. It's a brutal environment that over a few years will destroy an unmaintained piece of track.

When he was president of the Southern Railway, L. Stanley Crane said that there are three secrets to successful

Amtrak's Northeast Corridor is home to the highest-speed trackage in North America, where 140-mile-per-hour *Acela* trainsets are found in daily service. This view shows Pandrol clips in use on concrete ties at Bristol, Pennsylvania, on July 1, 2006. The *Silver Star*, blistering past the station on an express track, is powered by an AEM7. The clips are necessary because the tie plates must be mounted on the concrete ties at the factory. The tracks in this view are all long-section welded rail with very few joints in view. *Kevin EuDaly photo*

Few railroad bridges are as spectacular as the Chesapeake & Ohio's through-truss span over the Ohio River at Sciotoville, Ohio. Due to the Corps of Engineers' restriction of one pier in the river, this bridge wound up with the distinction of having the highest load capacity in the world. On May 2, 1963, F7A 7015 exits the south portal on the Kentucky side of the river at Limeville. The train is completely dwarfed by the bridge. *James F. EuDaly photo*

railroading: "Drainage, drainage, and drainage." A good bed of ballast and system of drainage ditches will make any railroad easier to maintain.

Section gangs patrol every piece of railroad, intensely or casually, depending on the traffic, to keep the ties level and the rails in alignment. A few sweating laborers can replace a tie with picks and shovels, but more likely today the job will be done by impressive mechanized track gangs with hydraulic machinery that can lift up the track underneath itself and swap out a tie in a couple of minutes and tamp it back into its place in the ballast.

Everyone is amazed by the super-high-speed passenger trains in Europe and Japan: their secret isn't the train but the track. The Japanese Bullet Train system is shut down every midnight, and for the next six hours, hundreds of track gangs literally rebuild the entire railroad every night! Amtrak's Northeast Corridor gets almost as much attention to maintain the smooth 150-mile-per-hour *Acela* service.

Bridges

When the railroads encountered barriers such as rivers, streams, deep valleys, and mountain ridges, they turned to bridges and

Stone-and-mortar bridges were an early form used where a significant bridge was needed over a long distance. The most famous of all stone bridges is Starrucca Viaduct, located at Lanesboro, Pennsylvania, and was built by the 6-foot-gauge New York & Erie Railroad in 1848. It is still in use by Norfolk Southern today. In October 1985, Conrail SD40 No. 6321 crosses over the historic structure, which is on the National Register of Historic Places. *Jim Boyd photo*

tunnels. These were expensive investments for a fledgling rail line and weren't undertaken lightly; in some cases, however, they were unavoidable.

The first significant bridges built in North America were the classic masonry arch construction. Using stone and mortar, this design, much older than the concept of railroading itself, proved to be an extremely stable and durable means of crossing over a river or deep valley. So durable, in fact, that some examples of these bridges built in the 1800s still survive and carry main-line trains to this day. They were costly and time consuming to build, and the piers did not fit well in navigable waterways.

With the great untapped forests in North America, railroad builders soon turned to timber as a much cheaper and easier way to build bridges. Of these early bridges, the wood pile trestle was the most common. These consisted of multiple framed piers supporting the horizontal stringers that supported the track. Though cheap to build, they required much maintenance and prevented any traffic from either navigable waterways or roadways.

In 1820, Ithiel Town patented the wood lattice truss bridge. Since these were built mostly as covered bridges, many survived well into the twenty-first century, protected by the lattice work, roofs, and walls. In 1838, William Howe developed the Howe Truss, and that's when railroads really began to embrace the truss bridge. It gave railroads the ability to span deeper chasms that the timber trestle was less suited for, and was cheaper and easier to build than the masonry bridges. The truss bridge did not require the multiple piers of the masonry bridge, thus it was less of an impediment to traffic below.

In 1845, the Philadelphia & Reading built the first metal bridge using iron to replace the framework of the Howe Truss.

The most inexpensive bridges came in the form of wooden trestles, which ranged from tiny spans over creeks to massive structures over large valleys. There are thousands of these scattered across North America—this one is located at Stamping Ground, Kentucky, and has Montpelier & Barre 70-ton locomotives rolling across it in November 1969. *Jim Boyd photo*

A classic steel arch bridge in Canada is located on the Canadian Pacific and crosses Stoney Creek high up on Rogers Pass through the Selkirk Mountains in British Columbia. Three SD40-2s cross high over the creek canyon on August 11, 1983. *Kevin EuDaly photo*

The Kansas City Southern strikes out of the Little Blue River Valley and crosses several ravines on its way south out of suburban Kansas City. This concrete arch bridge crosses Gregory Boulevard, and is one of three like it. The bridge over Highway 50 (now Highway 350) is longer and the similar bridge over 67th Street is smaller. A fourth bridge in the area is a large steel deck trestle over 63rd Street. Four EMD units are carrying southbound freight on July 4, 1982. *Kevin EuDaly photo*

As different versions of the truss bridge were developed, the science of bridge building also improved with a better understanding of the stresses imparted on all aspects of the bridge by the load they carried, as well as the natural elements they withstood.

In the early 1900s, the steel plate–girder bridge came into vogue, and it's still one of the most prevalent of railroad bridges in North America. It's made up of several pieces of steel structural shapes to form an I-beam that is larger than one that could be produced as a single piece. These types of bridges tend to be in lengths of 40 to 125 feet.

There are two basic ways of laying track on a bridge; the first and most common method is to apply the cross ties directly on the longitudinal stringers. If steel girders were used, they would usually be directly under the rails. Since the ties were usually notched or anchored in place, this made a simple and rigid structure, but if anything needed adjustment, it could be a difficult task.

The second type was a ballasted deck bridge. Here the bridge deck was a solid trough into which a normal depth of ballast was placed, with the track laid in the ballast. The ballasted deck permitted the track to be leveled and adjusted

The Southern Pacific crosses over the Sacramento River in Redding, California, on a large curved steel deck trestle. Four EMD units are rolling westbound across the bridge in June 1999 (the SP classes everything as westbound that's headed toward San Francisco), on their way southeast toward Sacramento. *Jim Boyd photo*

Deep in Feather River Canyon in Pulga, California, the westbound *California Zephyr* crosses the river running eight hours late in July 1969. High above the right-of-way, State Highway 70 crosses both the railroad and the river on a steel arch bridge. The construction of the railroad bridge is typical—through-truss spans, the ends of which sit on concrete piers. *Jim Boyd photo*

just as it would on solid ground. Both ballasted and open-deck bridges are in common use today.

One of the biggest challenges railroads faced was spanning the waterways used by riverboat traffic. Before the railroads came, it was the up-and-coming riverboats that had the lion's share of freight traffic, and they weren't going to give it up without a fight. Small drawbridges started showing up on the railroad scene as early as 1835, and swing bridges came along by 1850. It wasn't until 1856 when the Chicago & Rock Island built the first railroad bridge to span the Mississippi River that the riverboat interests began to take notice. Built between Rock Island, Illinois, and Davenport, Iowa, the 285-foot truss draw span, which pivoted at the center and allowed the bridge to be swung open, provided a channel 120 feet wide for river traffic. Fifteen days later, a side-wheel packet boat named the *Effie Afton* collided with the bridge and burst into flames. The owner of the boat sued the railroad, claiming "wild currents" generated by the new structure drove the boat into the bridge, and it was an obstruction to navigation. The railroad disagreed and even suspected the whole incident had been staged. It

took a young lawyer named Abraham Lincoln, hired by the railroad, to prove once and for all that one man had as much right to cross the river as another had to sail upon it.

Since then, railroads have employed a wide range of moveable bridges to cross navigable waterways. In 1874, the first vertical lift bridge was employed to cross the Erie Canal. The design of the bridge allowed for the entire span to be lifted straight in the air between two towers, thus eliminating the center pivot span and reducing the danger of the bridge being struck by river traffic.

Another variation was the bascule bridge that was built not unlike a drawbridge from medieval times. By utilizing heavy counterweights, a large span could be tilted to a 90-degree angle, allowing for a larger channel for river traffic.

Opposite: Railroad alignments are often such that they cross navigable rivers at a relatively low level, resulting in the need for lift or swing bridges. The ASB Bridge in Kansas City takes traffic across the Missouri River, and can lift to allow barge traffic to pass underneath. This train of empty hoppers bound for Wyoming has brand-new BNSF SD70ACe operating on the rear as a distributed power unit (DPU), crossing the bridge northbound on May 4, 2008. *Kevin EuDaly photo*

The Appalachian region is also rife with tunnels, and the C&O had its share. GP40-2 No. 4389 leads a smoking GP38 roaring out of Eccles Tunnel near Beckley, West Virginia, at a crawl. Behind the cloud of smoke in the tunnel are another GP38 and a trailing GP40-2. This tunnel was restricted to first-generation diesels until bored out in the late 1970s, allowing these units access to the mines at the end of the Surveyor Subdivision. *Kevin EuDaly photo*

The "Hole" Story

What railroads couldn't go over or around, they sometimes had to go through. The concept of tunneling wasn't new, and, in fact, it predated railroading by some 3,500 years.

The Allegheny Portage railroad opened a 901-foot bore near Johnstown, Pennsylvania, that became the first railroad tunnel in North America when it was finished in 1832. Eighteen years later there would be 48, and by 1945 there would be over 1,500. In the mid-nineteenth century, the technology of tunneling was still in its infancy. Holes were bored into the hard rock with nothing more than a hammer and a chisel, and then black powder was used to blast away a section. It was then cleared out, using horses and wagons. In most cases, the tunnel also required additional support, with timber or stone as a lining. These were huge, time-consuming, expensive, and dangerous projects.

By the 1890s, compressed-air drills and dynamite replaced the chisel and black powder. Timber linings also had fallen out of favor, as concrete and masonry linings proved to be safer and more durable. So durable, in fact, that many of these tunnels are still in service today.

During this time, the Grand Trunk Railroad was working on a project that was at the forefront of tunnel technology. It would connect Ontario with Michigan by going under the St. Clair River at a length of 6,050 feet. By utilizing a moveable circular shield that maintained the integrity of the tunnel, as well as compressed air for ground support, the builders were able to overcome the hydraulic pressure as well as the soft soil under the river. A cast-iron lining was then quickly applied behind the tunneling shield to stabilize the whole affair. The tunnel was completed in 1891.

Less than two decades later, the Michigan Central built a tunnel under the Detroit River to connect Windsor, Ontario, with Detroit. Rather than using the moveable-shield method, they simply dredged a trench in the river and then sunk pre-fabricated tunnel sections in place.

With continued improvements in the equipment required to build tunnels, the Great Northern completed the Cascade Tunnel in 1929. Close to 8 miles in length, it remained the largest tunnel in North America until the Canadian Pacific completed a tunnel that was just over 9 miles long through Mount Macdonald in British Columbia in 1989. Both are still in use today, as are many other tunnels that are now over a century old.

Opposite: The Denver & Rio Grande Western had the slogan "Through the Rockies, not around them." The Moffat Road drilled tunnels nearly everywhere it went, primarily because of the incredibly rugged nature of the Rocky Mountains west of Denver. Although less storied than the Moffat line west of Denver, the route over Tennessee Pass also had tunnels. An eastbound approaches the portal of Pando Tunnel with SD40T-2 No. 5395 in the lead on September 24, 1993. *Kevin EuDaly photo*

Standard semaphore signals had the blade pointed up for a clear indication, and the blade for this southbound has just started to drop as lead Family Lines U30C gets ready to pound across the B&O diamond in Mitchell, Indiana. The train is running on former Monon rails that once linked Chicago with Louisville, and the northbound signal, sitting in the horizontal stop position, is for a passing siding there. *Kevin EuDaly photo*

Signals

A signal means many things to a railroader. It directs traffic, and it can warn the crew of approaching hazards such as another train, a broken rail, a landslide, or a signal failure. Contemporary signal devices also can let a train know if a wheel is overheating or if a car is dragging something.

This wasn't always the case. In the very early years of railroading, signals were not used at all, and those that were used were extremely crude. The first type of signal was simply a lit candle in the window of a station, alerting a passing train that all was clear as far as the station agent knew. Traffic, for the most part, was directed solely with the use of a timetable that indicated where trains should be at a certain time. And, of course, this required each crew member to have a very accurate pocket watch. There was a major flaw in this system, however. If anything went wrong—including bad weather or a mechanical failure causing a train to be delayed and thus operating behind schedule—there was no way to alert other trains operating on the same route to the change in plans.

Perhaps the most famous train wreck that was a direct result of the drawbacks of these early systems was the collision that caused American folk hero Casey Jones to lose his life. As the popular engineer on Illinois Central's train No. 1, the *New Orleans Special*, Casey was trying to make up time to get his late train back on schedule. Unbeknownst to him, two

freight trains ahead of him in the little hamlet of Vaughan, Mississippi, were having their own problems. The passing track they were attempting to use to get out of his way was too short, and to make matters worse, one of the trains had broken in two (came uncoupled), resulting in the airbrakes going into an emergency stop.

Without lineside signals, Casey Jones was unaware of the freight train stopped directly in his path, and as he came around a curve, he was suddenly staring at the rear marker lights of a caboose. Shouting to his fireman, Slim Webb, to jump, Casey laid on the whistle to warn the freight crew and stayed at the throttle, working the brakes, attempting to slow down his passenger train with no hope of stopping it. He died in the cab when his train collided with the standing freight, but his whistle had saved the lives of the freight crew men.

In 1900, when this collision occurred, these kinds of wrecks were far too common, and in fact, over 2,500 railroaders died in just that year alone. Not all of these deaths were caused by a lack of an adequate signal system, but the increasing loss of life and equipment forced the railroads to start looking at alternatives.

The first breakthrough came with the advent of the telegraph. By connecting all the wayside stations via the telegraph with a dispatcher, messages could be sent to these lineside stations and then passed off to trains to alert them to changes of meeting points or other unscheduled movements. The employees who manned the wayside stations were called "operators," and the messages they handed up to the trains were called "train orders." The very first train order was sent by Charles Minot, the superintendent of the Erie Railroad, on September 22, 1851.

Over the years, the system of governing the movement of trains with train orders has become standardized, and the telegraph has been replaced by the telephone and even the cell phone, but for all practical purposes, the system the Erie pioneered in 1851 is still in use today on many low-traffic rail routes.

For routes with higher density, though, a fail-safe system was imperative. This would allow for the safe movement of trains and maximize the use of a given section of railroad. A common term among railroaders is "highball," meaning to go or go fast. (Among nonrailroaders it's also used to reference an alcoholic drink that might just get one going, as well.) Its origin dates from one of the earliest forms of railroad signaling. In 1832, the New Castle & Frenchtown developed a system by which a ball suspended on a cable would alert train crews to what lay ahead. A lowered black ball indicated an obstruction was in their path, whereas a ball at half mast alerted them to be prepared to stop at the next station. A white ball at the top of the mast indicated that the way was clear and the train could proceed at top speed—thus the term highball was born.

The drawback to this system was that in the best of conditions the signals were hard to read until a train was almost right on top of them. In conditions such as fog or a moonless night they were very hard to read, indeed. Sometimes, the balls were replaced by lanterns for operation at night.

Another problem with ball signals is that they are not self-explanatory. Each crew of each railroad involved had to know what the signal display meant. The last ball-signal junction in the United States was where the Boston & Maine crossed the Maine Central at Whitefield, New Hampshire. Two red balls up on the mast gave the crossing to the Maine Central, while one ball up authorized the B&M. There was no way for a stranger, however, to interpret their meaning.

A signal that displayed a colored light was the next step in development. This would allow a train crew to see the signal indication well in advance of the actual signal's location. The first type was a semaphore with an illuminated set of color lenses that was joined with a long plank, or blade. When set to a stop indication, the blade would be horizontal, and the light would show red. If all was clear, the blade would be vertical with a clear lens. If the train was to slow down, the arm would set at a 45-degree angle with a yellow-light indication.

This system worked well, but there was still room for improvement. If, say, the red lens was broken, when the signal was set to stop the train, it would display a clear light, indicating

The Southern Pacific employed what was termed lower-quadrant semaphores, where a clear indication had the blade pointed at about a 20 degree angle from straight down. As with regular semaphores, the horizontal blade was the stop indication. A semaphore signal had a light that shone through colored lenses, which can be clearly seen in the northbound signal in this view of a southbound Central Oregon & Pacific freight operating on the Siskiyou line south of Talent, Oregon, on March 10, 2000. *Kevin EuDaly photo*

that the route was clear, when, in fact, it was not. By the late 1890s, railroads started to adopt a green lens, rather than clear, to indicate that line was clear—in other words, "go."

Another improvement was the illumination of the signal itself. The first semaphore signals used a kerosene lantern to light the lens. This resulted in almost daily maintenance, as well as a rather dimly lit signal. In signals illuminated by lanterns, they actually used a blue glass to make the yellow flame look green. In the first few decades of the 1900s, the semaphore was improved with electric light, thus allowing it to be seen from a much greater distance, as well as significantly reducing maintenance costs.

After the semaphore came the electrically powered color light signal. Using the basic red, yellow, and green lenses, they could be mounted in a variety of ways, most commonly in a

The Pennsylvania Railroad was populated with yellow position light signals, where a horizontal row of lights meant stop, a diagonal row meant proceed with caution, and a vertical row meant proceed. In this view on July 2, 2006, in Devon, Pennsylvania, the two right-hand tracks have clear indications, while the third track from the right has a stop indication. The left track has no signal on this signal bridge. *Kevin EuDaly photo*

lights," with green lenses at the top and bottom of a round background to make a vertical "clear," yellow lights at the 45-degree position for "caution," and red on the horizontals for "stop." The Pennsylvania Railroad used all yellow lenses and gave indications by illuminating the vertical, 45-degree or horizontal patterns, along with a center light.

In the 1940s, the Pennsy developed the single-lens searchlight signal that had an intense focused light beam with three small moving color lenses inside that imparted the color to the light at its focal point, creating a very intensely colored beam.

With the advent of signals, railroads began to adopt a manual block system. By dividing a piece of railroad into sections, commonly called blocks, operators positioned on the borders of these blocks could control the movements of trains through the operation of the signals, allowing only one train to occupy a block at one time.

In 1872, Dr. William Robinson invented the first track circuit. By running a small direct-current charge through the rails and connecting it with a relay, it provided the basis of the first automatic block signal (ABS). When a train came on to one of these blocks, the metal wheels and axle would complete the circuit, causing signals at either end of the block to turn red. If something failed in the system, such as a broken rail or a failed battery, it would break the circuit, causing the signals at either end of the block to turn red, creating a fail-safe signal system.

vertical row. Unlike highway traffic lights with the red on top, the railroads stuck with the traditional "high green," with the green light on the top above the yellow and red. There were numerous variations on the color lights, however, and some railroads, such as the Norfolk & Western, used "color position

The majority of signals in current service in North America are variations of the standard three-color signal. The signals shown here are in service on the NS former Nickel Plate main line in Gary, Indiana, where the line crosses Clark Road. An Indiana Harbor Belt train is westbound on September 28, 2007, coming past signals that control the interlocking where a small EJ&E yard is accessed off the main line. *Kevin EuDaly photo*

On the Norfolk & Western main line across southern West Virginia, color position signals not only give the various rows of lights, but accent those with color. This one at Vaughn on November 4, 2006, is lined up for a westbound on the right-hand track. Semaphores and position lights allow color-blind engineers to read the indications, while searchlight signals that depend totally on color can't be read by those who are color blind. *Kevin EuDaly photo*

Failsafe, that is, except for human error. Signals still had to be seen by the train crew, sometimes in the worst of conditions, and responded to properly. If a crew was distracted for any reason, a missed signal could mean disaster.

By 1923, the Pennsylvania Railroad was experimenting with a completely new system that incorporated vacuum tubes that actually displayed the lineside signal indications inside the cab. This relieved the train crew of watching for wayside signals and also allowed them to respond more quickly to changing operating conditions. In the event that a train crew failed to reduce speed for a restrictive signal, the system (called Automatic Train Control, or ATC) would activate the airbrakes. This almost completely removed the possibility of human error and once again allowed the railroad to use a section of track more efficiently with shorter distances between trains, thus increasing the volume of traffic that could be handled on the route at any given time.

This theme of improving safety while increasing efficiency became very popular with railroads as their systems and traffic grew. Railroads tended not to embrace new ideas based solely on safety, evidenced by their foot-dragging response to George Westinghouse's airbrake system in 1869 and the Janney automatic knuckle coupler patented in 1873. But when faced with the possibility of increased efficiency as well as safety, the railroads could hardly say no.

Interlocking

At the same time that the Janney coupler and the airbrake were entering the scene, a new type of signal and operating system was also being tested. In 1870, on the United New Jersey Canal & Railroad Companies, a new control system, called an interlocking, was imported from England. It was used at junctions with heavy traffic and multiple routes or when one line crossed another at grade. The system was designed so that the operator could not accidentally route one train onto the path of another.

In its original form, an interlocking plant was completely mechanical. Tall levers connected to long pipes operated

This CB&Q westbound bangs across the diamonds at Mendota, Illinois, in October 1965, where the Q crossed the Illinois Central and Milwaukee Road. The classic interlocking tower stands to the right, and the rods that controlled the switches can be seen along the tracks to the right. There were thousands of such interlockings across North America, guarding crossings of main lines and branch lines alike. Few interlocking towers remain standing today. *Jim Boyd photo*

This view shows the inside of one of the interlocking plants in Penn Station in New York City in May 1991. The levers and pushbuttons control dozens of switches and signals, allowing the operators to move traffic through the plant safely, which in this case involves scores of Amtrak trains. *Mike Schafer photo*

signals, derails, and switches. The levers were linked to a mechanical matrix (often 10 feet high) of locking bars that forced the operator to manipulate the levers in a certain sequence that prevented him from lining two trains on the same route. Because of the size of the interlocking frame at ground level, the levers were usually on the second floor of the building, known as a tower. This elevated room also usually gave the operator a good overall view of the tracks around the plant. In the more complex plants, an operator was in command and handled the train orders and paperwork, while a leverman actually operated the levers. Though gone today, some of these "Armstrong plants" remained in service until the 1990s.

The drawback to these manual interlocking plants was that the farther away a switch or signal was, the harder it was to

move it through the system of pipes and pulleys. These systems also required a great deal of maintenance and usually had a full-time maintainer on hand. By the mid-1880s, some railroads were experimenting with electropneumatic controls that allowed an operator to control switches, signals, and derails at a greater distance by using electrically controlled air cylinders. A short time later, interlocking plants became entirely electrically controlled.

The next step was obvious. With an electrically controlled interlocking, it became possible to completely automate some railroad junctions. The most common was where two railroads crossed at grade. When a train approaches one of these intersections, the interlocking automatically lines the route unless another train is currently occupying it.

Opened in 1925, Chicago Union Station was a classic example of a Beaux Arts–style terminal, incorporating the neoclassical look of ancient Roman temples. CUS was owned by the Pennsylvania Railroad, The Milwaukee Road, and Burlington Route; Gulf, Mobile & Ohio was a tenant. CUS comprised two buildings. The larger of the two contains the Great Hall waiting room and offices; razed in 1970, the smaller in this 1969 scene housed the concourse. Amtrak owns the complex today. *Mike Schafer photo*

On July 25, 1927, the New York Central placed into service what was in essence a much larger version of the interlocking machine. Instead of controlling a single junction, this new system, called Centralized Traffic Control (CTC), allowed a single person to remotely control a much larger segment of railroad. In this case, it was a 40-mile section of a busy main line between Toledo and Berwick, Ohio. Allowing all train movements over a large section of railroad to be controlled from a single location eliminated the need for lineside operators, thus reducing cost and making more efficient use of the trackage.

Today, the large green panels of the CTC board, with lights that follow the train movements and small levers and push-buttons to route them, have been replaced with computers, but for the most part, CTC hasn't changed much since the

New York Central first used it back in 1927. Contemporary railroads now have large dispatching facilities where a team of dispatchers can control hundreds of miles of railroad from just one location halfway across the continent.

Stations, Depots, and Terminals

Though often used interchangeably, the words "station," "depot," and "terminal" actually each have a unique meaning. A station is a location called out as such in a railroad timetable. This may be the name of a large city that includes facilities for passenger and freight traffic, or it could simply be a junction or passing track that has no such facilities.

A depot is a structure that acts as a conduit for inbound and outbound passengers and/or freight. Almost immediately, this conduit became the most important place in a community, especially in small, isolated communities that were springing up along the new rail lines in North America.

The small-town depot was a place where people came and went. Local folks would gather just to watch when the passenger train was due. Newspapers would have a cub reporter there at train time to record who was coming and going. In this world, the station agent ruled supreme. In his office, usually located in a bay window, he was in charge of ticket selling and the distribution of local freight and express. The agent took care of the retail-sales side of the railroad in town. An operator would often share the office with him to handle train orders and movements on the railroad itself. Smaller stations had a single agent-operator. Over the telegraph lines, the agent was the first to learn of major news events and handled personal telegrams. In a time before telephones, television, and the Internet, this position was one of vital importance to a small town.

The station agent handled the paperwork for the freight business in town. As local coal dealers and lumberyards moved more to trucks in the latter half of the twentieth century, the railroads began to employ mobile freight agents to handle the business in more than one town. The mobile agent would have his office in a van that he would drive from customer to customer, providing service at the front door. Towns with big industries retained the agent in the depot, although he would also often drive to the customer for his work.

Larger towns required larger facilities to accommodate the traffic flow. If it was warranted, the freight, express, and passengers were all handled at different facilities.

In some cases there was a "union station," a single depot owned and used by more than one railroad. They were commonly consolidated into Union Station Company in which all the railroads using the station shared ownership. In other cases, such as La Salle Street Station in Chicago, the facility was owned by the Rock Island, and the New York Central and Nickel Plate Road paid a rental fee.

These larger passenger facilities, usually stub-ended, were referred to as terminals and were located in the largest cities. These terminal buildings tended to consist of a head house that contained the waiting rooms, ticket offices, and vendors that catered to the passengers. It also consisted of a train shed shelter over the tracks used for inbound and outbound trains. Possibly the greatest example of a big-city passenger terminal is New York's Grand Central Terminal with its 34,375-square-foot grand concourse under a 125-foot-high vaulted ceiling displaying the constellations of the zodiac in gold leaf. In 1946, 204,000 passengers passed through here while embarking or disembarking from the 550 trains that served it every day.

Whatever one chooses to call them, a station, depot, or terminal, these were the gateways for people leaving or coming

Every small town with a railroad running through had a depot. This former Chicago & Eastern Illinois depot lies in Princeton, Indiana, on the main line to Evansville. It has been restored and is currently operating as a small museum. The tracks outside the bay window carry trains of both CSX and NS, which operate jointly through town, splitting apart at either end of town. *Kevin EuDaly photo*

home, for news and for freight, as well as the public face of the railroad for the community. As railroads moved into the twenty-first century, they did so with significantly fewer depots, due to the decline in passenger service and local freight shipments, and advances in dispatching technologies that have all but replaced the operator. Nonetheless, for communities that are still served by passenger trains, the depot is an important part of many people's lives.

Yards

A location with tracks used for rolling stock sorting and storage is called a "yard." These can be as simple as just a few tracks or may include hundreds of tracks spread out on thousands of acres of land. The most common of these is the flat yard, with multiple parallel tracks that are joined together at one or both ends with switches arranged in what's called a "ladder." In larger yards, this ladder track is joined by a switching lead that allows for the yard to be worked without interrupting trains passing by on the main line.

To work a yard, a switch engine sorts the cars onto different tracks, making up blocks of cars that are destined for the same location. While flat switching, the crew may carefully place each car in a crowded situation, coupling and securing the airbrakes for each move. Or, in an open classification yard, they will bleed the airbrakes to release them and "kick" cars from the lead into their appropriate tracks. While kicking, the locomotive will abruptly slow down while a crew member lifts the uncoupling lever, allowing the car to roll freely into the track that has been aligned for it. It takes a talented crew to do this efficiently, without damaging lading or equipment by having the cars come together too hard.

Flat switching, however, is too slow when a large volume of cars needs to be sorted. The solution was the "hump yard." It has the same parallel tracks connected by ladders, but instead of being flat, it's bowl shaped, and the switching lead is on a hill (or hump) that's on average 30 feet high. When switching, the locomotive pushes the cars over the hump as a crew member on the ground uncouples the cars, letting them roll freely down the hump and into their appropriate tracks using nothing but gravity to power them.

The Pennsylvania Railroad was the first to experiment with the hump yard. In 1902, it built the Youngwood, Pennsylvania, yard, southeast of Pittsburgh, for sorting cars in coal service. As cars were uncoupled at the top of the hump, crew members

rode them down, using the brake wheel to slow the cars' descent, ensuring that they didn't couple too hard at the bottom. Called "rider yards," their main drawback was getting the riders back to the top of the hump after they accompanied a car down. It took a large crew to keep the cars rolling down the hump, and much of that time was spent walking back up the hill. The work was also very dangerous.

Enter the retarder, a mechanical device on the downslope rails that grips the flange of the car rolling off the hump, slowing it down (or retarding its movement) so it couples onto the cut of standing cars at an appropriate speed. This eliminated the need for the riders but provided less flexibility, as the cars could be slowed down only at the retarders, compared to the judgment of the brakeman riding the car and controlling the brakes. Considering that cars of different sizes and weight roll at different speeds, the air-actuated retarders were manually controlled by an operator in the hump tower.

The DM&IR yard at Keenan, Minnesota, is a small flat switching yard that houses all the essential elements of a yard. The BNSF GP30 at left is on a local run on August 3, 2006, that interchanges cars here. There are 14 yard tracks, primarily for interchange and marshalling freight in this area of the Iron Range. At the very far right a single Missabe unit sits in the engine facility, and behind it is the yard office. *Kevin EuDaly photo*

With freight cars as far as the eye can see, Chicago & North Western's major Chicago-area classification yard at Proviso is shown during World War II in late 1942. For many years, Proviso had the distinction of moving the highest quantity of freight cars through per year and remains one of the busiest yards today. It has been extensively rebuilt several times and remains Union Pacific's key yard in the Chicago area. *Jack Delano photo, U.S. Library of Congress collection*

Today, the computer has solved most of the problems of the hump yard. It can weigh each car on its way up the hump, calculate its "rollability" down the first part of the drop, and adjust the retarders farther down the yard tracks for a perfect coupling, even keeping track of how many cars are on each track and where the coupling points are. The computers even compensate for wind speed and direction, as well as temperature and weather conditions.

The contemporary hump yard handles 2,000 to 2,500 cars per day. The typical car arrives on a train in the receiving yard. Here the road locomotives are pulled off and taken to the servicing area. Then the hump engine will couple on to the cars and push them over the hump for sorting. At the other end of the yard another locomotive pulls these now-sorted blocks of cars and makes up new trains with them in the departure yard. Couple up the trainline air hoses, make an inspection and brake test, and the new train is ready to go.

Locomotive Maintenance and Fuel Facilities

As railroad building marched across North America, it left in its wake a myriad of facilities for the fueling and upkeep of the growing fleet of locomotives and rolling stock. Unlike today's diesels, the steam locomotive had to be continuously restocked with fuel and water. Almost every town along the line had facilities to take on water. This was usually achieved with the use of a water tower, essentially a large wooden structure that was built like a wooden barrel on stilts with a pull-down water spout. In some cases, the water tower fed pipes that led to vertical water stand pipes, or pentstocks, with a downspout that swiveled.

The main drawback to this system was that the train had to stop to take on water. In an attempt to increase efficiency, some big railroads, such as the Pennsylvania and New York Central, used track pans that allowed a train to take on water without stopping. This was achieved by pumping water

from the lineside tank into a raised trough that sat centered between the rails. The tender of the locomotive was fitted with an air-actuated scoop that was lowered into the water as the train passed overhead. In early experiments, the scoops worked remarkably well; however, the tenders filled so fast that the water hit the inside of the top deck, and the tremendous hydraulic pressure blew the sides right out of the tender! High-capacity overflows thus became a standard part of the tender systems.

Towns with track pans no longer had as many trains stop there, and they became derisively known as "jerkwater" towns, where the trains would jerk water and just keep on going.

Fueling a steam locomotive was an entirely different matter. The first steam locomotives burned wood, and cordwood was simply loaded by hand into the tender from piles located along the route. Wood, though cheap and easy for railroads to acquire, was thermally inefficient, and by the 1870s most railroads had switched to coal.

The coal was shipped to strategically placed coaling stations in hopper cars. Materials used in the construction of these coaling facilities varied from timber to steel to reinforced concrete, but they all utilized the same basic principal of storing the coal in a large raised container above or beside the track. They were commonly called "coal chutes," as they had one or more gravity-fed chutes that could be lowered over the tender. The coal was loaded into the coal chutes from hopper cars placed on a ramp that had a conveyor or bucket system to the top of the coal chute.

Most steam locomotives burned a reasonably good grade of bituminous coal, while some Eastern roads used a bituminous-anthracite mix. A few Western roads burned locally mined low-grade lignite that was little more than messy dirt. The fireboxes and smokeboxes had to be adjusted for each railroad's preferred type of coal.

In areas where coal was scarce, particularly in the West, many railroads in the late 1800s began to burn heavy Bunker C fuel oil instead of coal. The heat content was about the same, and sometimes engines were swapped back and forth between oil and coal fuel by replacing the grates and burners and bunkers in the tender. One Shay locomotive in tourist service today at Cass, West Virginia, was built as a wood burner and then converted to oil at its home in the Pacific Northwest. When it moved to Cass in the 1980s, it was converted to burn coal like the rest of the Cass engines.

One advantage of an oil-burning locomotive was that the required fueling facilities were much easier to build and maintain, consisting of just a steel tank and pump and a heater in case of cold weather.

Regardless of what they burned for fuel, all locomotives required dry sand. Still used today in the same fashion, the sand is fed to a pipe in front of the driving wheels and placed directly on the rail to increase traction on slippery rails or when getting a heavy train started. The steam locomotive did not require sand as often as it did water and fuel, but it was still vitally important to its operation. Therefore, at every locomotive terminal there is a sand house equipped with dryers and a delivery system of pipes and hoses.

When railroads began to replace the steam locomotive, one of the key advantages of the diesel was that it could go much greater distances without having to pause for fuel. No longer was there a need for multiple lineside water towers and coal chutes, resulting in significant savings to the railroad in time, maintenance, and building construction. Not only could the new diesels go a greater distance without stopping for fuel, but when they did need to be fueled it was a much easier process. At modern diesel facilities today, multiple units can be fueled and filled with sand at once.

A second major advantage to the diesels is that they require significantly less maintenance. A steam locomotive, with all of its moving parts exposed to the elements, not to mention the servicing of a high-pressure mobile boiler, required a significant amount of light and heavy repairs. The most common place where this work occurred was the roundhouse. This consisted of a circular structure with individual interior tracks that radiated from a turntable. The turntable (built much like a bridge with a center pivot and wheels located at the bottom of each end) allowed for access to each track and provided the means to turn a locomotive around.

Inside the roundhouse, locomotives were spotted over pit tracks to be inspected, cleaned, and lubricated. Routine maintenance was conducted on all aspects of the boiler, firebox, and running gear. This work was required every time a locomotive came in from a run. Most roundhouses had a "house" steam supply that could keep an engine's water hot even if the fire had been dropped for maintenance work.

Roundhouses could be wonderful, atmospheric, and mysterious places, with hissing and breathing locomotives alive like dragons in their lair. They became part of American folklore. "Run for the roundhouse, Nelly; he can't corner ya there!"

Opposite: The huge wooden coaling chute at Proviso, Illinois, was one of the first mechanical hoist chutes built on the C&NW, and was captured in this view in December 1942. It was built by Ogle Company in 1912 and lasted into the mid-1950s. There was a continuous line of engines waiting to take coal at this facility, and at between 10 and 20 tons for each locomotive, the 500-ton capacity could only service about 30 engines before being refilled. The cylindrical structure to the right is a sanding tower for delivering sand to locomotives, and the worker is operating the water plug used to deliver water to locomotive tenders. *Jack Delano photo, U.S. Library of Congress collection*

Morrison-Knudsen power sits at the fuel racks and sanding towers in the engine facility in BN's Interbay Yard in Seattle on December 5, 1993. This is a typical diesel-era facility where locomotives are cut off trains and brought in for servicing. Many large modern yards have fuel racks and sanding towers right on main-line tracks, where engines are serviced quickly, crews change, and priority trains roll out of the yard never leaving the main line. *Gary Muehlius photo*

Not all roundhouses were round, however. The C&O was famous for its Mallet houses, rectangular buildings with parallel tracks long enough to hold two 2-6-6-2s each inside. And where a turntable wasn't available, locomotives or entire trains could be turned on a three-sided track arrangement known as a wye.

By their design, steam locomotives also required much more extensive repairs and replacement of heavy components on a regular basis. Besides the roundhouse, most railroads also constructed back shops at the largest of their terminals. Here, gantry cranes could lift boilers off their frames or frames off the running gear for servicing. These shops also included large and extensive metal-fabrication equipment such as forges, lathes, milling machines, and grinders, not to mention a small army of specialized workers. This force made up a large part of the entire railroad's payroll, and they spent

hours maintaining a steam locomotive for every one hour of its operation.

All of this was fundamentally changed with the coming of the diesel age. The diesel didn't require nearly as many heavy or light repairs and could go much longer between shoppings. Furthermore, the components that make up a diesel are standardized and for the most part are much lighter in weight. The joke among mechanics was that a problem on a steam engine would take two minutes to find and two weeks to fix, while trouble on a diesel would take two weeks to find and two minutes to fix.

All this meant a big savings for railroads. Maintenance and shop crews were drastically reduced. Many roundhouses and servicing areas were eliminated or streamlined, and back shops that sometimes covered acres of land and employed thousands were closed altogether. The contemporary diesel shops still have much in common with the steam shops of the past. In fact, some of these shops that were originally built for maintaining steam locomotives were retrofitted, so they now service the motive power that replaced them. In most cases, however, the turntable is gone, but the concept of a repair bay with a drop pit to allow access to the underside of the locomotive as well as the gantry crane are still in use. The bays have changed, though, with the inclusion of a parallel platform that is roughly level with the locomotive frame and allows easy access to the prime mover and generator. Mobile fork lifts make easy work of moving heavy components around the shop.

As the design of the diesel has improved over the years, the newest engines require less and less routine maintenance.

Some railroads have even closed what few locomotive shops they retained after steam was retired and instead have had outside contractors or the locomotive builders themselves handle the major repairs or rebuilds.

As North American railroads came into the twenty-first century, they handled more traffic than ever before. What is more astonishing is that with the advances in technology, this was accomplished with significantly reduced route miles, fewer employees, and an overall smaller infrastructure. Yet the basic elements still remain. Switches and signals still route trains operated by locomotives utilizing the flanged wheel on the steel rail to pull their trains. The show goes on, thanks to a very important supporting cast.

The roundhouse was where steam locomotive maintenance occurred and consisted of radial tracks in stalls arranged around a central turntable. Small roundhouses often were built with only a few stalls, while large roundhouses could be nearly a complete circle. This view captures the mood and mystique of the steam-era roundhouse—this one is in C&NW's Proviso Yard in December 1942. *Jack Delano photo, U.S. Library of Congress collection*

Railroading Today

by Steve Jessup

The former Santa Fe main line between Chicago and the West Coast is predominantly dedicated to providing a right-of-way for endless strings of piggyback trailers and double-stack containers. This early-morning westbound has four units with trailers in tow at East Perrin, Arizona, on May 25, 1995. Every trailer in sight is a semitruck not on the highway, and trains like this offer considerable relief to the nation's crowded roads. *Kevin EuDaly photo*

If James J. Hill, William Van Horne, Ed Harriman, and other such illustrious railroad pioneers were alive today, assessing the state of affairs on today's rails, an echo of something like, "That's what I'm talkin' about!" would be heard throughout the land.

What's happening in North American railroading today is truly staggering. Seven "supersized" Class 1 railroads (with operating revenues exceeding $346.8 million), numerous regional railways, and a collection of short lines control a vast network of trackage spanning coast to coast, Canada to Mexico, totaling well over 160,000 miles.

Stand trackside today somewhere between North Platte and Gibbon, Nebraska, and you'll see three main-line tracks instead of one. You'll see an average of around 130 trains a day, nearly double the total from 25 years ago, which was an astounding amount of traffic for the day. Granted, not every main line in America generates such a number, but it is a trend as major carriers scramble to accommodate industry growth.

One of the public's primary interfaces with railroads today is through Amtrak, whose ridership set a new record at 25,847,531 in 2007. This marked the fifth straight year of gains and set a record for the most passengers using Amtrak trains since it was formed in 1971. This northbound is train No. 760, the *Mt. Baker International,* and is rolling along Puget Sound at Edmonds, Washington, on May 23, 1999. *Steve Jessup photo*

On the issue of trackage, the busy main lines of the East have been double-tracked for years, but out West, single track and sidings have handled the flow, and that's beginning to change.

It's been about 80 years since the railroads, as a whole, have pushed for more track and additional improvements in infrastructure. The expansion to handle the anticipated traffic by 2035 will cost an estimated $148 billion, according to railroad sources. The railroads will spend about two-thirds, while the rest is to come from the federal government and the states. The railways are expected to dole out $10 billion this year alone to handle the forthcoming onslaught.

Regarding traffic, the railroads handled record amounts during World War II, then experienced a decline in business all the way into the early 1980s. From that point to today, the rail industry has rocketed to astonishing heights.

So what's caused the explosion? Beyond the deregulation issue (from 1980), one word sums it up nicely: trade. North American ports ship and receive millions of containers stuffed with billions of dollars' worth of merchandise. Once on land, the majority of the containers are loaded into well cars and transported in unit trains to their destination. The growth of containerized traffic is so intense that major ports are desperate to find additional space. Ships are now forced to call on new port locations that are pretty much unknown to the intermodal world. For example, readers of this book are likely to be familiar with Los Angeles/Long Beach or perhaps Seattle/Tacoma. But in cases where those facilities are congested, how about sending a ship to Prince Rupert, British Columbia? On the East Coast, not everyone knows that Wilmington, Delaware, handles container freight—not just New York.

The intermodal market, which also includes truck trailers shipped by train, now accounts for a whopping 22 percent (2003 figure) of the railroads' overall revenue. And the rival trucking industry has already formed a few partnerships with the rail roads partly because of soaring fuel prices and driver shortages.

Another big reason rail traffic has surged is coal—hardly an unfamiliar commodity to the railroads. It accounts for the most tonnage hauled on the rails. Low-sulfur coal is in high demand, and the major Western carriers have tapped into the world's largest single deposit of this coal in Wyoming's Powder River Basin (which also extends into southern portions of Montana). Railroads continue to move record volumes of coal from this region to power plants across the United States, and there's enough of the substance underneath these areas to keep the roads busy for a long time.

Besides coal, other bulk commodities such as grain and fertilizer have moved on the rails for domestic consumption and use, but this traffic has grown by leaps and bounds due to export demands.

These key areas in the railroad industry would likely account for about three-quarters of the rail traffic passing you by in Nebraska. And the railroads have millions of dollars' and tons' worth of other products to ship—all just as important—including petroleum, forest, automobile, and perishable materials, to name just a few.

It all runs behind some pretty sophisticated, high-tech, high-horsepower, diesel-electric locomotives. In the steam days, many trains were handled by one powerful locomotive. When diesel units came along, they were lashed-up together—two, three, perhaps four or more—pulling long strings of freight or speeding along with passenger trains. Even in the 1980s, it was common to see three or four 3,000-horsepower units on a main-line freight. Today, a pair of 4,300- or 4,400-horsepower locomotives will do the trick.

To say that engineers and conductors are pampered a bit with these new units would be a slight understatement. You won't see them with soot all over their faces or apparel. The two primary builders, General Electric and Electro-Motive Diesel, Inc. (formerly Electro-Motive Division of General Motors), equip these units with wider "comfort" cabs complete with air-conditioning and a work desk. Computer screens have replaced gauges and, in some cases, levers and flip switches have turned into press buttons. The units have such on-board features as a global positioning system (GPS), wireless communications packages, cab signaling (a readout of the signal color before reaching the actual post), and even a locomotive camera to record grade-crossing and right-of-way incidents.

The late twentieth- and early twenty-first-century railroad boom is not limited to freight business. Passenger service has picked up considerably, especially in the short-haul category. While Amtrak has posted five consecutive years of increased ridership nationwide, urban congestion has spawned commuter rail service in many cities. New York, Chicago, Washington, D.C., and Los Angeles were the noted metropolitan areas offering commuters an alternative transportation source to work a few years ago. Today, there are 32 North American cities with commuter trains in place—28 in the United States, 3 in Canada (Montreal, Toronto, and Vancouver), and 3 in Mexico (Mexico City).

Usually, the trains use existing freight main lines and are equipped with one locomotive and anywhere between 4 to 12 cars. The end car contains a small cab for the engineer to remotely control the locomotive when going the opposite direction (that is, push-pull operation).

Electric-powered light-rail transit systems provide additional service around some urban areas. One advantage to light rail is that, a vast majority of the time, it doesn't compete with other freight and passenger trains as it has its own trackage.

And then there's Amtrak—America's grossly under-appropriated rail passenger carrier since 1971. As much as Congress has tried to quietly escort Amtrak to its grave, it keeps rolling. On long-haul runs, riders are afforded a relaxing trip with some of the best views across the United States on such well-known trains as the *Coast Starlight*, *Empire Builder*, *Southwest Chief*, *California Zephyr*, and *Capitol Limited*. But where Amtrak has really made its mark in recent years is regional service where a car trip might be too long and an airline ticket would be too expensive.

The high-speed, electrified Northeast Corridor set the stage with fast, efficient transportation between Washington and Boston. Similar regional trains (though not as fast) are in place across the United States, using diesel locomotives and conventional passenger equipment. Newer Spanish-built Talgo sets with lighter cars are used on the Amtrak Cascades in the Pacific Northwest between Eugene, Oregon, and Vancouver,

For bulk commodities, nothing can move tonnage like trains. With hundreds of power plants consuming coal, the coal-moving industry in North America is a high-volume railroad conveyor. Though coal from the Powder River Basin dominates, there is still significant tonnage moving from Eastern carriers, including Norfolk Southern. Here three units move empty hoppers back to the coal fields, rolling through Eckman, West Virginia, on June 15, 2007, on the former Norfolk & Western main line. *Kevin EuDaly photo*

British Columbia. The cars were designed for higher speeds, although Amtrak is subject to the speed restrictions set by the railroads it operates on.

The bullet-train concept has never caught on in the United States for a variety of reasons, not the least of which are cost, infrastructure limitations, and perceived lack of population in areas where it might work. Highly popular in countries such as France and Japan, these trains routinely travel in the 200-mile-per-hour range over flat terrain. In the United States, mountain regions in the West and in the East would pose some route infrastructure challenges. The long-time perception that high-speed trains will only be successful in areas that are more densely populated than found in North America outside of the Northeast Corridor have been disproven. France, with its highly successful, world-renowned TGV system, is less densely populated than the American Midwest. So, as of 2008, several new proposals for high-speed service have surfaced. One proposal was the Magnetic Levitation Train project for the Los Angeles–Las Vegas corridor that, if built, would allow speeds up to 300 miles per hour on an elevated structure. It would come with a price tag of approximately $12 billion, and according to *USA Today*, there's only one country using this technology, and that's China.

Another proposal—far short of bullet-train status—comes from DesertXpress Enterprises at roughly one-third the cost ($3 to $5 billion) of Magnetic Levitation. A line would be built to handle 125-mile-per-hour trains between Victorville, California (northeast of the renowned train-watching location of Cajon Pass), and Las Vegas. Presumably, these trains would enter the Los Angeles Basin on conventional lines with lower speeds.

The CSX train at right is parked under the loadout at Coal Run, near Pikeville on February 27, 2008. To the left, a loaded coal train has stopped for a crew change at the small office, having come over the Coal Run Subdivision earlier in the day. This line replaced a twisted route over Pompey Mountain, and feeds coal to the former Chesapeake & Ohio Big Sandy main line in eastern Kentucky. *Kevin EuDaly photo*

Elsewhere, proposals for higher-speed (that is, 125 miles per hour) corridors abound in North America, with the mantra of incremental improvements. For example, these routes would use existing rail lines but upgrade with signaling or a global-positioning train-location system that would permit higher speeds. If those prove successful, then additional steps are taken to raise the bar and with it, higher speeds yet—perhaps up to the 150-mile-per-hour status already enjoyed by Amtrak's *Acela* trains, which run over rights-of-way dating from the 1800s! Speeds beyond that will likely require all-new dedicated rights-of-way such as those used by French TGV trains on the highest-speed portions of their runs. (Outside of those dedicated tracks, the TGVs use historic lines to reach city centers.) Currently, California is already attempting to fund a new, dedicated, high-speed rail passenger route linking L.A. with the San Francisco Bay Area via the Central Valley. If this endeavor is successful, it could spawn similar new starts all over the country.

Although not as prevalent as coal, another bulk commodity common in the upper Midwest is iron ore, in this case hauled out of the Iron Range of northern Minnesota by Duluth, Missabe & Iron Range. This train is moving southeast toward the port at Two Harbors, where the taconite (refined iron ore) will be loaded into a ship for travel through the Great Lakes to steel mills on the southern shore of Lake Michigan near Gary, Indiana. Iron ore also moves this way for export to the Far East. SD38AC No. 205 leads two CN units (CN purchased the DM&IR in 2004) through Fairbanks, Minnesota, on February 8, 2008. *Kevin EuDaly photo*

In one century, North American railroading has gone from the elite form of transportation to a largely unknown business.

It's an industry that built a nation and then seemingly faded in the front half of the twentieth century. The automobile afforded people with the most convenient way to get around, and in the mid-1900s, air travel allowed the public to go anywhere in the world—fast!

To most people, railroading exists, but only as an outdated form of transportation. They feel that there's no need to travel by rail, and in their minds, there isn't any freight that can't be hauled by truck. Basically, people have no real interaction with the railways, thus there's no reason for them to become acquainted with the business. After all, why spend their precious time learning about something they're not interested in?

Simply put, railroading is off the radar.

And yet, as outlined above, the reality is that railroading is as healthy, vibrant, and active as it has ever been.

The fact that the railroads are thriving without a lot of public awareness is probably just fine with the nation's carriers—they would just as soon shun the publicity. But in today's money-lust society, no railroad executive is going to turn down a pot-load of potential business that comes with an educated public.

When you think about it, it's hard to simply shrug off such an important industry. Take it away, though, and people who fail to comprehend the logistics of a highly effective and successful transportation source will quickly gain the necessary perspective of its value.

For instance, a passing train on either side of the highway may be of little importance to the average citizen behind the wheel. But take a 100-car, 10,000-ton coal train off the rails. Let's say one truck could handle one car load (actually it would take more than two). How would the driver react following 100 trucks on a highway already clogged with 18-wheelers?

What about the 100-car grain train that passed a half hour ago with 10,000 tons of grain? How would drivers react following 200 trucks?

But let's say there's an average of 20 trains a day on the line. Would they like to drive on a stretch of highway that had an additional *2,000* trucks per day? If the driver of that vehicle ran a shipping business, would he/she rather pay 40 employees or 2,000? What about fuel costs?

Then you look at how much the government feeds the highway system in comparison to the railways, and it's pretty easy to conclude that our nation's policymakers have no clue when it comes to prudent spending on transportation.

The fabric of our lives runs on the railroads. Coal is needed to supply power. Grain is needed to make food. Lumber is needed to construct homes and businesses. Merchandise is needed for commerce. Millions of tons of products and

Amtrak's eastbound *Illinois Zephyr*, with four cars, zips down the center main line of the former Chicago, Burlington & Quincy main line in the western suburbs of Chicago in Western Springs on September 28, 2007. On either side are commuter-heavy tracks that move incredible numbers of people in and out of the Windy City every day, and to the left is the small depot where thousands board and disembark. *Kevin EuDaly photo*

bulk commodities need to be shipped quickly, reliably, and efficiently, and the railroads were invented for this purpose.

And as we enter the twenty-first century, rail passenger service is clearly a necessity. More and more drivers are becoming irritated while trapped in city traffic. Metropolitan areas all across the nation have massive freeway, highway, and side-street traffic these days, and it's not getting any better. Everyone is complaining about rising fuel costs, and sitting in traffic burns more fuel, not to mention a hole in the pocketbook. The automobile—once looked at as a remarkable invention for the betterment of our lives—is fast becoming one of the greatest sources of stress and strain.

Fewer families are taking longer road trips based on fuel costs as well as highway safety and fatigue factors. And people are becoming increasingly frustrated with airline service—cancelled flights, lost baggage, incompetent security screening, and so on.

As America inches toward the tip of the frustration iceberg, we begin to search for alternative forms of getting around. Will it dawn on the public that the railroads are tried and true in this arena?

The bottom line is that railroads work—they work exceedingly well, and they exist to serve a busy, growing world. They are far from outdated—they are updated. They are safe. They are reliable. They are highly efficient and highly cost effective.

And they wait for the public to mature in order to exercise even greater potential.

Following pages: Railroads as a transportation network are unparalleled at moving large quantities efficiently. Perhaps no commodity demonstrates that as well as coal. In this view, three brand-new GE Dash 8-40CWs ease down York Canyon in northern New Mexico on September 18, 1992. Trailing the lead units are 110 cars of coal, and three pushers can be seen about three-quarters of the way back in the train. Once out of the canyon, the train will head north over tortuous Raton Pass, then across the prairie to a power plant near Milwaukee, Wisconsin. *Kevin EuDaly photo*

About the Authors

Kevin EuDaly was born a stone's throw from the Monon in Bedford, Indiana, and grew up chasing trains with his dad, Jim EuDaly, some of whose photographs appear in this book. A childhood move to Kansas City put Kevin in position to witness the many railroads of the 1960s and 1970s before merger mania erased so many names. Frequent treks around K.C. with his brother, Lon, helped build an early interest in railroad photography.

In 1992, he founded White River Productions and began publishing historical society magazines. He wrote and published *Missouri Pacific Diesel Power* that same year. He has authored dozens of articles and had hundreds of photographs published over the last two decades. WRP has grown to become the primary producer of historical society publications in the United States, and currently produces magazines, calendars, and books for 16 organizations, as well as *Railroads Illustrated* and *Passenger Train Journal* under the WRP flag.

Kevin resides on the east side of Kansas City near the former Rock Island in Raytown with his wife, Nadean, and four children, Sarah, James, Danae, and Ashley. This is the sixth book he has authored or co-authored.

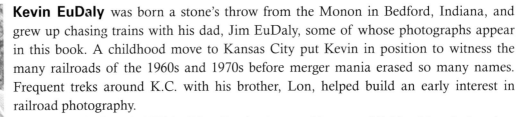

Mike Schafer hails from Rockford, Illinois, where he recalls his earliest train-watching experiences on the Illinois Central, Milwaukee Road, Burlington Route, and Chicago & North Western. He vividly recalls his first train rides, circa 1952, on IC's *Hawkeye* and *Land O' Corn* between Rockford and Chicago. Eventually he would declare the latter—America's railroad hub—his "honorary hometown."

Mike spent all of the 1980s art directing and editing *Passenger Train Journal*, *Prototype Modeler*, and a line of books for PTJ Publishing (later purchased by Interurban Press). In 1990, he became part owner of Andover Junction Publications, another railroad book and magazine publisher and production house. In 2005, White River Productions hired Mike to help edit and produce railroad magazines and books, including a revived *Passenger Train Journal*.

Mike and his little dog, Archie, reside in a house (which includes a 1,600-square-foot model railroad) next to BNSF's busy Twin Cities main line in a small town outside Chicago, where he also serves as village trustee and occasionally mayor pro tem.

Jim Boyd grew up in Dixon, Illinois, where he lived within sight of the Illinois Central that was still running steam during his early teen years. He made his peace with the black Geeps that replaced the Mikados, but began a lifetime of pursuing preserved steam operations. He attended the University of Illinois and Layton School of Art and began writing magazine articles in the early 1960s. In 1967, he got a three-year job as a field-service representative for the Electro-Motive Division of General Motors, delivering new diesel locomotives. After EMD, he worked for a year as a brakeman on the Ilinois Central before joining Carstens Publications in New Jersey as a magazine production editor.

When Hal Carstens created *Railfan & Railroad* magazine in 1974, Jim became its editor and held that title for the next 23 years. After retiring as editor, Jim stayed in New Jersey and began producing railroad books, and has completed or contributed to more than three dozen volumes. He still writes feature articles for numerous magazines and does a monthly "Camera Bag" column in *Railfan & Railroad*.

Steve Jessup is originally from Southern California and grew up on the Southern Pacific Coast Line in Atascadero. It was there he developed a passion for railroading in the late 1960s and 1970s, and took an interest in rail photography in 1980 with several trips to Tehachapi Loop and Cajon Pass.

Steve began his editorial career in Seattle in 1982 and spent 14 years as a sports editor. He jumped back into publications work in 2007, joining White River Productions following a decade's worth of experience in model railroad sales.

Steve has written many railroad features, and since 1981 his byline and photos have appeared in *Trains, Railfan & Railroad, Railroads Illustrated*, and *Rail Classics*. He and his wife, Julie, and daughter, Angela, reside in Lee's Summit, Missouri.

Andrew McBride was born in Dixon, Illinois, where he grew up with the sounds of the Chicago & North Western's main line and a branch of the Illinois Central Gulf floating through his bedroom window. His father, Mike McBride, a rail enthusiast and model railroader, as well as an employee of the C&NW, got him hooked early on. By the time he was 14, his photography had been published in a couple of railroad magazines and he was hard at work on his first HO scale layout.

Andrew has spent most of his life working in the railroad hobby field. His first job was at the local model railroad hobby shop. From there he worked for Interurban Press, FastTrack video, the NMRA, Kalmbach Publishing, Walthers, and Andover Junction Publications. Today, Andrew works for White River Productions as an editor and graphic designer for some of the many historical society magazines it publishes.

Besides a life of railfanning, Andrew also lives and dies with his beloved Chicago Cubs and is an avid collector of music and books. He lives in Paw Paw, Illinois, with his wife, Wendy, their three girls, a dog, two cats, and assorted tropical fish.

Steve Glischinski was born in St. Paul, Minnesota, in 1957 and has been interested in railroads since he was 10 years old. He began taking photographs of railroads in 1970. Since then, his photos have appeared in a number of books and numerous magazines, including *Pacific Rail News, Passenger Train Journal, Progressive Railroading, Railfan & Railroad*, and *Trains*. His first magazine articles on railroading were published in 1982, and his byline has appeared dozens of times, mainly in *Trains*, for which he serves as a special correspondent. He is the author of four books on railroading, including such topics as the Burlington Northern Railroad, Wisconsin Central, Milwaukee Road steam locomotive 261, and regional railroads.

Steve holds a bachelor's degree in political science with a minor in history from the University of Minnesota at Duluth. In 1991, he entered the field of freelance writing full-time, working with several clients, including one that handles public relations and communication programs for several short-line railroads. He and wife, Lori, and son, Andy, currently reside in the St. Paul suburb of Shoreview, Minnesota.

Index